"Owing to his broad spectrum of mission experiences — from the plains of Kenya to the halls of academia to the city streets of domestic church planting — Dr. Van Rheenen is uniquely qualified to prepare a work of this scope. He equips the reader with the tools necessary to navigate the waters of mission, guiding one from theological reflection to everyday praxis and back. The first edition of *Missions* was seminal in my early thinking about participating in God's mission — the kind of book that often gets dusted off and consulted. This revised edition promises rarely to gather much dust!"

— Andy Johnson, *Missionary among the Dagara of Burkina Faso*

"I have been indebted to Gailyn Van Rheenen for years — teaching his Missional Helix in seminary classes and using it in my own reflection. Now, in this updated volume, he does not disappoint — combining the heart of a practitioner with the mind of a scholar, Van Rheenen takes us to the text of Scripture and the context of culture, providing the guidance that practitioners and students alike will find invaluable."

— Ed Stetzer, *www.edstetzer.com*

"Too often, theology and mission practices are separated as if one does not inform the other. Dr. Van Rheenen brings theology and practice back together in clear and passionate prose. He knows that all mission practices say something theologically and that all good theology is good because it can be practiced. This book is a must read for everyone who finds themselves on mission with God!"

— Ben Langford, *Director of the Center for Global Mission at Oklahoma Christian University*

"Too often, those in the academy are not practical enough and those out on the mission are not theological enough. But Dr. Van Rheenen is an academic AND a missionary, and no one is better prepared to guide us from deep theology to workable strategy to sustainable practice. This book is the culmination of a lifetime of reflection and practice on how the Kingdom of God comes into the dark places in our world. And though it is not too late, there is no time to lose!"

— Randy Harris, *Bible Professor and College of Biblical Studies' Spiritual Director, Abilene Christian University*

"What is rare and what makes Van Rheenen's work in this volume so helpful is that he combines deep theological reflection on the mission of God with practical strategies which are not only commensurate with that good theology, but are tested in the field and timely in a world going through rapid global transformation. All of this is done in a way that is surprisingly comprehensive and accessible. If you are starting to build a bibliography for Missiology, this should be your cornerstone volume. No one has helped my understanding of missions more than Gailyn Van Rheenen, and I am grateful that his knowledge is now available in this more comprehensive edition."

— DR. DAN BOUCHELLE, *President, Missions Resource Network*

"Gailyn Van Rheenen is a missional polymath. A successful church planter in Africa, he subsequently established himself as a leading academic missiological voice. Recently he has birthed and leads an organization designed to equip churches for missional practice in North America. Because of this amazing confluence of missional capacities and experiences, you should pay close attention to the wise words in this revised version of his already outstanding 1996 text. Each chapter is extraordinarily accessible yet never dumbed-down. The addition of many new chapters makes this an even more valuable resource. Eminently practical. Grounded in personal experience enriched by informed historical, cultural, and theological analysis. There is simply no better introductory text for missional preparation today."

— DR. CHRIS FLANDERS, *Professor of Missions and Director, Halbert Institute of Missions, Abilene Christian University*

"Gailyn Van Rheenen is uniquely qualified to offer this work for those preparing to heed the call of God. He has the experience and skill to articulate the field in a practical manner. Most important, however, is the man himself. His description of the missionary is a portrayal of his own nature: 'The attributes of God — holiness, love, and faithfulness — form the character of those carrying this mission.' This book is intended to do much more than offer strategies for mission work. It is intended to encourage the shaping of the heart of the missionary."

— JACKIE L. HALSTEAD, *Director, Institute for Christian Spirituality, Lipscomb University*

"Dr. Van Rheenen is an experienced missional practitioner across multiple contexts. He combines this experience with an engaging narrative style to paint a picture of biblical mission that is both deeply theological and eminently practical. Highly recommended for anyone who wants to more deeply understand God's mission in the world!"

— MIKE BREEN, *3DM*

I first read *Missions* in college as I was preparing for church planting in North America. Many of Dr. Van Rheenen's insights impacted me deeply, and I carry them with me today as a missionary. I was particularly touched by Van Rheenen's emphasis on the missionary's heart and motivation, which helped me to confront some of the deficient motives I was carrying into the mission. I'm confident that the revised edition will serve others similarly as they seek to join God in his mission.

— CHARLES KISER, *Church Planter in Dallas, Texas; Director of Training, Mission Alive*

"Books on missionary strategy and methods abound. Books on mission theology are fairly numerous, but certainly not in commensurate supply. Books that combine strategy and theology are more rare and most welcome — especially when, as is the case here, the strategy grows out of the theology. Able both as theologian and strategist, Van Rheenen and his book are worthy of wide reading and serious consideration."

— DAVID J. HESSELGRAVE, *Ph.D., Professor of Mission Emeritus, Trinity Evangelical Divinity School*

"Everyone who claims to follow Jesus can — and on some level *must* — be a missionary; but not everyone does missions *responsibly.* Grounded in both rigorous critical theory and years of experience on multiple fields, Dr. Van Rheenen brings an updated toolkit to the table for both students and practitioners of mission. More than that, he helps refocus missions away from human agenda and onto the character of God. Here you will find sound resources to challenge and guide you through the multifaceted work of the missionary task so that the act of sharing Good News really will be *good news.*"

— JONATHAN W. STRAKER, *Missionary in post-disaster Ishinomaki, Japan*

"Van Rheenen has it right; he examines the 'why' of missions before the 'how,' where most activists prefer to begin. Solid biblical foundation must precede contemporary missionary strategies. Mission begins with the heart of God and then works its way out in opportunities for service the world over. Travel with Jim and Julie as they begin their mission journey in a university and proceed to the field where they encounter all of the normal missionary problems: culture shock, cross-cultural evangelism, ethnocentrism, the proper use of funds, contextualization, and reentry. This book is an introduction to missions on steroids; a must-read for anyone interested in Kingdom expansion."

— Doug Priest, *Executive Director, CMF International*

"When students tell me, 'I feel called to missions; what do I do now?' I often hand them the first edition of *Missions*. This updated edition with eight new chapters is as timely as it is broad. Dr. Van Rheenen's years of experience, continued study, and practical focus lend weight to the insights and reflections he offers. It is a great starting point for the missional journey."

— Dr. Gary L. Green, *Associate Director for Missional Formation, Halbert Institute for Missions, Abilene Christian University*

"Dr. Van Rheenen has done an outstanding job of revising and updating his excellent book on missions. This new edition will be a book I will require for all of my students considering God's missional call as their primary purpose for life. It is biblically founded, comprehensive, and extremely practical — a rare combination indeed!"

— Dr. Earl Lavender, *Director of Missions Studies, Lipscomb University*

"Anyone who coaches a sport knows that fans love spectacular plays, but that such outstanding plays can only happen after mastering the basics of the sport. Gailyn Van Rheenen has spent most of his adult life coaching disciples of Jesus Christ, whether new converts, potential evangelists and missionaries, or urban church planters. In this updated edition of *Missions*, Van Rheenen manages to major in the basics of cross-cultural ministry while addressing current issues. This is a thorough and biblically based textbook suitable for training disciples."

— Dr. Robert Reese, *Professor of Cross-Cultural Ministry, Mid-Atlantic University*

"Gailyn Van Rheenen has been a model, mentor, and teacher to a multitude of servants who have joined God in His global mission. I have been one of those blessed through the example of Gailyn and his wife, Becky, as they have taken steps of faith in following God's mission call. The first edition of *Missions* has been an essential tool I have consulted again and again in preparing missionaries and equipping those involved in the sending process. This updated volume promises to maintain the strong theological and practical mission foundation, but will also incorporate new insights gained from a journey of engaging an ever-changing world with a timeless message of good news."

— Jay Jarboe, *Vice President for Ministry Operations and Director for Church Equipping, Missions Resource Network*

Dr. Van Rheenen is able to weave profound topics (such as *missio Dei,* Incarnation, and missional helix) into practical matters (such as short-term missions and money) winsomely and interestingly.

— Dr. Enoch Wan, *President, Evangelical Missiological Society*

2nd Edition

missions

Biblical Foundations and Contemporary Strategies

Gailyn Van Rheenen

with Anthony Parker

ZONDERVAN®

ZONDERVAN

Missions

This title is also available as a Zondervan ebook.
Visit *www.zondervan.com/ebooks*.

Requests for information should be addressed to:

Zondervan, 3900 *Sparks Drive SE, Grand Rapids, Michigan 49546*

Library of Congress Cataloging-in-Publication Data

Van Rheenen, Gailyn, 1946–
Missions: biblical foundations and contemporary strategies / Gailyn Van Rheenen, with Anthony Parker. — Second Edition.
p. cm.
Includes bibliographical references and index.
ISBN 978-0-310-25237-5 (hardcover printed)
1. Missions—Theory. 2. Christianity and culture. I. Title.
BV2063.V35 2014
266.00—dc23 2014001162

Cover design: Tammy Johnson
Cover photo: Getty Images
Interior design & composition: Greg Johnson/Textbook Perfect

Printed in the United States of America

---

20 21 22 /DCI/ 22 21 20 19 18 17 16 15 14 13 12 11 10 9 8 7 6 5 4 3

Contents

Foreword

By the grace God has given me, I laid a foundation as an expert builder, and someone else is building on it. But each one should be careful about how he builds. For no one can lay any foundation other than the one already laid, which is Jesus Christ. If any man builds on this foundation using gold, silver, costly stones, wood, hay or straw, his work will be shown for what it is, because the Day will bring it to light. It will be revealed with fire, and the fire will test the quality of each man's work.

(1 Corinthians 3:10–13 NIV 1984)

With these words, the apostle Paul makes the case for missional strategizing. In the wake of the much-maligned Church Growth Movement, it is a timely call. Many of us—Dr. Van and me among them—rode the crest of the church growth wave to other nations in the decades of the 70s, 80s, and 90s and followed its principles in our church planting and maturing ministries in Africa. I understand and sympathize with the critique of that movement's excesses. Sometimes, however, I get the impression that when kingdom business is the topic of discussion, "strategy" itself is considered "unspiritual" at best and taboo at worst, a useless relic of the Church Growth era.

But I beg to differ. Paul, imitating Jesus, was deliberate, careful, visionary, and yes, strategic. His work was grounded in conviction about the nature and will of God embodied in Christ and driven by a long-term goal of bearing the gospel to the nations. A significant part of the approach was to establish churches that would multiply until the Lord's return, churches that could withstand the fire test; thus, Paul emphasized building with durable materials.

The book you hold in your hands is grounded in that same conviction, which Dr. Van Rheenen makes explicit throughout. The theology of mission presented in the first five chapters lays the groundwork for what follows. Then he expertly builds on that foundation—if I may appropriate Paul's metaphor in this way—by describing in accessible terms various types of missionaries, the missionary cycle, lessons current and future missionaries may learn from the history of missions, and the nuts and bolts of incarnational ministry—how to enter a culture other than one's own, overcome one's own ethnocentrism, and become an effective intercultural communicator. The final seven chapters address the most significant strategic challenges missionaries face—from the practical, day-to-day tasks related to planting and nurturing new churches (with a whole chapter devoted to church planting in North America), to the very real opportunities and challenges presented by missions funding and by the growing ranks of short-term missions and short-term missions participants. The nine new chapters constitute a significant and valuable update to the 1996 edition of this book.

Dr. Van Rheenen practices what he preaches. I have been privileged to serve alongside Gailyn as a "partner in the gospel" for nearly three decades, first in Kenya (where we speak the same language and minister in some of the same congregations), then as colleagues in the academic world as missions professors. Both of us were mentored at Trinity Evangelical Divinity School by the late Dr. Paul Hiebert, who wrote the Foreword to the first edition of this book. I watched as Gailyn and his wife, Becky, birthed "Mission Alive," a church-planting ministry designed to train and coach others to form "Missional Communities" in North America (see chapter 16) and have praised God with them and with their trainees as that ministry has grown.

Gailyn is eminently qualified to provide this comprehensive introductory text to students of missions. May the Lord Himself use it to further equip you, the reader, for the missional task to which He is calling you, to build on the foundation that is Jesus Christ, and lay atop that unshakable foundation only that which will endure.

Monte Cox
Harding University

Preface

THE STUDY OF MISSIONS IS A JOURNEY that expands our horizons and broadens our understandings in at least four directions. First, the study of missions is a *journey into the world* to see the world *as it really is* — as God sees it — culturally diverse and pluralistic, torn between the opposing forces of Satan and God. Second, it is a *journey above* to perceive the purposes of God — what he is about in his world and what he desires of us. Third, the study of missions is a *journey into Christian community*. Christians cannot live autonomously — disconnected from the church — but must unite as a community of faith for the purposes of God. The initial desire for mission, nurturing of new believers, and training for missions most effectively occurs within intimate Christian community. Fourth, it is a *journey within* — a journey of spiritual formation — of being formed as disciples of Jesus. During this journey of prayerful reflection, Christians ask, "Who am I in God's world? What is God calling me to be?" Thus the study of missions can never be a cerebral, academic exercise; it must be a transforming experience in which the heart and head are actively engaged in determining the will of God in the world and in our lives.

The text *Missions: Biblical Foundations and Contemporary Strategies* is a basic equipping tool for this journey. Each section provides a new building block to stretch monocultural horizons and equip Christian leaders to be Christ's messengers in his world.

Reading a significant introductory missions text should be the first task of the future missionary. This experience serves to form the conceptual infrastructure on which all subsequent studies and analysis of missions are based.

Some prospective missionaries, however, assume that general life training in their culture is adequate. Others realize their inadequacy to connect with searchers, model and communicate God's good news, spiritually equip new Christians as disciples, and train missionary leaders even in their own culture. Therefore, they seek training from those who have effectively carried the mission of God. Jim and Julie, for instance, went on a campaign to Haiti, their first trip outside of the United States. For the first time they realized how many people do not know the way of God in Jesus Christ and how this immense world is, to a large extent, socially broken and spiritually alienated from God. They decided that they must do something about it. But what? Consider the following two scenarios.

Scenario #1: Jim and Julie's impulse was to seek support from an agency or church and immediately return to Haiti as full-time missionaries. Had they not taught people while they were there on a campaign? Were they not greatly respected as American teachers? Could they not make significant differences in people's lives by serving them? Within a year they were able to raise support through their local church and began serving as missionaries in Haiti. Because of their lack of training, however, they did not learn the language, develop tools to learn the culture, or acquire the understanding to develop long-term strategies with local leaders. Although they desired to *Christianize* rather than *Americanize*, they did not have the basic training to understand the difference.

Scenario #2: Although Jim and Julie were tempted to return to Haiti as soon as possible, they realized their inadequacies. They realized that they knew little about the gospel and how to serve as missionaries even in their own context! They reasoned, "How can we teach what we only partially understand? What do we know about learning a language and culture, bringing searchers to faith, and 'equipping God's people for works of service'?" (Eph. 4:12). Therefore, they decided to get the best training available before returning to Haiti. They began working as youth ministers at a local church while studying Bible and missions at a local seminary. Almost immediately, they realized that North America was also a mission field! What they learned in seminary would be immediately applied to missionary ministry as they walked with high school students to minister in the two high schools of their city. They become missionaries in their own country in preparation for missionary ministry in Haiti. Over the years, Jim and Julie were used by God to bring many to Christ, nurture them to maturity, and equip them as leaders.

In Scenario #1, the missionaries ministered in Haiti as monocultual Americans without developing the conceptual infrastructure to develop and evaluate their ministries. They served as Americans who transplanted their language, culture, and message. They did not have the understandings of disciple making and mission to equip local leaders to transform their culture.

Missions: Biblical Foundations and Contemporary Strategies is written for people who have chosen the second option. The purpose of this text is to equip present and future missionaries, both domestic and foreign, with an understanding of the theological, cultural, and strategic foundations on which effective missions is based. This book guides missionaries (1) to attune their hearts to the missionary narrative of mission in the Bible — to live out the missional stories of *missio Dei*, kingdom of God, incarnation, crucifixion, and resurrection; (2) to spiritually transform their lives into God's likeness; (3) to discern personal motivations for carrying the mission of God; (4) to learn from missionaries who have gone before — in each of six epochs of the historical expansion of Christianity; (5) to learn how to be learners as they enter a new culture (even within their home culture); (6) to confront personal feelings of ethnocentrism so that they might communicate to those of another culture as equals; (7) to communicate God's eternal message in cultural categories that are both meaningful and effective; (8) to minister using a process of theological reflection, cultural analysis, historical perspective, and strategy formation within the context of spiritual formation; (9) to learn basic incarnational principles for planting churches, nurturing new believers, and training leaders; (10) to apply these principles to the specific contexts of Africa and North America; (11) to discern the wise use of money in missions; and (12) to determine fundamental criteria for selecting sites for missions.

My prayer is that this book will equip leaders to plant and renew hundreds of churches, thereby catalyzing movements of discipleship and mission.

I have been greatly blessed to partner with numerous coworkers in the writing of this book. First, and most important, is my wife Becky, who read and reread the manuscript, reflected on the content, and made suggestions. She has provided both inspiration and wisdom in forming the content of this text. Anthony Parker — my first graduate assistant at Abilene Christian University; long-term missionary to Benin and Togo, West Africa; and coach-trainer for Pioneer Bible Translators — has worked closely with us as researcher and writer. He worked tirelessly, searching for sources, organizing content, and suggesting revisions. His fingerprints are all over chapter 6 ("Types of Missionaries: The Many Faces of Missionary Ministry"); chapter 8 ("Epochs of the World Christian Movement — The Survival and Growth of Authentic Christianity through Mission"); and chapter 18 ("The Benefits and Challenges of Short-Term Missions: How Short-Term Ministry Can Have Long-Term Impact"). I am thankful to Bryan Ries, who did initial research on the chapter on "Epochs of the World Christian Movement," and Allen Diles, who wrote an initial draft of the chapter on "Short-Term Missions." My coworkers in Mission Alive have been of great encouragement. Charles Kiser, Director of Training, worked with me on the content of chapter 16 on "Planting, Nurturing, and Training: An Incarnational Model for North America." Tod Vogt, Director of Ministry Operations, has been a source of continued encouragement and a resource in areas of coaching and spiritual direction. Finally, I am thankful for the many mentors who have formed my theology and practice of missions. They include Dr. Ed Mathews and Wendell Broom of Abilene Christian University; Dr. David Hesselgrave and the late Dr. Paul Hiebert of Trinity Evangelical Divinity; and more recently, Mike Breen and Alan Hirsch, contemporary leaders of the missional movement in North America and Europe. Above all, I am thankful to God for providing the strength and focus in his Holy Spirit for writing this text. To him be glory and praise forever and ever.

Dr. Gailyn Van Rheenen
Executive Director, Mission Alive

List of Figures

chapter 1

The Biblical Narrative of Mission

Entering God's Story

JIM AND JULIE ANTICIPATED MARRIAGE and a life together serving God. As undergraduates at a Christian university, they looked forward to ministry in an existing North American church. Jim would serve as a youth minister; Julie would work vocationally as a government social worker but also assist in the youth ministry. Both had been profoundly influenced during their teenage years by youth ministers and wanted to emulate the ministry of these empathetic mentors.

During their senior year at university, a different vision began stirring their hearts: "Does God want us to become missionaries in another culture?" This question emerged when a missions professor encouraged them to go with him for a weeklong spring break mission trip to Haiti. Their lives would never be the same!

They were first impressed by Haiti's overwhelming poverty. "How could anyone live with so little?" they wondered. They were also surprised that authentic Christians were joyful despite their poverty. Life was given meaning through a loving relationship with God rather than through wealth, security, and entertainment.

They heard many sounds in Haiti: children crying, people arguing, horns honking, chickens squawking. But no sound touched them like the beating of voodoo drums — a throbbing of desperation reverberating in the night. They learned that thousands of Haitians live in fear of evil spirits and appease, manipulate, and coerce these spirits so that all aspects of life are harmonious, without illness or misfortune.

Learning the story of God's mission is a first step in becoming a missionary. The missionary learns from this story how to follow a missionary God, who sent his Son as a missionary.

The drumbeats haunted Jim and Julie, symbolizing the brokenness of a world without Jesus Christ.

During their final year at university, Jim and Julie made two commitments. They first made a commitment under God to be husband and wife. Second, and of even greater significance, they committed themselves to looking at the world through God's eyes.

A wonderful opportunity developed. A church asked Jim and Julie to serve as youth ministers. Because this church was within driving distance of an exceptional Christian seminary, they could minister full-time as they explored their developing interest in missions.

The Missionary Story of God

Their first class was an integrative course on theology of mission. In this class, they learned to read an ancient story in a new way.

The Bible, they learned, is not merely a book of dos and don'ts or a patterned guide to life. It is the story of a loving, holy, faithful God working through his people to accomplish his mission. Jim and Julie learned that this mission did not begin with Jesus or with the journeys of Paul; it began with God, who created the universe. Throughout history, people have been called to enter God's mission, to become participants in God's ongoing story. God was (and is) a missionary God!

GOD'S MISSION IN THE OLD TESTAMENT

Jim and Julie recognized that the first words of the Bible, "In the beginning God created the heavens and the earth" (Gen. 1:1), provide the roots of kingdom theology: God rules because he is our creator. God as creator is the starting point of all theology:

The earth is the LORD's, and everything in it,
the world, and all who live in it;
for he founded it on the seas
and established it on the waters.

(PSALM 24:1 – 2)

In creation, God gave form to formlessness, filled what was empty, and called light to dissipate darkness (Gen. 1:2 – 3). God continues this creation process: "God, who said, 'Let light shine out of darkness,' made his light shine in our hearts to give us the light of the knowledge of God's glory displayed in the face of Christ" (2 Cor. 4:6). Creation in many ways is similar to conversion, or re-creation. God, by his nature, brings light into darkness.

God created humans in his image, in his likeness (Gen. 1:26 – 27), expecting them to be reflections of him. They were created to replicate God's attributes — his holiness, love, and faithfulness. Although humans are earthly (i.e., created from dust), they were also inbreathed of God to become living beings (Gen. 2:7), created with eternal consciences (Rom. 2:15). Human attributes and morality should therefore be defined by the divine nature: humans must love, because God is love (1 John 4:16); they must be holy, because God is holy (1 Peter 1:15); they must be faithful, because God is faithful (2 Tim. 2:13); they are to be mirrors reflecting God.

Humans frequently, however, did not reflect God. They were created not as robots, manufactured to function according to the Master's will, but as individuals who were given the freedom to choose their direction in life. They were "free," for instance, to eat from both the tree of life and the tree of the knowledge of good and evil. God, however, gave them this instruction about the latter: "You must not eat from [it], for when you eat from it you will certainly die" (Gen. 2:17).

Humans, free to choose their way in life, often fell away from God and did not reflect God, their creator. Satan's lie convinced Eve that she would not die if she ate from the tree of the knowledge of good and evil (Gen. 3:4). She saw that the fruit was delightful to the eye and good for food and believed that it would make her like God. She therefore ate it and invited Adam to also eat.

This sin ruptured the harmony of God's world and resulted in alienation from God. Adam and Eve recognized their nakedness and hid from God. Human relationships were fragmented: they blamed others for their wrongdoing while trying to justify themselves (Gen. 3:11 – 13). People could no longer live in harmony with the land: it now produced thorns and thistles, forcing humanity to work it by the sweat of their brow (Gen. 3:18 – 19). From the beginning, sin has torn all relationships of the God-created social and environmental fabric.

After Adam and Eve acquiesced to Satan's temptations, God came searching for them, calling, "Where are you?" (Gen. 3:9). God, however, was not asking for their location. He knew where they were. He was calling them to renew their relationship with him. His question identifies his nature: he has been and is a missionary God. He continues to ask, "Where are you?" to people who are alienated from him. Throughout history, God has sought to reconcile people to himself so that they might live in a personal relationship with him.

A pattern was established with Adam and Eve: death comes to all people because they all sin (Rom. 5:12; 6:23); God, however, continues his mission of reconciliation in the midst of a sinful world.

When the people of Babel sought to make a name for themselves and avoid dispersion by building a city with a tower reaching to heaven, God confused their language and scattered them over the face of the earth (Gen. 11:1 – 9). He then elected one man, Abram, to become a great nation (Gen. 12:1 – 7) that would serve as his priest to all the nations (Ex. 19:6). This priestly nation was elected to be God's "light for the Gentiles," bringing "salvation … to the ends of the earth" (Isa. 49:6). God sent Joseph to Egypt ahead of this developing nation to save them from famine (Gen. 50:20). He later sent Moses to Pharaoh to deliver his people "with a mighty hand and an outstretched arm" (Deut. 26:5 – 9). God's mission is seen in his response to his people: he "heard their groaning and … remembered his covenant …, looked on the Israelites and was concerned about them" (Ex. 2:23 – 25). In the desert, God went ahead of them, guiding them with a pillar of cloud during the day and a pillar of fire at night (Ex. 13:21). God in his mission instituted a priesthood to stand before him on behalf of the people, laws so that they might be holy (Lev. 19), and atoning sacrifices for their forgiveness (Lev. 16:1 – 21). God sent prophets to speak to kings and to the people. In the Old Testament, God displayed his mission in the people's midst. They were in turn to be a missionary people reflecting God's light in the world.

God selected Israel as his chosen people not because they "were more numerous than other peoples" but merely because he loved them (Deut. 7:7). They were to be his holy people and thus draw all nations to him. They were to "give praise to the LORD, proclaim his name; make known among the nations what he has done" (Ps. 105:1). Thus the nations would say, "Come, let us go up to the mountain of the LORD, to the temple of the God of Jacob. He will teach us his ways, so that we may walk in his paths" (Isa. 2:3).

But God's chosen people were frequently rebellious. They sought to build up their own armies rather than trust in God. They became rich by trampling on the poor rather than remembering that they were once poor, wandering aliens. They insidiously worshiped the gods of the nations around them while still declaring their allegiance to God. In the midst of such great disobedience, God wept over his people as a husband mourning for his unfaithful wife or a father feeling the loss of an estranged child. He cried, "How can I give you up, Ephraim? How can I hand you over, Israel?... My heart is changed within me; all my compassion is aroused" (Hos. 11:8). Because of their great disobedience, God delivered the northern part of the nation, Israel, into Assyrian captivity (2 Kings 17:16–20), and the southern part of the nation, Judah, into Babylonian captivity (Jer. 5:19), to be refined as God's people.

I am extremely nearsighted. Without my glasses, I have difficulty seeing anything distinctly if it is beyond arm's reach. Likewise, perceiving the realities of the world without the lens of Scripture is spiritual nearsightedness. Scripture helps me perceive God's world through God's lens in relation to God's purposes.

Even in Babylonian captivity, the people of God learned that "the righteous will live by faith" (Rom. 1:17). Although many Jews accommodated to their new land, forgot God their savior, and adopted the gods of the land, God worked through Daniel to declare to Babylonian and Persian kings that he was sovereign over all the kingdoms of the world. God's gracious hand was on Ezra as he organized synagogues so that the people of God would not forget the law and helped organize the people for renewal both in captivity and in Jerusalem. God worked through Ezekiel, Zerubbabel, Jeshua, Nehemiah, Haggai, and many others to fulfill his mission of returning to Jerusalem a remnant, through whom a Promised One would come.

This missional reading of the Old Testament led Jim and Julie to memorize significant passages about God. These passages define his distinctiveness from other gods and reflect his nature.

Who among the gods
is like you, LORD?
Who is like you—
majestic in holiness,
awesome in glory,
working wonders?
(EXODUS 15:11)

He is the Rock, his works are perfect,
and all his ways are just.
A faithful God who does no wrong,
upright and just is he.
(DEUTERONOMY 32:4)

The LORD, the LORD, the compassionate and gracious God, slow to anger, abounding in love and faithfulness, maintaining love to thousands, and forgiving wickedness, rebellion and sin. Yet he does not leave the guilty unpunished; he punishes the children and their children for the sin of the parents to the third and fourth generation.[1] (EXODUS 34:6–7)

Holy, holy, holy is the LORD Almighty;
the whole earth is full of his glory.
(ISAIAH 6:3)

Jim and Julie learned to stand in awe of the Lord of glory, creator of the heavens and the earth, who seeks his people like a compassionate father searching for his lost child.

Their understanding of the Old Testament helped Jim and Julie comprehend the New Testament. The Bible, they realized, is like a long sentence with the first part related to the second. Both parts describe the history of God's work. The Old Testament narrates how Creator God formed a people to represent his nature in an idolatrous, alienated world where gods made by human hands were worshiped rather than the God who created the heavens and earth. The New Testament tells the story of God's Son who came to the earth to model kingdom living and commission his people to make disciples of all nations. They realized that Jesus Christ stands at the fulcrum of history, bringing light and life to all generations.

GOD'S MISSION IN JESUS

In the New Testament, Jim and Julie saw God's mission personified in Jesus Christ. The "one and only Son, who came from the Father, full

1. The ramifications of sin often pass from one generation to another. They can be stopped only by turning to God, who is merciful, always ready to forgive.

of grace and truth" (John 1:14), became God in human flesh by divine will. Born to a virgin, he was both wholly divine and fully human, and therefore called Immanuel, meaning "God with us" (Matt. 1:23). Jesus' life reflected God, who sent him. Jesus acknowledged that he could do nothing on his own. The words he spoke were not his own but from the Father, who was working within him (John 14:10). His attitudes of love and holiness reflected those of God.

He Touched the Untouchable

> *A man with leprosy came to him and begged him on his knees, "If you are willing, you can make me clean." Filled with compassion, Jesus reached out his hand and touched the man. "I am willing," he said. "Be clean!" Immediately the leprosy left him and he was cured. (Mark 1:40–42 NIV 1984)*

He Wept with the Weeping

> *Jesus said to [Martha], "I am the resurrection and the life. . . ." When Mary reached the place where Jesus was and saw him, she fell at his feet and said, "Lord, if you had been here, my brother would not have died." When Jesus saw her weeping, and the Jews who had come along with her also weeping, he was deeply moved in spirit and troubled. "Where have you laid him?" he asked. "Come and see, Lord," they replied. Jesus wept. Then the Jews said, "See how he loved him!" (John 11:25, 32–36)*

He Died for People Dying in Sin

> *Even the Son of Man did not come to be served, but to serve, and to give his life as a ransom for many. (Mark 10:45)*

> *God demonstrates his own love for us in this: While we were still sinners, Christ died for us. (Romans 5:8)*

Jesus' miracles testified to his divinity: he fed the multitudes, calmed storms, helped the blind to see and the lame to walk, cast out demons, and raised the dead. Nicodemus, the Jewish religious leader, confessed to Jesus, "No one could perform the signs you are doing if God were

The Great "I Am's" in the Book of John Affirm the Distinctiveness of Jesus

"I am the bread of life" (6:35).
"I am the light of the world" (8:12).
"I am the gate for the sheep" (10:7).
"I am the good shepherd" (10:11).
"I am the resurrection and the life" (11:25).
"I am the way and the truth and the life" (14:6).
"I am the true vine" (15:1).

not with him" (John 3:2). When the multitudes heard about salt and light, a righteousness that surpassed that of the Jewish teachers of the law, and other kingdom teachings in the Sermon on the Mount, they were amazed "because he taught as one who had authority, and not as their teachers of the law" (Matt. 7:28 – 29). This kingdom message was "not of coercive dominance but of liberating love, not of top-down domination but of bottom-up service, not of a clenched iron fist but of open, wounded hands extended in a welcoming embrace of kindness, gentleness, forgiveness and grace" (McLaren 2004, 83).

Numerous disciples gathered around Jesus, and from among them he prayerfully selected twelve apostles who would be "with him and that he might send them out to preach" (Mark 3:14). He personally nurtured them while "teaching in their synagogues, proclaiming the good news of the kingdom and healing every disease and sickness" (Matt. 9:35) and then sent them out on the Limited Commission. This commission was motivated by his compassion for the multitudes: they were pictured as "harassed and helpless, like sheep without a shepherd" (Matt. 9:36). He then told his disciples to "ask the Lord of the harvest ... to send out workers into his harvest field" (Matt. 9:37 – 38). These praying disciples were then sent out two by two to proclaim the message of the kingdom to their fellow countrymen, the Israelites (Matt. 10:1 – 6).

Jesus' ministry challenged the entrenched Jewish religious hierarchy, who sought to appease Rome and uphold the sectarian views of the religious elite. The religious elite imposed their own traditions and beliefs on the people but defined them as rules of God (Matt. 15:1 – 9). Jesus taught that righteousness of the heart is more to be desired than righteousness of the law, that mercy is preferred over sacrifice, and that the kingdom of God is greater than the dominions of this world. Jesus described his relationship with his Father: "I and the Father are one" (John 10:30), and "The Father is in me, and I in the Father" (John 10:38).

The religious establishment considered these teachings blasphemy, worthy of death. These religious authorities delivered Jesus to the political rulers and campaigned for his crucifixion. What a paradox! "He came to that which was his own, but his own did not receive him" (John 1:11).

The final week of Jesus' life is pivotal in human history. All history either points forward to the events of this week or reflects backward to them. These events took place during the Passover Feast, celebrated to remember God's deliverance of the Israelites from Egyptian captivity. During this remembrance, the Son of God, incarnated in human flesh, full of compassion, died to deliver people who trust him from the bondage of sin. Jesus demonstrated "the full extent of his love" by washing his disciples' feet (John 13:1 – 17 NIV 1984). He comforted his disciples after telling them of his betrayal and death (13:18 – 14:14). He promised to give them the Holy Spirit as comforter and counselor (14:15 – 16:33). He prayed for the faith and unity of his disciples (17:1 – 26). Knowing that his time was short, Jesus earnestly prayed that God would take away the impending "cup" of suffering but concluded his prayer with, "Yet not my will, but yours be done" (Luke 22:42). He prayed in anguish, so that "his sweat was like drops of blood falling to the ground," knowing that his death was near (v. 44). This perfect One of God was

Why did Jesus die? How do we clearly articulate what God did in the death of Jesus Christ? Answering these questions is an important missionary task.

- betrayed by Judas,
- denied by Peter,
- condemned by the high priest,
- sentenced by Pilate,
- flogged and mocked by soldiers,
- accused of sedition by Jewish leaders,
- nailed to a cross by the powers.

Despite his rejection, Jesus illustrated the heart of God from the cross by speaking words of forgiveness. Our wronged Savior in anguish cried, "Father, forgive them, for they do not know what they are doing" (Luke 23:34). He proclaimed that the way forward was not justice based on revenge but unconditional forgiveness. This forgiveness is illustrated by Jesus' response to the indicted criminal dying with him who asked, "Jesus, remember me when you come into your kingdom." Jesus replied, "Truly I tell you, today you will be with me in paradise" (Luke 23:42 – 43). Jesus as sovereign Lord has the power to forgive. By becoming a victim, he forgave and illustrated a way to live. Jesus as God's sovereign victim has the power and the right to forgive. He died to bring forgiveness to all people who come to God in faith.

Or, stated through an alternative metaphor, God in his Son came to the earth to die as a substitute for us as sinners, the holy for the unholy, the sinless for the sinful, a sacrificial lamb slaughtered so that we might live. Paul wrote, "God made him who had no sin to be sin for us, so that in him we might become the righteousness of God" (2 Cor. 5:21). God was on mission in Jesus Christ.

A third metaphor is Paul's description of Jesus' death and resurrection in cosmic terms. We participate in the death and resurrection of Christ by dying to our own sins and being raised to life. In this triumphal resurrection, Christ disarms "the powers and authorities" and makes "a public spectacle of them, triumphing over them by the cross" (Col. 2:13 – 15). This teaching of Christus Victor spoke powerfully to Jim and Julie as they contemplated the Haitian fear of gods, demons, and spirits. God, through Jesus Christ, defeats these powers and delivers people from their control to live as his children.

Jesus' death, as illustrated in these metaphors of atonement, is only the beginning of the story. Neither a guarded grave nor satanic shackles could hold the Son of God. God, by his mighty power, raised Jesus from the dead! After his resurrection, Christ appeared first to Peter, afterward to the Twelve, and eventually to more than five hundred brothers at the same time (1 Cor. 15:5 – 6).

Thomas, who was absent when Jesus first appeared to the other apostles, doubted. "Unless I see the nail marks in his hands and put my finger where the nails were, and put my hand into his side," he declared, "I will not believe" (John 20:25). A week later Jesus again appeared to the apostles, and Thomas was present. Jesus, feeling the struggles of Thomas, told him to put his finger in his wounds, saying, "Stop doubting and believe" (v. 27). Upon seeing the resurrected Lord, doubting Thomas could only reply, "My Lord and my God!" (v. 28). Jesus then concluded, "Because you have seen me, you have believed; blessed are those who have not seen and yet have believed" (v. 29).

Jim and Julie realized that Christ's ministry culminated in the Great Commission:

> *All authority in heaven and on earth has been given to me. Therefore go and make disciples of all nations, baptizing them in the name of the Father and of the Son and of the Holy Spirit, and teaching them to obey everything I have commanded you. And surely I am with you always, to the very end of the age.* (MATTHEW 28:18 – 20)

They acknowledged that the commission begins and ends with Christ's authority as resurrected Lord. By his authority, they were to "go and make disciples," and Christ would be with them in ministry until his second coming. The Great Commission defined their ministry: They were to make disciples — not adherents or church members but disciples! "Baptizing ..." and "teaching ..." are dependent clauses describing how disciples are made. Making disciples is accomplished by guiding believers to fully participate in Christ's death, burial, and resurrection and by teaching them to obey everything Christ has commanded. The fourfold use or inference of the word *all* illustrates Christ's supreme sovereignty in God's mission of disciple making: Christ is given "all authority" to make disciples of "all nations," teaching them to obey "everything" Christ has commanded, and he will be with his followers "always."

This missional reading of the Gospels led Jim and Julie to memorize significant passages about the role and ministry of Christ in redemptive history.

> *He appeared in the flesh,*
> *was vindicated by the Spirit,*
> *was seen by angels,*
> *was preached among the nations,*
> *was believed on in the world,*
> *was taken up in glory.*
> (1 Timothy 3:16)

> *God so loved the world that he gave his one and only Son, that whoever believes in him shall not perish but have eternal life.* (John 3:16)

> *The Son is the image of the invisible God, the firstborn over all creation. For in him all things were created: things in heaven and on earth, visible and invisible, whether thrones or powers or rulers or authorities; all things have been created through him and for him. He is before all things, and in him all things hold together.* (Colossians 1:15–17)

> *In Christ all the fullness of the Deity lives in bodily form, and in Christ you have been brought to fullness. He is the head over every power and authority.* (Colossians 2:9–10)

Having disarmed the powers and authorities, he made a public spectacle of them, triumphing over them by the cross.
(Colossians 2:15)

They concluded that "to be a Christ-follower is to become a character who contributes to the continual telling, retelling, and re-retelling of Christ's story" (Kallenberg 2002, 37 – 38).

GOD'S MISSION IN THE CHURCH THROUGH HIS HOLY SPIRIT

Jim and Julie soon realized that the stories of Jesus' life were written to provide a model for his disciples to emulate. While reading the book of Acts and the letters of the apostles, they learned how the early Christian church sought to live out the life of Christ, and they recognized how the story of Christ's life had similarly shaped them. They concurred with Paul in wanting "to know Christ — yes, to know the power of his resurrection and participation in his sufferings, becoming like him in his death, and so, somehow, attaining to the resurrection from the dead" (Phil. 3:10 – 11).

The book of Acts and the letters of Peter, Paul, and John caused Jim and Julie to grow in their desire to imitate the early Christians as they likewise imitated Christ (1 Cor. 11:1). These early Christians, gathered from multiple ethnic heritages, were to be God's redeeming light to the nations, inviting all people to journey with Christ in community, preparing for an eternity with God.

During the forty days after his resurrection, Jesus prepared his disciples for a Spirit-guided life without him. He had promised that he would ask the Father to provide them with "another advocate to help [them] and be with [them] forever — the Spirit of truth" (John 14:16 – 17). Jesus said, "I will not leave you as orphans; I will come to you" (John 14:18). He then "opened their minds so they could understand" what had occurred in his death, burial, and resurrection in light of the Scriptures (Luke 24:45), and he commissioned them to become his witnesses to the nations by the power of the Holy Spirit (Luke 24:46 – 49). His last words described his imminent mission through them by the power of the Spirit: "You will receive power when the Holy Spirit comes on you; and you will be my witnesses in Jerusalem, and in all Judea and Samaria, and to the ends of the earth" (Acts 1:8).[2] After these words, Jesus was exalted into heaven "before their very eyes" (Acts 1:9). Two angels in white asked his disciples, "Why do you stand here looking into the sky? This same Jesus, who has been taken from you into heaven, will come back in the same way you have seen him go into heaven" (Acts 1:10 – 11). Because Jesus had told them to wait in Jerusalem for the promised gift of the Holy Spirit (Acts 1:4 – 5), these early Christians, filled with anticipation, remained in the city. They prayed together and used Scripture to discern whom they should select to take Judas's place as the twelfth apostle.

Fifty days after Passover, during the Feast of Weeks, or Pentecost, Jews once again gathered in Jerusalem, to thank God for the abundant harvest. On this momentous day, God poured out his Holy Spirit on the apostles, who were gathered with the 120 in an upper room. They began to speak with other tongues. Jews from many nations who had gathered for this celebration observed this phenomenon and were amazed. They asked, "Aren't all these who are speaking Galileans? Then how is it that each of us hears them in our native language?" (Acts 2:7 – 8). "What does this mean?" (Acts 2:12). Joel's prophecy that the Spirit would be poured out on all people so that they would see visions, dream dreams, and prophesy, Peter testified, was being fulfilled (Acts 2:14 – 21). Peter then recounted the gospel, the story about the death, burial, resurrection, and exaltation of Christ.

> *Fellow Israelites, listen to this: Jesus of Nazareth was a man accredited by God to you by miracles, wonders and signs, which God did among you through him, as you yourselves know. This man was handed over to you by God's deliberate plan and foreknowledge; and you, with the help of wicked men, put him to death by nailing him to the cross. But God raised him from the dead, freeing him from the agony of death, because it was impossible for death to keep its hold on him.... God has raised this Jesus to life, and we are all witnesses of it. Exalted to the right*

2. This verse outlines the book of Acts. Chapters 1 – 7 describe their witness in Jerusalem, chapters 8 – 12 in Judea and Samaria, and chapters 13 – 28 to the ends of the earth. This passage illustrates the major theme of Acts: God's mission was to be accomplished not by human initiative but by the power of God's Spirit.

hand of God, he has received from the Father the promised Holy Spirit and has poured out what you now see and hear.
(ACTS 2:22 – 24, 32 – 33)

Peter's message to the Jews resounds throughout Christian history as the core of the gospel:

- Jesus' miracles testified to his nature.
- His death was according to God's eternal plan.
- God raised him from the dead.
- God has exalted him to his own right hand.
- Christ has received the promised Holy Spirit from God and has now poured it down on us.

The Jews, after hearing Peter's message and realizing that they had crucified God's Messiah and their Lord, asked, "Brothers, what shall we do?" (Acts 2:37). They were told to "repent and be baptized ... for the forgiveness of your sins"[3] and that they would "receive the gift of the Holy Spirit" (Acts 2:38). On that day, three thousand people were baptized, and as a community, they committed themselves to what has been called throughout history the basic Christian practices: "They devoted themselves to the apostles' teaching and to fellowship, to the breaking of bread and to prayer" (v. 42). The word *together* typified this early community. They shared what they had; the rich helped the poor. They met together publicly in the temple and privately in their homes. They witnessed the miracles of the apostles. "They broke bread in their homes and ate together with glad and sincere hearts, praising God and enjoying the favor of all the people" (vv. 46 – 47). The church became the community in which Christian teachings were explained and the way of God in Christ was illustrated. As a result, God "added to their number daily those who were being saved" (v. 47).

Because they proclaimed the resurrection and exaltation of Jesus and believed that "salvation is found in no one else" (Acts 4:12), these early Christians were a challenge to Jewish leaders. They could not be

3. Baptism is an act of grace in which believers participate in the death, burial, and resurrection of Christ (Rom. 6:3 – 10). The teaching that baptism is for the forgiveness of sin does not negate salvation by grace through faith. Salvation is "the gift of God," not achieved by human activity (Eph. 2:8).

silenced, even though they were considered "unschooled" and "ordinary" (v. 13). When commanded not to speak in the name of Jesus, they replied, "We cannot help speaking about what we have seen and heard.... We must obey God rather than human beings!" (Acts 4:20; 5:29). They asked for courage, and God filled them with his Holy Spirit so that they continued to speak the word of God boldly (Acts 4:23 – 31).

Missions 101
It's God's Mission
By His Power
With His Provision
Through His People
(Reppart 2006)

The early church was distinctively Jewish. They continued to observe Jewish feasts, circumcise their male children on the eighth day, and zealously keep the teachings of the law (Acts 21:20). They used Old Testament Scripture to affirm that Jesus was their long-awaited Messiah, and following him demonstrated their faithfulness to the covenant of Abraham.

God in Christ and his Holy Spirit, however, began to work through his people to expand the Christian mission to include the entire world. Persecution in Jerusalem caused Christians to be scattered among God-fearing Gentiles and Samaritans (Acts 8). Jesus appeared to Saul, the ardent persecutor, in a vision and set him aside to be his apostle to the Gentiles (Acts 9, 22, 26). An angel appeared to Cornelius, a God-fearing Gentile, in a vision, telling him to send for Peter. Also through a vision, God declared to Peter that he should not "call anything impure that God has made clean" and told him by the Spirit to go with three men sent by Cornelius (Acts 10:9 – 23). Peter, led by the Holy Spirit, acknowledged before Cornelius and his household God's actions in his life: "You are well aware that it is against our law for a Jew to associate with or visit a Gentile. But God has shown me that I should not call anyone impure or unclean" (Acts 10:28). He declared God's universal vision for all people to know God and to walk with him: "I now realize how true it is that God does not show favoritism but accepts from every nation the one who fears him and does what is right" (Acts 10:34 – 35). After Cornelius and his household heard the story of Jesus, the Holy Spirit miraculously fell on them, as with the apostles on the day of Pentecost (Acts 10:44 – 48).

When Jewish brothers in Jerusalem heard that Gentiles "had received the word of God," they confronted Peter, saying, "You went into the house of uncircumcised men and ate with them" (Acts 11:1 – 3). Their core struggle hinged on the question of table fellowship. Could they socially accept Gentiles as brothers and sisters in full community?

Peter responded by describing his vision, the Spirit's leading him to Cornelius's house, and the outpouring of the Holy Spirit on Cornelius and his household. He then concluded that "if God gave them the same gift he gave us who believed in the Lord Jesus Christ, who was I to think that I could stand in God's way?" (v. 17). Upon hearing this, the Christians realized that "even to Gentiles God has granted repentance that leads to life" (v. 18).

Although Acts 10 – 11 is typically described as the story of Cornelius's conversion, it also contains the story of Peter's conversion. Peter, a Hebrew-speaking Jew, was led by God to accept Greek-speaking Gentiles as his brothers and sisters in Christ. This story demonstrates that God's mission moves forward, not only by strategic planning or human ingenuity, but also by God's mighty actions in the lives of Christians and searchers alike. Peter had no plans to visit Cornelius. He was merely following God's leading through the Holy Spirit.

God's mission among Gentiles began in earnest when Jewish Christians, scattered by persecution, began telling the good news to Gentiles in Antioch, the fourth-largest city of the Mediterranean world. Luke affirms that this was God's work: "The Lord's hand was with them, and a great number of people believed and turned to the Lord" (Acts 11:21). When the Jerusalem church heard of this new movement, they sent Barnabas, the "son of encouragement" (Acts 4:36), to assess what was occurring. Barnabas, seeing "what the grace of God had done ... encouraged them all to remain true to the Lord with all their hearts" (Acts 11:23). Luke in Acts affirms that the proclamation of the gospel to the Gentiles was by God's leading — according to his will.

Barnabas, perhaps recalling that God had called Saul to become an apostle among the Gentiles, brought him to Antioch, and together they taught many people to know the way of God (Acts 11:25 – 26). As leaders of this newly founded church were "worshiping the Lord and fasting," the Holy Spirit said, "Set apart for me Barnabas and Saul for the work to which I have called them" (Acts 13:1 – 2). After fasting and praying, the Antioch church submitted to the Spirit's call and "placed their hands on them and sent them off" (v. 3). The church sought the will of God and implemented it.

The Antioch church illustrates that world mission flows from a vibrant relationship with God. Without spiritual formation, world mission stagnates. All mission endeavors — because they are God's work — must begin with worship and prayer.

Saul, now known as Paul (the Gentile equivalent of Saul), quickly becomes the major character of the biblical mission narrative. Paul is the historical prototype of a missionary sent to plant new churches via evangelism, equip young Christians to grow to spiritual maturity, and train leaders to work beside him in Christian service. As already noted, Barnabas, the encourager, played a significant role in Paul's life. He introduced this previous persecutor to the elders of the Jerusalem church after Paul was called to be an apostle to the Gentiles (Acts 9), brought him to Antioch to help launch the Gentile mission (Acts 11), and became his first coworker in God's missionary enterprise (Acts 13).

On their first missionary journey, Paul and Barnabas modeled "the apostolic band," a small group of evangelists who regard themselves as "envoys of God" sent out by the church "to the unbelieving world" (Glasser 2009, 150). Glasser uses Acts 14:21 – 23 to describe their sequence of activities as

- preaching the gospel,
- making disciples,
- modeling community in Christ,
- demonstrating how community members serve as custodians of the gospel and exemplifiers of the kingdom of God,
- organizing new disciples into local congregations in which individual members commit themselves to one another and to the order and discipline of the Spirit of God. (Glasser 2009, 150)

An apostolic band emerges when God calls missionaries into a common evangelistic ministry. Unlike the church (which is marked by continuity and reproduction), the band is ever changing, temporary, as evangelists fulfill their calling in God's mission. The first missionary band was composed of Paul and Barnabas, with Mark as their temporary helper; the second, of Paul and Silas, with Timothy as their apprentice; the third, of leaders representing various churches: "Sopater son of Pyrrhus from Berea, Aristarchus and Secundus from Thessalonica, Gaius from Derbe, Timothy also, and Tychicus and Trophimus from the province of Asia" (Acts 20:4).

The conversion of Gentiles created a significant stir among Jewish Christians. Christians from Judea visited Antioch and began teaching that "unless you are circumcised, according to the custom taught by Moses, you cannot be saved" (Acts 15:1). They advocated that in order to be a Christian, a believer must become a Jew through the ritual of circumcision. Paul and Barnabas sharply disputed this teaching, creating such dissention that a delegation was sent to consult with the apostles and elders in Jerusalem about the issue.

In the Jerusalem conference, Peter recounted what God had done through him in bringing Gentiles to repentance, and argued that God had made no distinction between Jew and Gentile. Both were saved by grace, not by law (Acts 15:7 – 11). Barnabas and Paul attested to the miraculous signs and wonders that God had performed among the Gentiles through their ministry (v. 12). Would God perform such miracles if he were not accepting Gentiles into his kingdom?

Finally, James quoted Amos, who had prophesied that "David's fallen shelter" would be restored and that both the remnant and "nations that bear [God's] name" would be included (Amos 9:11 – 12). All of the Christian leaders accepted James's conclusion: "It is my judgment, therefore, that we should not make it difficult for the Gentiles who are turning to God" (Acts 15:19). The council then decided that people from another culture should not be compelled to conform to the patterns of the sending culture.

Nevertheless, in order to allow Jews and Gentiles to have fellowship within one body, the Gentile Christians were asked to "abstain from food polluted by idols, from sexual immorality, from the meat of strangled animals and from blood" (Acts 15:20). These items, related to the worship of false gods, were repugnant to Jewish Christians and therefore disruptive of fellowship (vv. 20 – 21). Paul's writings about meat offered to idols demonstrate that these restrictions were not binding in all cases (Rom. 14:13 – 23; 1 Cor. 8:7 – 13). Although eating meat offered to idols was not wrong in itself, the act became wrong when it caused a Jewish Christian to stumble. Every culture has customs that, when practiced, disrupt fellowship between cultures. Since Christians value others above themselves (Phil. 2:3), they humbly submit to one another by discerning how God desires them to live.

The Jerusalem conference established a precedent for the relationships between sending churches and churches established in mission areas. Christian leaders did not require people receiving the gospel cross-culturally to adopt the culture of the sending church in order to be received into Christian fellowship. Specifically, in the early Christian culture, Gentiles were not obligated to undergo circumcision and thus become full-fledged Jews in order to be saved. Without this decision, Christianity would likely have remained a Jewish sect. God's mighty working, however, led Christian leaders from vastly different heritages to a mutual agreement.

Paul's writings continually reminded the churches of their apostolic calling. They were a people sent by God to preach the gospel beyond their immediate communities. This theme is evident in Paul's letter to the Romans. In his introduction, Paul acknowledged, "We received grace and apostleship to call all the Gentiles to the obedience that comes from faith" (Rom. 1:5). The letter was written after Paul's missionary tours in the eastern Mediterranean. He testified that "by the power of signs and wonders, through the power of the Spirit," he had preached the gospel "from Jerusalem all the way around to Illyricum"[4] (Rom. 15:19). He then planned to go to Rome so that they might send him on to Spain (v. 24). He envisioned the Roman church as "a second Antioch" (Glasser 2009, 152), a new sending church to launch God's mission through him in the western Mediterranean.

Paul's letter to the Romans gives a theological rationale for his ongoing missionary activity. All people, both Gentiles and Jews, have sinned against God (Rom. 1:18 – 3:20). But God reunites all people to himself, not because they obey the law but because of the sacrifice of his Son (Rom. 3:21 – 25). God "presented Christ as a sacrifice of atonement, through the shedding of his blood" (v. 25). This grace is extended to the believer who, having been a slave of sin, is freed from those shackles and becomes instead a slave of righteousness. He has moved from death to life (Rom. 6:1 – 23). The battle between flesh and spirit rages within the human soul. However, God by his Spirit emancipates the believer by "[putting] to death the misdeeds of the body" (Rom. 8:13), thus providing authentic life with God in Christ by his Holy Spirit (Rom. 7:7 – 8:39). Paul writes with assurance, "I am convinced that neither death nor life, neither angels nor demons, neither the present nor the future, nor any

4. An area northeast of Italy, somewhat comparable to present-day Slovenia.

powers, neither height nor depth, nor anything else in all creation, will be able to separate us from the love of God that is in Christ Jesus our Lord" (Rom. 8:38 – 39).

Paul emotionally writes about the dilemma of his own people, the Israelites. Their rejection of Christ, their failure to fulfill their role as a kingdom of priests (Ex. 19:5 – 6) and to serve as a light to the nations (Isa. 60:3), led to Gentiles being included in God's mission (Rom. 11:11). Gentile believers, however, must humbly acknowledge that they are like wild shoots grafted into an olive tree, and thereby receive nourishment from a heritage not their own. Israelite branches were pruned from the tree because of disobedience, and Gentile branches were grafted in because of faith (v. 20). God has not rejected Israel. He has merely extended his grace to the Gentiles.

Paul concludes his letter to the Romans with practical instructions that grow out of his theological principles. Christians should view their lives as spiritual sacrifices, no longer conforming to the world but being transformed by God (Rom. 12:1 – 2). They should humbly recognize the gifts that God has given them (vv. 3 – 8). God's love should permeate their lives so that they joyfully and harmoniously dwell in Christian community (vv. 9 – 21). They should submit to governing authorities, since these authorities have been established by God (Rom. 13:1 – 7). The strong in Christ should accept the weak "without quarreling over disputable matters" such as which foods to eat or which sacred days to observe (Rom. 14:1 – 12). They should not create obstacles to faith (v. 14) but should accept others in all their diversity. Paul writes, "Accept one another, then, just as Christ accepted you, in order to bring praise to God" (Rom. 15:7).

Paul finally comes back to God's missionary purposes — the reason, in fact, for his writing to the Romans. "Christ has become a servant of the Jews ... that the Gentiles might glorify God for his mercy" (Rom. 15:8 – 9). By God's grace, Paul had been set aside "to be a minister of Christ Jesus to the Gentiles ... so that the Gentiles might become an offering acceptable to God, sanctified by the Holy Spirit" (v. 16). Thus Paul's epistle to the Romans expressed his missional theology, with hopes that the Roman church would sponsor him in God's mission in the western Mediterranean, as the church in Antioch had done in the eastern Mediterranean.

The early Christian church, however, was weak and fallible, prone to accommodate to popular culture. For example, Colossian believers, although they had received Christ, were tempted to also follow the "elemental forces of the world" (Col. 2:8 HCSB), the *stoicheia*. The *stoicheia* were the cultural building blocks of traditional society, the directives through which spiritual powers had established legalistic control of society (Col. 2:6 – 8; Gal. 4:3). They included legalistic observances of the law, worship of angels, and other pre-Christian animistic practices (Col. 2:16 – 19). Colossian Christians who were tempted to slide back into their pre-Christian worldview were told to remember their conversion (v. 6) and not return to the old principles (v. 8). Rather they were to hold to Christ as "all the fullness of the Deity" (v. 9) so that "all things, whether things on earth or things in heaven" would come under his authority (vv. 19 – 20). He is to be "the head over every power and authority" (v. 2:10).

As Jim and Julie reflected on the Colossian church, they became aware of the tendency for God's people in all times and on all continents to blend their beliefs and practices with that of the dominant culture. They also reflected on how their own church, and even their own lives, illustrate such cultural accommodation. They asked, "How often have we followed the elementary principles of this world?"

The early Christians believed that they were standing between the times. The kingdom of God had more fully broken in with the coming of Christ, the King of Kings, but had not yet been consummated with his second coming. The parable in Matthew 13:24 – 30 shows that wheat and weeds grow side by side and look very much alike. The weeds, however, represent "the people of the evil one," and the wheat "the people of the kingdom" (v. 38). Since the two sets of roots have mingled, removing the weeds would endanger the harvest. The parable focuses on the command "Let both grow together until the harvest" (v. 30). Good and bad are not separated in the present age. When God consummates his kingdom with judgment, the weeds will be separated from the wheat, and "the righteous will shine ... in the kingdom of their Father" (v. 43). This parable thus gives a reason for the continuance of Satan's kingdom even though God's kingdom in Christ has broken into the world.

Christians, who have been "strengthened with all power according to [God's] glorious might" in the present age, anticipate "the inheritance of his holy people in the kingdom of light" (Col. 1:11 – 12). They have "tasted ... the powers of the coming age" (Heb. 6:5). The rule that God has initiated in Jesus Christ continues through people who believe in him, and will be consummated at the end of the age (Beasley-Murray 1986, 80). Christians are therefore to watch because they do not know when the Lord will come (Matt. 24:42; 25:13), prepare themselves by holy living (2 Peter 3:14), and proclaim with urgency the gospel (Acts 8:12).

This missional reading of God's work through his Holy Spirit in the early Christian church led Jim and Julie to memorize:

The Words of Jesus in Acts 1:8

You will receive power when the Holy Spirit comes on you; and you will be my witnesses in Jerusalem, and in all Judea and Samaria, and to the ends of the earth.

The Words of Peter in Acts 10:34 – 35

I now realize how true it is that God does not show favoritism but accepts from every nation the one who fears him and does what is right.

The Words of Jesus to Saul on the Road to Damascus in Acts 26:17 – 18

I am sending you to them to open their eyes and turn them from darkness to light, and from the power of Satan to God, so that they may receive forgiveness of sins and a place among those who are sanctified by faith in me.

The Words of Paul in Ephesians 2:4 – 6, 8 – 9

Because of his great love for us, God, who is rich in mercy, made us alive with Christ even when we were dead in transgressions — it is by grace you have been saved. And God raised us up with Christ and seated us with him in the heavenly realms in Christ

Jesus. . . . For it is by grace you have been saved, through faith — and this is not from yourselves, it is the gift of God — not by works, so that no one can boast.

The Words from Heaven Heard by John in Revelation 12:11

They triumphed over [Satan]
by the blood of the Lamb
and by the word of their testimony;
they did not love their lives so much
as to shrink from death.

Claiming the Story

Rehearsing the story line of the Bible challenged Jim and Julie and changed their lives. They now recognized that Christianity is a distinctively historical religion and can be understood only through hearing of God's ongoing work in human history.

They learned that missionaries are people sent on a mission. The mission, however, is not a human endeavor dedicated to some sort of human achievement. It is the undertaking of God for the glory of God. In fact, the mission was initiated by God himself, who is by nature a missionary God. Missionaries are merely God's servants who participate in his mission.

This mission is best described by the term *missio Dei*, "the mission of God" (see chap. 3). God is a missionary God who enters into human contexts and sends various sorts of missionaries to participate in his mission. God continues to call and send workers into his mission as he called and sent Abraham to a distant country and Moses back to Egypt. The greatest illustration of this sending is Jesus Christ, sent by God into the world to redeem us from sin and reconcile us to God. This Jesus, reflecting God's sending of him, said to his disciples after his resurrection, "As the Father has sent me, I am sending you" (John 20:21).

Missio Dei also infers the rule, or reign, of God. The God of mission rules because he is God! There is no other! He is our creator, the One to whom we give full allegiance. After the deliverance from Egypt, Moses, who knew the power of the gods of Egypt, professed,

Who among the gods
is like you, LORD?
Who is like you —
majestic in holiness,
awesome in glory,
working wonders?
(EXODUS 15:11)

The attributes of God — holiness, love, and faithfulness — form the character of people carrying this mission. The result is that his "kingdom [will] come" and his "will [shall] be done, on earth as it is in heaven" (Matt. 6:10).

God thus calls people into his mission to represent him in the world. Missionaries thus are people sent by God on his mission.

REFLECTION AND APPLICATION

Questions

1. How is God described in this chapter? How do these understandings form how we live?
2. What aspects of God's nature motivate you to join him in his mission? Give specific examples from Scripture.
3. Review the "I am" statements of Jesus. How does your belief in these statements motivate you to make Jesus known?
4. What is the central task to which the Great Commission (Matt. 28:18–20) calls us?
5. What was the "core gospel" that the Holy Spirit led Peter to proclaim on Pentecost?
6. In what sense was the conversion of Cornelius also part of the ongoing conversion of Peter and the church?
7. What was the role of the "apostolic band" in early Christian mission?
8. What did Paul hope the church in Rome would do for him after reading his grand exposition of "missional theology"?
9. How is it that God's kingdom is "already" but "not yet" present? What is our task as believers during this in-between time?
10. What is the significance for you that mission is *missio Dei*, the mission of God, and not a human endeavor?

Application

When Jim and Julie learned the narrative of God's mission in Scripture, their lives were changed. In what ways have you been transformed? Specifically, what did you learn from (1) God's mission in the Old Testament, (2) God's mission through Jesus, and (3) God's mission in the church through his Holy Spirit? How does this chapter form your identity?

chapter 2

Spiritual Awakenings for Mission

Reflecting God's Glory

JIM AND JULIE SOON REALIZED that they could not "become missionaries" by their own might and power. They needed to learn to rely on God, accept his sovereign reign over their lives, and be "transformed into his image" (2 Cor. 3:18).

From Caterpillar to Butterfly

They began to understand that they were like caterpillars. Frequently, they were crawling in earthly realms, consuming thoughts and fads of popular culture.[1] They needed a metamorphosis in order to be spiritually formed for God's mission. To soar in the heavenly realms like nectar-drawing, pollen-carrying butterflies, they had to undergo a transformation.

METAMORPHOSIS

Caterpillars, hatched from butterfly eggs, consume large amounts of leaves and fruit. Their task is to eat and grow—to consume and

1. This chapter uses "the earthly realms" to refer to a worldview that limits reality to the observable, physical, visible realm or that functionally behaves as if reality were limited to this realm. "The heavenly realms" is a domain that recognizes God's sovereignty, not only over the visible world but also over the larger, and even more real, unseen world. The book of Ephesians uses the expression "in the heavenly realms" *(en tois epouranois)* five times (1:3, 20; 2:6; 3:10; 6:12) to refer to the realm in which believers *presently* dwell with Christ and where spiritual powers are operative.

expand — shedding their skin several times as they grow large enough to pass beyond the larva stage of development.

When caterpillars reach full growth, they become pupas by attaching themselves to solid objects and covering themselves with chrysalises — cocoonlike shells that protect them during this transformation. Pupas do not eat and are almost completely inactive. Although it appears that nothing is happening, inside a great metamorphosis is taking place.

Inside the chrysalises, the caterpillars are becoming butterflies. This period of becoming changes both appearance and task. The unattractive, self-absorbed creatures become beautiful and giving. As these butterflies draw nourishment from nectar, they carry pollen from flower to flower, enabling them to produce fruits and seeds.

From consuming caterpillars to pollen-carrying butterflies — what an amazing transformation!

CATERPILLARS, PUPAS, AND BUTTERFLIES

Jim and Julie realized from this metaphor that there are three types of Christians.

Caterpillar Christians are by nature consumers, self-absorbed and self-concerned. Most of their resources are used for their own personal growth and development. They ask, "How is the church meeting my needs?" This self-absorbed focus displaces God as sovereign Lord. Because they function only in the earthly realms, they can neither see nor imagine the majesty of the heavenly realms. To caterpillar Christians, evangelism is a duty to be performed, an obligation to be discharged, a program to participate in. While claiming to be Christians, caterpillars have yet to die to self. Sadly, many Christians die as caterpillars.

Pupa Christians are in a state of transition — a transformation to become more like God. They ask, "What does God desire for us to *be* and *do*?" They realize their weakness: that they can do little to become holy, loving, and faithful without God working in their lives. They are learning to turn from self to God, by praying, by reading Scripture for their own spiritual growth, and by living in community with other Christians who are on a similar journey. A spiritual conversion is occurring.

The difficulties experienced by Christians going through the pupa stage should never be underestimated. Rethinking theological foundations and changing patterns of life to reflect God's purposes creates immense discomfort. It is therefore not surprising that some people stagnate in the pupa stage. They never open themselves to the world but merely live in their newfound spiritual cocoon. Others even revert to the caterpillar stage.

Butterfly Christians emerge from this time of spiritual reflection to view the world from God's perspective. Acknowledging human weakness, they draw nectar from God through active reading of Scripture, fervent prayer, and loving fellowship with one another. These spiritual resources enable God's people to spread his pollen. While soaring in the heavenly realms, they see the masses of caterpillars who try to find meaning and purpose by their own might and power. They understand and prioritize the purposes of God in personal life and ministry.

HOPE FOR THE FLOWERS

In her book *Hope for the Flowers* (1972), Trina Paulus tells the story of two caterpillars, Yellow and Stripe, who think there must be more to life than just eating and growing. They meet in a pillar of squirming, pushing caterpillars, each struggling to reach the top, all assuming that true fulfillment — the purpose of existence — will be achieved by getting there. Eventually Yellow and Stripe become disillusioned with the climb, descend from the pillar, and enjoy crawling together in the sunlight and breeze. Stripe, however, driven by curiosity, regularly crawls to the foot of the pillar and wonders what is at the top. The pillar haunts him. He is soon drawn back to the pillar and, with tears, leaves his beloved Yellow behind.

Yellow is desolate without Stripe. Where is he? Will he ever return? She crawls daily to the foot of the pillar, looking for him, and returns home sad. One day, Yellow is surprised by a grey-haired caterpillar who is hanging upside down on a branch. He seems caught in some "hairy stuff." Yellow, assuming he is in trouble, asks, "Can I help?" "No, my dear," the grey-haired one answers. "I have to do this to become a butterfly." She leaps inside. "That word 'butterfly,' what does it mean?" As the grey-haired caterpillar spins his cocoon, he explains.

> "*It's what you are meant to become.* It flies with beautiful wings and joins the earth to the heaven. It drinks only nectar from flowers and carries the seeds of love from one flower to another." (Paulus, 1972, 70)

Yellow is fascinated that inside "a fuzzy worm" are the makings of a beautiful butterfly. She first doubts. "It can't be true! How can I believe there's a butterfly inside you or me when all I see is a fuzzy worm" (1972, 72). She asks, "How does one become a butterfly?" "You must want to fly so much that you are willing to give up being a caterpillar," the grey-haired one responds as he continues spinning his cocoon. "You mean to die?" retorts Yellow.

> "Yes and No," he answered. "What *looks* like you will die, but what's *really* you will still live. Life is changed, not taken away. Isn't that different from those who die without ever becoming butterflies?" (1972, 75)

With courage, Yellow decides to become a butterfly and hangs beside the grey-haired caterpillar to imitate what he is doing. "What do I do?" Yellow asks hesitantly. The caterpillar answers,

> "Watch me. I'm making a cocoon.
>
> It looks like I'm hiding, I know, but the cocoon is no escape.
>
> It's an in-between house where the change takes place.
>
> It's a big step because you can never return to caterpillar life.
>
> During the change, it will seem to you or to anyone who might peek that nothing is happing — but the butterfly is already becoming.
>
> It just takes time!
>
> And there's something else!
>
> Once you are a butterfly, you can *really* love — the kind of love that makes new life. It's better than all the hugging caterpillars can do." (1972, 76–77)

Yellow's first inclination is to crawl to the pillar and try to find Stripe. But she knows that is impossible. The grey-haired caterpillar suggests different thinking.

> "If you change, you can fly and show him how beautiful butterflies are. Maybe he will want to become one too!" (1972, 78)

In the meantime, Stripe has almost reached the top of the pillar. But at this height, there is little movement. The caterpillars at the top, resisting pressure from below, hang on for dear life. Those underneath know they can succeed in reaching the top only by throwing off the top layer. The struggle is intense. The whispers from the top are the most haunting: "There's nothing up here at all!" Then Stripe is able to look out from his pillar to see dozens of caterpillar pillars, and realizes that "millions of caterpillars [are] climbing nowhere!" (Paulus 1972, 94).

The caterpillars on the top level are then distracted by a majestic, yellow-winged creature circling the pillar. Stripe wonders how it can get so high without climbing (1972, 101). The yellow-winged creature seems to recognize him and extends its legs to grab him. Stripe pulls back so that he will not fall from the pile. The brilliant creature lets go but looks sadly into his eyes. Stripe is shocked! Can this be Yellow? Is it possible that caterpillars are made to fly in the heavenly realms? Is Yellow calling him to a different existence? These thoughts race through his mind as he seeks to escape his entrapment by descending the pillar. On his way down, all he can remember is the love he saw in the creature's eyes. He tries to share the good news: "We can fly! We can become butterflies! There's nothing at the top, and *it doesn't matter*!" He "[looks] at each caterpillar inebriated with joy that there could be a butterfly inside" (1972, 114). Stripe's joy turns to doubt when one crawler sneers, "How could you swallow such a story? Our life is earth and climbing. Look at us worms! We couldn't be butterflies inside. Make the best of it and enjoy caterpillar living!" (1972, 128). But he continues to testify, "I saw a butterfly — there can be more to life" (1972, 120).

When Stripe reaches the bottom, he crawls to the old place where he and Yellow used to play. Yellow is nowhere to be found, and exhausted from the descent, he falls asleep. Upon awakening, he finds the yellow butterfly "fanning him with wings of light." "Is this a dream?" he wonders. He can feel her love as she "[strokes] him with her feelers and most of all [looks] at him so lovingly that he [begins] to trust that what she had said about becoming a butterfly might be true" (1972, 128). Yellow flies from him to two torn sacks, keeps inserting her head and then her tail and then flying back and touching him (1972, 130). Stripe slowly begins to understand, hangs beside the other sacks, and "[lets] go of ... everything" (1972, 137) in order to become what God intends him to be.

"Whoever has ears, let them hear" (Matt. 13:43).

Christians must also undergo a metamorphosis to become God's butterflies. They must abandon their endeavor to climb into the heavenly

Message to ...

Caterpillars: "You are not meant to crawl in the earthly realms, oblivious to God in the heavenly realms."

Pupas: "You are not meant to merely focus on self, on your own personal transformation. You must stretch beyond your cocoon to spread God's pollen in the world."

Butterflies: "You are fragile. You need nectar to spread pollen."

realms by their own power, and allow God to mold them. Attempting to achieve God's purposes solely through human effort leads to disillusionment, because there is no transformation of self.

Missionaries called by God into his mission must be transformed people who reflect his nature — his love, holiness, and faithfulness. As butterflies, they draw divine nectar in order to spread life-giving pollen.

From *Solitude* to *Community* to *Ministry*

Jim and Julie realized that the greatest example for them to follow was Jesus, who demonstrated how to live in intimate relationship with his Father. Jesus habitually sought time alone with God. He had come from the Father and continually wanted to be with him.

One day, when the sun was setting, people brought the sick and demon-possessed to Jesus, and he healed them. At daybreak, even though the people were searching for him, Jesus "went out to a solitary place" to prepare for a day of ministry (Luke 4:40 – 42). Jesus, seeking power and strength from the Father, "*often* withdrew to lonely places and prayed" (Luke 5:16, emphasis added). This was Jesus' rhythm of life!

Early in his ministry, as Jesus prepared to make one of his most momentous decisions, he went to a mountain to pray and spent the entire night conversing with God. At daybreak, he called together his disciples and chose twelve of them to be his apostles. Jesus sought God's divine guidance while selecting the twelve who would become his apostles (Luke 6:12 – 16).

Henri Nouwen draws from Luke 6:12 – 19 to describe three central disciplines in the life of Christ: solitude, community, and ministry. First, Jesus sought *solitude* when he "went out to a mountainside to pray, and spent the night praying to God" (v. 12). Second, Christ's communion with God led him to choose his twelve apostles, thus creating *community* (vv. 13 – 15). Third, Jesus went down from the mountainside with his disciples and began to *minister* with divine power (vv. 17 – 19). These "three disciplines are important for us to remain faithful, so we not only become disciples, but also remain disciples" (1995, 81).

Imagine life as a big wheel with a rim as ministry, many spokes as community, and solitude as the hub. Nouwen observes that often "we are running around the rim trying to reach everybody. But God says,

'Start in the hub; live in the hub. Then you will be connected with all the spokes, and you won't have to run so fast'" (1995, 83). Like Jesus, Christians find community after times of solitude. Nouwen observes that "it's precisely in the hub, in the communion with God, that we discover the call to community" (1995, 83). In the community, there is spiritual equipping for ministry. The order is significant. These disciplines, Nouwen says, move from solitude to community to ministry. There is no other way! Without time with God, without formation of community, there can be no effective ministry! Christian discipleship "moves from *solitude* to *community* to *ministry*" (1995, 81 – 87).

Jim and Julie dreamed again and again about this process and personalized it with these words:

Dream the dream ... again.

Walking with God—personally, intimately, faithfully.
 Being transformed into God's likeness.
 Absorbing God's love, seeing His holiness, witnessing His faithfulness.
 Shedding anger, losing lust, giving up personal advantage.
 Reframing ego—from ***our*** glory to ***His*** glory.
 Praying, fasting, worshiping ... communing with God.
 Bowing before Him, acknowledging that He alone is Lord.
Walking in community—personally, intimately, faithfully.
 Journeying together with God to become like Him.
 Putting on love, which binds us together in perfect unity.
 Loving the unlovable, accepting the unacceptable—within each of us.
 Encouraging the young, listening to the old, growing together in Christ.
 Expecting the miracle—bondage broken, addictions cured, bodies healed.
 Confessing sins to one another—feeling freedom, love, and acceptance.
Walking on mission with God—personally, intimately, faithfully.
 Emulating the ministry of Jesus.
 Becoming God's ministers of reconciliation.
 Becoming spiritual friends with searchers and skeptics.
 Equipping God's people for works of ministry.
 Doing church ***God's*** way—not ***my*** way.
 Training leaders to plant churches that plant churches that ...
Dream the dream ... again.

Jim and Julie grew to realize the need to discipline their lives so that they would become devout disciples of Christ. They knew that the words *discipline* and *discipleship* come from the same root. They

"Prayer needs no passport, visa or work permit. There is no such thing as a 'closed country' as far as prayer is concerned.... Much of the history of mission could be written in terms of God moving in response to persistent prayer."
(Stephan Gaukroger, n.d.)

concurred with Nouwen: "Once you have made the choice to say, 'Yes, I want to follow Jesus,' the question is, 'What disciplines will help me remain faithful to that choice?' If we want to be disciples of Jesus, we have to live a disciplined life" (1995, 81).

Therefore Jim and Julie restructured their days to include early morning, midday, and evening periods of solitude. They consciously took one day a week as a Sabbath, a day of rest from other labors in order to better focus on the purposes of God. They valued their time within an equipping community in their local church, as well as fellowship within the missional community in their neighborhood. The fellowship they experienced and the spiritual steps they were taking amplified their ministry in evangelism and with youth in ways they could not have anticipated. They felt their lives moving from solitude to community to ministry. Jim and Julie, seeking to be spiritually formed as Christ's disciples, began to understand what they read in the Bible about the role of prayer in missions.

Prayer and Missions

Before sending his disciples on the Limited Commission, Jesus looked with compassion at the multitudes around him, seeing that they were "harassed and helpless, like sheep without a shepherd" (Matt. 9:36). There was a field to be harvested. The harvesters, however, were few. Would the grain rot in the field for lack of harvesters? Jesus commanded, "Ask the Lord of the harvest, therefore, to send out workers into his harvest field" (v. 38).

Jesus did not merely ask them to pray; he sent them out in pairs to "the lost sheep of Israel" (Matt. 10:1 – 20). As this prayer worked on their hearts, centering the harvesters on God, they became reapers in the harvest field. Prayer prepared the harvesters to trust God for their welfare, seek worthy people (or "persons of peace") to sponsor them in teaching the good news, and continue despite opposition along the journey (vv. 5 – 16).

This kind of prayer life was reflected in the early Christian church. When the church experienced persecution, they "raised their voices together in prayer to God," pleading, "Lord, consider their threats and enable your servants to speak your word with great boldness" (Acts 4:24, 29). After the believers prayed, "The place where they were meeting was

Life is war. That's not all it is. But it is always that. Our weakness in prayer is owing largely to our neglect of this truth. Prayer is primarily a wartime walkie-talkie for the mission of the church as it advances against the powers of darkness and unbelief. It is not surprising that prayer malfunctions when we try to make it a domestic intercom to call upstairs for more comforts in the den. God has given us prayer as a wartime walkie-talkie so that we can call headquarters for everything we need as the kingdom of God advances in the world. Prayer gives us the significance of front-line forces, and gives God the glory of a limitless Provider. The one who gives the power gets the glory. Thus prayer safeguards the supremacy of God in missions while linking us with endless grace for every need. (Piper 2010, 65)

shaken. And they were all filled with the Holy Spirit and spoke the word of God boldly" (v. 31). Likewise, the Gentile mission was launched when Antioch leaders prayed and fasted and, in response, the Holy Spirit told them, "Set apart for me Barnabas and Saul for the work to which I have called them" (Acts 13:1 – 2).

The apostle Paul, realizing the importance of prayer, begged the Ephesians, "Pray also for me, that whenever I speak, words may be given me so that I will fearlessly make known the mystery of the gospel, for which I am an ambassador in chains. Pray that I may declare it fearlessly, as I should" (Eph. 6:19 – 20). It is evident that we cannot progress in mission until we spend time in prayer.

> *Ask the Lord of the harvest, therefore, to send out workers into his harvest field.* (Matthew 9:38)

> *Brothers and sisters, my heart's desire and prayer to God for [them] is that they may be saved.* (Romans 10:1)

> *I appeal to you, brothers, by our Lord Jesus Christ and by the love of the Spirit, to strive together with me in your prayers to God on my behalf, that I may be delivered from the unbelievers in Judea, and that my service for Jerusalem may be acceptable to the saints.* (Romans 15:30 – 31 ESV)

> *Brothers and sisters, pray for us that the message of the Lord may spread rapidly and be honored, just as it was with you.* (2 Thessalonians 3:1)

The leaders of The Hills Church[2] in Fort Worth, Texas, testify that prayer is a vital part of local evangelism and world missions. In the early 1990s, their elders dedicated themselves to prayer during a time of financial and congregational struggle. This prayer life rippled through the congregation and became part of their DNA. Don Box, a church elder and past missions ministry chair, said, "Everything we have been able to do is because of our prayer focus" (1999). The missions committee has become not just a decision-making body but also an ardent fellowship that prays for missionaries. Each missionary family also has its prayer group, whom they supply with a thirty-day prayer plan. My wife and I recall a meeting with the missions ministry during the spring semester of 2000 while I was researching *The Status of Missions: A Nationwide Survey of Churches of Christ* (ACU Press, 2002). We and the committee spent an hour in prayer before any discussion and concluded by praying for each other. The church also prayed for forty thousand local people for forty days. At the end of this period, they sent cards to these people, telling them of their prayers, and then made personal connections with them.

I got up early one morning,
And rushed right into the day!
I had so much to accomplish,
That I didn't take time to pray.

Problems came tumbling about me,
And heavier came each task,
"Why doesn't God help?!" I wondered.
He answered, "But you didn't ask."

I wanted to see joy and beauty,
But the day toiled on, grey and bleak.
I wondered why God didn't show me.
He said, "But you didn't seek."

I tried to come into God's presence.
I used all my keys in the lock.
God gently and lovingly chided,
"My child, you didn't knock!"

I woke up early this morning,
And paused before entering the day;
I had so much to accomplish,
That I had to take time to pray.

(Author unknown)

Many churches, however, make missions decisions without significant emphasis on prayer. In our survey of Churches of Christ, 59 percent of the members revealed that they "hardly ever" or only "sometimes" prayed for their missionaries during public service. One large church confessed, "We do not communicate with the congregation well enough, and we do not pray enough." Only 7 percent of the churches

2. Formerly Richland Hills Church of Christ.

Figure 2.1 Percentage of Churches That Pray for Their Missionaries During Public Services

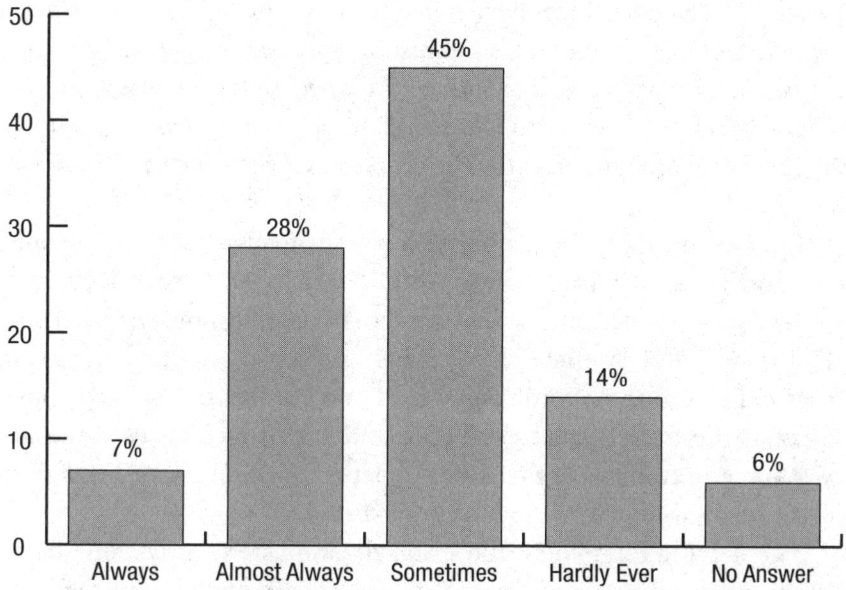

could affirm that they "always" prayed for their missionaries, and 28 percent that they "almost always" interceded publicly for them.

As a result of their learning, Jim and Julie made three commitments. First, they formed a prayer team within the missions ministry of their local church to pray for a missionary family planting churches in a largely Muslim area of West Africa. Second, they worked with the worship leaders of their church to have prayer times for their missionaries during their Sunday morning services. Third, they developed a weekly prayer time with missions-focused people, as described in the following section.

Student Power in World Missions

Jim and Julie learned that for the past three centuries, educational institutions had taken the lead in providing the motivation and understandings for cross-cultural missions. Jim and Julie were, in fact, feeling these influences in their own lives.

The modern missionary movement traces its roots back to Moravian missions and the influence of Count Nicolaus Ludwig van Zinzendorf. From 1710 to 1716, Zinzendorf, still a teenager, joined four other boys to form the Order of the Grain of Mustard Seed in their school in Halle, Germany. "They purposed to witness the power of Jesus Christ, to draw other Christians together in fellowship, to help those who were suffering for their faith, and to carry the gospel of Christ overseas" (Howard 2009, 305).

Charles and John Wesley's interest and involvement in missions began at Christ Church College in Oxford. In 1726, they formed a student group that some fellow students contemptuously called the "Holy Club" and "Methodists" (because of their disciplined approach to life). The group not only worshiped and studied but also compassionately ministered among the poor and imprisoned. These times of devotion and study were the initial impetus for the Wesleys' becoming missionaries to the New World (Howard 1999, 278).

The driving force for world evangelization frequently came from significant university professors being personally involved in the lives of their students. At Cambridge, Charles Simeon influenced a generation of Christian leaders who served both in England and throughout the world. During his forty-four years of teaching, he gathered undergraduates in his home for Bible study and prayer. In the personal atmosphere of these meetings, his students, sometimes called Simeonities, learned not only the Word of God but also its implications for their lives. In 1827, Simeon's students organized the Jesus Lane Sunday School, through which many young people in the community became church leaders. The Cambridge Union for Private Prayer, founded by Simeon's students in 1848, brought revival to hundreds. Missionaries and evangelists such as David Livingstone and D. L. Moody built on the foundations of Charles Simeon's revival (Howard 1999, 279).

In North America, Samuel Mills, whose father was a Congregational minister and whose mother reportedly consecrated him "to the service of God as a missionary," enrolled in Williams College in Massachusetts. His custom was to pray with other students on Wednesday and Saturday afternoons. In August 1806, Samuel and four other students were praying that God would awaken the mission interest of students. Suddenly rain began to fall, and thunder echoed in the background. Samuel and the others hid under a haystack to protect themselves and continued to pray. In the haystack, Samuel exhorted his fellow students to personal responsibility for world missions. He said, “We can do this if we will,” a phrase that became the motto of the ensuing missionary movement. “Bowed in prayer, these first American student volunteers for foreign missions willed that God should have their lives for service whenever he needed them, and in that self-dedication reality gave birth to the first student missionary society in North America” (Howard 2009, 307). From this initial prayer meeting, the impetus for world evangelization spread from campus to campus, leading to the Student Volunteer Movement (SVM). Their goal was “the evangelization of the world in this generation” (Howard 2009, 307). At the movement’s height in 1920, its quadrennial convention in Des Moines was attended by 6,890 people, and the next year, 637 volunteers sailed for the field (Howard 2009, 309).

The Student Volunteer Movement focused on spiritual preparation for missions. The theological, cultural, and strategic preparation for representing God in his mission, however, was lacking. When these “well-educated amateurs” arrived on the field, they “took one look at the level of education of many African pastors and declared them unqualified. They pushed real leaders out of the pulpits. Serious setbacks resulted in most fields. It took twenty, thirty, forty years for the volunteers to relearn much of what earlier missionaries had already discovered,” because “the volunteers did not read the earlier writings” (Winter 1996).[3] Thus prayer movements for world evangelization must be coupled with basic preparation to minister in a cross-cultural context.

Many continue to be called into missions through spiritual renewal on college campuses. My Christian faith and character were nourished while I was studying at Crowley’s Ridge Academy, a Christian high school in northeastern Arkansas. The yearbook for my senior year states that my career goal was “to be a missionary.” I was nurtured to understand the world, the Bible, and ministry at Harding University in Searcy, Arkansas. During these years, I participated in prayer groups, attended an Asian missions fellowship, and led campaigns to churches in Arkansas and Iowa. Graduate education in missions at Abilene

3. Winter (1996) cautions against the “re-amateurization of missions” in this generation through ill-prepared short-term missions.

Christian University provided the theological, cultural, historical, and strategic preparation for the fourteen years that God worked through us in East Africa. Bible and missions teachers from each of these schools became my role models. The World Mission Workshop, which rotated from campus to campus in our religious fellowship, inspired me as a missionary. Many of the speakers during these conferences became my heroes, the people whose examples I wanted to follow.

Jim and Julie likewise experienced missions as undergraduates in a Christian university. Their hearts were stirred by devotional speakers who shared personal stories of God's mission in their lives. Jim and Julie took their first missions course, which provided basic understandings. They became part of a missionary fellowship. Their trip to Haiti heightened their interest by providing a context for understanding cross-cultural missions. They also attended the triennial Urbana meeting *(www.urbana.org)*, the missionary renewal movement of InterVarsity Christian Fellowship. This movement, the contemporary counterpart of the Student Volunteer Movement, draws students from secular and Christian universities in North America. Amazingly, Jim and Julie's undergraduate experiences took missions from a point of little exposure in their lives to a viable option for ministry.

Now, as graduate students, Jim and Julie made a commitment to develop their own prayer team for world evangelization. Would God lead them to become his missionaries?

REFLECTION AND APPLICATION

Questions

1. Would you consider yourself a caterpillar, a pupa, or a butterfly? Why? How is God leading you to become a butterfly, one who is drawing nectar while spreading pollen?
2. Describe how Jesus moved from solitude to community to ministry. How could you employ this pattern practically in developing your daily rhythm of life?
3. What is the correlation between prayer and missions? Give a contemporary example of this relationship.
4. Dave Davidson has written, "In our lifetime wouldn't it be sad if we spent more time washing dishes or swatting flies or mowing the yard or watching television than praying for world missions?" (2006). Realizing the truth of this statement, how should we reprioritize our time to give God space?
5. Describe the role of colleges, universities, and Bible schools in the spiritual nurturing for world evangelization. Have such schools formed your passion and motivation for world missions? If so, how?

Application

1. Outline a personal prayer and devotional pattern for your day. If you are married, you should develop these spiritual patterns with your spouse and children. What spiritually formative activities might you do in the morning, in the midday, in the evening?
2. Remember that spiritual formation is most effectively done within a community of faith. Define your role as God's person in your community of faith. How might an enhanced commitment to community guide you in your quest to know God and live out his mission in your life?
3. Surf the Web to find references to the 1806 Haystack Prayer Meeting at Williams College. How could you put together your own prayer group for world evangelization?
4. The ancient church father Bernard of Clairvaux wrote, "Learn the lesson that, if you are to do the work of a prophet, what you need is not a scepter but a hoe." The kingly scepter symbolizes power and pride; the hoe signifies service and humility.

The Decision: The Hoe or the Scepter?

How does spiritual formation for ministry help us grasp the humble handle of service and reject the power and pride of the scepter?

Strangely enough, many of us have little experience with the hoe but anticipate using some type of churchly scepter.

Teach us, O God, service and humility as we minister in your world. Help us to know that we have much to learn. Empower us to overcome pride and the desire for power.

Personal Inventory

How has God spoken to you through this chapter? What is God calling you to do about it?

chapter 3

Theological Foundations of Missions

Developing a Theology of Mission

A THEOLOGY OF MISSION describes the heart and motivation of God and thereby defines the rationale of mission. It describes what God is about in his world and why he is doing what he is doing. These reflections enable missionaries to understand God's purposes and thereby determine God's will for their lives. Reflecting on these theologies leads missionaries to ask, "How do our lives and ministries reflect that of God?" or "How do we design patterns of life and models of ministry which reflect the kingdom of God?"

Two "ship" metaphors help us discern this relationship between theology and practice.

> As Jim and Julie studied these theologies within the context of the biblical narrative, they realized that Scripture was shaping their identity and that biblical theology was giving them new categories for interpreting the world.

First, a theology of mission, like the rudder of a ship, guides the mission of God and provides direction. My wife is fond of remembering how our children frequently wanted to "drive" when we took them on pedal boats. At times, they were so intent on pedaling — making the boat move — that they held the rudder in an extreme position, and we went in circles. Realizing their mistake but still intent on pedaling, they would move the rudder from one extreme to the other, so that we zigzagged across the lake. Without the foundation of a missional theology, missionaries likewise zigzag from fad to fad, from one theological perspective and related philosophies of ministry to another. A theology of mission, like the rudder of a ship, provides practical direction for Christian ministry.

A theology of mission is also like the engine of a ship, propelling forward the mission of God. One spring, my wife and I taught at Abilene Christian University's campus abroad program in Montevideo, Uruguay. During the semester, we traveled with our students to Iguazu Falls, a spectacular waterfall between Brazil and Argentina. One highlight of our visit was a motorboat excursion against the mighty current of the river almost to the foot of the falls. I was impressed not only by the immensity of the water's flow but also by the power of the engine to push the boat up the river against the surge. A mission theology, like the engine of a ship, provides the power that enables finite humans to carry God's infinite mission against the currents of popular cultures.

As these metaphors illustrate, theology is indispensable to the mission of God. A theology of mission provides both direction and empowerment for developing practices of missions.

Stuart Murray says that often "mission work is done naively out of human planning rather than beginning with understandings of the nature and purposes of God and then moving from these theological frameworks to practice." Church planters, he says, "operate within theological frameworks, but often these are assumed rather than articulated and adopted uncritically rather than as the result of reflection. Theological principles may influence strategy and practice less than unexamined tradition or innovative methodology" (2001, 39). Paul Hiebert asserts,

> Too often we choose a few themes and from there build a simplistic theology rather than look at the profound theological motifs that flow through the whole of Scripture. Equally disturbing to the foundations of mission is the dangerous potential of shifting from God and his work to the emphasis on what we can do for God by our own knowledge and efforts. We become captive to a modern secular worldview in which human control and technique replace divine leading and human obedience as the basis of mission. (1993, 4)

Developing a theology of mission is both a primary and an ongoing activity in missionary practice. This chapter will define four formative understandings of such a theology.

Imagine the mission of God as a beautiful mountain with various ski runs extending down its slopes. The runs are interconnected theologies that illustrate the nature of God and his work in his world. Your unquenchable desire to know God and his purposes draws you to the assorted runs down God's mountain. These ski paths are labeled

- *Missio Dei*: God calls and sends his people, guided and empowered by his indwelling Spirit, into mission.
- *The Kingdom of God*: God rules over the world he created.
- *Incarnation*: God comes to us, embodying himself in forms that we can understand.
- *Crucifixion and Resurrection*: God brings to life what has been dead. Following the way of Christ results frequently in suffering.

These and other themes, which form a theology of mission, prepare missionaries to emotionally and spiritually represent God in his world.

Missio Dei: A Theology of God Who Calls and Sends

Missio Dei, the first run down the ski slopes of God's mountain, "express[es] the conviction that mission is not the invention, responsibility, or program of human beings, but flows from the character and purposes of God" (Murray 2001, 39). "All mission or missions which we initiate, or into which we invest our own vocation, gifts, and energies, flow from the prior and larger reality of the mission of God" (Wright 2006, 531).

Missio Dei involves two related movements. God, the source of mission, calls and sends his people to carry out his purposes. God's people, as finite humans, question and doubt their abilities and calling along the journey.

God, for instance, called Abraham to become the father of an elect nation and sent him to a land that he did not know (Gen. 12:1 – 7). He promised Abraham that all nations on earth would be blessed through him (Gen. 12:3), a promise so significant that Paul would later call it "the gospel in advance" (Gal. 3:8).

Abraham, however, doubted God's promises. Why could he not settle in Haran, where some of his own people lived, rather than going on to Canaan (Gen. 11:31)? Would God protect him (Gen. 12:10 – 20)? How could he become a great nation, since he had no son (Gen. 15:2 – 6)? What sign would God give him that he would possess the land

The biblical narratives of God's mission invite us to participate. How do these stories describe our lives, provide motivation for ministry, and shape us to become representatives of God's mission?

of Canaan (Gen. 15:8 – 21)? Despite these doubts, Abraham believed God (Gen. 15:6). His faith grew so that he was willing to obey God's command to sacrifice his son (Gen. 22). He believed that God, who is faithful to his promises, would raise Isaac from the dead (Heb. 11:17, 19). God's justification of Abraham by faith became the paradigm by which God would bless all peoples (Gal. 3:6 – 8). This story of blessing Abraham to become God's chosen people to bless all nations, according to Wright, is "arguably ... the single most important biblical tradition within a biblical theology of mission and a missional hermeneutic of the Bible" (2006, 189).

God called the reluctant Moses to go back to Egypt (Ex. 3:1 – 12) to lead the Israelites from captivity. Moses, however, felt inadequate. Forty years earlier, Moses, the adopted son of Pharaoh's daughter, had identified the Israelites as "his own people" and felt the injustice of their bondage. He killed an Egyptian slave master (Ex. 2:11 – 15), expecting that the Israelites "would realize that God was using him to rescue them" (Acts 7:23 – 25). God's timing, however, was not the same as that of Moses. After Moses spent forty years in Midian, God called him to return to Egypt as his agent of deliverance. Moses feared God's call. He felt insufficient, afraid that he could not accomplish the task. Had he not tried to deliver the Israelites earlier? He failed to realize that the mission was not his but God's, something to be accomplished according to God's timing so that God's "name might be proclaimed in all the earth" (Ex. 9:16). Moses was merely the emissary carrying out the mission of God.

Moses' misunderstanding led him to object, "Who am *I* that *I* should go?" (Ex. 3:11, emphasis added), "What if they do not believe *me*?" (Ex. 4:1, emphasis added), and "*I* have never been eloquent.... *I* am slow of speech" (Ex. 4:10, emphasis added). These objections illustrate the human tendency to make God's mission a mission of self. Each objection was based on human deficiencies or misunderstandings. God's responses, however, proclaimed that the mission was greater than the missionary. The ever-present I AM WHO I AM was behind it.

God's calling and sending is reflected throughout Scripture. He called Isaiah by revealing his holiness, helping Isaiah realize his sinfulness, leading him to repentance and cleansing, and then sending him to Jerusalem as his spokesman (Isa. 6:1 – 10). God called Jeremiah to prophesy to and weep over a disobedient nation (Jer. 1:4 – 8; 8:21 – 9:2) that would soon go into captivity (Jer. 5:18 – 19). God called Zerubbabel, Ezra, and Nehemiah at various times and sent them to organize his captive people and lead them back to Jerusalem. God sent his only Son to earth to reveal his glory, full of grace and truth (John 1:14), "to seek and to save the lost" (Luke 19:10), and "to destroy the devil's work" (1 John 3:8). Jesus in turn sent his disciples, stating, "As the Father has sent me, I am sending you" (John 20:21, cf. 17:18). After Jesus ascended into heaven, God sent his Holy Spirit as another advocate so that his people would not be left as orphans (John 14:15 – 18).

The calling and sending by God was also evident in the early Christian church. By his authority as resurrected Lord, Jesus commissioned his disciples to "go and make disciples of all nations" (Matt. 28:18 – 20). These disciples were sent by divine power for divine purposes. God, through the Holy Spirit, called Peter and sent him to the house of Cornelius, thus opening the door to the Gentiles (Acts 10). God called Saul as he traveled from Jerusalem to Damascus in order to persecute Christians. In a vision, Jesus told him, "I am sending you to [the Gentiles] to open their eyes and turn them from darkness to light, and from the power of Satan to God, so that they may receive forgiveness of sins and a place among those who are sanctified by faith in me" (Acts 26:17 – 18). Paul invited Timothy to join Silas and him as they traveled on Paul's second missionary journey (Acts 16:1 – 4). Titus accompanied Paul and Barnabas to Jerusalem (Gal. 2:1). These early Christians defined themselves as apostles (Rom. 1:1, 5; 1 Cor. 1:1; cf. Gal. 1:15 – 17) or ambassadors (2 Cor. 5:18 – 20), people sent to represent God in his mission.

Sometimes God enters into the human situation himself and becomes the Sent One, the Missionary. For instance, when Adam and Eve sinned, God himself walked in the Garden of Eden seeking his fallen creation (Gen. 3:8 – 19). God, perhaps in the form of an angel, fought all night with Jacob, the deceiver who stole his brother's blessing and birthright, and changed his name to Israel, meaning "one who struggles with God" (Gen. 32:22 – 29). God in Jesus became flesh and entered human culture (John 1:14). God, through his Holy Spirit, indwells Christians to set them free from sin and to lead them forward as witnesses to the world (Acts 1:8).

Understanding God's Trinitarian nature amplifies our understanding of *missio Dei*. God, Christ, and the Holy Spirit, though separate personalities, operate in perfect unity. The church, living in communion with the Trinity, is called to reflect the harmony and qualities of this union (John 17:20–23). Bosch describes this Trinitarian unity of God's mission: "The classical doctrine of the *missio Dei* as God the Father sending the Son, and God the Father and the Son sending the Spirit, is expanded to include yet another 'movement': Father, Son, and Holy Spirit sending the church into the world" (Bosch 1991, 390).

The church, God's called-out people on the earth, becomes a finite participant in God's Trinitarian nature. God reigns over the church as sovereign Lord, Christ cleanses the body by his blood, and the Holy Spirit liberates the church from sin to become holy and empowers its mission. The church, then, is "a temporal echo of the eternal community that God is" (Gunton 1991; cf. Bosch 1991, 390).

God continues to call and send his disciples into his mission, and these disciples continue to question and doubt their calling and ability to fulfill the mission. My wife, Becky, and I have both received the callings and experienced the doubts. Sometimes I am so filled with insecurity that I question every step I take, even as God calls me forward. I have been surprised to find how much I am like Moses, asking God, "Who am I that I should go?" I struggle to listen to God when he says, "I will be with you!"

Early in life, I received the call to be a missionary. It was rooted in my upbringing, much as in Timothy's case (2 Tim. 1:5), from parental encouragement to experiences in a Christian high school and university to graduate studies. Becky made a decision to be a missionary by marrying one. We felt the hand of God in times of blessing and when Christian leaders spoke into our lives, encouraging us as messengers of God. We doubted our ability to leave our parents and friends and form new relationships in another land, to raise our young son (and children to come) in a foreign land, to learn new languages and cultures, and to serve as God's messengers opening a new area to his gospel. I especially worried because of a disability that hinders language learning. But God was faithful in the midst of our doubts and struggles.

While working among the Kipsigis tribe in Kenya, we learned to be apostolic church planters. We partnered with local people with open hearts and leadership abilities, whom we called "people of peace" (Luke 10:5–7), to plant multiple local churches. These churches began in homes, then met under trees, moved to the local schools whenever permission was granted, and then built their own buildings as they were able. They were locally led and financially self-sustainable from their inception. We feel blessed that despite our weaknesses, God worked through our team with local leaders to plant one hundred churches, an endeavor that has now become a major church-planting movement in southeastern Kenya.[1]

After we spent fourteen years of ministry in Africa, God called us to Abilene Christian University, where we used our experience to equip new missionaries. During the next eighteen years, my wife and I worked within the Department of Missions and then the Halbert Insitute of Missions to train missionary teams through academic training, internships and practicums, mentoring groups, and continental fellowships with the focus on beginning church planting movements in various areas of the world. During these years, our understandings of missions and church planting deepened as we worked with church-planting teams going into various nations.

Then, unexpectedly, God called us to begin Mission Alive *(www.missionalive.org)*. The call came during a sabbatical, while we were studying missions in local North American churches and writing a book called *The Status of Missions: A Nationwide Survey of Churches of Christ* (ACU Press, 2002). We saw the nominalization of local churches that unconsciously adopt the felt needs of popular culture rather than live as holy people who reflect the kingdom of God in the world. We discovered the great need for both the planting of new churches and the renewal of existing ones in North America. We discerned that the frontier of Christianity is blazed when and where disciples of Christ meet not-yet Christians in school events, neighborhoods, and social clubs, especially in vortexes of dialogue, and invite them into disciple-making communities shaped by this theology of the kingdom of God.[2]

Looking back, we are awed by God's leading and power. He was leading us in mission in ways that we could not fully fathom. Frequently, we questioned and doubted our abilities and even God's leading along the journey.

---

1. Chapter 15 describes an incarnational model for planting, nurturing, and training in developing a church-planting movement in Africa.
2. Chapter 16 describes an incarnational model for planting, nurturing, and training in developing a church-planting movement in North America.

Figure 3.1 The Flow of the Mission of God

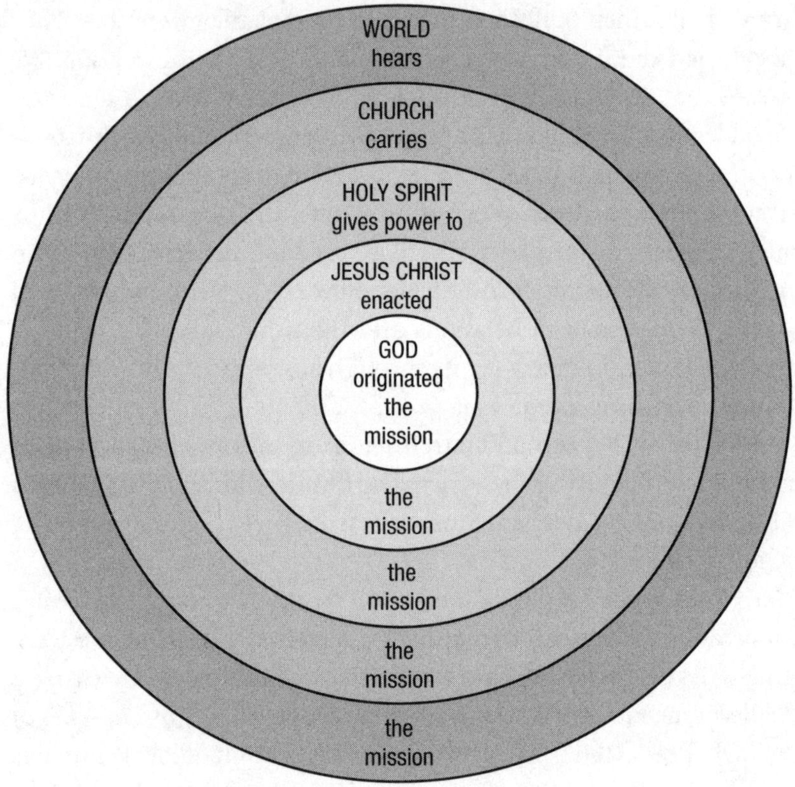

Figure 3.1 illustrates *mission Dei.* God is the source! Christ, because of who he is — the Son of God — and his willingness to die for sinners, became the very *message of mission.* The Holy Spirit empowers the church to become God's messengers from Jerusalem to the "ends of the earth" (Acts 1:8). Christians within local churches embody God's mission and are empowered by the Holy Spirit to convey it to the world. Thus, God's mission flows from God to Christ to the Holy Spirit, who empowers the church, who carries the mission to the world. Mission, therefore, is derived from the very nature of God, who sends and saves, and it is carried by finite humans who doubt and struggle along the journey.

What are some applications of *missio Dei* to Christian life and practice?

First, if mission flows from the character and nature of God, it cannot be neglected by the church. Mission, because it is of God, cannot be aborted!

Second, since the mission is of God, God will equip people for the task. If God's messengers are afraid to speak, God will be with their mouths. If they feel inadequate, he will empower them to become capable communicators. If they are afraid of the world's response, they must remember God's power to reshape people in his image.

Third, *missio Dei* enables Christian missionaries to understand themselves under God's sovereignty. Christians should undertake God's mission not for self-glorification but for the glorification of God. Paul wrote to Christian leaders in Philippi, concerning dissension there, "Do nothing out of selfish ambition or vain conceit. Rather, in humility value others above yourselves" (Phil. 2:3). The missionary must preach not "to gain personal glory" but to "[seek] the glory of the one who sent him" (John 7:18). Such an other-centered, God-oriented perspective leads the Christian communicator to realize that the mission is greater than self. It is God's enterprise! He is the spring of mission, pouring forth living water upon the world.

Fourth, *missio Dei* implies sacrifice. It is a mission worth living for and dying for. Consequently, many missionaries have entered fields knowing that their life expectancy would be severely affected. One missionary in Eastern Europe was told by the people there that because he had come to that part of the world, his life span would probably be shortened by five years because of pollution, radiation, and ecological mismanagement. Early missionaries to Africa packed their belongings in caskets, knowing that they would likely die in the land they were entering.

Finally, the perspective of *missio Dei* enables the Christian communicator to recognize that because the mission is God's, it will succeed. Even though messengers fail and people reject the message, the mission of God continues. God, the source of mission, will raise up new people like Moses to carry his message.

The Kingdom: A Theology of God's Ever-Present Rule

The theology of the kingdom of God is a second theme that flows through the biblical text. This theology does not stand apart from *missio Dei* but interpenetrates and enhances its meaning. Kingdom and *missio Dei* are like parallel ski runs converging, enveloping, and enriching each other.

These two themes illustrate that the God who calls and sends also reigns over the world he created. Sovereign God is carrying out his mission!

KINGDOM DEFINED

The term *kingdom*, as illustrated and defined in both the Old and New Testaments, means "a rule or reign, an exercise of authority." Applied to the reign of God, the term means "the rule or sovereignty of Creator God." Two passages will be used to define *kingdom*, one from the Old Testament and another from the New Testament.

Psalm 145 describes the greatness, goodness, and love of God our King. We exalt and praise him because he faithfully rules over us. The synonymous parallelisms of this psalm define the nature of God's kingdom.

> *All your works praise you,* L*ORD;*
> *Your faithful people extol you.*
> *They tell of the* glory *of your kingdom*
> *and speak of your* might,
> *so that all people may know of your* mighty *acts*
> *and the glorious* splendor *of your kingdom.*
> *Your kingdom is an* everlasting *kingdom,*
> *and your* dominion *endures through all generations.*
> (PSALM 145:10–13, EMPHASIS ADDED)

God's kingdom is exemplified by glory and splendor. The synonymous parallelism equates the kingdom with power, mighty acts, and dominion. God "does not merely sit on a throne, but he reigns by performing mighty deeds ... expressed in acts of power" (Ferguson 1989, 7). The kingdom of God is illustrated by *what the King does*!

These acts of power reflect his nature. Thus this description of God's kingdom is framed by two descriptions of God's love: he is "gracious and compassionate, slow to anger and rich in love ... good to all" (Ps. 145:8–9) and "righteous in all his ways and loving toward all he has made" (Ps. 145:17 NIV 1984). God's mighty acts reflect his love. The kingdom of God is thus defined by *who the King is*!

The Lord's Prayer gives the most fundamental definition of kingdom in all Scripture. According to Beasley-Murray, the first three petitions of the Lord's Prayer provide the essence of kingdom life, with the fourth statement modifying each description (1992, 23–24).

Hallowed be your name,
your kingdom come,
your will be done,
on earth as it is in heaven.
(Matthew 6:9b–10)

The first phrase reflects the awe with which people of the kingdom should regard the name of God. God's reputation was not to be defiled by sin and acts of disbelief but to be glorified by obedient, holy living. The phrases "your kingdom come" and "your will be done" both express the desire that God's kingdom values operate in our lives. The phrase "on earth as it is in heaven," applying to all three statements, expresses God's ultimate design that he reign as the exclusive Lord in both heaven and earth, that he once again become the Lord of Lords, the King of Kings (Beasley-Murray 1992, 23–24). The phrase "kingdom of God" is thus defined by the Lord's Prayer as "God's will being done on earth as it is in heaven."

In recent years, we have too frequently defined the kingdom of God as "the church" or "heaven." These two descriptions are not wrong. They are simply too small! Both take the kingdom of God out of the world (Robinson 2007). God does not rule merely in his church or ultimately in heaven. God rules over the entire world. How is this understood historically?

GOD'S KINGDOM NARRATIVE

The history of the world is a story of God's rule. This kingdom theme is, in fact, like a "scarlet thread" woven through the fabric of the "biblical testimonies" (Moltmann 1981, 95).

The kingdom narrative begins with creation. God established his right as King because he created the heavens and the earth. God in his sovereignty created Adam and Eve in his image, in his likeness (Gen. 1:26–27), with the expectation that they live in relationship with him, reflecting his love, holiness, and faithfulness. He commissioned them as vice-regents over what he created (Gen. 1:26), so they would care for his universe (Gen. 2:15). The psalmist testifies that the earth, and everything in it, belongs to Yahweh, "for he founded it on the seas and established it on the waters" (Ps. 24:1 – 2).

God is incomparable; no other gods are like him. After God delivered the Israelites from Egyptian captivity, Moses praised him, saying, "Who among the gods is like you, LORD? Who is like you — majestic in holiness, awesome in glory, working wonders?" (Ex. 15:11).

God's rule is demonstrated throughout the Old Testament, in his raising up judges to deliver the Israelites (Judg. 2:10 – 19), in his instituting priests to intercede for the people of Israel (Ex. 28 – 29; Lev. 8 – 9), and in his sending prophets to proclaim his message to the kings and the people (Jer. 1:5 – 6; 15:19; Ezek. 3:17; Amos 7:16). God chose Israel to become "a kingdom of priests and a holy nation" to represent God before the world (Ex. 19:5 – 6; Deut. 7:6 – 8), and to be a light to the nations (Isa. 42:6; 49:6). The Israelites were frequently, however, inclined to worship the gods of the nations around them rather than represent God to the nations. Because of Israel's inclination to follow pagan gods, God disowned his elect people and sent them into Assyrian and Babylonian captivity (2 Kings 17:7 – 23; Jer. 5:19).

God's insistence that his people — and all nations — turn away from false gods was not merely an assertion of his sovereignty; it was also an expression of his love. "The blessing of the nations must ultimately include ridding them of gods that masquerade as protectors and saviors, but are actually devouring, destroying, disappointing deceptions. The battle to do so is a battle of divine love" (Wright 2006, 178).

Although Israel was God's special kingdom of priests, God ruled over all nations. All nations — not merely Israel — were accountable to God for their sins (Amos 1 – 2; Ezek. 25 – 32). God, who freed the Israelites from Egyptian captivity, also delivered the Philistines from Caphtor, and the Arameans from Kir (Amos 9:7). God not only gave Canaan to the Jews, but also allotted the Moabites and Ammonites their lands (Deut. 2:16 – 19). God sent the Jewish prophet Jonah to save the Assyrian city of Nineveh. The theme of Daniel is, "the Most High God is sovereign over all kingdoms on earth" (Dan. 5:21). "The LORD has established his throne in heaven, and his kingdom rules over all" (Ps. 103:19). These claims of God's sovereignty lead to the conclusion that "there is not an inch of the planet that belongs to any other god, whatever the appearances" (Wright 2006, 112).

With the coming of Jesus Christ, the word *kingdom* took on new meaning. *Kingdom* began to connote God's ultimate, decisive reign through his Son. Jesus' ministry is summarized in each of the Synoptic Gospels by the statement "Repent, for the kingdom of heaven has come near" (Matt. 4:17; cf. Mark 1:15; Luke 4:43). The phrase "come near" has connotations of both the present and the future. It means "'drawing near,' 'breaking in,' 'in process of becoming'" (Ferguson 1989, 24). The synonymous parallelism of Mark 1:15 helps to clarify the meaning of "come near": "The time has come" is synonymous with "the kingdom of God has come near." The first phrase "looks backward, while the second looks to the present and future; the first announces the end of the old era, the second proclaims the beginning of the new" (Ambrozic 1972, 21 – 22). In Jesus Christ, God has broken into the world to initiate a rule that will never be destroyed. In a sense, the kingdom was "coming" but was also "in their midst" in the person and ministry of Jesus Christ. When Christ the King came, the kingdom began to break more fully into the world.

Christ proclaimed the kingdom in both word and deed. He preached "the good news of the kingdom" (Luke 4:43). His parables described the nature of the kingdom. During the last days, the kingdom of God and the dominion of Satan would coexist — like weeds and wheat, only to be separated in the final harvest. Christ gave a rationale for the continuance of the kingdom of Satan even though the ultimate reign of God in his Messiah had been consummated (Matt. 13:24 – 30, 36 – 43). This kingdom is like a pearl of great price, so precious that a merchant would give all he has to possess it (vv. 45 – 46).

Casting out demons was a demonstration of the kingdom. When Jesus sent seventy-two disciples out on the Limited Commission, he commanded them to proclaim that "the kingdom of God has come near to you" (Luke 10:9). They returned with joy, saying to Jesus, "Lord, even the demons submit to us in your name" (Luke 10:17). Jesus said, "I saw Satan fall like lightning from heaven" (Luke 10:18). This defeat of Satan during Jesus' ministry was a foretaste of his disarming Satan's power on the cross (Col. 2:15).

After Satan tempted Jesus, and before Christ began his public ministry, Jesus spoke in his hometown synagogue. He described his kingdom ministry by quoting from Isaiah:

The Spirit of the Lord is on me,
because he has anointed me
to proclaim good news to the poor.
He has sent me to proclaim freedom for the prisoners
and recovery of sight for the blind,
to set the oppressed free,
to proclaim the year of the Lord's favor.
(LUKE 4:18 – 19)

Jesus' words echo the theme of the servant songs of Isaiah describing God putting his Spirit on the Messiah so that he will "bring justice to the nations" (Isa. 42:1), be "a light for the Gentiles,... open eyes that are blind,... free captives from prison and ... release from the dungeon those who sit in darkness" (Isa. 42:6 – 7). Jesus quoted directly from Isaiah 61:1 – 2, but inserted "to set the oppressed free," from Isaiah 58:6, into the reading. Isaiah 58 compares prideful fasting with loving and caring for the poor (vv. 6 – 7), that is, to "spend [ourselves] in behalf of the hungry and satisfy the needs of the oppressed" (v. 10).

The gospel of Luke describes this ministry of compassion for the poor, the prisoners, the blind, and the oppressed. In the kingdom of God, the poor, the crippled, the lame, and the blind are invited to our feasts (Luke 14:1 – 24). In God's kingdom, the rich are compassionate, rather than indifferent, to the poor (Luke 16:19 – 31). The "eternal life" desired by a certain ruler is more than obeying God's commandments; it is giving all for the sake of his kingdom (Luke 18:18 – 25). When people embrace God's kingdom, they generously give to the poor and make restitution for ill-gotten gain (Luke 19:1 – 8). Luke compares two responses of the wealthy: the Rich Young Ruler cannot comply with these demands of the kingdom (Luke 18:23). Zacchaeus, the tax collector, however, gives "half of [his] possessions to the poor" and makes restitution to the people he cheated (Luke 19:8).

The Sermon on the Mount describes a way of life under God's reign. People of the kingdom of God

- display the character described in the Beatitudes (Matt. 5:1 – 12),
- show people the goodness of God's reign in this world (5:13 – 16),
- strive to continually listen to the words of Jesus (5:17 – 20),
- value other people by showing them gentleness (5:21 – 26),

- value other people by honoring them (5:27 – 28),
- avoid sinful actions and motivations at all cost (5:29 – 30),
- value other people by keeping commitments to them (5:31 – 32),
- value other people by always speaking the truth to them (5:33 – 37),
- value other people by refusing to use violence (verbal or physical) for protection (5:38 – 48),
- pursue righteousness by giving to the needy (6:1 – 4), praying for themselves and their world (6:5 – 15), and fasting from their excess (6:16 – 18),
- invest in things that really matter (6:19 – 24),
- seek to submit to God's reign in their daily lives (6:25 – 34),
- show people a better way of life instead of judging their way of life (7:1 – 6),
- ask, seek, and knock for opportunities to help others experience the reign of God (7:7 – 12),
- strive with intensity to keep submitting to God's reign throughout their lives (7:13 – 27).

Kingdom living is thus a countercultural lifestyle reflecting the love, holiness, and faithfulness of God. Christians "enter into this lifestyle . . . to the extent that they have submitted to the reign of God" (Robinson 2007).

The kingdom was also proclaimed in the ministry of the early church. When Philip went to Samaria and "proclaimed the Messiah there" (Acts 8:5), his message was "the good news of the kingdom of God and the name of Jesus Christ" (Acts 8:12). Paul "[went] about preaching the kingdom" (Acts 20:25). His ministry reflected his conversion experience. Christ sent him to the Gentiles "to open their eyes and turn them from darkness to light, and from the power of Satan to God" (Acts 26:18). Paul in Rome declared to the Jews the kingdom of God (Acts 28:23). Pauline epistles proclaim deliverance "from the dominion of darkness . . . into the kingdom of the Son" (Col. 1:13). Apostolic preaching was kingdom proclamation.

Christians stand between the times. They experience the temptations and onslaughts of Satan while living as ministers of the kingdom of God. Thus Peter exhorts Christians to "be alert and of sober mind. Your enemy the devil prowls around like a roaring lion looking for someone to devour. Resist him, standing firm in the faith" (1 Peter 5:8 – 9).

A tension exists between the already and the not yet. The kingdom has been inaugurated but has not yet been completed. Christians, who have been "strengthened with all power according to [God's] glorious might" in the present age, anticipate "the inheritance of his holy people in the kingdom of light" (Col. 1:11 – 12). They have "tasted ... the powers of the coming age" (Heb. 6:5). The concept that the kingdom has already broken into the world but has not yet been consummated is termed *inaugurated eschatology.* God's reign, which was initiated in Jesus Christ, continues through people who believe in him, and will be consummated at the end of the age (Beasley-Murray 1986, 80).

A clear vision and expectation of the ultimate kingdom determines how Jesus' disciples, who live between the times, respond to others in the here and now. In Matthew 8, a Roman centurion showed greater faith than did people in Israel. Jesus told his disciples that "many will come from the east and the west, and will take their places at the feast with Abraham, Isaac and Jacob in the kingdom of heaven" (Matt. 8:11). Jesus "rather shockingly uses texts that originally spoke of God gathering in Israelites from exile, 'from the east and the west' (Ps. 107:3; Is. 43:5 – 6; 49:12), and implies that they will be fulfilled when Gentiles like this centurion arrive at the banquet" (Wright 2006, 243 – 44).

This inaugurated eschatology is illustrated in Christ's parables of the kingdom. These parables make clear the nature of God's rule in a world where the powers of Satan continue to exist. As we saw in chapter 1, in the parable of Matthew 13:24 – 30 the weeds and the wheat grow side by side. The good and the bad are not separated in the present age. That will be God's final work when he consummates his kingdom: the weeds will be separated from the wheat. This parable explains why Satan's kingdom continues even though God's kingdom in Christ has broken into the world.

Within this context, the church is God's eschatological community for people living between the ages. As mentioned, two prevalent assumptions about the kingdom have been made in recent times. The kingdom is equated either with the church or with heaven. There is truth in both assumptions. The church must serve as God's agent or representative of the kingdom (see chap. 4). The final consummation of the kingdom occurs when, after Christ "has destroyed all dominion, authority and power," all authority is placed into the hands of God

(1 Cor. 15:24 – 28). These two descriptions are "not wrong" but merely "too small" because they "take the kingdom of God out of the world" (Robinson 2007).

THE KINGDOM DILEMMA

Kingdom understandings pose a major dilemma. In many instances, God does not appear to be in charge of the world he created. If God is Lord, why does he allow so much evil to permeate the world? Where do sin and death come from?

Two truths help provide an answer to these difficult questions. First, "all things" have been created as creatures of free choice. Second, Satan's dominion arose to challenge the kingdom of God.

The presence of God's kingdom has not negated the presence of sin and evil in the world. God is pictured as a father, and we are his children; he is our husband, and we are his bride; he is the vinedresser, and we are his vineyard. These parenting, marriage, and vineyard metaphors imply relationship. Within relationship with God, there are varying degrees of closeness or distance, obedience or disobedience, walking *with* or walking *away*. As a parent, God disciplines us because of his love (Heb. 12:5; Prov. 3:11 – 12); as a husband, he woos us back when we stray (Hosea 1 – 3); and as a vinedresser, he prunes us so that we bear more fruit (John 15:1 – 2; Isa. 5:1 – 7).

Like humans, angels and other heavenly beings had a choice. The heavenly hosts could either walk with God or establish their own autonomous, rebellious journeys apart from God (Ps. 82; 86:8 – 11; 88:5 – 7). The Psalms acknowledge the presence of these celestial beings and declare that they should never equate or compare themselves with God. At some point, Satan rebelled against God and declared his own kingdom,[3] and from the beginning of human creation, he challenged the rule of God. Satan tempted Adam and Eve to seek solutions independent of God (Gen. 3:1 – 5). Israel consistently provoked God's jealousy by

---

3. Colossians 1:15 – 20 implies a cosmic rebellion. Paul says that "all things" (v. 16) were created by Christ. "All things" are generally called the principalities and powers. They are "things in heaven and on earth, visible and invisible, whether thrones or powers or rulers or authorities" (v. 16). All these things were "created through [Christ] and for him" (v. 16). The reconciliation of all things to Christ, then, could only occur "by making peace through his blood, shed on the cross" (v. 20).

abandoning him as the rock of their salvation, in favor of the gods of the nations (Deut. 32:15 – 18). Because of Israel's proclivity for these gods, Jehovah God disowned his elected people and sent them into captivity to Assyria and Babylon (2 Kings 17:7 – 23; Jer. 5:19). God's kingdom was frequently rejected by human-created, Satan-induced sovereignties standing in opposition to God. God thus responded as a parent both punishing and loving his child, or as a husband unconditionally loving his wife in times of closeness or distance. The Old Testament prophets anticipated a time when God would send a Savior to not only redeem Israel, but also bring together what was broken apart (Isa. 11).

The Gospels picture two kingdoms opposing one another. The kingdom of God came with power to defeat the dominion of Satan. When Jesus healed a demon-possessed man, multitudes of Jews began to wonder if Jesus was the Messiah, the Son of David. The Pharisees, becoming jealous, retorted that Jesus was casting out demons by Beelzebul, the ruler of demons. Jesus replied by describing two opposing kingdoms. The demons were not cast out by Beelzebul, because Satan would not fight against himself (Matt. 12:22 – 27). Then Jesus said, "But if it is by the spirit of God that I drive out demons, then the kingdom of God has come upon you" (Matt. 12:28). Deliverance from demon possession demonstrated the emancipating power of God, which had entered the world to defeat the power of Satan.

In Matthew 12:29, Jesus gives the analogy of binding a strong man in order to carry off his property. In this context, Satan is the strong man; however, Jesus, the implied stronger man, is able to bind him. When healing the spirit-possessed, Jesus entered the house of Satan, bound him, and took possession of his property. This defeat of Satan was characteristic of Christ's ministry. He was breaking down the authority of Satan by entering his domain, a world controlled by his power (1 John 5:19).

It must be noted that the stronger man "first ties up the strong man" before he proceeds to "plunder his house" (Matt. 12:29). The satanic in a person must be defeated before God can take possession of him. "The plundering of the Strong Man's house takes place only after he had been defeated" (Beasley-Murray, 1986, 109).

The defeat of Satan during Jesus' ministry was a foretaste of what Jesus did in breaking the chains of death and rising from the dead (Col. 2:15). The entire ministry of Jesus was characterized by triumph over

Satan. This has become a testimony to later generations that "the one who is in you is greater than the one who is in the world" (1 John 4:4).

Thus the kingdom was proclaimed not only by word, but also by deed. Jesus proclaimed the message of the kingdom while at the same time casting out demons and helping the blind to see and the lame to walk (Matt. 11:5). The kingdom in the New Testament is seen as the "dynamic activity of God, operative in, with, and through" Jesus Christ (Beasley-Murray 1986, 74).

THE MISSIONARY AND THE KINGDOM

It is essential that missionaries view their work in terms of participation in God's kingdom. What then is the role of the missionary in relation to the kingdom of God?

First and foremost, missionaries must be *citizens of the kingdom*. They must be people who embrace the reign of God in their lives. They must yield their lives to the King of Kings and the Lord of Lords. This yielding happens first on a heart level but necessarily is manifested in their lives. Missionaries who are citizens of the kingdom live out the values Jesus proclaimed in the Sermon on the Mount. They experience Jesus' triumph over darkness, by confronting darkness in their own lives and triumphing over it through the power of the Holy Spirit. They live with humility that allows them to confess their sins so that this victory becomes an ongoing experience. As citizens of the kingdom, they live within the reality that they "have been given fullness in Christ, who is the head over every power and authority" (Col. 2:10 NIV 1984), and they resist the powers of darkness in their own culture, the "elemental spiritual forces of this world" (Col. 2:8), that pull them away from the kingdom of God.

They realize that they have grown to become participants in God's kingdom over a period of time. Jarrod Robinson describes the process in three stages. Seekers begin by *experiencing God's kingdom*, much like a child learning to experience life. This is a time of observing the nature of kingdom life in community. While living in community, they naturally begin *participating in the kingdom*, like a child learning to eat solid food or stand up and walk. There comes a point at which searchers begin *submitting to God's kingdom*, living totally for him. What is heard and observed and then practiced becomes their allegiance for living (Robinson 2007). Participating in Christ's death and resurrection in baptism becomes a living illustration of this submission to the kingdom of God. Over a period of time and much struggle, we move from *observing* to *participating in* to *submitting to* the kingdom of God.

Missionaries who experience God's reign in their lives become *ambassadors of God's kingdom*. Speaking with the full authority of the King, they invite others to enter the kingdom. Like Jesus, they proclaim through word and deed that God is king over all the earth. As people reflecting the mission of Jesus, they "proclaim good news to the poor" and "proclaim freedom for the prisoners and recovery of sight for the blind" and "set the oppressed free" (Luke 4:18 – 19). They take seriously Jesus' call for Saul on the road to Damascus to become his follower and apostle: "I am sending you to [the Gentiles] to open their eyes and turn them from darkness to light, and from the power of Satan to God, so that they may receive forgiveness of sins and a place among those who are sanctified by faith in me" (Acts 26:17 – 18). They acknowledge Christ's kingdom authority in the Great Commission to "go and make disciples of all nations, baptizing them in the name of the Father and of the Son and of the Holy Spirit" (Matt. 28:18 – 19). As ambassadors, they consider these kingdom callings precious. Their message has credibility, because their lives and ministries reflect God's reign.

As citizens of and ambassadors for the kingdom of God, missionaries learn to spiritually discern kingdom activity where it exists. They believe that God is already at work in their context, and they seek ways to join him. Rather than forging ahead with plans based on human initiative, they seek the initiative of the Spirit and then respond obediently. At the same time, they recognize the weeds that grow in the fields they cultivate. They look for the ways in which Satan is active in their own hearts and in their cultural context and in opposing their kingdom work. They stand against him with the power and authority of Jesus, while trusting God to separate the weeds from the wheat in his own time.[4]

4. In *Communicating Christ in Animistic Contexts*, I say that kingdom proclamation has four functions: kingdom theology (1) provides an interpretive model based on the Word of God for explaining the world, (2) introduces the reign of God, which equips believers to attack and defeat the powers of Satan, (3) acknowledges that the encounter between God and Satan is actively taking place in this world and in the process makes no dichotomy between the natural and the supernatural, and (4) aims to Christianize the entire cultural system, broadening our focus from individual conversion to systemic Christian involvement in all of culture (1991, 139 – 41).

We ski down the mountain of God with the realization that we have eyes that see but cannot yet behold the wonderful dimensions of the kingdom of God. We understand the meaning of the kingdom parables only partially. We can say only, "The kingdom of God is like ..."

Incarnation: A Theology of God among Us

The theology of incarnation is a third theme that flows through the biblical text and enriches our understanding of both *missio Dei* and the kingdom of God. It is another ski run that helps us envision God and his work in this world. This theme is exceptionally practical because it illustrates how sovereign God is coming to us to carry out his mission.

It is easy for us to live as if God does not exist. Pride warps our hearts, lust enslaves our flesh, the world presses us into its mold, and Satan tempts us to follow him (James 4:1 – 10). We are tempted to live autonomous lives, separate from God. The great paradox is that when we forget God, he comes to us! God, because of his nature, personifies or embodies himself in his creation. This "God coming to us" is *incarnation.*

We must remember that God always takes the initiative in coming to us. His coming is a display of his grace, not based on our merit. God's coming to us is rooted in his nature of love and faithfulness. Moses reminded the children of Israel in Deuteronomy 7:7 – 9,

> *The* Lord *did not set his affection on you and choose you because you were more numerous than other peoples, for you were the fewest of all peoples. But it was because the* Lord *loved you and kept the oath he swore to your ancestors that he brought you out with a mighty hand and redeemed you from the land of slavery, from the power of Pharaoh king of Egypt. Know therefore that the* Lord *your God is God; he is the faithful God, keeping his covenant of love to a thousand generations of those who love him and keep his commandments.*

THE INCARNATION FORESHADOWED

In what ways has God come to us? Sometimes God comes to us *personally*, as he did with Adam and Eve in the Garden of Eden. When Adam and Eve acquiesced to Satan's temptations, God came searching for them, calling, "Where are you?" (Gen. 3:9). Their sin led them to fear God, hide from him, and seek to live without him. God came to them seeking reconciliation.

God likewise came to Jacob in a vision at Bethel to open his mind to his sovereignty (Gen. 28:10 – 22), fought with him all night and gave him a new identity by changing his name from Jacob ("he who grasps the heel" or "deceiver") to Israel ("one who struggles with God") (Gen. 32:22 – 30), and finally sent him back to Bethel to purify his household (Gen. 35:1 – 4). Our lives are transformed as God comes to us and meets us at the point of our rebellion so that we will begin to walk intimately with him.

There is also an incarnational element in God's self-revelation through *prophets*. The writer of Hebrews says, "In the past *God spoke* to our ancestors *through the prophets at many times and in various ways*" (Heb. 1:1, emphasis added). These prophets were uniquely called and sent by God to speak his words. God told Jeremiah, "I have put *my words* in your mouth" (Jer. 1:9, emphasis added; cf. Deut. 18:18). Ezekiel was commanded to eat the scroll that God had given him and then "go ... to the people of Israel and speak [his] words to them" (Ezek. 3:1 – 4). These prophets of God are contrasted to false prophets, who spoke "visions from their own minds, not from *the mouth of the LORD*" (Jer. 23:16, emphasis added). They spoke what the people or kings and nobles wanted to hear (Jer. 23:9 – 32; Ezek. 13:1 – 9). Ezekiel said, "Their visions are false and their divinations a lie" (13:6). Although God spoke to Moses "face to face," he typically spoke to prophets through dreams and visions (Num. 12:6 – 8).

THE INCARNATION REVEALED

The ultimate expression of God's incarnation, however, is *Jesus Christ*. God in Christ is like an artist who creates a multidimensional reality and enters into that reality to serve as a loving, holy participant. The writer of Hebrews says, "In these last days he has spoken to us by his Son, whom he appointed heir of all things, and through whom also he made the universe" (Heb. 1:2). Christ is the ultimate expression of incarnation, because he is "the radiance of God's glory and the exact representation of his being" (Heb. 1:3).

God in Christ is like an artist who creates a multidimensional reality and enters into that reality to serve as a loving, holy participant.

In the incarnation of God in Jesus of Nazareth, the most stunning miracle in the history of the world occurred: humanity and divinity mingled to become the God-man, "the One who is both the complete God and a perfect man, possessing the divine nature and the human nature distinctively, without a third nature being produced" (Lee 1995, 283). This incarnation is encapsulated in the name *Immanuel* or *Emmanuel*. This Hebrew name לֵאוּנָּמִע (*'immânû 'çl*), meaning "with us [is] God," consists of two Hebrew words: לא (*El*, meaning "God") and ונמע (*Immânû*, meaning "with us"). Who then is Jesus? The answer revealed by the incarnation is, Jesus Christ is fully God and fully man in one person. In other words, he is *God incarnate*.

Several passages of Scripture help us to better grasp the incarnation of God in Christ. With clear echoes of the creation account of Genesis, the gospel of John begins with the powerful revelation that "in the beginning was the Word, and the Word was with God, and the Word was God" (John 1:1). The Word, the *Logos*, God's revelation of himself, is identified with and yet somehow distinct from God. The Word is also "the true light that gives light to everyone," that was "coming into the world" (John 1:9). The very world that the Word/Light had created failed to recognize him, even though he entered into it (John 1:10). The Word/Light is not just a spiritual concept but also a physical reality. John claims, "The Word became flesh and made his dwelling among us. We have seen his glory, the glory of the one and only Son, who came from the Father, full of grace and truth" (John 1:14). The word John uses for "made his dwelling" could be rendered "pitched his tent." John reminds us of how the glory of God entered the Old Testament tabernacle (Ex. 40:34 – 35). In Jesus, the glory of God entered human flesh.

In Philippians 2, Paul quotes what appears to be an early Christian hymn as he calls Christians to imitate the humility displayed by Christ. The incarnation reveals to us that our glorious God is also a humble servant. Faith in the incarnation presupposes that the divine Word/Light existed before the incarnation event. He who was "in very nature God … *made himself* nothing" (Phil. 2:6 – 7, emphasis added). Again, we see God's incarnation as a display of his grace. By becoming human, God himself became subject to suffering and death (Phil. 2:8).

Luke 5 provides several illustrations of what the incarnation meant for Jesus' earthly ministry. Near the conclusion of the chapter, Jesus reminds his questioners that the time that he, the bridegroom, was with them was indeed a unique moment in history (Luke 5:33 – 35). Because God was in the flesh, he could stand beside a lake he had created, feel (and smell!) the crowd around him, speak in an audible voice, and float in a boat (Luke 5:1 – 3). He could impart healing through a physical touch and a spoken word (Luke 5:13). Because Jesus was human, physical limitations, like a crowded room, restricted people's access to him. Yet people who had faith could always find a way to get to him (Luke 5:17 – 19). At times, Jesus took advantage of this ability to separate himself from people, by withdrawing to a lonely place to pray (Luke 5:16). He needed prayer to sustain his human spirit. Because he was in the flesh, he ate and drank, yet eating and drinking were not merely ways to sustain his physical body; they were social activities by which he touched the lives of "tax collectors and sinners" (Luke 5:29 – 31).

Still, even in his humanity, the divinity of Christ shone through. He knew just where there were fish to be caught — knowledge so indicative of holiness that Peter felt unworthy to be in his presence (Luke 5:4 – 9). The Pharisees and the teachers of the law were astonished by Jesus' claim to forgive sins, because they recognized that such a prerogative belonged to God alone (Luke 5:20 – 21). No mere man could expect unconditional obedience to the command "Follow me" (Luke 5:27 – 28).

Without the incarnation, God's plan to redeem humanity would have been impossible. Stuart Murray writes, "If mission originates in the character and activity of God," the incarnation of Christ is the most significant "means by which God engages in mission" (2001, 42). Jesus' death on behalf of every human being was possible only because he entered fully into the human condition.

The writer to the Hebrews explains in Hebrews 2:9:

> *We do see Jesus, who was made lower than the angels for a little while, now crowned with glory and honor because he suffered death, so that by the grace of God he might taste death for everyone.*

Erwin McManus offers this insight into the incarnation:

> Jesus did not come into this world and live His life on a mountaintop isolated from human suffering. He walked among us, ate with us, and shared in our humanity. He did not heal lepers from a distance, but touched them into wholeness. He pressed His disciples and prayed for

> them to be in the world but not of the world. The focus of their three years together was not the salvation of the Twelve, but their ministry to the entire planet. (2003, 11)

THE CONTINUING INCARNATION

The incarnation of God in Christ shows just how far God is willing to go to identify with people he wants to serve and to save. In a less profound but equally true sense, Christian missionaries must similarly "incarnate" the gospel among people to whom they proclaim the good news. This was the strategy of the apostle Paul, who wrote,

> *Though I am free and belong to no one, I have made myself a slave to everyone, to win as many as possible. To the Jews I became like a Jew, to win the Jews. To those under the law I became like one under the law (though I myself am not under the law), so as to win those under the law. To those not having the law I became like one not having the law (though I am not free from God's law but am under Christ's law), so as to win those not having the law. To the weak I became weak, to win the weak. I have become all things to all people so that by all possible means I might save some. I do all this for the sake of the gospel, that I may share in its blessings.*
> (1 CORINTHIANS 9:19–23)

Paul was willing to meet people where they were and adjust to their culture in order to help them grasp the gospel. Jewish followers of Christ continued to circumcise their children and live their lives within the covenant practices of Abraham. Gentiles who came to Christ were not bound by these Jewish customs but nonetheless were expected to live holy, loving, faithful lives within Christian community. In a city where some people felt they could not eat meat that had been ceremonially sacrificed to idols, Paul was willing to live with sensitivity, saying, "Be careful ... that the exercise of your rights does not become a stumbling block to the weak" (1 Cor. 8:9). Paul was able to say, "I have become all things to all people so that by all possible means I might save some. I do all this for the sake of the gospel" (1 Cor. 9:22–23).

The implications of the incarnation for Christian missions are discussed more fully in subsequent chapters. The role of the church in mission will be explored more deeply in chapter 4. The very understanding that the church is "the body of Christ" (1 Cor. 12:27; Eph. 1:22 – 23; 4:15 – 16) produces vivid implications of how the church should conceive of herself and her mission to the world. An incarnational model of practice is introduced in chapter 9. This way of ministry, standing in contrast to contemporary extractional models, imitates the life and ministry of Christ and is characterized by compassion, interpersonal rapport, and reciprocity.

Crucifixion and Resurrection: A Theology of Life in Death

The cross is recognized almost universally as the symbol of Christian faith. Christians display it in their meeting places, wear it as jewelry or on clothing, and even tattoo it onto their bodies. At least one Christian marketer has produced a line of "Empty Tomb Gear," encouraging Christians to announce their faith in the resurrection in the same way that we point to the centrality of the cross.[5]

Although the crucifixion and resurrection are distinct events, each derives its meaning from the other. The resurrection proves that the atoning death of Jesus was a victory, not a defeat. The crucifixion and resurrection function together as yet another theological foundation of missions, a fourth theme that helps us envision God and his work in this world.

Scripture is clear that Jesus' crucifixion provides a model for the Christian's life. Jesus anticipated his own crucifixion by saying that a disciple must "take up their cross" (Matt. 16:24; Mark 8:34; Luke 9:23). Peter told Christians who were suffering insult and persecution to "rejoice inasmuch as you participate in the sufferings of Christ" (1 Peter 4:13). The word *participate [koinôneô]* has as its most basic meaning "to share." When Christians suffer for the sake of the gospel, they enter into the sufferings of Christ.

Before his conversion, the apostle Paul found his identity in seeking justification through personal righteousness by keeping the law. When

5. *www.emptytombgear.com* (Accessed December 4, 2011).

he described his abandonment of this pursuit in favor of justification by grace through faith, he declared, "I died to the law" (Gal. 2:19). This was not a simple death; it was a crucifixion. He affirmed, "I have been crucified with Christ and I no longer live, but Christ lives in me" (Gal. 2:20). Paul also told the Philippians that he had forsaken self-righteousness in exchange for "participation *[koinônia]* in [Christ's] sufferings," which meant "becoming like him in his death" (Phil. 3:9 – 10).

Yet just as Christ's crucifixion served as a prerequisite for his resurrection, so Paul's identification with the death of Christ resulted in new life for him. Paul told the Galatians, "The life I now live in the body, I live by faith in the Son of God, who loved me and gave himself for me" (Gal. 2:20), and he told the Philippians that he sought also "to know Christ — yes, to know the power of his resurrection ... and so, somehow, attaining to the resurrection from the dead" (Phil. 3:10 – 11).

When we look at a model missionary like Paul, we wonder what fueled his tremendous drive and willingness to suffer for the sake of bringing the good news to others. Paul himself says that he was inspired by the prospect of fellowship with Christ by sharing both in his death and in his resurrection.

Missionaries must fully surrender themselves to God and embrace a cruciform life. Only then will they be prepared to receive God's fruitfulness. In the divine order, death precedes life. Jesus anticipated his own death and resurrection when he said, "Very truly I tell you, unless a kernel of wheat falls to the ground and dies, it remains only a single seed. But if it dies, it produces many seeds" (John 12:24). But he also applied this death-to-life order to all who would follow him: "Anyone who loves their life will lose it, while anyone who hates their life in this world will keep it for eternal life" (John 12:25).

Evangelists, church planters, and missionaries imitate Jesus through their willingness to suffer and even die for others. Their lives are a sacrificial giving of self for the sake of saving others. Their lives are shaped by the cross. They experience resurrection power in the context of suffering and death because they are walking so personally with God that he shapes how they think and live. No longer do they live their own carnal lives; they live a new life empowered by God's Spirit.

Figure 3.2 A Process of Theological Engagement in Ministry

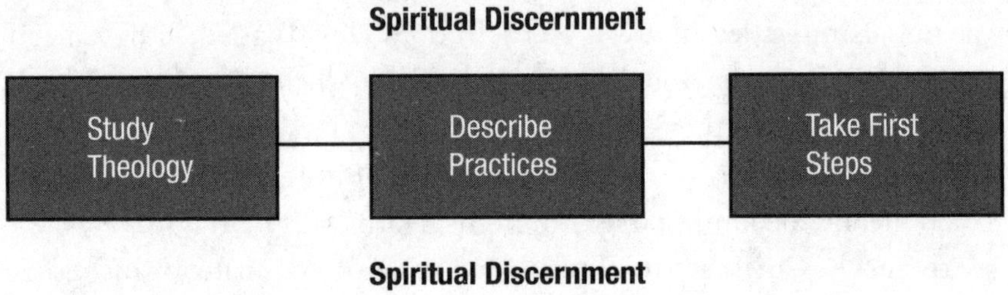

RELATIONSHIP BETWEEN THEOLOGY AND TRANSFORMATIVE SPIRITUAL PRACTICE

Well-meaning and busy evangelistic activity that lacks a theological foundation is like a cut flower. It may appear attractive for a while, but it is destined to wither and die. At the same time, theological reflection that does not result in missional practice is like a dead stump. The roots may run deep, but there is no life and no fruit. All too often, even people who understand the theological foundations of missions form their practices based on contemporary modes of business (selling, advertising) and schooling (conveying knowledge). The challenge for today's students and practitioners of cross-cultural missions is to develop continuity between our missional theology and our missional practices within the context of spiritual formation.

This simple diagram (Figure 3.2) outlines a useful process for ensuring such continuity. Even as students study theology, they must continually ask, "What practices flow out of this understanding?" or "If our theology has helped us to better understand the nature of God, how do we imitate God's nature in our practice?" or "If this is really the Word of God, what does obedience to it look like in our context?" Once such a vision for obedience has been discerned, Christian disciples take the first steps toward the realization of the vision. Disciples hold themselves accountable to their Christian community, discuss how to overcome obstacles, and together evaluate their progress. When they sense that they have gotten off course or that their steps are not leading in the right direction, they return to Scripture and reenvision how they can act more consistently with God's nature and his purposes in the world.

REFLECTION AND APPLICATION

Questions

1. What metaphors describe a theology of mission? How do these metaphors help us understand the mission of God?
2. How does understanding that God is the source of mission prepare our hearts for missions?
3. Tell the story of the mission of God in the life of one biblical character. How does this story spiritually form you as a person who wants to carry the mission of God?
4. Use Scripture to define *kingdom* and *the kingdom of God.*
5. Why is kingdom living a countercultural lifestyle? How does living in the kingdom help you prioritize the decisions you make in life?
6. What is the meaning of the phrase "inaugurated eschatology"? Use this phrase to describe how Christians stand between the times.
7. How does a theology of the kingdom of God shape how we live and minister?
8. Use Scripture to define *incarnation.*
9. Describe how a theology of incarnation shapes practical missionary life and ministry.
10. Use Scripture to define a theology of the cross (a theology of crucifixion and resurrection).
11. How does this theology of the cross shape how we live and minister?

Application

Creatively outline, draw, or diagram the biblical story line of the *missio Dei.*

Personal Inventory

How has God spoken to you through this chapter? What is God calling you to do about it?

chapter 4

The Church

God's Embodiment of Mission

LIKE MANY OF THEIR GENERATION, Jim and Julie struggled with the nominalism of the church in North America. Many church fellowships, they believed, were being swept along by culture currents and had begun to look more like social fraternities than communities of disciples on mission with God. When the church reflects the world, its distinct nature is lost and it has little to offer the world. Jim and Julie believed the words of the apostle John: "Do not love the world or anything in the world. If anyone loves the world, love for the Father is not in them. For everything in the world — the lust of the flesh, the lust of the eyes, and the pride of life — comes not from the Father but from the world" (1 John 2:15 – 16).

They realized that this cultural accommodation had occurred because in order to attract and retain members, many contemporary churches try desperately to satisfy appetites created by worldly society. The tone and content of their preaching, worship, small groups, and community service are shaped by "what works" to attract people to their public gathering.

Jim and Julie had attended an evangelical Bible church planted by their friend Bill Stephens. Bill's training led him to develop strategies responding to the question, "How can we meet the needs of the people of this community and make this church grow?" Bill developed a core team, launched with an attendance of two hundred after six months of planning, and now has an average attendance of seven hundred people each Sunday. By all appearances, he is very successful. However, as Bill's friends, Jim and Julie knew that he was inwardly perturbed. He acknowledged that his church attracts people because it caters to what they want. It is more a vendor of goods and services than a community of the kingdom of God. They discussed the members' mixed motives: attending is their duty; church is a place to meet people of influence or where children receive moral instruction. Church attendance assuages guilt and declares to others (and to self) that "I am religious." A spiritual responsibility has been discharged; therefore all is well. One day Bill, confiding in Jim and Julie, exclaimed, "What have I created!"

Jim and Julie also noted a competing and equally destructive trend in North American churches. Seeking to avoid the pollution of the world, some churches culturally withdraw from the world but publically protest practices such as homosexuality and abortion. They vie within the political system for laws and customs that uphold Christian values. Frequently, they idealize the past, believing that the nation was built on Christian principles and that these values must be protected in a decaying culture. To outsiders, who become increasingly resistant to such rhetoric, they sound angry, frustrated, and belligerent.

David Kinnaman's books *Unchristian* (2007) and *You Lost Me* (2011) amplified Jim and Julie's understanding of what was taking place in North America. In 2007, Kinnaman studied a cross section of people in the United States aged sixteen to twenty-nine, that is, the leading edge of the mosaic generation and the trailing half of the baby buster age group. These young people viewed Christians as antihomosexual, with 91 percent of survey respondents agreeing that "Christians show contempt for gays and lesbians." Most saw Christians as judgmental, "prideful and quick to find faults in others" (87%). Nonbelievers found Christians hypocritical (85%) and described them as old-fashioned (78%), too political (75%), out of touch with reality (72%), insensitive to others (70%), and boring (68%) (2007, 21–40).

Many Christians thus began to feel this anti-Christian stigma: "When you introduce yourself as a Christian to a friend, neighbor, or business associate who is an outsider, you might as well have it tattooed on your arm: anti-homosexual, gay-hater, homophobic. I doubt you think of yourself in these terms, but that's what outsiders think of you" (2007, 93). Believers began to hide their Christian convictions and felt that it would be better to lead by example than by speech.

Caught between these extremes of cultural accommodation and Christian elitism, Jim and Julie began to ask, "How can the church resist the allure of worldliness while still maintaining a relevant and convincing witness in the world? How do Christians avoid living by the world's standards yet remain gracious toward and connected with people who do?"

This chapter attempts to answer Jim and Julie's questions. It revisits the theological foundations from chapter 3 — *missio Dei*, the kingdom of God, incarnation, and crucifixion and resurrection — to examine their impact on the church.

The church is not merely a human organization. It is the result of a mission or sending that began with God.

The Church: The Result of *Missio Dei*

The church is not merely a human organization. It is the result of a mission or sending that began with God. The mission of God was initiated the moment humans fell into sin, reached its climax in sending Jesus Christ into the world, and continued through his disciples and the formation of the church. Christ prayed about this sending in John 17:18: "As you sent me into the world, I have sent them into the world." He reiterated the statement after his resurrection: "As the Father has sent me, I am sending you" (John 20:21). In other words, both Christ and his disciples were ambassadors sent by God, the source of mission. The church, then, must see herself as "the outcome of the activity of God who sends and saves" (Vicedom 1965, 80).

Had God not sent his Son, there would be no church. Since God's mission through Christ gave birth to the church, it must be seen as *his* institution, under *his* jurisdiction, set aside to fulfill *his* purposes in the world. Never should *his* body be considered a social fraternity with little relationship with the One who initiated it.

In a practical sense, the church has always been the result of mission. Faithful servants of God bring together searchers open to listening to the gospel, group those who respond into a fellowship of the faithful, then nurture them to grow in the Lord. Churches have always been planted by people led by the mission of God.

I encourage you to learn the history of your home church. How did it start? Who led in starting the church?

I spent my teenage years in northeastern Arkansas, where mission and evangelism were a part of life. One of my fondest memories is working with my father and other local Christians to plant the Center Hill Church of Christ. I remember visiting many people in the community.

I helped to lay the cement blocks that became the meeting place of a new church. Boyd Morgan, a lifelong itinerate evangelist exemplifying the pioneering spirit of church planting in Churches of Christ, became the first preaching minister of this new church. In *Arkansas Angels*, he described the early missionaries who planted the first churches in northern Arkansas.

> These men loved the cause for which they labored more than their lives. They toiled, they walked, they traveled by horseback or by train, just a few went by early autos. They laughed, they cried, and they prayed over their problems. They worked with their own hands to support themselves. Their families also worked to supplement the meager preacher's pay when they got any.... Disappointments, hardships, perils of life, hard times were legion. [These hardships] meant nothing to these men whose faith in the Bible and their God ... was the directing force of their lives. These men were alive and active. They ceased only when the flesh failed. Their work lives. (1967, iv)

During my early years, I saw church planting as natural to the life of the church. To be a Christian was to reproduce, and the ultimate type of reproduction was the planting of new churches. This church of my youth nurtured within me the desire to become a missionary.

For thirteen years, our family served as church-planting missionaries among the Kipsigis in Kenya. We witnessed God's mighty hand as churches were planted via evangelism, new Christians were nurtured to maturity, and leaders were trained to evangelize and plant other churches, pastor and shepherd the communities of faith, and train still other leaders. These communities have brought God's witness to thousands of homes, hundreds of village counsels, and various parts of local and district governments. They foster love and unity within families, represent the mission of God in village counsels, and challenge corruption and graft in public offices.

The Church: The Manifestation of the Kingdom of God

The church is not equated with the kingdom, since God's rule is from eternity to eternity and is exercised even over people who do not consciously submit to his reign. The church, however, must obey Jesus' teaching concerning the kingdom of God and manifest its presence in the world today. Robert Webber says, "The church's mission is to *show the world what it looks like when a community of people lives under the reign of God*" (2002, 133, italics added). Because the kingdom of God runs counter to the cultures of the kingdoms of this world, the church that is faithful to Christ will always be distinct from the dominant surrounding culture.

The church is God's people called out from the world to be his witness in the world. As an institution, it appears fallible and weak, but paradoxically, it has outlasted states, nations, and empires (Newbigin 1989, 221). The church reflects the eternal nature of the kingdom that cannot be destroyed (Dan. 2:44; 7:13 – 14). Its survival is rooted in being God's people under his eternal sovereignty.

Often, Christians fail to recognize the difference between the values and ethics of God's kingdom and those of the world. The world so permeates the church that Christians no longer recognize biblical allusions to its separateness. How are disciples of Christ *in* the world but not *of* the world (John 17:14 – 16)? How can people of God live in the heavenly realms while dwelling in the earthly realm (Eph. 1:3; 2:6; 3:10 – 12)? What does Paul mean when he says that the believer's citizenship is in heaven (Phil. 3:20)? Why do two Christian scholars define the church as "a colony, an island of one culture in the middle of another"? "In baptism," they say, "our citizenship is transferred from one dominion to another" (Hauerwas and Willimon 1989, 12).

Israel illustrates a nation's struggle to be God's distinctive people. God's covenant with Israel set them aside as "a kingdom of priests and a holy nation" within God's world (Ex. 19:5 – 6). Their designated purpose was to become God's light to the nations (Isa. 42:6; 49:6) and God's priests mediating his purposes. Unfortunately, Israel forgot that they were chosen and imitated the nations around them by going after their gods (Deut. 32:15 – 18). As a result, God sent them into captivity (2 Kings 17:7 – 23). The church, like Israel, is called to be a distinct, separate people, personally relating to the God who chose them.

Peter defines the church's separateness from the world in words that call to mind God's election of Israel. The church, God's new Israel, is to be "a chosen people, a royal priesthood, a holy nation, God's special possession" (1 Peter 2:9). Such separation from the world led Peter to

You cannot live in Northern California very long before you encounter the largest trees in the world, the Sierra redwoods. These giants can live two thousand years, may weigh upwards of five hundred tons, reach over 350 feet in height, and drink thousands of gallons of water to stay alive. Ironically, one would think that because these enormous trees have no taproot, they would topple over during a heavy storm. But they have a little secret which keeps them safe and healthy—they don't grow off by themselves. Each tree's root system is intertwined with the roots of all the surrounding redwoods. It is literally an underground fellowship which anchors them to the earth. And if one does fall, it still has life to produce another redwood from its base!

What a picture of the church! The more we are connected to one another in love, wisdom, faith, and good works, the better we will thrive in the kingdom of God. And if we do fall, the body of Christ will continue to pump life into us so we can rise again, to the glory of God.

describe Christians as "foreigners and exiles" (v. 11; cf. 1:1, 17). They have entered into Christ through a fundamental change of life, called a "new birth," which gives them an eternal inheritance with God (1:3, 23). As strangers in a world not their own, they must be holy because their God is holy (v. 15), and they must not imitate the vain ways of their forefathers (vv. 13–19). Because they are God's distinctive people, they are able to suffer as Christians without shame, knowing that they are participating in the sufferings of Christ (4:12–16).

Unfortunately, the church often loses its identity as God's distinctive people. Vicedom has written that the greatest problem with Christians is that "they do not know that they are Christians" (1965, 80). Rather than permeating the world with God's eternal message, the church is being permeated by the world. Philip Kenneson believes that the church in the United States, although numerically strong, is seriously ill. He says,

> It is quite possible for the church to be both growing and yet not bearing the fruit of the Spirit. What is happening in many cases is that the church is simply cultivating at the center of its life the seeds that the dominant culture has sown in its midst.... Stated another way, the church that is being cultivated in the United States looks suspiciously like the dominant culture rather than being an alternative to it. (1999, 11–12)

In light of Kenneson's statements, Christians must discern whether the church reflects the purposes and mind of God.

Peter describes the church as "a chosen people, a royal priesthood, a holy nation, God's special possession, that [we] may declare the praises of him who called [us] out of darkness into his wonderful light" (1 Peter 2:9). The last part of this verse is contingent on the first part. The church as God's chosen possession calls sinners to holiness in God. However, a church without a distinct nature, partaking of the world, calls people into a fraternity with Christian trappings. This group, because it is not sufficiently connected to the Vine, is unable to bear the fruit of God's Spirit.

How do Christians testify to people in the world while not being of the world? The Quaker missionary Thomas Kelly wrote,

> He plucks the world out of our hearts, loosening the chains of attachment. And He hurls the world into our hearts, where we and He together carry it in infinitely tender love. (1996, 20)

The Church: The Continuing Incarnation

The credibility of the church's witness to the world is determined by the extent to which the body of Christ exemplifies the life of God. The church's understanding of herself as *the body of Christ* (1 Cor. 12:27; Eph. 1:22 – 23; 4:15 – 16) profoundly impacts how she sees her mission. The church is to continue the mission of Jesus to seek and save the lost and to impart abundant life in his name. We must share the message of Christ's sacrifice so that others can be saved by it through faith in him. God's people, like Christ, are called to lives of obedience and sacrifice, living for the sake of others, not merely for themselves. They must emulate all facets of Christ's ministry — healing, proclamation, deliverance, and identification with the poor.

Mission is to the church what blood is to the body. As the body cannot survive without blood, so the church cannot survive without

> There is only one actual incarnation of God and that is in Jesus Christ, but the church, being his body, sustains an incarnational dimension. The church is a witness to the presence of Jesus in the world as it embodies and lives out its faith. . . . The church is the continuation of the incarnation. It is the earthed reality of the presence of Jesus in and to the world. Herein lies the ancient apologetic. (Webber 2002, 95)

As the body cannot survive without blood, so the church cannot survive without mission.

mission. Without blood, the body dies; without mission, the church dies. As the physical body becomes weak without sufficient oxygen-carrying red blood cells, so the church becomes anemic if it does not express its faith. The church most frequently establishes the reason for its existence while articulating its faith. An unexpressed faith withers. A Christian fellowship without mission loses its vitality. Mission is the force that gives the body of Christ vibrancy, purpose, and direction. It is the lifeblood of the church. When the church neglects its role as God's agent for mission, it is neglecting its own lifeblood.

The concept of sending, integral to the *missio Dei*, is also grounded in the incarnation (John 20:21). As the Father sent the Son into the world on a mission of redemption, so God sends his church into that same world to continue that mission. Likewise, local churches are to send emissaries as representatives of God into places the entire church cannot go. These messengers "believe and therefore speak" (2 Cor. 4:13). They have been given the "ministry of reconciliation" and are ambassadors sent by God. Through these emissaries, God makes his appeal for unbelievers to be reconciled to him (2 Cor. 5:18 – 20).

The Antioch church illustrates how God used a church attuned to the Holy Spirit to launch his mission. Antioch was a praying and fasting church. Acts 13 describes how they sent out two of their own: "While they were worshiping the Lord and fasting, the Holy Spirit said, 'Set apart for me Barnabas and Saul for the work to which I have called them'" (v. 2). Sensitive to the Spirit's moving, and after prayer and fasting, the church laid their hands on Barnabas and Saul and sent them out (v. 3). This sending was not a human endeavor! When Christians turn their hearts and lives to God through worship and fasting, he hears and acts. God, through his empowering Spirit, used this church to evangelize from Antioch to the remotest parts of the world. Churches today must follow Antioch's example of seeking God's guidance through fervent prayer, fasting, and obedience to God's direction.

In Romans 10:14 – 15, Paul describes the significance of mission and uses rhetorical questions to show the role of mission in the church.

> *How, then, can they call on the one they have not believed in? And how can they believe in the one of whom they have not heard? And how can they hear without someone preaching to them? And how*

can anyone preach unless they are sent? As it is written: "How beautiful are the feet of those who bring good news!"

The basis of all mission is sending. Messengers, whose feet are beautiful to people hearing and receiving the word of Christ, cannot go unless they are sent.

The Church: A Cross-Formed yet Hopeful Community

The early Christian church was called into existence by urgent proclamation of the death, burial, and resurrection of Jesus. Peter stood before people witnessing the outpouring of the Holy Spirit on the day of Pentecost and testified,

> *Fellow Israelites, listen to this: Jesus of Nazareth was a man accredited by God to you by miracles, wonders and signs, which God did among you through him, as you yourselves know. This man was handed over to you by God's deliberate plan and foreknowledge; and you, with the help of wicked men, put him to death by nailing him to the cross. But God raised him from the dead, freeing him from the agony of death, because it was impossible for death to keep its hold on him.*
> (Acts 2:22 – 24)

This message of the death and resurrection of Christ is the most fundamental reference point of the Christian faith, the apostolic *kerygmya*, the gospel! Paul highlights this core message to the Corinthian church in what is one of the earliest Christian confessions:

> *I want to remind you of the gospel I preached to you, which you received and on which you have taken your stand. By this gospel you are saved, if you hold firmly to the word I preached to you. Otherwise, you have believed in vain.*
>
> *For what I received I passed on to you as of first importance:* that Christ died for our sins according to the Scriptures, that he was buried, that he was raised on the third day according to the Scriptures, and that he appeared to Cephas, and then to the Twelve.
> (1 Corinthians 15:1 – 5, emphasis added)

This teaching of God's work of reconciling sinful humankind to himself by the death and resurrection of Jesus Christ is called *atonement*. What happened when God sent his Son to die on the cross? What is the significance of the resurrection? Without a thoughtfully developed theology of atonement, the church loses her focus as a distinctive people of God in the world.

Many contemporary forms of Western Christianity, however, leave little room for the cross and the empty tomb. Molded by modern, secular thinking, "Christians have been tempted ... to alter the radical message of the cross into something more in harmony with human reason, human sensibilities, and human wishes" (Allen 2006, 126). "The dominant vision of the good life that holds sway everywhere around us today simply excludes the cross" (2006, 126). This exclusion of the cross and the empty tomb results in the taming or domestication of Christianity. The result is an "anemic and distorted gospel" (2006, 125).

Leonard Allen, in his chapter titled "The Church under the Cross" in *The Cruciform Church*, poignantly asks the question, "What does it mean for the church to live under the cross?" (2006, 126). In his Christian heritage, there was an assumption by some formative leaders that everyone in North America understood the atonement. The major challenge was calling people into Christian union based on restoring the "ancient order of things." Focusing on the process of coming to Christ rather than what God had done by his great goodness to reconcile us to himself led to a movement "preoccupied with form, structure, and the setting in order of what was lacking." In the process, "the 'word of the cross,' in its New Testament fullness, was partially displaced.... The cross was simply a historical fact; one should believe that fact, then concentrate on one's proper response to it" (2006, 129–30). In this process, the transformative power of God's atoning Spirit and power, his very identity as God, has been lost.

> The cross ... challenges and breathtakingly alters our human conceptions of what God must be like. We think of God as high and lifted up, enclosed in glory; the cross reveals God as stooping and lowly, enduring shame. We think of God as omnipotent, invulnerable, and unaffected; the cross reveals God as making himself vulnerable because of love, exposing himself to all the world as one who appears weak and powerless. We think of God working his will through sheer almightiness; the cross

> shows us that God has chosen to work his will through the power of suffering love. (Allen 2006, 146)

Without a thoughtfully developed understanding of atonement, the church loses her focus as a distinctive people of God in the world.

This cross-formed, or "cruciform," vision of the church resets our identity in three fundamental ways.

> 1. *The cross reveals the heart of God most clearly, thereby putting all our human conceptions of God to the test.* The cross reveals the depth of God's suffering love.
> 2. *The cross reveals to us the true nature of human sin and the depth of divine grace.* We do not truly see our sin until we see something of what our sin cost God. We cannot know the extent of our estrangement from God until we see something of the distance God had to travel to reach us. We do not confess our sin, then turn to the cross. Rather we see Jesus lifted up on the cross and find ourselves moved to confess our sin.
> 3. *The way of the cross provides the model for God's new social order, the messianic community.* In proclaiming the kingdom of God and in calling people to follow him, Jesus summoned people into a new kind of community, an alternative social order. (Allen 2006, 145–48)

Thus we walk counterculturally, understanding that "the message of the cross is foolishness to those who are perishing, but to us who are being saved it is the power of God" (1 Cor. 1:18). The Christian walk is about dying to Christ and allowing him to raise us to transformative life! This understanding of the cross and the empty tomb defines the nature of the church.

Today's church, like the church in Corinth, may be tempted to bypass the cross and move straight to the resurrection. Paul told the Corinthians that while Christians have been raised with Christ, they still live in the body with all its humbling limitations (2 Cor. 4:8–13). He stresses that "Christ alone has been raised in glory thus far—the Christian's resurrection to glory remains in the future" (Allen 2006, 154).

But the resurrection must never eclipse the cross. Unbalanced triumphalism (an emphasis on Christian victory without suffering) may cause the church to think that suffering and setbacks indicate that certain endeavors are not God's will. Without a theology of the cross,

The church is *the distinctive people of God called by him through his mission and set aside for his mission.*

some churches, wanting to get the most bang for their missions buck, withdraw financial support from works that fail to quickly yield visible fruit. Encountering opposition and obstacles may in fact indicate that the church is in the center of God's will. The church must prayerfully discern the best ways to manifest God's kingdom among unreached people groups. At times, this will mean setting aside our desire to see them quickly turn to God. Among some peoples, it will take unconditional love extended over a long period of time to break down the barriers that have kept them from hearing the gospel as good news.

Though we have not experienced the ultimate victory, we confidently expect it. Therefore we can endure the suffering that comes with the way of the cross. We enter into difficult circumstances because we expect God to call out a people for himself. We know that he has gone before us and is at work before we arrive. We believe that where the church sends, Christ's ambassadors will preach. Where they preach, people will hear. Some who hear will believe, and those who believe will call on the name of the Lord and be saved (Rom. 10:13 – 15).

Allen suggests that following the way of the cross will mean "intentionally nurturing a community standing in sharp contrast to the dominant secular ethos of our time" (2006, 155). Although this cross-shaped community is distinct from secular society, the church must not assume an attitude of arrogant superiority toward the world. Rather the church must seek ways to love and serve the surrounding culture in concrete, incarnational ways.

How then should the church be defined from a biblical perspective? The church is *the distinctive people of God called by him through his mission and set aside for his mission*. The purpose of the church is not merely to interpret history but to become God's instrument for shaping the future he intends for the world. It is through the church that "God brings history to its goal, and only because this is so does it provide the place where the goal of history can be understood" (Newbigin 1989, 131). The church embodies the very essence of the mission of God.

For this reason, committing one's life to Christ's mission does not include the option of saying yes to Jesus but no to the church. Despite one's frustrations toward the institutional church or disillusionment with her failures, the church remains God's instrument for his mission in the world. Missionaries must appreciate all that is good about the church, be thankful for the heritage of faith she provides, and help the church become an even more faithful agent of God's mission.

Just as Christ was *in* but not *of* the world (John 1:10), so his body, the church, must dwell in the world yet not be of it (John 17:15 – 16). This tension of being in but not of the world allows the church to avoid the competing currents of secularism and isolationism. A church that surrenders to the surrounding culture is both in and of the world; a church that preaches only condemnation fails to love and engage the world.

The church must understand that she is the result of God's relentless pursuit of humanity. She must manifest the reign of God, represent Christ in the world, be shaped by the cross, and live in hope of the resurrection. God will then use his body as his instrument to accomplish his purposes in the world.

REFLECTION AND APPLICATION

Questions

1. What is the significance of each statement below in describing the relationship between the church and mission?
   a. "The church is the result of mission."
   b. "For the church to effectively minister, it must be God's distinctive people in the world."
   c. "The church most frequently establishes its rationale for being — its purpose for existing — while articulating its faith. An unexpressed faith withers."
   d. "The purpose of the church is not merely to interpret history but also to become God's instrument for shaping the future he intends for the world."
2. How do you think your church is perceived by its non-Christian neighbors? How would you know?
3. Contrast how the world sees itself with how the church molded by the mission of God sees the world. How do Christians live "in the world" yet not be "of the world" (John 17:14 – 16)?

4. What is the significance of the question, "What does it mean for the church to live under the cross?"

Application

1. Talk to someone who knows how your congregation began and write a paragraph summarizing the story.
2. Ask three non-Christians what words they would use to describe people who follow Christ. If their descriptions are negative, don't argue but ask forgiveness. Write a short description of your experience.

Personal Inventory

How has God spoken to you through this chapter? What is God calling you to do about it?

chapter 5

Motives for Missions

Reasons for Participating in God's Mission

RECOGNIZING THE SIGNIFICANCE OF *MISSIO DEI*, the kingdom of God, the incarnation, and the crucifixion and resurrection leads to personal reflection. What motives spur participation in God's mission? Do they flow from the mind of God or from human desires and egos? Are they primary or secondary to the heart of God?

Motives are heart allegiances that lead missionaries and ministers into action but sometimes render them to inaction. Most frequently, the human psyche is made up of motives that compete against each other. Prayerful consideration of motives enables people who carry the mission of God to overcome, or at least compensate for, deficient motives while also deepening the foundations of primary Christian motivations.

During the course of their studies, Jim and Julie began to ask, "Why do we want to be missionaries?" They were touched by the theologies of *missio Dei*, the kingdom of God, the incarnation, and the crucifixion and resurrection! They realized that these theologies must shape their motives and asked, "Do our motives reflect God's heart or our own desires?"

For example, Isaiah indicted the Israelites because even as they went through all the motions of religion — sacrificing burnt offerings, attending convocations and assemblies, and spreading out their hands in prayer — they were mistreating the people around them (Isa. 1:10 – 17). They were like silver that was covered with dross, the scum that forms on the surface of molten metal (v. 22). God, however, promised to "purge away [their] dross and remove all [their] impurities" (v. 25).

This purifying process occurs when Christians evaluate their motives. God works to purge deficient motives and makes people who are his "as white as snow" (v. 18). He weighs all motives (Prov. 16:2), wanting to purify, not destroy. In this process of reflection, primary motives increasingly become the driving force of the missionary's life.

In prioritizing motives, Christian ministers must search the heart of God and make his motives their motives.

All a person's ways seem pure to them,
but motives are weighed by the LORD.
(PROVERBS 16:2)

Types of Motives

Motives of mission can be grouped into three categories. *Primary* motives reflect the will of God. *Secondary* motives reveal personal or cultural impulses. *Deficient* motives echo selfish purposes.

PRIMARY MOTIVES: REFLECTING THE NATURE OF GOD

Primary motives of mission mirror the mind of God; they reflect his attributes and his will. In prioritizing motives, Christian ministers must search the heart of God and make his motives their motives. They do this by diligently studying the Word, fasting and praying, and meditating on God and his message. As they practice these Christian disciplines, God works in their lives to form primary motives and to re-form negative ones. Motives change as they move inward and upward.

Primary motives of mission include the compelling love of God incarnate in human life, a living acknowledgement that God is sovereign over time, and thankfulness for what God has done.

God's Love and Compassion

God's dominant attribute is love. Old Testament Hebrew captures this quality in the word *hesed*, "steadfast love." God describes himself to Moses as "compassionate and gracious ... slow to anger, abounding in love and faithfulness, maintaining love to thousands, and forgiving wickedness, rebellion and sin" (Ex. 34:6 – 7; cf. Num. 14:18; Neh. 9:17; Ps. 86:15; 103:8; 145:8; Joel 2:13; Jonah 4:2). God can therefore be described in a single word: *love* (1 John 4:7 – 8).

Love motivates God to minister within human cultures. The Bible testifies how he raised up *judges* to deliver the Israelites (Judg. 2:10 – 19). He instituted *priests* to intercede for the people of Israel (Ex. 28 – 29; Lev. 8 – 9). He sent *prophets* to proclaim his message to kings and the people (Jer. 1:5 – 6; 15:19; Amos 7:16; Ezek. 3:17). He gave his

Son, *Jesus Christ*, the Messiah, to die for humankind (John 3:16). He chose Israel because he *loved* them (Deut. 7:7–8) as a father loves his son (Hos. 11:1–11). He compassionately taught Israel to walk (v. 3) and led them "with cords of human kindness, with ties of love" (v. 4). When Israel's disobedience forced God to forsake them, he shed divine tears. He cried,

How can I give you up, Ephraim?
How can I hand you over, Israel?...
My heart is changed within me;
all my compassion is aroused.
I will not carry out my fierce anger,
nor will I devastate Ephraim again.
For I am God, and not man—
the Holy One among you.
(HOSEA 11:8–9)

God's steadfast love moved him to send Jesus to die for humanity: "God so loved the world that he gave his one and only Son" (John 3:16). "God demonstrates his own love for us in this: While we were still sinners, Christ died for us" (Rom. 5:8). "This is how God showed his love among us: He sent his one and only Son into the world that we might live through him" (1 John 4:9). Jesus, sent from God, reflected the love of God. He touched the untouchable (Mark 1:40–45), cried with the crying (John 11:32–37), and died for those dying in sin.

The LORD does not look at the things people look at. People look at the outward appearance, but the LORD looks at the heart.
(1 SAMUEL 16:7)

Christian compassion also motivates missionaries. Paul describes how Christ's love "compels us." Christ died for all. Therefore his followers must die to self. That is, they can "no longer live for themselves but for him who died for them and was raised again" (2 Cor. 5:14–15). Just as love compelled God to reconcile sinners to himself, his love propels Christians to minister to people broken by sin, alienated from him, and living without hope in the world. Like parents entering a burning house to save their children, Christians urgently enter human contexts, compassionately seeking the lost. The dominant characteristic of God in Scripture becomes our fundamental motivation for mission: "We love because he first loved us" (1 John 4:19).

In my living room hangs a picture that depicts the mission of God. At the top are two hands — relaxed, compassionate, inviting — gently reaching down. Other hands — shackled, tense, desperate — are urgently reaching up. This portrait symbolizes God's loving hands reaching down to grasp the anxious hands of the world. It could also connote Christian hands, toned by a loving Father, reaching down to the lost of the world. *Missions is the loving hands of God reaching through compassionate Christian hands to release the shackled hands of the lost.*

God's Sovereignty Over Time

Before Christ's ascension, the apostles asked him when God would restore the kingdom to Israel. Jesus responded that *God is in charge of time*: "It is not for you to know the times or dates the Father has set by his own authority" (Acts 1:6 – 7).

Scripture affirms that time is in the hand of God. The Bible begins with God initiating human time (Gen. 1:1) and ends with Christ promising to come soon to conclude time (Rev. 22:20). God brought the world into existence and will bring it to an end. Although God is "from everlasting to everlasting" — that is, beyond time — he is to be praised because he created "the whole world" (Ps. 90:2). He sent Christ to the earth at the appointed time (Gal. 4:4) and will determine the time of his second coming (Matt. 24:36). The duration of nations, the span of kings, and the length of lives are all in the hand of God.

God sets the boundaries of time in terms of his loving nature. Before bringing judgment, he is waiting patiently for sinners to repent (2 Peter 3:9), and he will change his mind about punishment if there is repentance (Jonah 3:10). As discussed in chapter 3, Christians today live in the *in-between times* — the age between the first and second comings of Christ. God's kingdom came into the world in the person of Jesus of Nazareth, who was anointed by God to be the Savior of the world. People who believe in Christ live under God's sovereignty and have access to his power and blessings.

Paradoxically, Satan continues to be active in this age. As we saw earlier, the parable of the wheat and the weeds teaches that even though the kingdom of God has come into the world, the dominion of Satan continues (Matt. 13:24 – 30, 37 – 43). The wheat and the weeds represent two different domains. The good and the bad are not separated in the present age. This separation will be the final work of God when his reign is fully manifest.

How does the belief that Christ is sovereign over time serve as a motivation for mission? During this in-between period, Christians are called to both prepare themselves and prepare the world for Christ's second coming. Christ calls his followers to "watch" (Matt. 24:42 – 43; 25:13) and "be ready" (24:44), since they "do not know the day or the hour" that Christ will come (25:13). Peter reiterates and expands this theme of watchfulness in anticipation of Christ's second coming: "You ought to live holy and godly lives," he writes, "as you look forward to the day of God.... Since you are looking forward to this, make every effort to be found spotless, blameless and at peace with him" (2 Peter 3:11 – 12, 14).

The realization that time will end also motivates Christ's followers to teach people broken by sin and alienated from God. All people will ultimately stand before Christ and be judged for deeds during their lifetime. Knowing "what it is to fear the Lord," Christians must make every effort to persuade people to be reconciled to God (2 Cor. 5:10 – 11).

The ultimate work of Christians is to prepare themselves and the world for Christ's second coming. Contemporary Western Christians often reject this eschatological plea by living for the present and not preparing the world for Christ's second coming. The consequences of Christianity lived for the here and now are frightening! Christianity should not be merely a way to meet human needs but a heart-to-heart, intimate relationship with the sovereign God who sets the boundaries of time.

An Outpouring of Thanksgiving to God

Mission, in its essence, is an outpouring of thanksgiving to God for what he has done in human lives. The psalmist sang,

Give thanks to the Lord, proclaim his name;
make known among the nations what he has done.
Sing to him, sing praise to him;
tell of all his wonderful acts.

Glory in his holy name;
let the hearts of those who seek the Lord *rejoice.*
(Psalm 105:1 – 3)

This passage indicates the function of praise literature. Praise speaks not only to God but also to the nations. They hear of God's mighty acts and glorify his name. The spontaneous praise of the faithful becomes a testimony to the nations. People who praise God cannot refrain from speaking of him. Thus Paul writes that people who speak because they believe will "cause thanksgiving to overflow to the glory of God" (2 Cor. 4:13 – 15).

These three motivations — God's love and compassion, God's sovereignty over time, and an outpouring of thanksgiving to God — lead us to give our lives to pursuing the will of God. C. S. Lewis says that Christians not only see the beauty of God, but also become beautiful. "We want something else which can hardly be put into words — to be united with the beauty we see, to pass into it, to become part of it" (1949, 12 – 13).

SECONDARY MOTIVES: PREACHING CHRIST FOR HUMANITARIAN AND PERSONAL REASONS

Many secondary motives, although neither deficient nor primary, lead people to the mission field. These motivations are usually humanitarian and personal. They include a desire to help people physically, a yearning for adventure, and a desire for a deeper faith.

A Desire to Help People Physically

Westerners are frequently touched by the poverty of the world in comparison with their own wealth. Their response to this poverty is a desire to use their medical, technical, and teaching skills to upgrade the physical and socioeconomic conditions of the poor. This response may be rooted in the compassion of God and thus reflect the mind of God, becoming a primary motive for Christian mission. Sometimes, however, the impulse is no different from that of philanthropists who want to improve the world.

If the desire to help the poor is rooted in God's compassion, Christian medical practitioners will seek to minister to the human soul as well as to the body. Prayer and reflection on evil will be integrated into medical missions. Building Christ-centered lives will be part of lessons on carpentry. Helping the world run under the sovereignty of God will be part of mechanics. The church, God's distinctive people in the world, will be emphasized over human (including parachurch) organizations. Compassion will lead missionaries to make their ministry holistic—integrating the message of God and prayer to God into social ministry. Without such integration, these social ministries are no different from services performed by governments and secular organizations. Thus, being moved by poverty is a Christian motivation only when it is related to God's compassion for the poor and reaches beyond the physical to touch the spiritual.

Compassion will lead missionaries to make their ministry holistic—integrating the message of God and prayer to God into social ministry. Without such integration, these social ministries are no different from services performed by governments and secular organizations.

A Yearning for Adventure

Many, if not most, prospective missionaries feel the excitement of seeing the world and experiencing new and unusual customs and foods. Their spirit of curiosity propels them beyond the boundaries of their own culture to learn why other people think and act as they do. They are enthralled by the challenge of learning new languages, visiting in the homes of people of the land, and questioning the traditional spiritual leaders of the culture. Missionaries benefit from a spirit of adventure and curiosity.

A Desire to Build a Deeper Faith

Others enter the mission field because of a desire to build a deeper faith. They view missionaries as spiritual giants who have learned to rely totally on God. Wanting to surrender completely to God but feeling that their faith is insufficient, they are drawn to the mission field to increase their faith and reliance on God. They view missions as a personal faith-building experience. Again, the emphasis is on self, not on others. Although such faith-building as a motivation for missions may be deficient, it inevitably *is* a benefit of missions. John Wesley made this entry in his diary: "I went to America to convert the Indians but oh! who shall convert me?" (Telford 1898). Most missionaries will, at some point, pose a similar question.

Secondary motives are inadequate to sustain missionaries on the field. If people are to carry the mission of God, their motives must, to some degree, reflect the mind of God.

DEFICIENT MOTIVES: PREACHING CHRIST FOR SELFISH PURPOSES

All Christian missionaries and ministers must confess deficient motives that do not reflect the heart of God. These motives are intermingled with secondary and primary ones. The existence of deficient motives, however, should not reduce Christian servants to despair or inaction. God, because of his great mercy, sees these motives within the hearts of his servants and helps us by his Holy Spirit to develop new ones, which more clearly reflect his nature.

Paul reflects on the radical changes that occur in people who are in Christ. He describes Moses, who reflected God's radiance after communing with him on Mount Sinai. Christians, like Moses, are being transformed into the image of God as they intimately commune with him (2 Cor. 3:18). Deficient motives must be transformed by the shaping hand of God.

Making a Name for Oneself

Paul acknowledged that not all who preach do so from pure motives. Some preach Christ "out of selfish ambition, not sincerely" (Phil. 1:17). They are concerned about proclaiming the gospel, but they also want to make a name for themselves, to be recognized for their accomplishments. Paul contrasts preachers with selfish motives with those who preach "out of goodwill" (v. 15). The former are motivated by ego, the latter by love (vv. 16–17). Becoming well known means little to those motivated by love; they unselfishly want to lead the lost to the Redeemer, to glorify God, not themselves.

Paul exhorted the Philippians to "do nothing out of selfish ambition or vain conceit" (Phil. 2:3). They were to be "not looking to [their] own interests but ... to the interests of the others" (v. 4). This other-directedness is portrayed by Christ's becoming human. In his incarnation, he "humbled himself;" he gave up equality with God and "made himself nothing" (vv. 6 – 8). Paul states that this attitude of humility, this willingness to seek others' interests, should become our nature (v. 5). Harrell writes,

> The hinge on which this section of the letter turns is the contrast between the empty glory of man who willfully grasps at what he does not have and the glory of Christ who willingly emptied Himself of that which was always His. (1969, 85)

Just as Christ emptied himself and became human, Christian ministers and missionaries must strive to empty themselves of selfish ambition and acknowledge that they are only "jars of clay" filled and empowered by God (2 Cor. 4:7).

This self-emptying is difficult, however. Jesus encountered this problem even with his apostles (Mark 10:35 – 45). James and John came to him, asking to be given places of importance in his kingdom — one on his right hand and one on his left. The other ten were indignant: why should James and John expect to be given significant positions of authority? Hearing of their indignation, Jesus called the apostles together and described the nature of Christian leadership. He then contrasted leadership in the world to his model of servant leadership: the greatest in the kingdom of God is not one who rules but one who *serves*! Jesus himself exemplified this servant leadership. He said, "For even the Son of Man did not come to be served, but to serve, and to give his life as a ransom for many" (v. 45). Thus Christian leaders are not to "preach [themselves], but Jesus Christ as Lord, and [themselves] as ... servants for Jesus' sake" (2 Cor. 4:5).

Building Personal Kingdoms

Similarly, a feeling of superiority causes some to use missions to create little kingdoms where they are in control. They dominate a new endeavor and establish their own rules and regulations. In effect, they become rulers over their own kingdom. Charles Landreth recounted such motives when describing certain ministers in inner-city North America: "Sometimes people go down to the very poor because they can have power over them. They set themselves up as *gods* to these people. They intimidate them" (Lamascus 1989, 2).

Escaping from One's Own Culture or Church Situation

Some view missionary work as an escape from highly traditional or lukewarm churches within their own country, or from a culture that they consider flawed. Their dissatisfaction with the church in their home country prompts them to leave behind a disappointing situation, with plans to establish a "perfect" Christian movement in some other area of the world. Or perhaps their disdain for their own homeland provokes them to seek a more congenial society.

Rejecting one's culture and church situation is both highly idealistic and selfish. The problems one is seeking to escape will likely reappear in the new culture, since propensities for nominalism and sin are universal. In reality, missionaries cannot escape the cultures that have molded their lives.

Healthy missionaries do not desert their own culture when going to another. They strive to become bicultural, able to relate to both their home culture and their adopted culture. They realize that both cultures have strengths and weaknesses — that the dominion of Satan and the kingdom of God are present in each. Paul, for example, was a Jewish leader called to be an apostle to the Gentiles. He was not seeking, however, to escape his culture. Before their first missionary journey, Paul and Barnabas visited Peter and John in Jerusalem. These pillars of the Jerusalem church gave Paul and Barnabas "the right hand of fellowship," agreeing that they "should go to the Gentiles" (Gal. 2:9). Later, to show the unity of the Christian church, Paul took up a contribution to help Jewish Christians during a time of famine (Rom. 15:25 – 28). After the final missionary journey, Paul purified himself in the temple to demonstrate that he was walking orderly as a Jew and that he was not teaching Jews of the dispersion to forsake the law of Moses (Acts 21:17 – 26). Despite being chosen by God as an apostle to the Gentiles, he continued to feel "great sorrow and unceasing anguish" in his heart because his own people did not follow Jesus (Rom. 9:1 – 3). Paul did not reject the Jewish church but attempted to bridge the cultural and theological gaps between the Christian fellowships in the two cultures.

Reacting to Guilt

One missionary, obsessed with his parents' failure in cross-cultural ministry, wanted to erase a failure and bring honor to his family. This motivation, however, increased the already great pressures of adapting to another culture. Another missionary, strongly aware of his sinfulness — the utter brokenness of his own life — sought to offer recompense by committing his life to missions. *I'll become a missionary to try to atone for my sins,* he felt. This motive is depicted by Robert De Niro, as a sinner turned priest, in the movie *The Mission*. He repeatedly stated that he would endure any hardship that God put before him in order to "buy" atonement for his many sins.

Ministers and missionaries can be effective only if their personal spiritual motives are well defined. Conflicting motives will ultimately reduce them to inaction.

Paradoxically, God may use deficient motives to produce great good. Joseph's brothers certainly had deficient motivations when they sold him into Egyptian slavery. But God turned that evil into good so that Joseph saved his family from the subsequent famine (Gen. 50:20). Likewise, God may use ministers with faulty motives to carry his message. Faulty motives are frequently transformed as ministers themselves grow to reflect the image of God.

Motive Transformation

Missionaries whose motives are secondary, or even deficient, may feel discouraged and unfit for the task. The stories of Scripture, however, illustrate that God is able to transform and use people whose initial motives are primarily deficient.

FROM JACOB TO ISRAEL: A CASE STUDY OF TRANSFORMATION

Jacob entered the world grasping the heel of his twin brother Esau. His name, in fact, literally means "he who grasps the heel." In Jewish culture, this was an idiomatic expression that meant "a deceiver." This name became symbolic of much of Jacob's life. Jacob took advantage of Esau's hunger and convinced him to sell his birthright (Gen. 25:24 – 34). Aided by his mother, he disguised himself as Esau and deceived his father Isaac so that he received the blessing that should have gone to his older brother (Gen. 27). Paradoxically, after Jacob fled the wrath of his brother and settled with his mother's family in Haran, his father-in-law Laban deceived him as Jacob had deceived his father and brother. Jacob fell in love with Laban's daughter Rachel, but when the wedding day came, Laban substituted Leah, Rachel's older, less attractive sister. Jacob then had to pledge another seven years' work for Rachel (Gen. 29). Laban agreed to give Jacob certain sheep, lambs, and goats as payment for working for him but changed the rules (Gen. 31:6 – 7). Even years later, when meeting Esau and his army on the way back to Canaan, Jacob failed to keep his promise to follow Esau. He decided not to live with Esau as part of an extended family but to settle elsewhere in Canaan (Gen. 33:12). Deceit was embedded in Jacob's character.

God was working, however, to transform Jacob's life. After Jacob fled from his brother, God appeared to him in a dream in a place called Bethel, meaning "house of God." In this dream, Jacob saw angels ascending to and descending from heaven. The Lord stood above, saying, "I am the LORD, the God of your father Abraham and the God of Isaac" (Gen. 28:12 – 13). Then God reaffirmed the covenant of Abraham and Isaac with Jacob, saying,

> *I will give you and your descendants the land on which you are lying. Your descendants will be like the dust of the earth, and you will spread out to the west and to the east, to the north and to the south. All peoples on earth will be blessed through you and your offspring. I am with you and will watch over you wherever you go, and I will bring you back to this land. I will not leave you until I have done what I have promised you.*
> (GENESIS 28:13 – 15)

Jacob's response, however, was conditional — an "if ... then" statement:

> If *God will be with me and will watch over me on this journey I am taking and will give me food to eat and clothes to wear so that I return safely to my father's household,* then *the LORD will be my God and this stone that I have set up as a pillar will be God's house, and of all that you give me I will give you a tenth.*
> (GENESIS 28:20 – 22, EMPHASIS ADDED)

Instead of thankfully accepting God's grace and trusting him, Jacob wanted to make a deal with God.

But God was not finished with Jacob. Eventually Jacob decided to return to his home country to face his brother Esau, who had earlier vowed to kill him. Jacob proceeded in fear, apparently forgetting God's promise at Bethel to safely return him to his homeland (Gen. 28:15). He sent messengers ahead with gifts for his brother, seeking favor. But the messengers returned saying that Esau was coming to meet him with four hundred men. In great fear, Jacob divided his family and their flocks into groups, thinking, "If Esau comes and attacks one group, the group that is left may escape" (Gen. 32:8). Jacob began to pray, confessing his unworthiness, acknowledging God's gracious blessings of family and wealth, confessing his fear, and asking God to save him (vv. 10 – 12). He then sent his servants with flocks of livestock as gifts, hoping that these would pacify his brother. He thought, "I will pacify him with these gifts I am sending on ahead; later, when I see him, perhaps he will receive me" (vv. 13 – 20).

That night, "a man" appeared and engaged Jacob in a wrestling match. The two wrestled all night, but neither could overpower the other. Finally the opponent touched Jacob's hip, wrenching it from its socket. Jacob, recognizing that this was no mere human adversary, hung on tenaciously and demanded a blessing. The opponent, after asking his name, replied, "Your name will no longer be Jacob, but Israel, because you have struggled with God and with humans and have overcome" (Gen. 32:28).

Jacob, "the deceiver," became Israel, "one who struggles with God." This struggle, the constant wrestling match between God's pure and perfect will and humanity's impure and imperfect motives, characterized not only the man Israel but also the nation that bore his name. In better moments, the name Israel had a positive connotation — one of struggling not *against* God but *with* or *alongside* him, of being used as his agent in the world to accomplish his purposes.

Later God commanded Jacob to cleanse his household of all false gods and return to Bethel, where he had received the promise of God's protection and blessing. There Jacob made sacrifices to the Lord. God then affirmed that his name was to be Israel and reiterated his blessing. This time, Jacob built an altar where God had been speaking to him and poured sacrifices on it. From that point on, he would be known not for his deception but for his intense engagement with God.

At the end of his life, Jacob pronounced blessings on his descendants, showing that he was able to discern God's unique calling for each of them (Gen. 49). When we, like Jacob, submit our deficient motives to God, he will transform us and use us to accomplish his purposes.

BIBLICAL METAPHORS FOR GOD'S ROLE IN MOTIVE TRANSFORMATION

The Bible reveals God's transforming power through vivid word pictures which illustrate both his nature and how he expects us to be transformed into his image — holy, loving, and faithful.

God Is a Gardener Who Prunes the Branches

First, God is like a gardener who planted and nurtured a vineyard on a fertile hillside. He "dug it up and cleared it of stones and planted it with the choicest vines," anticipating great harvest. But "it yielded only bad fruit" (Isa. 5:1 – 2). In response, he allowed the vineyard to become "a wasteland, neither pruned nor cultivated" (Isa. 5:6). This vineyard was "the nation of Israel, and the people of Judah" (Isa. 5:7), who forsook Creator God and followed the gods of the nations. A major theme of Isaiah, however, is that God pruned his people so that he might welcome them back as people of his vineyard.

Jesus used this metaphor when saying, "I am the true vine, and my Father is the gardener. He cuts off every branch in me that bears no fruit, while every branch that does bear fruit he prunes so that it will be even more fruitful" (John 15:1 – 2). This important passage says that we must live in Christ, understand that our Father is the gardener who prunes and shapes us, and realize that this pruning is for our good, that we might bear more fruit within his kingdom. The key understanding of the passage is that there is no life unless we remain in the vine. Jesus says, "Remain in me, as I also remain in you" (John 15:4). Remaining in Christ gives us sustenance and life.

Although a branch may need to be completely removed, that is never the gardener's desire. Some pruning, however, is necessary so that the branch can be as fruitful as possible. Such pruning experiences are also necessary, but painful, in human lives. Missionaries and people considering missions often find that God prunes deficient motives and burdensome attachments from their lives so that they can become more fruitful in ministry.

God Is a Father Who Disciplines His Children

Second, God is like a father who loves his children, and because of this love disciplines them.

My son, do not despise the LORD's discipline
and do not resent his rebuke,
because the LORD disciplines those he loves,
as a father the son he delights in.
(PROVERBS 3:11 – 12)

The author of Hebrews quotes this passage and adds that God disciplines us as children "for our good, in order that we may share in his holiness" (12:10). Just as the vinedresser trims branches to make them more fruitful, God the Father prunes Christians so they produce "a harvest of righteousness and peace" (12:11).

This discipline must be from God, not people. When humans take on God's work, the result is usually manipulation, control, and alienation.

God Is a Refiner Who Purges Impurities

Third, God is like a refining fire burning away impurities. Isaiah, seeing intrinsic value in the people of Jerusalem, lamented their corruption, saying, "Your silver has become dross" (Isa. 1:22).

This dross consists of solid impurities which rise and then float on top of molten metal. It must be skimmed off the surface before the metal is poured into a mold. God, the Mighty One of Israel, declared that he would do this for his people.

I will turn my hand against you;
I will thoroughly purge away your dross
and remove all your impurities.
(ISAIAH 1:25)

God's words "I will turn my hand against you" indicate that the process would be painful. The precious metal had to be heated far beyond its natural state, its "comfort zone," in order to be purified. This painful process ultimately demonstrated grace as God removed the pollution and restored the metal's purity.

God — always motivated by his love and his grace — allows, and sometimes even causes, his people to go through this process. He compares our value to that of silver and longs to purify us by removing corruption.

From 1980 to 1994, the frescoes of the Vatican's Sistine Chapel underwent significant restoration. A team worked meticulously to clean away the centuries of grime, which had fallen from the candles illuminating the chapel, without harming the original paint. Pictures taken before and after the cleaning show amazing contrasts in color and detail! In our spiritual walk, Jesus, God's restorer, works to return our souls to their original beauty. Jesus' work of removing the grime of sin from our lives, like that of the restorers in the Vatican, must be done carefully. There is, however, one difference: we are coworkers with Christ in the restoration of our souls, which continues throughout our lifetime.

Psalm 51:10–12 describes this process: "Create in me a pure heart, O God, and renew a steadfast spirit within me. Do not cast me from your presence or take your Holy Spirit from me. Restore to me the joy of your salvation and grant me a willing spirit, to sustain me." Since God considers our souls worth restoring, even at the expense of Christ's death, we need to have a steadfast spirit that always rejoices in the Lord!

HOW GOD TRANSFORMS MOTIVES

God transforms our deficient motives through at least three means. First, God transforms our motives in worship. During worship, God molds us into people who know him, have a relationship with him. Worship reminds us where we stand in relation to God and therefore humbles us. It opens our hearts to the transforming work of the Holy Spirit.

Second, God transforms our motives as we serve others. Expressing love makes us more loving people. A common English proverb says, "Practice makes perfect." The French equivalent says, "It's by blacksmithing that one becomes a blacksmith." We might say, "It's by serving that one becomes a servant." This is not an excuse for hypocritical action. Rather we must recognize that if we want to develop certain qualities, we must put ourselves in situations where those qualities can develop. If we ask God for purity of heart, for love for others, or for a desire for his glory, and act as though he has already answered our request, we will see these qualities develop.

Third, God transforms our motives through times of crisis. God works through critical incidents in our lives to call forth the character he wants to develop in us. Few crises, national or personal, could match Judah's exile into Babylonian captivity. Few moments in history have looked darker for the people of God. Yet God used the experience of captivity to purge the idolatry that the people had practiced for centuries. Though Jeremiah lamented over the tragedy of the exile, he could sense God's grace.

Because of the LORD's great love we are not consumed,
for his compassions never fail.
They are new every morning;
great is your faithfulness.
I say to myself, "The LORD is my portion;
therefore I will wait for him."

The LORD is good to those whose hope is in him,
to the one who seeks him;
it is good to wait quietly
for the salvation of the LORD.
(LAMENTATIONS 3:22–26)

God works in human beings, though our motives are deficient, to transform us into vessels fit for his service. When we engage in genuine worship, serve others, and recognize crises as opportunities for growth, we open ourselves to God's transforming work.

Prayer for Transformation

God, work on our hearts. Transform empty conceit into compassionate love. Help us taste your infinite glory and thereby partake of it. Touch our hearts with your grace so that we become like you — holy, loving, faithful. In the name of Jesus, amen.

REFLECTION AND APPLICATION

Questions

1. What is meant by "Motives are heart allegiances that lead missionaries and ministers into action but sometimes render them to inaction. Most frequently, the human psyche is made up of motives that compete against each other"? Why is it important to evaluate personal motives?
2. What is the relationship between compassion and action?
3. In what way is *God's sovereignty over time* a primary motive of mission?
4. With which of the secondary motives of missions do you struggle most? Why?
5. With which of the deficient motives of mission do you struggle? Why?
6. How have you seen God transform your motives to reflect his qualities of holiness, love, and faithfulness? How might your story of transformation be important to others?

Personal Inventory

How has God spoken to you through this chapter? What is God calling you to do about it?

Imagine ...

Imagine that you have served as a missionary in a certain country for twenty-three years—the prime working years of your life. During these years, you struggled to learn the language, raise your children away from their grandparents, and nurture the initial Christians. When you were ready to return to your home country, the churches you planted were still small and struggling. You remember thinking, *I wonder if these churches will be able to continue without me?*

Five years later, Biwott, who was converted during your ministry, began a revival movement among the weak churches of this country. When you lived and worked there, Biwott was a weak Christian, frequently a thorn in your flesh. His own revival had begun after he experienced a time of prayer, fasting, and reflection. Then the church, after a period of intense revival, began to grow rapidly. Eventually you saved up enough money to visit your former mission field, but when you arrive, everyone praises Biwott and seems to have forgotten that you were instrumental in Biwott's conversion and that you initiated the church in this part of the world.

With what emotions would you struggle? Why might you have a difficult time recognizing the hand of God and praising him for what he has done through Biwott? How would you feel about God using your life the way that he did?

chapter 6

Types of Missionaries

The Many Faces of Missionary Ministry

IN THE PAST, MISSIONARIES TENDED TO BE GENERALISTS. They planted churches, developed training schools for church leaders, organized public or private education, fed the poor, began the first translations of Scripture, and perhaps became local veterinarians as well. Their skill set was broad because workers were few, finances limited, and Christian movements small. They were also overtaxed and frustrated, as they felt compelled to engage in ministries for which they may not have been particularly gifted.

We have entered, however, an era of specialization in which there are multiple expressions of mission throughout the world. This chapter describes these types of ministries. Some missionaries plant churches among unreached and lightly churched people; others train church leaders, translate Scripture, serve as agents of transformational development, seek justice for the oppressed, and provide logistical support for fellow missionaries on the field. Some missionaries work in multidisciplinary teams, in which different "specialists" combine their ministries to produce a more complete expression of the kingdom of God.

Many missionaries today still serve multiple functions, either simultaneously or during different periods of their missionary careers. They may initially learn languages and cultures, discover how to connect with local peoples, and develop the first communities of faith in their areas—

Jim and Julie came to believe that God was calling them to participate in the *missio Dei* as cross-cultural missionaries. As they began to look at specific opportunities for service, they discovered that one size does not fit all. They asked, "What types of missionaries has God called us to become?" They discerned God's calling and the particular gifts that God had put within them.

the classical approach of church planting. In later years, however, they may become trainers of leaders and/or compassionate advocates of the poor by launching ministries of transformational development.

Creating a strong movement of God requires that certain ministry tasks be prioritized: First, initial evangelism must lead to planting new churches. Second, Christians must be nurtured to maturity within these churches. Third, leaders must be trained to evangelize and plant other churches, pastor and shepherd the community of believers, and train still other leaders. Other tasks may amplify these but cannot take their place.

At the inception of missions in a particular area, these primary tasks are essential. Incoming missionaries must ask questions such as, "What is the status of the mission of God in my particular area?" and "How do my ministry skills fit into God's mission in this area?" In some cases, missionaries will discern a calling to a particular field and will adapt their ministries to the needs of that field. In others, they will discern a calling to a particular type of ministry and select a field where that type of ministry is most appropriate.

Planters of New Churches

Jeff's Story

As I looked down at the endless expanse of Africa from my seat in the airplane, the immensity of the tasks before me really hit home. Our team was flying to Africa to plant churches among a people group considered to be unreached. Our plan was based on basic principles: learn the language and culture, make disciples that would meet together as the body of Christ (churches), intentionally allow the spread of the gospel to become the responsibility of the nationals, and ultimately phase out of the missionary endeavor to the point that the church would function on its own. Thousands of feet above the earth, those goals no longer seemed basic. They seemed overly ambitious.

For many months after arriving on the field, we were learners. We spoke a new language like babies. Through blunders, intense time with the locals, and an intentional "non-leader" role, we learned cultural taboos, gender and leadership requirements, as well as religious beliefs. Having formed relationships over many months, we started testing our new language and culture learning by telling stories from Scripture.

> Many of the early believers invited us to their home villages and other places. Soon we saw small groups of people meeting to hear the Word of God. We found that it was often difficult for individuals to become Christians and that family groups providing support to one another often converted together. Churches often formed around clans. Others seemed to spring up in areas of new settlements, where people felt less pressure to conform to long-held religious traditions.
>
> Even before churches developed, we watched God start developing leaders. As the churches began, the missionaries taught leadership skills, culturally relevant teaching methods, and evangelistic principles which followed familial and friendship bonds. From the beginning, an emphasis was placed on the nationals teaching and evangelizing—even when they were new believers struggling with various sins and inabilities.
>
> Teaching the new leaders was endless. The leaders, young in their faith, needed a solid foundation, occasional rebukes, and spiritual motivation. Although our team did not pay local leaders, we intentionally found ways to address physical needs around us. We helped dig wells, address medical concerns, and develop an agricultural program. By the grace of God, we watched churches grow, plant new churches, and provide their own assistance to others.
>
> After fourteen years of missionary presence, our team phased out of on-site work. The phaseout process started the day we arrived. In reality, it continues. Each year, missionaries return to ask the leaders about what they want to learn and what struggles they encounter. Our prayer is that the seeds we planted will continue to grow and that a continual harvest will occur. It was an ambitious endeavor. We failed many times. So did the nationals. However, we praise God that he had the grace to do more than we could ask or imagine, and we pray that the good work which was started will be brought to completion.
>
> (Jeff Holland, *Togo*)

Some missionaries serve as church-planting pioneers in unreached or lightly churched areas. This happened naturally in the early Christian church. For example, the Jerusalem church, scattered because of persecution, "preached the word wherever they went" (Acts 8:4). Although Paul and Barnabas were sent out by the church in Antioch of Syria without a specific church-planting mandate, church planting resulted from their proclamation. As they preached the Word in the cities of Asia Minor, people came to faith in the Lord Jesus. As part of their ministry of strengthening and encouraging these new disciples, "Paul and Barnabas appointed elders for them in each church and, with prayer and fasting, committed them to the Lord, in whom they had put their trust" (Acts 14:23).

Acts 14:21 – 28 provides a close look at the practice of these early church planters. The church in Antioch became a church-planting church by prayerfully sending out godly, Spirit-filled teachers who

- preached the Word,
- were faithful in adversity,
- emphasized dependence on God,
- entrusted leadership to others,
- maintained contact after departure,
- remained accountable to those who sent them.

These elements are all important for effective church planting today. Indeed, the Word must be proclaimed! But before that is done, missionaries must understand the culture in which it was originally revealed, their own cultures, and the culture of people who hear the message. They must then work with their hosts to contextualize the message in linguistic and liturgical forms that preserve the meaning of the original message in the host culture.

Church planters today, like Paul and his companions, will encounter adversity. It takes many forms — separation from the familiarity of one's home culture and loved ones, adaptation to living conditions, frustration with learning another language and culture, dealing with hostile or corrupt governments, challenges of cross-cultural and multicultural relationships, outright persecution, and sometimes death. Church planters will be judged by their faithfulness in adversity, not only by God, but also by the people they are trying to reach. Missionaries' response to adversity is a critical part of their Christian witness.

These challenges require that church planters learn to depend on God. They must pray, seek God's direction, hear his voice, and obey him. Only then can they have the confidence to persevere in spite of difficulties.

Church planters serve as *initiators* of movements. They are apostolic servants sent by God to train local leaders to establish churches, help them come to maturity, and equip leaders as servants of God. Their task, according to David Watson, is to model, equip, watch, and leave (2009a).

Though they may move to other locations of service, church planters should never abandon the movements they have helped initiate. Maintaining contact and making periodic visits provides ongoing support and encouragement for the churches they planted. Church planters, as faithful servants, also report to those who have sent them and eventually become resource people and equippers for sending churches and agencies.

The goal of many church-planting missionaries is not merely to birth a church but to start *church-planting movements.* This requires that they model simple, replicable modes of ministry which are then copied by local leaders, who in turn teach others. In other words, missionaries *model* ministry, *equip* others for ministry, *watch* as the local leaders do ministry, and then *leave* them with God's missionary task (Watson 2009a). God often uses these simple, reproducible methods to produce a church-planting movement — "a rapid multiplication of indigenous churches planting churches that sweeps through a people group or population segment" (Garrison 2004, 21).

David Garrison's book *Church Planting Movements* (2004) cites ten elements that are found in every church-planting movement (CPM) (2004, 172 – 98). They are:

1. extraordinary prayer
2. abundant evangelism
3. intentional planting of reproducing churches
4. the authority of God's Word
5. local leadership
6. lay leadership
7. house churches
8. churches planting churches
9. rapid reproduction
10. healthy churches

People who serve as catalysts for church-planting movements must labor in prayer, understand local language and culture, submit to and teach the authority of God's Word, and train local leaders who both serve pastorally and plant new churches. They must develop intentional strategies to ensure that the churches planted in this movement are both rapidly reproducing *and* healthy. In most contexts, megachurches are not the norm. Healthy churches are defined not by size, by infrastructure, or by academically credentialed leaders but by the same elements that are vital to the existence of church-planting movements.

Trainers of Church Leaders

Without mature, indigenous leaders, church-planting movements flounder. Effective church-planting missionaries therefore begin early to serve as trainers of leaders. As the work grows and matures, other missionaries, whose primary calling and ministry is to equip church leaders "for works of service, so that the body of Christ may be built up" (Eph. 4:12), may carry the work forward.

Paul, for example, was both a pioneer missionary and a trainer of leaders. His custom was to quickly entrust church leadership to local elders, even when he ministered with a church for an extended period. Paul spent over two years in Ephesus as an evangelist-equipper by holding "discussions daily in the lecture hall of Tyrannus," and he left the church with well-established local elders (Acts 19:8 – 10; 20:17). Later Timothy continued the work in Ephesus, which involved preparing and equipping elders (1 Tim. 3:1 – 7; 5:17 – 20). Paul also left Titus in Crete to appoint elders in each town (Titus 1:7). He described his pattern for perpetuating capable church leadership: "The things you have heard me say in the presence of many witnesses entrust to reliable people who will also be qualified to teach others" (2 Tim. 2:2).

Paul's training model, reflecting the life of Christ, was not only informational but also imitative. He consistently selected Timothys and Tituses to journey with him and to minister alongside him. He journeyed and taught within a missionary team. Paul (then called Saul) was teamed with Barnabas by the Holy Spirit on the first missionary journey, and John Mark accompanied them as their "helper" (Acts 13:5). On the second missionary journey, Paul and Silas worked together and called Timothy to become their missionary apprentice (Acts 16:1 – 5). Later Paul ministered within a missionary band including Sopater from Berea, Aristarchus and Secundus from Thessalonica, Gaius and Timothy from Derbe, and Tychicus and Trophimus from the province of Asia (Acts 20:4; cf. Col. 4:7 – 14). Training was done experientially, within the context of community. These leaders were then expected to innovate what they had learned in other cultural contexts.

Mike Breen and Steve Cockram describe the movement from *information* to *imitation* to *innovation*. (See Figure 6.1.)

Figure 6.1 The Pathway of Learning

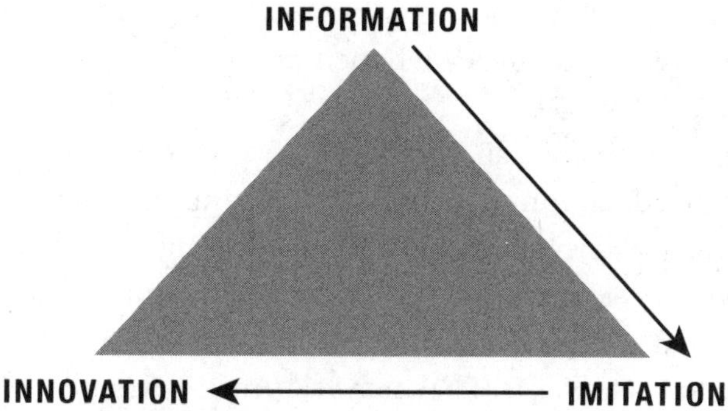

> We suggest that if you want to be a disciple, and if you want the people you disciple to be able to disciple others who then disciple others, you will need to follow the path of Information to Imitation to Innovation. Information is incredibly important, but having it right in our heads isn't enough. We need to see how that Information becomes knowledge and is incarnated in the everyday life of another person. We then apprentice ourselves to that person, learning not only the Information but also how to do what he or she does. And finally, after becoming confident in knowledge and practice, we have the capacity to innovate new ways of discipleship and mission. (2011, 48–50)

This movement from *information* to *imitation* to *innovation* infers that missionaries become learners within the local culture and adapt teaching and ministry models to cultural environments, education patterns, and learning styles. In some cultures, leadership training may occur during a weekly meeting with a group of evangelists beneath a tree in a remote village, followed by ministry that illustrates how the message is caught and taught. In other contexts, mature leaders are taught in classrooms in a well-equipped national seminary, followed by internships that illustrate the teaching and living of the message.

Cultures also vary in their attitudes toward learning. Do students learn better through trial and error or by rote? Do the students or the teachers ask the questions? What constitutes a proper student-teacher relationship? Do students learn best by listening to a lecture or by engaging in dialogue, individually or in groups? The answers to these questions are generally cultural. Cross-cultural teachers must learn and

"Nothing is learned until it is practiced."
(Dr. Ed Mathews)

respect the norms of their host cultures before attempting to innovate. Their goal should be to "create a learning context that is familiar to students yet stretches them beyond their previous experiences" (Lingenfelter 2003, 52).[1]

Missionaries cannot simply replicate the training models used in their own education. Ministry practicum experiences are now common, but Western education still places a high value on academic preparation. Missionaries whose preparation is primarily academic may be tempted to train new church leaders as they were trained, with a strong academic emphasis. They may lecture, for example, when group exploration would be more appropriate. They may give heavy reading assignments to students who learn better through personal interaction with experienced church leaders. They may mistakenly think that all students who can reproduce a body of information on an exam have internalized it. Dr. Ed Mathews, my former colleague and department chair at Abilene Christian University, says, "Nothing is learned until it is practiced."

The learning environment must be appropriate for academic objectives as well as ministerial and vocational needs of learners. Requiring leaders-in-training to attend a school may mean that they spend several years removed from their context of ministry. When these leaders complete their training, they may be less capable of making disciples and planting churches than they were before entering the classroom. In some cases, theologically educated leaders forget that lay members do not understand the vocabulary they have learned, and lay leaders may view them as less approachable.

Truly, many Western missions have initiated work in unreached areas by opening schools to train national evangelists who have in turn planted thousands of God-honoring churches. Often, however, these otherwise good works have remained dependent on external funding and, sometimes, under foreign control. Culturally appropriate and locally sustainable models allow newer churches to remain free from foreign dependence. They provide testimony to God's power to work within the resources he has given to his people.

---

1. Judith and Sherwood Lingenfelter's book *Teaching Cross-Culturally* (2003) provides an excellent introduction to recognizing important cultural differences in education.

THEOLOGICAL EDUCATION BY EXTENSION

Many missionaries educate and train national church leaders and evangelists in ways that allow them to remain at their homes and in their jobs, and to avoid dependence on foreign subsidies. Theological Education by Extension (TEE) is one such training method.

TEE was devised by Jim Emery in Guatemala as an attempt to overcome the obstacles inherent in residential training models. According to Ralph Winter, Emery's primary goal was "to educate the right people"—mature individuals, already engaged in church leadership, who could not easily leave their homes to attend a distant seminary (Winter 1999b). Thus TEE delivers seminary-level education in modular format, so that candidates can continue to work in their home areas.

Other missionaries have adapted the original TEE model. "Obedience-oriented education" places a high priority on experiential learning. It requires that the trainee be engaged in pastoral ministry while continually honing his knowledge and skills. This model is similar to a traditional trade apprenticeship. The theoretical aspect is taught and reinforced through the practice of ministry, which is also shaped by feedback from experienced ministers. People practicing obedience-oriented mentoring recognize that academic credentials are not a prerequisite for effective pastoral ministry and evangelism.

Kenneth Mulholland, reflecting on his experience in Central America, refers to obedience-based education as "the very soul of theological education itself" (1999, 7). George Patterson, a pioneer of this method, notes that obedience-oriented mentoring must be directly related to a local church and that the curriculum must fit the local situation. He further proposes that trainers encourage the spontaneous development and expansion of the church while working with small, highly disciplined groups that hold members accountable (1980, 120–28).[2]

The content of obedience-oriented education is derived from the Great Commission—not just the command to make disciples but also the charge to teach everything that Jesus commanded. Mark Moore has identified 110 commands of Jesus, while acknowledging that we do not

2. Websites which feature materials suitable for use in obedience-oriented mentoring include *www.trainandmultiply.com*, *www.paul-timothy.net*, *www.mentorandmultiply.com*, and *www.dci.org.uk*. Supporting articles can be found at *www.mentornet.ws*.

have a complete collection of Jesus' teaching and are looking not for "a shopping list of tasks, but for a template of priorities" (2012, 65). Moore collects the commands of Jesus under the following categories.

- Following Jesus
  - –Believing and abiding
  - –Listening to Jesus
- Religious piety (including prayer)
- Money
- Treatment of others
- Preaching and persecution

Such priorities, presented with Patterson's emphasis on relevance to the local context, could provide the themes for an obedience-oriented approach to leadership training.

ADVANCED THEOLOGICAL STUDIES

There is, however, a significant place in every culture for advanced biblical scholarship and theological training. In many contexts, missionaries fill this need until local Christians are equipped to provide such training. Often, missionaries teach alongside highly trained local professors.

Indigenous scholars are important because they bring new perspectives that help local Christians understand and apply Scripture in their contexts. Indeed, the global church is enriched by contributions from non-Western scholars. In cultures where well-educated leaders are highly valued, where governments closely examine religious leaders' credentials, or where national churches want to promote scholarly research, advanced theological training for local leaders is appropriate.

Bible Translators

Greg's Story

When my wife and I first made our home in a small West African village to translate the Bible for a minority people, we had to begin by learning a language the people had not yet written down. We had already spent a year learning French so we could communicate with the few educated men in the village to learn how to say key questions like, "What do you call that?" in the local language.

Then we spent all day every day with the people, asking questions and jotting down and analyzing the answers. After two years, we could speak well enough to begin the work.

We started by developing an alphabet and a system of writing for the language and literacy materials, to teach people how to read their own language. In the beginning, we knew of only forty Christians among the seventy thousand or so speakers of that language in the country where we lived. These believers provided some talented minds to translate the first draft from the French Bible.

We would then compare the meaning of the drafts to the original Greek or Hebrew Scripture and propose ways the translation could be made more accurate to the meaning of the original text. Together we struggled to craft the clearest, most natural wording as close as possible to the meaning of the original.

After we considered the translation perfect, we would conduct a comprehension test by reading it publicly. When the listeners were struck by a hunger to know Jesus and could answer content questions accurately, the translation passed the test.

Occasionally, people misunderstood the translation, like the time they thought the Bible taught that John the Baptist was a great sorcerer who could eat people's souls. That's when we would back up and try again. After the comprehension testing, the Scriptures would be checked by a translation consultant and then published.

After fifteen years of endeavor, this West African language group finally has the whole Bible! With God's help, we have also recorded a dramatized audio version of the New Testament so the new Christians who can't read in the five new churches that have been planted can grow spiritually. Now the Christians are struggling to use the Scriptures to multiply the churches.

(Greg Pruett, *Guinea*)

Reading and hearing God's Word in one's own language is essential in cultivating churches that devotedly embody Christian faith in their unique cultures.

(Lamin Sanneh)

Some missionaries, motivated by the importance of the Bible to Christian faith, serve as Bible translators. They recognize that God's Word is not tied to a single language. They are also aware that translating the message into a new language while preserving the meaning of the original message requires careful discernment. They realize that reading and hearing God's Word in one's own language is essential in cultivating churches that devotedly embody Christian faith in their unique cultures (Sanneh 2009, 252ff).

Even before the coming of Jesus Christ, God's people saw the need to make God's Word available in other languages. New Testament authors frequently quote from the Septuagint, the Greek translation of the

Hebrew Scriptures. In the earliest days of the expansion of Christianity, believers in Jesus translated their Scriptures into languages such as Syriac, Latin, and Coptic.

Missionaries in the modern era have also seen the importance of making God's Word available to people in their own language. William Carey, frequently called the Father of Modern Missions, was continuously involved in drafting preliminary translations of the Bible into various Indian languages, including Bengali, Sanskrit, and Marathi, and eventually became the professor of oriental languages at Fort William College in Calcutta (Tucker 2004, 127). The late Ghanian theologian Kwame Bediako acknowledged the value of Bible translation to Africa:

> It is to the undying credit of the modern missionary enterprise from the West, and to the lasting benefit of the newer churches which have resulted, that the value of the vernacular Bible for converts was generally recognized quite early. There is probably no more important single explanation for the massive presence of Christianity on the African continent than the availability of the Scripture in the many African languages. By rejecting the notion of a sacred language for the Bible, Christianity makes every translation of its Scriptures substantially and equally the Word of God. Thus, the existence of vernacular Bibles not only facilitates access to the particular communities speaking those languages, but also creates the likelihood that the hearers of the Word in their own languages will make their own response to it and on their own terms. (Bediako 1995, 62)

More than 2,000 languages and dialects have Scripture portions available. Only 469 of those, however, have a complete, printed edition of the Bible, and 1,231 additional languages have the New Testament available (UBS 2011). According to the United Bible Societies, "There are estimated to be 6,600 spoken languages in the world and most people would assume that the Bible is available in the vast majority. The fact that fewer than 500 have a Bible shows how little of the real story of Bible translation the statistics alone tell" (UBS 2011). About 340 million people speak the 2,000 languages for which translation projects have not yet begun (Wycliffe Bible Translators 2011). Most of these are part of small, unreached people groups, that is, those who have little contact with the way of God in Jesus Christ.

Translating any document, including Scripture, is a complex process of communicating the meaning of the original text in language that is

Figure 6.2 Overview of the Translation Task

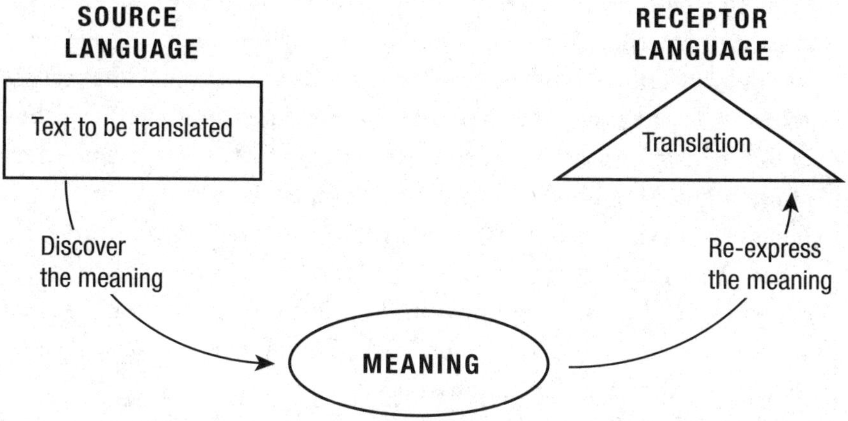

comprehensible to native speakers. The diagram above (Larson 1998, 4) depicts this process. (See Figure 6.2.)

SIL International (2011) maintains that the ideal translation should be:

- Accurate: reproducing as exactly as possible the meaning of the source text.
- Natural: using natural forms of the receptor language in a way that is appropriate to the kind of text being translated.
- Communicative: expressing all aspects of the meaning in a way that is readily understandable to the intended audience.

In addition to allowing Christians to understand the Bible, having the Scriptures in their own language shows believers that neither God nor the Christian faith are foreign. They begin to understand that God speaks their language, that his Word is spoken in terms of their cultural realities. People begin to value their own language and culture.[3] Sherry Farris, a Bible translator in Guinea, West Africa, notes that the Sankaran people she lives among "do not think they matter much to God. By putting God's Word into their language, we are affirming them as a people loved by God" (Farris 2009).

3. Because the use of vernacular languages affirms local cultures, Sanneh credits Bible translation with subverting colonialism in Africa (2009, 149).

Missionaries who serve as Bible translators must prepare thoroughly. Ideally, they will be competent in the original languages of the Bible. At a minimum, they should be able to use original language reference tools. They often need to learn a Western or trade language that serves as a bridge to the language they plan to translate the Bible into. They may be the first to put a language into written form. They need, then, to study linguistics, phonetics, and orthography. In addition, they need to be able to develop relationships with people in the host culture who can help them learn the new language and express biblical concepts through local idioms. They must build relationships with and solicit participation from Christian groups already in the area, who will assist in producing the new translation and assuring its use.

The work of Bible translation extends beyond the process of putting Scripture into a vernacular. Richard Chowning, one of my colleagues among the Kipsigis of Kenya, later planted churches and helped translate the New Testament and significant portions of the Old Testament into the Aja language of Benin. Chowning, who now serves as a church-planting consultant for Pioneer Bible Translators, says, "Translating scripture into the vernaculars of the world is not enough. These scriptures have to be put to use." Bible translation agencies speak of "what is variously called scripture impact, scripture engagement, and scripture use. There is the understanding that translating scriptures is just the beginning. They must be introduced in ways that transform lives and societies" (Chowning 2008). The objective, however, is not merely a translated Bible but disciples of Christ who follow the God of the Bible. Thus many translators become church planters as the seed of the kingdom takes root and grows among the people they serve.

The ministry of Bible translation is also necessary for the kingdom transformation produced by the gospel (see following section). Greg Pruett argues,

> It is not enough to have church and Scripture; the churches must be using Scripture to transform their communities for Christ.... Therefore, the next major benchmark I see on the pathway to obeying the Great Commission is this: churches with Scripture transforming every language community on earth. We must cross every language barrier on earth with church, Scripture, and transformation. (2012, 215)

Agents of Transformational Development

Lori's Story

I traveled to Honduras for the first time in 1999. Every day I met women who prayed the Lord's Prayer, "Give us this day our daily bread," with a conviction I could never know. Through spending time with these women and through listening to their cries, God gave me a desire to understand poverty and injustice and to understand how people are forgotten.

I wanted to know not only how to speak the Word of God, but also how to live out and show the love of God. I wanted to show the women and children that they were not forgotten by God or by his people. I began praying about how I could effect change in women's lives that offered a different future for them and for their children.

With that thought, the mission of Mi Esperanza was born. We began the ministry with six women. We know that in developing countries, when the family income is in the hands of the mother, the chance of survival for children increases by 85 percent. By distributing "micro" loans to these women, we enabled them to begin businesses that are a consistent and stable source of income for their family, an income that could be spent on nutrition, education, and health care. We provided loans to women for a variety of businesses, from tortilla making to village stores.

The natural next step in our program was education so that women could turn their new opportunities into viable businesses. We opened a training facility where we offer skill training along with additional education. The women have four choices of skill training: sewing, computers, hairdressing, and piñata making. By providing a variety of skills, we target young and old, from people with no education to people with basic reading and writing skills. When the women finish their training, we help them explore how they can use their new knowledge to generate income.

Through our activity in the lives of these women, and as we help them to meet their basic human needs, we are showing them and touching them with the very love of God.

(Lori Connell, *Honduras*)

A heightened awareness of inequality and injustice leads to reflection on Isaiah's words that were quoted by Jesus in the synagogue in Nazareth.

The Spirit of the Lord is on me,
because he has anointed me
to proclaim good news to the poor.

He has sent me to proclaim freedom for the prisoners
and recovery of sight for the blind,
to set the oppressed free,
to proclaim the year of the Lord's favor.
(LUKE 4:18 – 19 [CF. ISA. 61:1 – 2])

In a real sense, this verse is God's missionary call to every Christian in every culture. It expresses God's heart — his compassion for people marginalized by poverty, discrimination, violence, and addiction. It is God's call for social justice in every world context — urban, suburban, or rural. It provides the rationale for Christians bringing *shalom*, or God's peace, into human culture. God, however, raises up certain ministers who focus on social transformation, or what Bryant Myers calls "transformational development" (1999, 3).

Missionaries engaged in transformational development must respect and believe in all people, including those who are poor and suffering. As the title of Myers' book *Walking with the Poor* implies, ministers of transformational development walk alongside the poor on a "journey of transformation" that aims to "recover our true identity as human beings created in the image of God and to discover our true vocation as productive stewards, faithfully caring for the world and all the people in it" (Myers 1999, 3). These missionaries seek solutions *with* local people and learn *from* them, rather than bringing prefabricated projects from the outside (McVey 2009).

Andrew Gordon, who seeks to integrate community health evangelism with chronological Bible storying among Muslims in West Africa, offers this observation:

> There seems to have been a definite shift in the past two decades from a "Let's get out there and help those poor folks!" mentality to a "Let's be God's agents in helping to bring transformation to these communities" way of thinking.... [We] have seen the problems with dependency and are being more intentional about empowering people, under God, to provide for themselves. So there's much more stress on the holistic, transformational, participatory nature of Christian development ministry. (Gordon 2009)

Though historically many missionaries have attempted to provide relief and facilitate development, success has been limited. Missionaries have unconsciously assumed a posture of superiority and failed to solicit local investment. Because projects were viewed as belonging to outsiders, many well-intentioned efforts have been beset by waste and mismanagement and have proven unsustainable. When missionaries view the people as their greatest resource, and the people view themselves as valued partners, such consequences can be avoided.

The local community must look to themselves, and to the work of the Holy Spirit among them, as the primary solution to their problems.

Missionaries who serve as agents of transformational development must seek to engage the poor and suffering in discovering and implementing solutions to their own problems. Reflecting on the Isaiah passage, Myers says that "when the poor hear the good news and receive freedom and release, they become 'oaks of righteousness . . . that rebuild the ancient ruins and restore the places long devastated.'" He insists that "people, not money or programs, transform their worlds" (1999, 116). Myers argues that a kingdom framework considers "the physical, social, mental, and spiritual manifestations of poverty, and so all are legitimate areas of focus for transformational development that is truly Christian. . . . Whatever heals and restores body, mind, spirit, and community, all can be part of the better future toward which transformational development should point" (1999, 113).

The affected community is key to discerning the needs that should be addressed. Myers adds, "Therefore, immunizing children, improving food security, and providing potable water can be part of a kingdom future *if the community says they need to be*" (1999, 113, emphasis added). The local people might also choose to address reconciliation and peace building, the need for counseling services, discovering ways to improve agriculture, facilitating community health development, or advocating for women's and children's issues.[4] As needs are identified, the local community must look to themselves, and to the work of the Holy Spirit among them, as the primary solution to their problems. Outside resources and partnerships, even when essential, must be only part of the solution.

This perspective requires maturity typically found only in a strong, indigenous national church movement. It is usually preferable therefore to focus initially on church planting and leadership development before confronting social needs.

4. A list of related resources and agencies engaged in development ministries can be found at *http://mislinks.org/practical/rdorgs.htm* (Accessed December 8, 2011).

This type of work requires openness, patience, flexibility, and vulnerability on the part of missionaries (McVey 2009). They must be good neighbors who maintain a humble spirit. They need professional competencies, but these must be practiced with a genuine Christlike spirit (Myers 1999, 153 – 56). Many countries also require missionaries to supply professional credentials before granting permission to engage in some types of development work.

Needs and opportunities for transformational development are almost limitless. The following two subtypes of missionaries could be viewed as representing opposite ends of this spectrum — those who serve to provide immediate relief from suffering and those who engage in for-profit business.

COMPASSIONATE SERVANTS

The Gospels speak often of Jesus' compassion. He had compassion on people who, "like sheep without a shepherd," needed direction and guidance (Matt. 9:36). He looked on the crowds with compassion and healed their sick (Matt. 14:14; 20:34). He fed the hungry (Matt. 15:32). Jesus told the story of a father who, "filled with compassion," ran to welcome home his prodigal son (Luke 15:20).

As agents of God's kingdom see suffering and hurting people, they, like Jesus, are filled with compassion. Ideally, they will work with God and with local people to battle against the principalities and powers and to transform the structures that perpetuate suffering. Systemic change, however, takes time, and long-term solutions may do little to alleviate present suffering. Compassionate missionaries, then, provide immediate relief while continuing to search for and implement long-term solutions.

Some cross-cultural servants respond compassionately to natural disasters such as earthquakes, floods, and famines to supply food, shelter, and medical care. Others work in hospitals and clinics to provide both preventative and curative medical care to people who would not otherwise receive it. Still others care for orphans and the socially disenfranchised. Their actions bear witness to the love, compassion, and servant nature of Christ. As they serve, they also give verbal testimony that God loves each hurting person and invites them into his kingdom.

Offering relief or aid requires cultural sensitivity. Attitudes of superiority should be discarded and aid offered in ways that maintain the recipients' dignity. Servants should seek the cooperation and advice of local leaders so that services are fairly distributed. They must also seek to understand how local people view their suffering. They can then speak God's Word to them in a relevant way.

As missionaries are confronted with profound physical needs, they must remember the paramount need: to know Jesus. Aaron Burk, who served among the Dagara people of Burkina Faso, describes a conversation with church leaders about how to best use funds for famine relief. Initially the leaders, overwhelmed by the responsibility, preferred that the missionaries make the decisions. Further discussion and a time of focused prayer, however, revealed new understandings. Burk wrote,

> They said, "You know, food is great, but you can't take it with you, and we need to be praying for and talking with our neighbors and family members that are still in the darkness about our faith." Wow! Sometimes, as a missionary in one of the poorest countries in the world, you worry that you focus too much on teaching Christ and not enough on just helping people. It took a group of Dagara Christians to remind me ... that those things aren't necessarily separate and that fellowship with God really is our deepest need. (Burk 2009)

BUSINESS MISSIONARIES

The theology of business as mission is rooted in creation. In creation, God worked, and when he created humans, he gave them work — creative, God-honoring work. Christians who conduct business "in agreement with his law and his character," with integrity and for the benefit of others, honor God by imitating him (Russell 2006, 117 – 19).

Abraham, Joseph, Moses, Daniel, and Amos are "examples of people who supported themselves financially ... while working in a foreign land" (Russell 2006, 120). It is from Paul and his coworkers, Priscilla and Aquila, that we derive the term *tentmaking*, which often refers to "the use of business skills in a ... ministry setting for the advancement of the Kingdom of God" (Russell 2006, 121).[5] As a tentmaker, Paul was able to identify with both religious scholars and common working people. He was viewed as credible because he did not "peddle the word of God" (2 Cor. 2:17) and modeled a work ethic often absent in segments of ancient society (Russell 2006, 123–26).

Various terms designate the different ways business and mission are integrated in contemporary practice. *Tentmaking* promotes "the evangelistic potential of individual Christians in a workplace setting." *Business as Mission* stresses the redemptive potential of business itself, and *Marketplace* (or *Workplace*) *Ministries* equip Christians to be more effective ambassadors of Christ in the workplace. *Enterprise Development* primarily involves the use of loans to empower local people to develop micro-, small-, and medium-size business enterprises. Funds from repaid loans are made available for others (Johnson and Rundle 2006, 20–21).

Working with local people to establish ethically operated, financially feasible businesses enables missionaries to demonstrate the good news of Jesus Christ being lived out in terms of economic realities. While many local people have valuable skills and products to market, they may lack the expertise to operate a business, especially as a Christian, because the models they have seen are non-Christian. Corruption and exploitation may have been the norm. Missionaries therefore have an opportunity to offer a different model. The business reflects the goodness and graciousness of God both within its corporate structure and in its relationship to the broader community. Within the company, Christian workers are living testimonies to the way of God in Jesus Christ.

In many ways, all missionaries are committed to the work of transformational development. When God's kingdom truly comes into a new culture, his people work to alleviate suffering, and kingdom values

---

5. The Tentmaking Task Force of the Lausanne II Congress outlined nine considerations in defining the term *tentmaker*. Tentmakers, according to the task force, are people who are called to ministry, engage in religious ministry, maintain a secular identity, are intentional about their life and work, receive training for their role, serve cross-culturally, work in creative/restricted access nations (CAN/RAN), and reside in those countries. Task force members could not agree as to whether the tentmaker should be entirely self-supporting or could be partially supported by churches (Lai 2005, 14–21). Such nuanced definitions are useful to committees who need to assure that they are all talking about the same thing, but bivocational missionaries should be able to search for the best model for their situation instead of adhering to a particular definition of tentmaking.

transform both individual lives and societal structures. God calls some missionaries to herald the inaugurated kingdom by working through transformational development.

Ministers of International Justice

Missionaries all over the world encounter injustice — government corruption, police brutality, child slavery, or dangerous working conditions. Some are called to serve as ministers of international justice, advocates for the oppressed. These ministers must learn both how people view their present situation and how to communicate the changes that the ministers advocate in appropriate and culturally comprehensible ways. Only then can local people see a need for change.

The International Justice Mission (IJM, *www.ijm.org*) is devoted exclusively to this cause. IJM highlights abuses such as slavery, sex trafficking, illegal property seizure, illegal detention, police brutality, and sexual violence. They also supply relief to victims, hold perpetrators accountable, provide aftercare to help victims rebuild their lives, and work to transform the structures that permit such abuses to continue.

IJM's statistics about the pervasiveness of injustice are startling. For example, the United Nations estimates that the total market value of illicit human trafficking exceeds $32 billion. Each year, the global commercial sex trade exploits more than two million children. Twenty-seven million men, women, and children live as slaves. One in five women is a victim of rape or attempted rape in her lifetime, and more than one million children live in detention, the vast majority awaiting trial for minor offenses (IJM 2011).[6]

Victims of oppression cry out to God for justice. God hears, he remembers, and he is concerned (Ex. 2:23 – 25). He calls on his people to "seek justice" (Isa. 1:17) and is appalled when they fail to intervene on behalf of the downtrodden (Isa. 59:15 – 16). God listens to the cry of the afflicted, and he defends the fatherless and the oppressed "so that mere earthly mortals will never again strike terror" (Ps. 10:17 – 18).

6. The IJM website cites statistics from the U.N., including the U.N. Development Fund for Women and UNICEF, as well as Kevin Bales's work *Disposable People: New Slavery in the Global Economy* (Berkeley: University of California Press, 2004).

As Gary Haugen documented atrocities that occurred in the 1994 Rwandan genocide, he was convicted that Christians must have a role in international justice. Haugen notes that "while the kingdom of God will be complete only in the coming of Christ, today our great joy and privilege is to work as co-laborers with the Creator in extending his kingdom over one more life, one more family, one more neighborhood, one more community" (1999, 35).

Missionaries long to play a part in ushering in the reign of God, seeing the Father's will done on earth as it is in heaven. All missionaries, including those who labor in church planting, leadership training, Bible translation, and so on, can give voice to the stories of the oppressed, and they can work alongside culture experts, public justice professionals, and international businesspeople to assure that those voices are heard (Haugen 1999, 181 – 91).

Missionary Support Personnel

The primary task of missionary support personnel is to encourage, enable, and empower other missionaries. These missionaries, while serving other missionaries, must also have frequent contact with the local culture and learn to relate to nationals effectively. Their Christlike manner of life then serves as a witness in their host culture. Their primary task, however, is to serve other missionaries. Opportunities for this kind of service are many, including:

- *Hospitality.* Arriving missionaries need someone to meet them at the airport, help them transport their luggage, and offer them a place to stay. Mission guesthouse hosts and hostesses facilitate passages in missionary life — from initial arrival, to departure, to home assignments and breaks for rest and renewal. They are often the first point of contact for both long-term missionaries and short-term visitors and workers.
- *Administration.* In many agencies, support personnel handle the paperwork and make necessary trips to government offices to secure and renew visas and work permits or conduct other official business. They may arrange housing and/or other logistics, such as payroll for both expatriate and national missionaries.

- *Supervision and strategy.* Some mission agencies have on-field supervisors whose primary responsibility is to coach, coordinate, and supervise the missionaries who are more actively engaged with the local populations. These strategists must see the big picture for ministry in a region or nation so that the mission and the national churches channel their energies into appropriate areas.
- *Technology.* Computers have become universal, even in remote mission locations. Missionaries use computers to learn language, prepare lessons, and communicate with local friends, team members, and family and ministry partners in their countries of origin. Today's Bible translators rely heavily on technology. However, some areas lack local technicians who can maintain hardware or help missionaries troubleshoot problems. The need for IT personnel on the mission field, whether to maintain computers or to support Christian radio stations, is growing.
- *Aviation and transportation.* Missionary pilots transport personnel and supplies to remote areas. They are often the first responders in times of natural disaster and famine. Missionary boats and ships reach villages that are connected to the outside world only by water highways. The International Association of Missionary Aviation (IAMA) lists over fifty participating organizations.[7] Many of these also provide other transportation and technical services.
- *Missionary care.* People working in missionary care offer spiritual, psychological, and emotional support to missionaries. They may offer coaching and counseling to help missionaries serve effectively in stressful cross-cultural environments or deal with traumatic crises.
- *Education.* In some mission areas, local schools do not provide the education that missionary parents desire for their children. Many want their children's education to be consistent with that in their home culture, expecting them to be part of that system in the future. Many cross-cultural missionaries homeschool

7. A list of participating organizations as well as other relevant information can be found on the IAMA website: *www.iamanet.org* (Accessed March 2, 2012).

their children. Others, however, find it valuable to bring expatriate children together, whether by sending them to boarding schools, enrolling them in locally available international schools, or forming their own collective schools. These schools all require teachers and administrators.

This list, though not exhaustive, illustrates how God can use diverse gifts to serve his purpose of taking the good news of his reign to the nations.

Although missions has become more specialized, it should never be entirely so. Church planters also train leaders, while looking for opportunities to offer sustainable development alternatives to local people. Medical personnel offer immediate, compassionate relief, while they educate for prevention and train village-based health care workers. Bible translators share the gospel as they introduce Scripture portions, and churches are born. They teach literacy classes so that people can read the Bible, and thus transform cultures. Mission business managers gain a big-picture view of the mission's work by interacting with missionaries over a large geographical area, and thus can contribute information that is invaluable in strategy discussions.

Missionaries must have a clear sense of the work they have been called to do. Otherwise, they will be overwhelmed by the needs and opportunities. They should also be open to discovering new ways to serve, without neglecting their primary calling. Such balance can be maintained only by consistent communication with God and with other stakeholders in the missionary enterprise. Missionaries must seek God's priorities as they determine how to use their gifts, and respect the wisdom of their fellow missionaries, supporters, and national coworkers.

There are innumerable opportunities for missionary service, from church planting to Bible translation to support services. May God use our gifts for his glory!

REFLECTION AND APPLICATION

Questions

1. What questions should new missionaries ask when determining the role they will fill?
2. What is the major goal or focus of apostolic church-planting missionaries, both domestically and internationally?
3. Describe the characteristics and practices of church-planting missionaries in the book of Acts.
4. Describe how the role of a church-planting missionary differs from that of a local church pastor.
5. In what ways does the task of Bible translation testify to the love of God for all people?
6. How should transformational development workers determine ministry priorities?
7. In what ways do missionary support personnel encourage, enable, and empower other missionaries?

Application

1. You have just joined a mission effort serving an indigenous people in West Africa. Most people are farmers, most of whom have elementary school educations, with a few who went on to high school. Their families' survival depends on them being present to work the family farms, but the people do have more time free during the dry season and between planting and harvesting. A network of churches exists, and you have been invited to develop a training program for local church leaders. Your sending agency will provide funding for whatever method you choose. You must decide whether to establish a school for advanced theological studies, provide training for clergy through TEE (Theological Education by Extension), or establish a network of obedience-oriented mentoring. Which of these methods would you choose for this context? Would some other method, or a hybrid approach, be better? Explain your answer.
2. List some possible advantages and disadvantages of missionary specialization.

Personal Inventory

How has God spoken to you through this chapter? What is God calling you to do about it?

chapter 7

The Missionary Cycle

Predeparture through Reentry

ALL PEOPLE EXPERIENCE TRAUMA AND TENSION during major transitions in their lives. Beginning a new job or moving to a new city or state creates stress. Getting married or having a new baby causes a disruption of the norm and requires a lifestyle adjustment. During these times of transition, people struggle with their identities. They ask, "Who am I in the midst of all these changes? What does the future hold for me?"

International missionaries go through the trauma of transition both when they enter another nation and when they reenter their own country. Domestic missionaries feel a similar disequilibrium when entering new cultural environments, adapting to life and ministry in these contexts, and then returning to places more similar to their traditional cultural heritage. This chapter describes phases that missionaries and missionary families encounter from the time of their decision to become missionaries, through their years of experience on the mission field, until their reentry into their home culture. The cycle is typically recurring, because many missionaries and their families enter multiple mission fields both internationally and domestically during their lives.

> Learning about the missionary cycle helped Jim and Julie ready their hearts and minds to enter another culture. They began to prepare themselves for each stage. They realized that the stages are not clear-cut and sequential but overlapping and would be revisited frequently during their lives as missionary servants. They gave this chapter to their supporters and partners to help them understand some of the adaptations they would go through.

It is important during these transitions to realize that the struggles are normal and are experienced by all missionaries. Understanding the cycle enables future missionaries to culturally and spiritually prepare themselves for each phase of the cycle. These perspectives likewise help field missionaries to understand what they are going through and enable them to both adjust and minister with heightened intentionality.

The cycle of missionary service can be divided into seven stages.

1. Initial Commitment
2. General training
3. Field selection
4. Focused training
5. Initial adjustment
6. Long-term missionary service
7. Reentry to the home culture

Each of these stages has its own distinct challenges requiring spiritual discernment. (See Figure 7.1.)

Initial Commitment

The first step in the missionary cycle is an initial commitment to be God's missionary. This involves both receiving and accepting God's

Figure 7.1 The Missionary Cycle

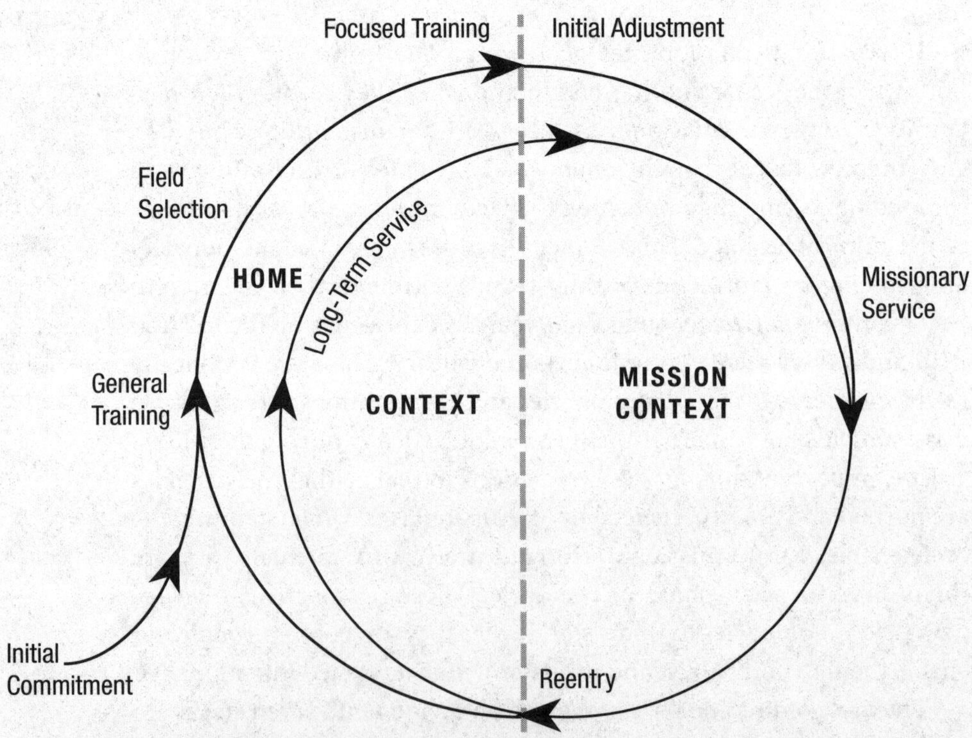

call to missions. During this stage, missionaries-to-be are frequently questioned by friends, family, and coworkers about the need to move into a new context or to go so far away. They ask, "Why would you move to live among the poor? Why would you go over there, when there is so much to do right here at home?" Parents want their children and grandchildren close enough for frequent visits. They also fear disease and political instability in some places chosen for ministry. Before we went to Uganda with our ten-month-old son, several friends told us, "We understand your wanting to go, but is it fair to take a baby to Africa?" We were encouraged, if we really wanted to be missionaries, to select a mission area in the United States. Such remarks lead prospective missionaries to question whether they have indeed received the call of God.

Future missionaries are often torn between the need to prepare and the urgency to begin their ministry. They can fathom only partially the role of training in missions. In-depth training is essential for long-term (or lifetime) service in the kingdom of God.

General Training

Commitment to go leads missionaries to seek training to better prepare for the task of evangelizing in a new context. At this point, training should be general, exploring what is involved in the work of a missionary. This training should include both textual Bible classes, to help internalize the story of God and develop the core allegiances of the Christian life, and core missions classes such as Introduction to Missions, Missionary Anthropology, and History of Missions.

Missionaries in this stage of the missionary cycle should participate in local apprenticeships to walk with experienced people of God, learning to imitate them as they imitate Jesus. Families will learn about keeping house, raising children, and going on mission as a family. Husbands and wives will learn what it means to work together as a team for the kingdom of God. Together they will explore opportunities in ministry, including teaching unbelievers, training leaders for Christian service, developing curriculum for youth education, and offering seminars in family health and nutrition. Learning to be God's missionary in one's own culture is preparation for ministering in another.

During this stage, future missionaries are often torn between the need to prepare and the urgency to begin their ministry. They can fathom only partially the role of training in missions. They typically ask, "Why do I need training? Why can I not just go?" Frequently, the value of training becomes apparent only later in the missionary cycle. In-depth training is essential for long-term (or lifetime) service in the kingdom of God.

Field Selection

During the early stages in the missionary cycle, a decision will be made concerning where missionaries will serve. Frequently, missionary candidates are certain of God's call to missions but unsure of the place to which God is leading them. Some feel called to a particular continent — their own or another one — but have not determined the specific country, city, and ethnic area. The first step on this journey of discernment is for candidates to prayerfully ask the Lord of the harvest — the source of mission — to place them where he desires them to be. On this journey, short-term mission experiences, both domestic and foreign, give exposure to different peoples and their cultures. Many candidates wisely choose to serve as interns for two or three months, to follow and imitate mature missionaries. Some may also choose to apprentice for approximately two years with an experienced missionary, to learn about ministry in a specific field. In this longer time, they also have the experience of learning a new language, adapting to a new culture, and learning from both local leaders and missionaries.

God often puts a burden for a certain city or ethnic group on the hearts of future missionaries during campaigns, internships, and apprenticeships. Missionary candidates begin to ask themselves, "Could we be part of God's mission in this context?" They also come face-to-face with questions concerning the selection of a place to serve: "How do we choose a place from all these possibilities? Where does God want

> Learning to be a missionary is more than gaining information. The process is most effective when information is understood within experiential contexts, both in the general training stage and in the field selection stage. Jesus said, "Come, follow me, ... and I will send you out to fish for people" (Mark 1:17). Paul said, "Follow my example, as I follow the example of Christ" (1 Cor. 11:1; cf. 4:16). Academic training is essential because it provides a disciplined environment and framework for learning and growing. Internships and apprenticeship concurrent with and subsequent to academic learning provides an experiential context for learning from experienced missionaries.

us to minister?"[1] In addition, they try to determine how God wants them to serve on the mission field. They ask, "What will be my ministry there?" Seeking answers to these questions leads the future missionary to begin focused training.

Focused Training

During the focused training stage, future missionaries are engaged in both formal and informal preparation. Their formal training includes courses geared exclusively for people involved in long-term missions. These courses may be offered through Christian universities, mission agencies, or missionary training organizations. Class assignments address specific issues that missionaries will encounter in their new cultural contexts. Future missionaries begin to ask focused questions such as, "How do we go about learning this particular language and culture?" "How do these people view reality?" "How do we make disciples in this new culture, communicating the gospel with such impact that it not only creates interest, but also touches the heart?" "How do we introduce the gospel with such clarity that it invites people to 'open their eyes and turn ... from darkness to light, and from the power of Satan to God, so that they may receive forgiveness of sins and a place among those who are sanctified by faith in [Christ]'" (Acts 26:17 – 18)? "What discipling models will we use to plant the church, nurture new Christians to maturity, and train leaders?"

Additional training takes place informally when missions teachers and student leaders invite learners to become part of missional communities for learning and laughter, for spiritual formation and ministry. They group together for prayer and planning and then go on mission in neighborhoods or networks to which they are called. The ministry might be on the campuses where they are studying, among the poor, in a local prison, or in a neighborhood where students and/or teachers live. What is learned in the classroom is immediately applied to life and ministry. Consulting with missionaries on furlough or recently returned missionaries also provides insight into the future work.

Team development frequently begins during this stage. In team

1. Chapter 18 provides specific guidelines for field selection.

Missionary candidates must learn to be missionaries in their home culture before attempting the much more difficult task of becoming missionaries in another culture. Becoming a missionary has little to do with crossing national or continental boundaries. It's about imitating others on mission with God.

formation, committed Christians with various gifts and ministries purpose together to catalyze a movement of God in some part of the world. This group works together to become a listening, caring, ministering team. Teams may develop among those who are studying together, who then together select a mission field and/or agency with whom to work. They may also form as part of an agency or group already interested in a specific field. The team develops patterns of decision making, seeks the collaboration and support of local churches or mission agencies, and applies mission principles to the specific culture where God is leading them to minister. Most teams continue to develop, in terms of both personnel and process, after arrival on the field. Mature teams seek the counsel and advice of mission resource people during this stage of focused training and during their time of missionary service.

Initial Adjustment

After months of planning and preparation, missionaries bid farewell to family and friends and travel by plane, train, or car to their new home. There is sadness because of separation from their families but also excitement because a new phase of life and ministry is beginning. The first weeks are partially consumed with setting up house, opening a bank account, purchasing a car, determining where to buy groceries, and learning to get from place to place. Missionaries also begin language and culture learning immediately upon arrival in the host culture. It is exciting — meeting new people, eating new foods, hearing a new language. Everything is great!

It is important to note that while this initial adjustment is less overt in a domestic mission context, it is still occurring. All contexts have their own languages and ways of interpreting their own world, the world beyond, and newcomers moving into the city. Missionaries come as newcomers needing to learn.

New missionaries, after several weeks (or even months) of glamorizing the new culture, suddenly find themselves annoyed that people cut in front of them at the bank or post office, frustrated that shopping takes so long (going to one shop for meat, another for canned goods, and still another for vegetables), irritated that people stare at them when they walk down the street, and downright angry because a beggar asks them for money. "These are the most inconsiderate, disorganized, rude people I've ever met," they say to themselves. "Why can't they be like people ought to be?" For a time, they reject their new culture and want everything to be like their own culture. They may withdraw, taking forays out of their home only when necessary. They see very little good in their host culture and no wrong with their home culture. They experience *culture shock*! During this stage of adjustment, some missionaries, deciding that they can never adapt to this new lifestyle, return home. Others begin looking for positive elements in the host culture and learn to accept the differences as part of life. They begin to adapt their lifestyle to their host culture and participate in the community where they live. They learn the language; visit with neighbors and cultural leaders, who become mentors; eat local food; make friends; and share the saving grace of Jesus. They begin to feel at home in the new culture.[2]

Missionary Service

The goal of this stage for church-planting missionaries is to plant a community of spiritually formed churches with equipped leaders who are called to be God's instruments of his mission in that particular area or region of the world. Other types of missionaries come in to encourage the church and equip it to fulfill its central tasks of disciple making and mission.

During this stage, missionaries progressively learn to minister in their new cultures. Occasions that were dreaded in the early days of missionary service are seen as wonderful times of fellowship. For example, in our early years working among the Kipsigis, I would return from a three-day period of working with some local Christians in establishing a church. These people came back with me, planning to go on to their destination the next day but expecting to spend the night at our house. At first, this was very frustrating to both my wife and me. After all, I had been gone for three days and wanted to come home and relax. I wanted to speak English and eat American food! We felt that our privacy was being invaded (which I soon learned was a very Western concept!). Later, when we had been with the Kipsigis for some time, we

2. Chapter 10 defines three stages of a typical missionary acculturation process.

Paradoxically, it is sometimes more difficult to learn the language and culture in a domestic context. Missionaries can naively assume that they know how people think and live.

began to view those evenings as welcome pleasures. Sharing our lives with Christians in our own home became a joy rather than something to be endured. Missionary families slowly develop friendships with local people and feel blessed by the time they spend with them. They learn to rejoice with them, cry with them, and grow with them. They come to anticipate times of fellowship.

Just as missionaries change personally during their years of service, so do their roles. Understanding how their roles change as they progress through the periods of learning, growing, collaborating, and phasing out — that make up this stage of the missionary cycle — can help missionaries form strategies that spur their work forward. The following discussion envisions a ministry of church planting, multiplication, and maturation, but these periods can be adapted for other missionary service roles as well.

THE LEARNING PERIOD

The first two years on the mission field are appropriately called the *learning period* or the *adaptation period*. Missionaries, both domestic and foreign, are learning to live in and adapt to new contexts. During this period, four interrelated types of learning take place. Missionaries learn to (1) speak the *language*, (2) understand the *culture* of the people they are working among, (3) form personal *relationships* within the culture, and (4) develop *models of ministry* appropriate to the context.

Paradoxically, it is sometimes more difficult to learn the language and culture in a domestic context. Missionaries can naively assume that they know how people think and live, without intentionally learning how words are distinctively used to form thinking and customs.

Two extremes are common during this period. On the one hand, some missionaries assume that they should not begin communicating the gospel until the learning period is completed — until language and culture learning are accomplished. However, since following Christ is the core of who they are, missionaries must not lay aside their identity even during the early stages of adaptation. Thus language and culture learning is done while living distinctively as Christians. Sharing and living out the Christian story is part of the language and culture learning process. Often, people find Christ and a church is planted because language and culture students released the "fire in their bones" (see Jer. 20:9). New missionaries must, however, understand their communicational limitations and learn to relate the story of God in Scripture to life in the new cultural context. They should also take great care when using illustrations derived from their host cultures.

On the other hand — quite the opposite — some missionaries bypass the learning period, naively asserting that "people are people all over the world, and the gospel can be presented in the same way in all contexts." They therefore want to be teachers without learning first. Forgoing language and culture learning during the first months on the field significantly reduces missionaries' ability to effectively minister in the new cultural context.

Effective missionaries are *incarnational*, a concept developed more fully in chapter 9. Briefly, missionary incarnation infers modeling the life of Christ, who "became flesh and made his dwelling among us" to reveal "the glory of the one and only Son, who came from the Father, full of grace and truth" (John 1:14). The nature of incarnation varies, however, depending on the ability of missionaries to model the life of Christ within their new cultural context. It also varies from stage to stage as the Christian movement matures. In this early adaptation phase, missionary incarnation is broadly focused and may be defined as *learning the general patterns of a new recipient culture and how to effectively carry out the mission that God has given missionaries to do.* The major role of missionaries during this period is *learner.*

Paradoxically, the first church planted among the Kipsigis people was started in a village called Chebongi during this learning period. The first Christians were a language and culture tutor and his family and friends. Our relationship was reciprocal: they taught us the Kipsigis language and way of life; we taught them the story of the Bible and the essence of living a Christian life. The developing leaders of this church worked with us over the years to plant numerous churches. We walked together as coworkers in the Lord, learning from one another.

THE GROWTH PERIOD

As they learn language and culture and share their faith, effective missionaries develop the cultural and linguistic understandings to effectively communicate God's eternal message in cultural metaphors and forms that both make the message intelligible and stir people's hearts. People are then inspired to follow the way of God in Jesus Christ. They also develop the skill of forming unique strategies for disciple making and mission appropriate to the cultural context. As they begin the growth period with these tools, they envision their task not as merely planting a church but as initiating a God-empowered movement of churches planting churches.

Developing a strong movement of God in a new city or ethnic area requires that three interrelated tasks be accomplished during the growth period. First, initial evangelism leads to planting new churches. Second, Christians are nurtured to maturity within these churches. Third, leaders are trained to evangelize people and plant other churches, pastor and shepherd the community of believers, and train still other leaders. Effective missionaries develop models for accomplishing these central tasks (see chaps. 14 and 15). Though these tasks may be amplified by other missionary endeavors, they are essential to a mighty movement of God coming into being.

During the growth period, the nature of incarnation becomes more focused: missionaries empathize with (1) the brokenness of *unbelievers* in order to lead them to Christ, (2) the struggles of *new Christians* in order to nurture them to maturity, and (3) the needs of *developing leaders* in order to model the way of Christ in equipping other leaders. In this period, missionaries are more than just learners; they are *evangelists* and *church planters, nurturers of new Christians,* and *trainers of developing leaders.* They partner with local leaders in developing processes of disciple making and mission that lead to a church-planting movement.

Garrison describes in some detail church-planting movements in various areas of the world. For example, Southern Baptists began missionary work in a certain Latin American country over a century ago. For the first seventy-five years, missionaries planted churches, trained leaders, and organized a Baptist union consisting of about 3,000 members. Soon after a military coup, however, all missionaries were imprisoned and then expelled, and almost all the local church leaders and half the church fled the country. Church members were persecuted, tortured, and imprisoned, but in the midst of opposition the church flourished. Between 1989 and the end of the century, the Northern and Southern Baptist Unions in this country grew from 229 churches to 4,075 meeting places (including house churches) and from 12,800 to 33,000 baptized members, with thousands more awaiting baptism (Garrison 2004, 133–35).

THE COLLABORATIVE PERIOD

A Christian movement established through heartfelt response to the proclamation of the kingdom of God — rather than through financial inducements — produces mature local leaders who stand as coleaders with the church-planting missionaries. As these devout, responsible leaders mature, the movement enters the third phase — the *collaborative period* — of church planting and development.

Understanding the relationship between missionaries and local leaders is essential to perceiving the need for this phase of church planting. Frequently, local leaders become disillusioned because of missionary paternalism, inappropriate or misunderstood strategy models, missionary turnover, and inadequate equipping of local leaders to assume traditional missionary tasks. Heightened tension leads local leaders to challenge — sometimes covertly, sometimes overtly — missionary roles and methodologies. Alex Araujo of Brazil graphically characterizes this relationship as *pororoca*, a loud noise heard when the massive waters of the Amazon meet the rising tide of the Atlantic Ocean. Like two gigantic bodies of water colliding, missionaries and developing local leaders clash, creating havoc for anyone caught in the maelstrom (1993, 362–63).

Such a clash between missionaries and local leaders can often be avoided when local Christians are nurtured as evangelists, elders, and collaborative decision makers in the developing movement. A process of leadership maturation is thus understood and employed from the inception of the missionary movement. Alex Araujo illustrates the merging of two leadership streams by describing two large rivers which become one as they flow into the Amazon River near Manaus, Brazil. The Negro River is dark and clear, like Coca-Cola seen through a glass. The Solimoes River, however, is full of sediment and appears grayish white. For miles downstream, they appear as two rivers sharing the same riverbed — dark on one side, grayish white on the other — but gradually the waters intermingle to become one mighty river. Local and missionary streams of leadership must flow together and intermingle to become one (1993, 362–63).

This intermingling results in changing roles for both missionaries and maturing local leaders. Missionaries who were culture and language learners in the learning period become teachers, evangelists, and church planters in the growth period and then become equippers, encouragers, and advisers in the collaborative period. Local leaders, who were converts during the learning and growth periods, become colaborers and fellow resource people — full participants in the collaborative process.

During the collaborative period, local leaders come to *own* their movement and make decisions for its continuity. Often, however, paternalistic missionaries thwart local initiatives, believing that the locals are out of line, usurping authority, or acting naively. Effective missionaries, on the other hand, serve as encouragers and advisers — co-facilitators in decision-making processes. Local leaders and missionaries thus work together to lay the foundations for eventual missionary phaseout and for the movement's continuity.

Cooperatively developing *structures of continuity* for the future is the major focus of the collaborative period. Monte Cox asserts that the "organization ambiguities" of certain anti-institutional movements like Churches of Christ have "dampened morale and perhaps stunted the growth of the church" in rural areas in Kenya (1999, 216). When churches reach what is here called the collaborative period, they begin to ask *structural* questions: "How do we plan events involving more than one congregation?" "Who do we recognize as legitimate spokespeople for our movement?" "Who controls church property?" "How do we strategize together and share resources to evangelize new areas?"

Two extremes are possible in regard to the collaborative period. At one extreme, missionaries phase out before local leaders mature and structures of continuity develop. Local Christians generally become discouraged in this situation because they are not ready for the missionaries' departure. Some may, consequently, revert to their pre-Christian patterns, some may affiliate with other Christian groups, and still others maintain their cohesion as a Christian movement by effectively developing simple, reproducible structures of continuity. Premature phaseout ignores the need for collaboration.

At the other extreme, some missionaries attempt to bypass the growth period and create training institutions before new churches are adequately nurtured and leaders equipped. These schools almost always reflect the worldview and economics of the sending culture. Missionaries in this scenario generally assume that Bible knowledge alone enables local leaders to effectively minister in their own culture. They presuppose that cognitive information without contextualization and application is adequate for ministry preparation. Both early phaseout and premature development of institutions imply inadequate understandings about the progressive development of Christian leaders. In life, all people pass through developmental stages; local church leaders grow to maturity in the same way.

When structures of continuity have been mutually developed by missionaries and local leaders, the stage is set for missionary phaseout.

THE PHASEOUT PERIOD

Paul concluded his letter to the Romans by describing how he had preached the gospel from Jerusalem to Illyricum, laying new foundations wherever he ministered (Rom. 15:19 – 20). His practice was to appoint elders and, through prayer and fasting, commit them to the Lord (Acts 14:23). His words to the Romans demonstrate the heart and motivation of an apostolic leader: "Now that there is no more place for me to work in these regions, and since I have been longing for many years to visit you, I plan to do so when I go to Spain.... It has always been my ambition to preach the gospel where Christ was not known, so that I would not be building on someone else's foundation" (Rom. 15:20, 23).

Phaseout is thus the farewell period when missionaries overtly and intentionally pass the baton of leadership to local leaders as they transition to other mission contexts. During this period, missionaries serve as *encouragers* and *advisers* of local leaders on both the congregational and associational level. As encouragers, missionaries affirm the locals' ability to carry the mission of God in responsible, reproducing ways. Elders and evangelists in local churches are affirmed as God's ordained servants. Equippers on the associational level are confirmed as leaders with godly dedication and experience. As advisers, missionaries affirm local initiatives and suggest models of teaching, ministry, and administration to the relatively new Christian movement and its leadership. A good rule of thumb is to make five affirmations for every suggestion. In other words, the role of encourager should surpass that of adviser.

A significant danger during this period is inadvertent paternalism. Without realizing it, missionaries are tempted to control the structures that they have developed collaboratively with local leaders. They work at disengagement with one hand while developing structures of control through money and placement of personnel with the other. Like parents of young adults, they know that they should not dominate, but have difficulty letting go.

"Ownership," Cox writes, "should be the main criterion by which missionaries and nationals determine the timing of disengagement" (1999, 227). This ownership is a process. During the growth period, Christian leaders assume leadership roles in their home churches and learn how to plant and develop other churches. During the collaborative period, missionaries and local leaders envision and plan together to develop the structures of continuity appropriate to the church in their context, and locals are equipped and empowered to lead those structures.

> Ideally, church-planting missionaries should stay until they have accomplished their task of planting a movement that "builds itself up in love." (Eph. 4:16)

It has been a joy to see the church planting movement among the Kipsigis grow and mature without missionary involvement. Twelve years after leaving, I journeyed by public service vehicle and by foot to an area where I had ministered many years before. During the time that I was ministering in this particular area of Kipsgis, the church was weak. I had worked with local evangelists to start a small church, which in turn established a second. But during this visit, I found ten much larger churches in this area. A crowd of 489 gathered in a cluster meeting from all the churches now existing in this area. Later, 120 vocational preachers ministering in these churches participated in an equipping seminar for leaders. These ministers are farmers and businessmen who receive no financial support for their Christian ministry but nevertheless provide leadership for Christian ministry. I stood amazed at their mature faith in God, in-depth knowledge of the Bible, and incisive plans for ministry. All I could say was, "Praise God! May he use the Kipsigis churches as missions-sending and missions-mobilizing churches!"

Reentry

Why do returning missionaries feel like strangers in their own culture? In reality, they are not the same people who left their culture several years before.

Missionaries enter their area of service expecting to have difficulty in learning a new language and adjusting to a new culture. They go knowing that they are entering a new world. They expect little trouble, however, when they complete their time of service and return to their home country or home area of their own country. Are they not returning *home*? They soon find that the home they had known no longer exists (Thompson 1992, 52). Excitement turns into frustration. They experience reentry shock—the trauma of learning to readapt to their own culture.

Why do returning missionaries feel like strangers in their own culture? In reality, they are not the same people who left their culture several years before. They have been changed by their experience in another culture and return home looking at their own culture with different eyes. And just as they are different, so also their home culture has significantly changed.

A color analogy may help readers grasp the changes that occur in missionaries while they are overseas or in a different part of their own country. Their home culture may be pictured as blue, and their host culture as yellow. After years in the foreign culture, the missionaries' own culture has been blended—in their lives and in their personalities—with the host culture, making them different people. A new color, green, emerges. Green missionaries do not identically match either their own or their adopted culture. The home culture has also changed while the missionary has been gone; it is no longer the same shade of blue. Returning missionaries have difficulty reconciling their greenness with the new shade of blue.

Although almost all missionaries struggle with reentry, many eventually flourish because they have developed the flexibility to adapt and have cross-cultural experiences that help them in their home culture. Some of the greatest Christian writers, evangelists, and teachers, exhibiting a high level of maturity for Christian service, have developed that maturity in mission contexts. Other reentering missionaries, however, who may have been less prepared or received less support, struggle and are able to adapt only after a long period of time.

Reentry has two phases: the *farewell phase* and the *hello phase*. The farewell phase includes last visits to churches with which missionaries have worked, family vacations to favorite places, selling belongings, and packing. Before our return to the United States, we had a *chaikab saisere* ("a tea to say farewell"), a Kipsigis tradition for when people move from one location to another. Three hundred Christians from numerous churches spent most of one day with us, singing, praying, and exhorting us to remain true to God in our new place and new ministry. Of course, the actual goodbyes in churches, friends' homes, and at the airport were also part of this phase. The hello phase begins with greeting family and friends in the early days of returning to the home culture. It continues as children begin school, new jobs are found, a house and furnishings are procured, and a new ministry is developed.

Missionaries must make adequate preparation for reentry. Part of this preparation is to realize that they have been changed by their years on the mission field and that their home culture has also changed. Our family memorized Psalm 37:5: "Commit your way to the LORD; trust in him and he will do this." We defined the word *this* as God's helping us to readapt to North American culture. Supporting churches and mission agencies must also make adequate preparation for their missionaries' reentry. They must listen attentively to reports of God's work in the missionaries' lives and praise God for his work in other world contexts; they must help the returned missionaries find ministries fitting their gifts; and they must provide counseling and time for readjustment into the home context.[3] A number of mission agencies and parachurch organizations in North America offer retreat and counseling opportunities for returning missionaries. Sending churches and agencies should encourage and financially support these experiences.

Conclusion

Clyde Austin says, "The formidable challenge confronting the missionary and the sending organization is to keep our missionaries whole

3. Clyde Austin's reader *Cross-Cultural Reentry* (1986) and Neal Pirolo, *The Reentry Team: Caring for Your Returning Missionaries* (2000) provide valuable information on missionary reentry.

through the international cycle" (1986, 123). By understanding the missionary cycle and the struggles associated with each stage, returning missionaries are better able to cope with readapting to their home culture.

REFLECTION AND APPLICATION

Questions

1. Describe each of the seven stages of the missionary cycle. What distinctive struggles occur during each stage?
2. During which stages do *culture shock* and *reentry shock* occur? Briefly compare these two types of cultural disorientation.
3. Describe the changing roles of missionaries during each of the four periods of missionary service. In your answer delineate how missionary roles change from one stage to another in the development of a church-planting movement.
4. Ideally, how long should church-planting missionaries stay in an area?

Application

Answer one of the following two questions.

1. How will understanding the missionary cycle help you nurture a domestic or foreign missionary whom your local church is sponsoring?
2. How will understanding the missionary cycle help you prepare for missionary life in a domestic or foreign context?

Personal Inventory

How has God spoken to you through this chapter? What is God calling you to do about it?

chapter

8

Epochs of the World Christian Movement

The Survival and Growth of Authentic Christianity through Mission

THE CHRISTIAN CHURCH HAS GROWN from a few disciples of Jesus to hundreds of millions of adherents today. Christian faith has endured—and has even thrived—during times of social and political upheaval. Most world religions, such as Buddhism and Islam, are predominately localized geographically and/or culturally. "Christianity, on the other hand, has throughout its history spread outwards, across cultural frontiers, so that each new point on the Christian circumference is a new potential Christian centre. And the very survival of Christianity as a separate faith has evidently been linked to the process of cross-cultural transmission" (Walls 1996, 22). Mission has been key to the survival of authentic Christianity!

Mission has been key to the survival of authentic Christianity!

Throughout the ages, mission has been the vehicle for this cross-cultural transmission.

The efforts of God's people to expand the kingdom of God have a unifying quality that is found in a continual focus on Christ and in a common influence on believers over the millennia. Their examples provide inspiration and instruction to the current and future church.

The history of the church is the history of mission. This chapter illustrates how the Christian movement survived turbulent times. This historical perspective helps us better understand the current state of world Christianity and gives us hope that, through the power of God, Christianity will spread and thrive in the future.

In the drama of the world Christian movement, God himself is the lead actor. Humanity knows God because he has revealed himself. God has pursued humanity, redeeming people created in his image from the death brought about by sin. This pursuit began at humanity's fall in the Garden of Eden, continued through the patriarchs, Israelite kings, and prophets of the Old Testament, and culminated with the incarnation of Jesus Christ — his powerful ministry, life-giving sacrifice, and triumphant, death-defeating resurrection. With the ascended Lord Jesus enthroned at the right hand of the Father and pouring out the Holy Spirit, God has continued to pursue humanity through the establishment of the church and through centuries of bold witness by faithful Christians.

The growth of the Christian movement, however, has often met with opposition. The forces of evil, both human and spiritual, have repeatedly sought to destroy the body of Christ (cf. Rom. 8:38 – 39; Eph. 6:12). God, however, works within his people to overcome the forces of Satan and to expand God's kingdom on earth (Winter 2009, 209 – 10). Christianity is a true world religion, with adherents among the vast and diverse racial, political, and socioeconomic groupings of humankind (Neill 1986, 14).

Scholars interpret the history of missions through different frameworks, as illustrated in Figure 8.1.

David Bosch (1991) views the history of missions as a series of paradigm shifts, in which changes in cultural worldview produced radical changes in the approach to mission. Andrew Walls (1996) sees the history of church and of mission as movements in the "center of gravity" of Christian power and influence. As the influence of once-prominent centers of Christianity declined, new centers, with little or no previous influence, arose. Ralph Winter (2009) looks at the history of mission as the history of peoples subjected to "conquest" by the gospel.[1]

This chapter, drawing insights from each of these perspectives, notes important transitions that took place during each epoch, as well as key figures from each period, as outlined in Figure 8.2.

1. In an insightful integration of Bosch and Winters, Stephen Burris (2012) considers paradigm shifts that have occurred in each of Winter's eras.

Figure 8.1 Comparison of Christian History Perspectives

<table>
<tr><th>Century</th><th>1st</th><th>2nd</th><th>3rd</th><th>4th</th><th>5th</th><th>6th</th><th>7th</th><th>8th</th><th>9th</th><th>10th</th><th>11th</th><th>12th</th><th>13th</th><th>14th</th><th>15th</th><th>16th</th><th>17th</th><th>18th</th><th>19th</th><th>20th</th><th>21st</th></tr>
<tr><td>Bosch (1991)</td><td>Primitive</td><td colspan="3">Patristic</td><td colspan="11">Medieval</td><td colspan="2">Reformation</td><td colspan="3">Modern</td><td>Postmodern</td></tr>
<tr><td>Walls[1] (1996)</td><td></td><td colspan="3">Hellenistic-Roman</td><td colspan="4">Barbarian</td><td colspan="7">Western Europe</td><td colspan="4">Expanding Europe & Christian Recession</td><td colspan="2">Cross-Cultural Transmission</td></tr>
<tr><td>Winter (2009)</td><td colspan="4">Romans</td><td colspan="4">Barbarians</td><td colspan="4">Vikings</td><td colspan="4">Muslims?[2]</td><td colspan="5">The Ends of the Earth</td></tr>
<tr><td>Van Rheenen (2013)</td><td>Jewish Emergence</td><td colspan="4">Gentile Engagement</td><td colspan="7">Institutional Entrenchment</td><td colspan="4">Evangelistic Exploration</td><td colspan="3">Colonial Expansion</td><td colspan="2">Global Embracing</td></tr>
</table>

1. Walls does not designate specific years for each epoch. Those represented in this chart are approximations based on historical references in Walls's description.

2. By placing a question mark next to the Muslims, Winter indicates his hesitancy to label the Crusades, which he calls "the great abortion," as a period of Christian mission (Winter 2009, 213).

Figure 8.2 Transitions in Christian History

Epoch	Major Transition	Key Personalities
Jewish Emergence (32–100)	From Jewish to Gentile	Paul
Gentile Engagement (100–500)	From Minority to Majority	Polycarp, Patrick
Institutional Entrenchment (500–1200)	From Mission Outposts to State Institutions	Boniface, Charlemagne, Cyril and Methodius
Evangelistic Exploration (1200–1600)	From Church-Centered to Gospel-Centered	Francis of Assisi, Raymond Lull, Francis Xavier
Colonial Expansion (1600–1900)	From Inward Focus to Outward Awakening	William Carey, Charlotte "Lottie" Moon, Samuel Crowther
Global Embracing (1900–present)	From Northern/Western to Southern/Eastern	Donald McGavran, David Bosch, Lesslie Newbigin, Paul Hiebert, Ralph Winter

The Jewish Emergence (AD 32–100)

The Christian church was birthed within Jewish religious culture during the extraordinary events in Jerusalem on the day of Pentecost. The outpouring of the Holy Spirit allowed "God-fearing Jews from every nation under heaven" to hear the apostles' testimony about Christ in their own language (Acts 2:5). Thousands were baptized that day! Many returned to their homelands, while others remained in Jerusalem and became part of the community of believers that was learning to follow Christ as "the Lord added to their numbers daily" (v. 47).

In those early times, the movement was exclusively Jewish. These disciples viewed Christianity as a continuation of Judaism — not as a different religion — that recognized Jesus as Messiah.[2] Believers still met at the temple, kept the Jewish law, and maintained Jewish customs. It was not long, however, before Spirit-led, Christ-devoted Jews took the gospel to non-Jewish audiences and areas.

The Holy Spirit led the apostle Peter to Cornelius, the first Gentile believer to join the Christian movement (Acts 10). Soon after this watershed event, "men from Cyprus and Cyrene" introduced Greek-speaking pagans in Antioch to the Lord Jesus (Acts 11:19–20). The church in Antioch was later called to "set apart" Barnabas and Saul (later called Paul) to carry the gospel more deeply into the Roman Empire (Acts 13:2–3).

While church tradition holds that the apostles of Jesus went to different parts of the world to evangelize, there is no biblical record of these efforts. Instead Paul's mission efforts and the letters he sent to churches and coworkers dominate the New Testament record. Because of his pioneering efforts in sacrificial ministry and his passionate teaching, Paul is the greatest missionary example of this opening period. Indeed, his example and teachings set the standard for missionary work in subsequent epochs of world mission.

KEY PERSONALITY: PAUL

Born in Tarsus, Paul — or Saul, as he was then known — was a strict Pharisee (Phil. 3:4–6) who studied under Gamaliel in Jerusalem (Acts

2. Each of the early public proclamations recorded in Acts 2–5, 7 emphasize Jesus as the one glorified by "the God of Abraham, Isaac and Jacob" and the one whom Jewish prophets declared would come.

22:3). His zeal for the Jewish law led him to persecute the church, imprisoning men and women and consenting to the stoning of Stephen. God, however, had other plans for Saul. While Saul was on his way to persecute believers in Damascus, Jesus Christ himself appeared to him in a vision and commissioned him to preach the gospel among the Gentiles. Obeying Jesus, whom he now embraced as Lord, Saul accepted this mission and adopted his Gentile name, Paul.

Paul was uniquely qualified for his role as a missionary. As a Pharisee, he was able to engage in dialogue and debate with Jews and their leaders. He spoke convincingly about Christ's fulfillment of Jewish prophecies and about Israel's ordination to be a blessing to the nations. Paul saw the gospel as being "first [for] the Jew, then [for] the Gentile" (Rom. 1:16) and regularly began his evangelistic efforts in Jewish synagogues.

Paul was also able to meet Gentiles on their ground. He was a Roman citizen and spoke Greek. He was familiar with Gentile poets, as evidenced in his discourse to the Athenians, recorded in Acts 17.

Paul's letters reveal that his ministry was motivated primarily by Christ's love, as well as by a sense of obligation and urgency for the lost (Bosch 1991, 133 – 39). These passions and the fruit they bore in Paul's ministry greatly informed his theology. David Bosch states, "It is today widely acknowledged that Paul was the first Christian theologian precisely because he was the first Christian missionary" (Bosch 1991, 124).

Paul's method was to focus his evangelistic efforts on main cities. His view of the world was more regional than ethnic. On his missionary journeys, Paul and his companions stayed in key urban centers and taught in places of public discussion, such as synagogues and markets. He trained and mentored local leaders and followed up these efforts by making pastoral visits and writing letters.

Paul was a pioneer in contextualization. As more Gentiles became believers, Paul championed a view that allowed Gentiles to become Christians without adopting Jewish customs or observing Mosaic rituals. He "based his work on the radical biblical principle (unaccepted by many Jews to this day) that it is circumcision of the *heart* that counts (Jer. 9), and that the new believers of a new culture did not have to speak the language, wear the clothes, or follow all the customs of the sending church" (Winter 2009, 214). This stance prevailed at the council at Jerusalem (Acts 15), allowing unity in the diversity of the growing movement.

Paul's dedication to spreading the gospel has served as an inspiration to later missionaries. He described the ordeals and suffering he endured in service to Christ:

> *I have worked much harder, been in prison more frequently, been flogged more severely, and been exposed to death again and again. Five times I received from the Jews the forty lashes minus one. Three times I was beaten with rods, once I was pelted with stones, three times I was shipwrecked, I spent a night and a day in the open sea, I have been constantly on the move. I have been in danger from rivers, in danger from bandits, in danger from my fellow Jews, in danger from Gentiles; in danger in the city, in danger in the country, in danger at sea; and in danger from false believers. I have labored and toiled and have often gone without sleep; I have known hunger and thirst and have often gone without food; I have been cold and naked. Besides everything else, I face daily the pressure of my concern for all the churches.*
>
> — 2 CORINTHIANS 11:23 – 28

Ultimately, Paul lost his life in service to the gospel. Tradition holds that he, as well as Peter and many other Christians, was martyred during the persecution led by Emperor Nero in AD 64.

In the decades following the establishment of the church, there was sporadic persecution of Jews by the Roman government. Many Jews (and Christians) were driven out of Jerusalem during these persecutions. Jerusalem was destroyed by the Romans in AD 70, and the Roman reaction to a Jewish revolt in AD 135 effectively ended the organized Jewish state.

This series of events might also have been disastrous for Christians had the Christian movement not already spread beyond the confines

> In their History of Missions course, Jim and Julie learned that the story of God's mission did not conclude with the New Testament age but carried on for two millennia. They heard stories of incredible dedication and sacrifice, of success and failure, and grew to appreciate the claim of Jesus that, in spite of Satan's attacks, the gates of Hades would never prevail against his kingdom. The more they learned, the more they realized that *they* were part of this ongoing story.

of Judaism. Its commitment to mission allowed the Christian movement to survive. Only this "diffusion of faith in Jesus" from the church's earliest days "gave that faith any continuing place in the world" (Walls 1996, 16).

By the end of the third century there was no area in the Roman Empire which had not been penetrated to some extent by the Gospel.
(Stephen Neill)

Gentile Engagement (AD 100–500)

As Christians dispersed throughout the world, whether by political force or evangelistic zeal, the church continued to grow beyond Judea, spreading deeper into Asia, Africa, and Europe. Christianity ceased to be a Jewish phenomenon and became increasingly at home in the Gentile world. The rapid growth of the church was enhanced by the Roman Empire's remarkable infrastructure of roads, trade routes, and communications. Since most of the known world was united under a common political structure (the Roman Empire) and because a common language (Koine Greek) was used for trade and communication, the gospel was more easily disseminated and messengers more easily sent.

In addition to missionaries sent out by churches, God used traveling or displaced believers such as merchants, slaves, and refugees to reach out to the world. A general acceptance of different cultures led to high receptivity. A widespread desire for immortality, the "burning conviction" and pure lives of Christians, as well as the brave witness of the martyrs, opened even more doors and influenced many to become Christians (Neill 1986, 35–38).

Aided by the written Scriptures (including the letters of Paul, John, and Peter, and the Gospels), the Christian movement continued to spread, while the emergence of Christian apologists and philosophers such as Justin, Tertullian, Clement, and Origen gave legitimacy to Christianity. Early Christian leaders engaged the Gentile cultures, sometimes expressing Christian theology through familiar philosophical frameworks and at other times holding Christian belief in sharp contrast to the prevailing cultures. Neill states that the Christian movement's growth was so rapid and widespread "that by the end of the third century there was no area in the Roman Empire which had not been penetrated to some extent by the Gospel" (1986, 35).

Despite riding this wave of tremendous growth, the church faced many challenges. Christians were persecuted by both Jews and pagans.

Persecution by Roman authorities was largely a reaction to Christianity's sole allegiance to divine authority, which was viewed as a threat to the loyalty demanded by the empire. In AD 112, Emperor Trajan, for example, responded to a letter from Pliny, governor of Bithynia, outlining imperial policies toward Christians. The Christians, he said, "ought not to be sought out," but "if they are brought before you and convicted, they ought to be punished." If they deny that they are Christians and prove this by "making supplication to our gods, however much [they] may have been under suspicion in the past," they should be pardoned. Attention should not be paid "to anonymous charges, for they afford a bad precedent and are not worthy of our age" (Petry 1962, 44). Christians also posed a threat to cultural moral standards. Practices such as the Lord's Supper were misinterpreted or misrepresented. Countless believers died during these times of persecution. One martyr was Polycarp, who served for fifty years as the bishop of Smyrna during the early second century.

KEY PERSONALITY: POLYCARP

Polycarp was a learned and influential teacher, dedicated to preserving and passing on the faith he witnessed in the apostles. He may have been a disciple of the apostle John. His letter to the Philippian church indicates that he held Paul in high esteem. Ruth Tucker describes Polycarp as "an evangelist and missionary who conveyed a deep sense of urgency in his interaction with the pagan culture around him. He was known in Smyrna as a teacher who could be found sitting in his special spot with believers and unbelievers, listening and debating" (2004, 31).

When persecution against Christians flared up in the province of Asia around AD 156, Polycarp was arrested. Because he was a very old man, however, the authorities were reluctant to execute him. Instead they hoped that he would deny his faith. The authorities brought Polycarp into a stadium filled with spectators and repeatedly implored him to renounce Christ. Polycarp refused, responding, "For eighty-six years I have been his servant, and he has done me no wrong. How can I blaspheme my king who saved me?" (Lightfoot and Harmer 1989, 139).

The authorities continued to press him to renounce his faith, threatening to feed him to wild beasts, but Polycarp stood firm. Finally, the proconsul said,

> "I will have you consumed by fire, since you despise the wild beasts, unless you change your mind." But Polycarp said: "You threaten me with a fire that burns only briefly and after just a little while is extinguished, for you are ignorant of the fire of the coming judgment and eternal punishment, which is reserved for the ungodly. But why do you delay? Come, do what you wish." (Lightfoot and Harmer 1989, 139)

Polycarp was burned at the stake.

Although Polycarp was a victim of local persecution, the oppression of Christians became imperial policy beginning with Decius in AD 249. Decius's goal was not to kill Christians but to force them to renounce their faith by confessing that the emperor was Lord. He aimed to "make apostates, not martyrs" (Petry 1962, 38). Although large numbers of believers succumbed to Decius's efforts, others remained firm in their faith. Later, Christians would suffer under statewide persecutions by Valerian (257 – 59) and Diocletian (c. 303).

But the Christian movement continued to grow despite persecution, resulting in a radical change of policy. The edicts of Galerius (311) and Constantine and Licinius (313) granted tolerance to Christians and permitted them to assemble, worship as they pleased, and reclaim property seized during times of persecution (Petry 1962, 56 – 58). In AD 375, Constantine chose Christianity as his vehicle to unify the Roman Empire, making it the official religion of the empire. Amazingly, this deprecated minority sect quickly became the religion of anyone pursuing prestige, favor, or social advancement. The church's evolution from a severely persecuted cult to *the* state religion in just over seventy years is perhaps the most significant transition to occur in the Christian movement.

This change of status brought both great opportunities and limitations. As the state religion, Christianity lost the ability to reach people who did not identify with the Roman culture or agree with its politics. As it became more enmeshed with politics, the church adopted worldly qualities. Hellenistic thought exerted greater influence on the church and brought with it a growing concern with right doctrine and orthodoxy. Walls writes, "Of the new religious ideas which entered with the Christian penetration of Hellenistic culture, one of the most permeative for the future was that of orthodoxy, or a canon of right belief, capable of being stated in a series of propositions arrived at by a process of logical argument" (Walls 1996, 18).

The combination of an inward focus on orthodoxy and the accommodation to worldly ideas and practices greatly weakened the church's evangelistic zeal. Bosch reports that the church in the East "was still expanding and enlarging. This was, however, hardly mission in the Pauline sense; rather, it was Christian propaganda. To the church, paganism and the absence of 'civilization' were synonymous, and mission identical to the spread of culture" (Bosch 1991, 201).

Still, the Christian movement continued to spread into new areas. Winter posits that most of the missionary work done on the fringes of the empire and in frontier lands did not happen because of Rome's initiative but "came about mainly through unplanned processes involving Christians from the eastern part of the Roman Empire" (Winter 2009, 215). Patrick, missionary to Ireland, serves as one example of this type of mission work.

KEY PERSONALITY: PATRICK

Patrick was born in 389 to Christian parents in Britain, but at age sixteen he was captured by Irish marauders and sold as a slave to an Irish farmer. During these years of servitude, Patrick's life was transformed into one of prayer and devotion to God.

After six years, Patrick escaped slavery and went to a monastery in France before returning home to Britain. Soon afterward he had a vision — his "Macedonian call" — to return to Ireland as a missionary. He immediately began making plans to return to Ireland and, after some trials, arrived there in 432.

Ireland was an intimidating, isolated place populated with pagan peoples. In confrontations with druid and pagan leaders, Patrick engaged in a power encounter, using what he called "God's magic" to best their own magic. He won many converts, including some of the druid chieftains, but continued to face opposition "from the representatives of the old religion, from the kings whom he tried to convert, from British raiders who disrupted his work and massacred his converts" (Neill 1986, 50).

Because evangelism was Patrick's major goal, he did not linger in one place for very long. "After establishing a church," writes Tucker, "Patrick moved on to new areas where the gospel had never been preached; and by 447, after fifteen years of preaching, much of Ireland had been evangelized" (Tucker 2004, 39).

Although primarily an evangelist, Patrick also emphasized the spiritual growth of converts. Converts went through intensive training in the Scriptures and were encouraged to engage in ministry themselves (Tucker 2004, 40).

While legends about Patrick abound, his true legacy is his faithful response to God's call to evangelize Ireland. His mission efforts led to about two hundred churches, which together comprised almost one hundred thousand converts, and laid the foundation for the Celtic church, which carried out missions in Britain, deep into central Europe, and north into Iceland.

The Goths' invasion of the Roman Empire in the early fifth century signaled the beginning of the end for the empire. Christianity, which had benefited from being the religion of the largest empire in the world, now faced new challenges. The Christian movement had already, however, proven its ability to overcome great obstacles: the destruction of its birthplace, persecution from Jews and pagans alike, and the advances to new and difficult lands. Reflecting on Christianity at the end of the Roman age, Neill states, "It had manifested a versatility that could adapt itself to the needs of peoples on very different levels of civilization" (Neill 1986, 52).

This versatility, along with a genuine desire to participate in the ministry of reconciliation, helped Christianity grow after the fall of the Roman Empire. The Middle Ages challenged that versatility as barbarian invaders streamed in from the north and a new, powerful religion and culture — that of Islam — pressed in from the east.

Institutional Entrenchment (500–1200)

Even though Rome's political power diminished, the church grew in influence and control. This was possible because the church's dominance was tied not to the status of Rome as a city but to the church's claim that its bishop stood as successor to Peter (Todd 1977, 191–92). At a time when Western Christianity was threatened by the military power and pagan beliefs of barbarian invaders, it continued to look to the church in Rome for leadership.

Sometimes the popes, as religious leaders, were able to exert political leadership. Gregory the Great, for example, who became pope in 590, prevented Rome's total annihilation. He "provisioned the city and provided for its defense, sent orders to generals in the fields, negotiated with the Lombards, and finally concluded peace without the [Roman] Emperor's authorization" (Todd 1977, 195).

Although the invading forces of northern Europe largely won the battles for territory, power, and wealth, their cultures were eventually transformed by their encounter with Christianity. Todd notes that it was the Roman church, as "the principle surviving institution from the ancient world," that "transmitted Roman culture to the Middle Ages" (1977, 195). Because of its incarnational nature, Christianity could be expressed in the cultures of northern Europe, enabling the church not only to survive but also to conquer the conquerors. Winter writes that "while the Romans lost the western half of their empire, the Barbarian world, in a very dramatic sense, gained a Christian faith" (2009, 217).

This contextualization came about not through the church in Rome or Constantinople but through people converted on the periphery of the former empire. "Barbarian Europe was won more by the witness and labors of Celtic and Anglo-Saxon converts of the Celts — 'Third World missionaries' — than by the efforts of missionaries deriving from Italy or Gaul" (Winter 2009, 218).

The monastic movement also played a major role in the church's growth during this time. Monasteries established across Europe and North Africa became centers of culture and civilization as well as mission (Bosch 1991, 230). The monks, living in remote places, frequently had close connection with local peoples. Their understanding of local customs and beliefs enabled them to transform, rather than annihilate, pagan beliefs and ceremonies (Neill 1986, 66–67).

The monks also learned to speak and write the languages of northern Europe, which helped them to engage with local peoples on an even deeper level (Neill 1986, 67). Bosch writes, "Although the monastic communities were not *intentionally* missionary (in other words, created for the purpose of mission), they were permeated by a missionary *dimension*. Even without knowing it and without intending it, their conduct was missionary through and through" (Bosch 1991, 233).

KEY PERSONALITY: BONIFACE

Boniface, who has been acclaimed as "medieval Europe's most energetic and outwardly successful missionary" (Tucker 2004, 51), was shaped and informed by the monastery. Born in England around 680, Boniface entered the monastery at a young age and became a priest at thirty. Although his first missionary effort into Friesland (in the present-day Netherlands) in 715 was largely unsuccessful, it strengthened Boniface's desire to work in foreign lands.

Boniface returned to England and in 718 journeyed to Rome. He believed that new mission churches needed to be connected directly to the church in Rome in order to have a sustained and permanent presence (Neill 1986, 64). After his successful trip to Rome, Boniface went to Germany and Friesland with the blessing and support of the pope. Soon he was called back to Rome and consecrated by Pope Gregory II as a missionary bishop to Germany.

Boniface is remembered for his bold act of chopping down the sacred oak of Thor in Geismar, Germany, in 724. He and local believers were troubled that new converts were participating in pagan worship practices. To show that God was more powerful than pagan gods, he began chopping down this sacred tree. A crowd of pagans cursed him, saying that he would die for this act. Undeterred, Boniface felled the tree. All waited to see what would happen to this man who desecrated the sacred tree. Nothing occurred. Many became believers after witnessing the defeat of their gods by a stronger God (Petry 1962, 205 – 6).

Encouraged by the results of this power encounter, Boniface performed similar aggressive acts in other areas, destroying pagan shrines, totems, and holy places. These efforts were productive, though less dramatic than felling the sacred oak. Boniface later, however, questioned the effectiveness and validity of the practice (Tucker 2004, 50).

Boniface maintained the tradition of establishing monasteries to train and educate local believers. Though Boniface's methods were not new, one "truly innovative aspect of his ministry was his enthusiastic recruitment of women to serve the cause of missions," one of whom was Lioba, Boniface's cousin (Tucker 2004, 50).

After another visit to Rome in 737 – 38, Boniface returned to Germany to ordain bishops throughout the area. He aided in reforming the Frankish church (Neill 1986, 65) and founded the monastery of Fulda, which remains a key institution in Germany.

When he sensed another call to pioneer missionary work, Boniface returned in 753 to areas of Friesland which were not yet evangelized. The work was initially successful but encountered strong opposition. In fact, Boniface was killed by a mob of armed pagans as he was preparing for a service to confirm new converts.

KEY PERSONALITY: CHARLEMAGNE

Charlemagne appeared on the world scene a couple of decades after Boniface's death, ruling the kingdom of the Franks from 771 – 814. During that period, he also was crowned emperor of the Holy Roman Empire by Pope Leo II in 800. Charlemagne, like Constantine, was both a believer and a soldier. As a result, he used a mixture of religion and armed force to control his enemies, the Saxons. His practice of forcing conquered peoples to convert to Christianity or be killed produced a number of revolts, followed by military campaigns, which in turn led to more revolts and new campaigns (Neill 1986, 68). This cycle of violence characterized much of the Middle Ages.

Charlemagne initiated other reforms without the use of violence.

> Under his sponsorship a whole range of issues — social, theological, political — were soberly restudied in the light of the Bible and the writings of the earlier Christian leaders in the Roman period. Charlemagne was a second Constantine in certain respects, and his influence was unmatched in Western Europe during a half a millennium. (Winter 2009, 218)

"Christian nations" existed during Charlemagne's rule, but they became the norm as the gospel spread to other European countries. This was driven not by heavy-handed rule by conquerors like Charlemagne but by traditional understanding of communal decision-making.

> A communal decision to adopt the Christian faith might take some time in coming; there might be uncertainty, division, debate for a while, but once thoroughly made, the decision would bind everyone in that society. A community must have a single custom. It was not necessarily a case of strong rulers enforcing their own choice. (Walls 1996, 20)

As more and more nations in the Middle Ages found their new identity in Christianity, the two main churches — those of Rome and Constantinople — were trying to gain footholds in new areas through evangelization. Repeatedly, disputes arose regarding who had oversight over particular lands. Two influential missionaries were involved in one such dispute.

KEY PERSONALITIES: CYRIL AND METHODIUS

Around AD 860, the prince of Moravia (present day Slovakia) asked the Byzantine church in Constantinople to send missionaries to his country. Eager to gain a stronger foothold in Eastern Europe, the emperor selected two brothers, Cyril (also known as Constantine) and Methodius, for the task. Both men were well educated and experienced as missionaries, having worked among the Khazars in Russia. This experience, as well as their childhood exposure to Slavonic speech, uniquely qualified them for this mission.

As they prepared for the work in Moravia, Cyril and Methodius decided that the local languages would be the best medium through which to teach the Slavs the gospel. Before their departure, Cyril began creating an alphabet in which the languages could be written, and translated some important Scriptures. This translation, both of Scriptures and of the church liturgy, continued after the brothers arrived in Moravia.

Because the Roman church used only Latin for church liturgy, Cyril and Methodius's use of Scripture and liturgy in the local language was controversial. In the Byzantine church, "the desire for ecclesiastical centralization did not extend to language; and it always seemed natural to Byzantine churchmen that as new peoples were brought within the Church they should be encouraged to build up their Church and their national culture on the basis of their local language" (Neill 1986, 73).

Despite their successful work in using vernacular in liturgy, Cyril and Methodius soon found themselves caught between two political and religious forces as Rome and Constantinople argued over which church had the authority over Moravia. Even though the church in Constantinople had sent them to Moravia, Cyril and Methodius traveled to Rome in hopes of stabilizing the situation and ensuring the continuance of their work. During their visit, Pope Hadrian II recognized the brothers' work and gave the Moravian churches permission to use the Slavonic liturgy. Cyril, however, died before they could return.

Methodius continued the work he and Cyril had started and was later appointed bishop over the area. He continued to champion the use of Slavonic languages in worship but was maligned by other priests and monks and was continually caught in the middle of religious and political rivalries.

The mission work of Cyril and Methodius in the local Slavonic languages influenced Christian missions far beyond the Moravian borders. In fact, these two brothers "are seen as precursors to the translation work of Martin Luther and of translators of the modern missions era" (Tucker 2004, 56). As a testament to their resolve and pioneering efforts, both the Roman Catholic and Eastern Orthodox Churches recognize Cyril and Methodius for their efforts among the Slavonic peoples.

While these events were occurring in northern Europe and the British Isles, the development and advance of Islam were also exerting a major influence on the church. Within only a few decades, the new religion had grown vigorously and conquered the Persian Empire. By the turn of the eighth century, Islam had permeated northern Africa and entered southern Europe. In 732, a large Muslim army advanced as far as Tours in France, where it was defeated. Although this prevented a Muslim conquest of Europe, the Islamic movement continued to push into new areas.

As the Holy Roman Empire emerged in the year 800 with the crowning of Charlemagne, and as more nations forged Christian identities, the rulers decided to free the "holy lands" from Islamic hands. This led to a series of wars between 1095 and 1291 known collectively as the Crusades. Sponsored by Christian leaders and carried out by politically motivated kings and their armies, these wars brought death and disaster to both sides.

The Crusades also caused tremendous strain on Christian unity, driving a wedge between the Western and Eastern branches of Christianity. They established a tone of bitterness and mistrust in Christian-Muslim relations. "Far worse," notes Winter, "they established a permanent image of brutal, militant Christianity that alienates a large proportion of mankind, tearing down the value of the very word *Christian* in missions to this day" (Winter 2009, 221).

The violent acts performed in the name of God by political and religious powers during the Crusades overshadowed the noble efforts of monks and pioneering missionaries such as Boniface, Cyril, and Methodius. These missionaries sought to establish the Christian faith in new areas by fighting on a spiritual level, using the "weapons" of contextualization and power encounter. Their labor was not in vain. Even the tragic Crusades provided Christian mission with another opportunity to advance authentic Christianity into new areas.

Evangelistic Exploration (1200–1600)

Even though the Crusades enjoyed the favor of most of the Christian world, they permanently marred the image of Christianity in many parts of the world. There were, however, some believers who opposed the violent attacks on Islam and sought to engage Muslims by preaching the love and peace of the gospel. Two of these were Francis of Assisi and Raymond Lull.

KEY PERSONALITIES: FRANCIS OF ASSISI AND RAYMOND LULL

Francis, the son of a wealthy cloth merchant in Assisi, lived a high-spirited life typical of the wealthy. After serving as a soldier for Assisi, he returned home and gave up his worldly life and lived in poverty. Francis' new lifestyle and his zeal and passion for sharing Christ with the world led him to found the Franciscan order.

The emergence of the Franciscan order and similar orders "meant that a new spirit had come into the Christian world, and that a notable shift was about to take place in the missionary methods of the Christian Churches" (Neill 1986, 99). That shift was from fixed monasteries to the mobile ministries of the Franciscan, Dominican, and, later, the Jesuit orders. These orders dominated missions of this period as the Roman Catholic Church looked to extend its influence in Europe, North Africa, the Americas, and the Far East. One of the first Franciscan missionaries was Raymond Lull, whom Neill describes as "one of the greatest missionaries in the history of the Church" (Neill 1986, 114).

Lull was born in the early 1230s on the island of Majorca, just south of the Mediterranean coast of Spain. He grew up in a wealthy family, was well educated, and showed promise as a scholar and writer. As a young man, Lull served in the royal court. Although he grew up in the Roman Catholic Church, he lived an ungodly lifestyle. Repeated visions of Christ on a cross, however, led him to conversion and the decision to devote himself to a monastic life.

A few years later, Lull received a vision calling him to the Saracens, Muslim nomads in North Africa, who were known as fierce enemies of Christianity. He delayed his departure for North Africa for nine years, studying Arabic and developing a detailed plan for reaching the Muslim world.

Lull believed that there were three keys to reaching the Muslims. First, missionaries must have a thorough knowledge of the Arabic language in order to understand Muslim thought and doctrine and to engage them in discussion of religious matters. Second, a book that was written for Muslims and that clearly reasoned and demonstrated the truth of Christianity was needed. Finally, Lull believed, missionaries working among the Saracens should be above reproach and willing to face death for the sake of their witness for Christ. He wrote, "Such work will be entrusted only to the noblest and most devoted men, those ready to die for Christ, learned in philosophy and theology, and of well-regulated habits" (Petry 1962, 368–69).

Lull traveled throughout Europe, championing his plans to evangelize Muslims and seeking support from religious and political leaders. In 1276, Lull, with support from the king of Spain, opened a monastery on Majorca. Its main purpose was to train monks for ministry among Muslims by teaching them Arabic and Lull's mission philosophies.

Lull put his theories into practice during a missionary trip to Tunis, where he engaged in lively debates with Muslim leaders. Although the initial responses were promising, he soon was imprisoned, stoned, and kicked out of the country. Lull then returned to Europe, promoting his ideas and persuading new recruits to join him in his efforts.

In 1307, at age seventy-five, Lull returned to North Africa, to Bugia (presently Béjaïa), east of Algiers. Encouraged by his small measure of success in Tunis, Lull maintained his modus operandi of public debates and bold challenges with the Muslim leaders of Bugia. His efforts resulted in a six-month imprisonment, after which he returned to Europe for the last time.

Lull's final foreign mission effort was in Tunis in 1314. This work was more successful than his previous efforts, either here or in Bugia. Lull, however, wanted to make the ultimate sacrifice for Christ and become a martyr. He reentered Bugia and lived there secretly for ten months. When Lull presented himself publicly as the man they had banished several years earlier, the local officials were incensed and had him stoned. Lull died shortly afterward of the injuries sustained in the assault.

Raymond Lull left a legacy of systematic teaching and rational arguments, as well as a commitment to excellence in preparation for mission work. He also gave the church an example of living out one's beliefs and engaging the Muslim world with love, words, and deeds instead of swords, horses, and spears.

KEY PERSONALITY: FRANCIS XAVIER

Francis Xavier also left a profound mark on this era of missions. As a young man studying in Paris, Xavier met Ignatius of Loyola, founder of the Jesuit order. Through Ignatius's influence, he became a charter member of the Jesuits and is perhaps the best-known Roman Catholic missionary (Neill 1986, 128).

Xavier's call to missions was sudden. He accepted the call in 1542 to be a replacement on a team of two Jesuits going to Goa, India. The long voyage to Goa began a short, pioneering missionary career in the East.

Xavier moved up the coast from Goa to work with Hindu Paravas—peoples of a lower caste who were more receptive to the gospel. Xavier's methods of evangelism were simple but effective. He described some of them in a letter to Rome.

> We translated the Catechism into the Malabar tongue. This I learnt by heart and then I began to go through all the villages of the coast, calling around me by the sound of a bell as many as I could, children and men. I assembled them twice a day and taught them the Christian doctrine: and thus, in the space of a month, the children had it well by heart. And all the time I kept telling them to go on teaching in their turn whatever they had learnt to their parents, family and neighbors. (Manschreck 1964, 129)

Xavier also taught the Lord's Prayer, the Apostles' Creed, and the Ten Commandments at Sunday Mass through constant repetition. His work was so fruitful that he reported being physically exhausted by the work of baptizing and teaching people who accepted Christ. His words are inspirational, illustrating the great response to God's mission.

> As to the number who become Christians, you may understand them from this, that it often happens to me to be hardly able to use my hands from the fatigue of baptizing: often in a single day I have baptized whole villages. Sometimes, I have lost my voice and strength altogether with repeating again and again the Credo and the other forms. (Manschreck 1964, 130)

While he ministered to all people, Xavier found significant success among the children. These young people were often zealous for their new faith — destroying idols, evangelizing family members, and ministering to the sick and needy in Xavier's stead (Manschreck 1964, 130). This early shaping of the next generation of leaders would become a strong foundation for the church in India.

Even though his work with the Paravas was largely successful, Xavier moved to Japan in 1549. The work in Japan forced him to rethink the assumption that non-Christian worldviews or cultures are incapable of supporting the gospel.

Xavier had previously believed that one must repudiate all traditional beliefs and practices before becoming a Christian. However, "now that he was confronted by a civilization with so many elements of nobility in it," Neill writes, "[Xavier] saw that, while the Gospel must transform and refine and re-create, it need not necessarily reject as worthless everything that has come before" (1964, 133). Xavier's two years in Japan produced only a hundred converts. His efforts, however, paved the way for other Jesuits, so that by the end of the 1500s, the church had grown to three hundred thousand.

Xavier planned to go to China and returned to Goa to make preparations. However, he died of a fever during his journey to China. Though this pioneer's life was cut short, his example inspired hundreds of missionaries. According to Manschreck, "Xavier exemplified the dedication and perseverance of early Catholic missionaries" (1964, 462).

While mission efforts such as Xavier's expanded the Catholic Church abroad, the Protestant Reformation brought turmoil to the church in

Europe. Viewed by many as a reaction to the corruption and bureaucracy of the Roman Catholic Church, the Protestant Reformation was also the result of a widespread return to Bible study, transformed life, and evangelistic preaching (Winter 2009, 223–24).

The Reformation not only gave birth to Protestantism, but also transformed Catholicism. The Reformation, and the subsequent Counter-Reformation (revival within the Catholic Church), allowed the idea of individual decisions and application of faith — as opposed to group decisions and mass response to the gospel — to become the key characteristic of Western Christianity (Walls 1996, 21).

During this epoch, colonialism was birthed. Colonies were established through centuries of exploration and trading, as well as political ambition. Christianity was easily connected to this political and economic venture, since colonists brought their Christian religion with them.[3] This colonial wave saw the church — Catholic, Orthodox, and eventually Protestant — become a full participant in the new global reality.

Colonial Expansion (1600–1900)

In the sixteenth and seventeenth centuries, the Roman Catholic Church experienced global expansion. Protestants, on the other hand, focused more on reforming the church than on growing it, though the Swiss reformer John Calvin did send colonists to Brazil in 1555. The Protestant movement also battled for survival against both stern opposition and internal strife (Bosch 1991, 245).

Most Protestants, concentrated in the landlocked countries of Germany and Switzerland, had limited or no contact with non-Christians, since they lacked ready access to overseas travel. The emerging eschatological and soteriological beliefs of the new movement discouraged Protestant mission work as well. Manschreck writes, "As late as 1651, the theological faculty at Wittenberg insisted that the Gospel had in theory been carried into the world and that those who were still languishing in heathenism were obviously under the judgment of God" (1964, 462).

3. Christianity is often named as one of the three Cs — or three main "commodities" — brought to new worlds by colonialists. The other two Cs were civilization and commerce.

It was not until the early 1700s that Protestant Christianity began to develop an interest in missions. The efforts of Pietists such as A. H. Francke led to the establishment of the Danish-Halle Mission, which sent its first missionaries to Goa, India, where Xavier had worked almost two centuries earlier (Manschreck 1964, 462).

The Moravian Brethren, who were part of the early Protestant missionary movement, demonstrated much zeal and dedication in missions. The passion of Count Nicholaus Zinzendorf, an Austrian aristocrat and Pietist patron, spurred the Moravian Brethren to send vocational missionaries to Greenland, the Americas, the Caribbean, and South Africa. Zinzendorf's motto was, "Wherever at the moment there is most to do for the Savior, that is our home" (Bosch 1991, 287).

Missionary expansion during this period focused on areas with European colonies. The missionaries, however, were not puppets of their home governments. In fact, they often defied colonial authorities by standing against abuses to the local population. Moravian missionaries typically ministered to the lower strata of society, living among them, adopting their dress and food. Although this was frowned on by European colonizers, the Moravians were effective, not only in bearing witness to the gospel, but also in positively impacting the local economic and social conditions.

This new attitude and philosophy of these pietistic Moravian missionaries proved to be highly influential in Protestant missions. They emphasized forming communities of faith rather than transplanting the national churches of Europe. The responsibility for mission shifted away from the colonial government and onto the church. "Ordinary Christians" were encouraged to serve in foreign lands as missionaries with an ecumenical spirit (Bosch 1991, 255).

Neill writes, "The cool and rational eighteenth century was hardly a promising seed-bed for Christian growth; but out of it came a greater outburst of Christian mission enterprise than had been seen in all the centuries before" (1986, 477).

KEY PERSONALITY: WILLIAM CAREY

Because of the great enthusiasm his work generated, William Carey is often called the Father of Modern Missions. His ministry initiated the "Great Century" of Christian missions and "marks the entry of the English-speaking world on a large scale into the missionary enterprise" (Neill 1986, 222).

Expect great things from God; attempt great things for God.

(William Carey)

While apprenticed to a cobbler in England, Carey was converted by a co-apprentice at age eighteen and became an active member of the Baptist church. He taught himself five languages, including the biblical languages, and pastored two small churches. In 1792 he published a small book, *An Enquiry into the Obligation of Christians to Use Means for the Conversion of the Heathen*, which argued convincingly for the church to engage in mission work abroad.

Shortly after Carey made his famous exhortation, "Expect great things from God; attempt great things for God," to a gathering of ministers, the Baptist Missionary Society was formed. Carey, who volunteered to be one of the society's first missionaries, was confirmed and commissioned to go to India with coworker John Thomas.

The team arrived in India following a long period of preparation and fundraising, discouragement within Carey's family, and an arduous sea voyage. Upon arrival, they faced opposition from the East India Trading Company, which led Carey to move his family to the interior of the country. They settled in Malda, where he worked as a foreman in an indigo factory. Despite his demanding job and much family turmoil (the children were often sick, one child died, and Carey's wife suffered mental illness), Carey devoted himself to language learning, translation, and evangelism during his five years in Malda. In 1799, Carey and his family joined new missionaries, Joshua Marshman and William Ward, in Serampore. Their collective ministry produced local schools, a printing establishment, churches, and the Serampore College.

During their pioneering work, "Carey and his colleagues were conscious of communicating the gospel effectively in the Indian culture — though ever recognizing that their efforts were trifling in comparison to what native Indians themselves would be able to do" (Tucker 2004, 128). Carey continued his diligent work in the study of the local beliefs and customs, Bible translation, evangelism, and church planting — missionary practices that put Carey and his colleagues ahead of their time (Tucker 2004, 130).

Despite his tremendous work in translation and evangelism, "the significance of Carey's ministry lies in its influence on Protestant missions more than on its influence on the Indian people" (Tucker 2004, 121). This wide influence became possible because "the letters that Carey sent back to England were widely publicized and inspired Christians in Europe and America to undertake missionary programs" (Manschreck 1964, 463). Stirred by Carey's example and determination to succeed, many missionaries of the Great Century (and since) have dared to "attempt great things for God."

KEY PERSONALITY: LOTTIE MOON

Throughout history, women of faith have contributed to the expansion of the kingdom by serving as missionaries. This was especially true during this colonial period. Neill notes that by the first part of the 1900s, "women in missions greatly outnumbered men" (Neill 1986, 217). A large portion of this female missionary force was composed of wives who worked with their husbands on the field. Other female missionaries, however, were single women who bravely faced many obstacles — at home and abroad — in order to bring Christ to the nations. One such woman was Charlotte "Lottie" Moon.

Lottie Moon was born in 1840 and grew up in a Baptist home in Virginia. Always an excellent student, Moon graduated from Hollins College and went on to Albermarle Female Institute in 1857, where she graduated with a master of arts degree. She was particularly skilled in languages, being fluent in Spanish and French and able to read Greek, Hebrew, and Latin.

Moon's interest in missions was sparked at a spiritual revival she attended as a student. Because the Southern Baptist Convention (SBC) did not send out single women, however, she taught at a school in Kentucky and later ran a school for girls in Georgia.

In 1872, Moon's younger sister went to China with an SBC mission team. Soon afterward, Moon was asked to join the missionaries. She answered the call and moved to Tengchow of the Shantung Province, where she lived for forty years.

Initially, Moon's work was strictly "woman's mission to woman." The SBC had a general prohibition of women teaching, preaching, or exercising authority over men, so Moon's work was focused on women and children. From 1873 to 1885, she supervised a girls' school and learned the Chinese language. She also worked at personal evangelism, traveling both in town and into the surrounding country.

Moon's diligence resulted in "an excellent command of Chinese that coworkers envied. She developed a near-obsession for honoring Chinese customs unless they were blatantly incompatible with Christianity" (Allen 1994, 208). Her drive to learn and honor the Chinese culture became a hallmark of Moon's ministry.

As a missionary living in a remote province, Moon faced harsh physical and spiritual conditions. She lived a balanced, healthy life by exercising, eating well, and adapting to her surroundings. Most important, she was consistent in her daily devotions and her near-constant awareness of the presence of Christ.

In 1885, Moon moved to Pingtu, where she worked for seven years. In Pingtu, Moon lived among the local people, taught those who invited her in, and grew a large number of contacts in the city and surrounding villages. The fruit of this labor included planting a small church. One of her first converts became a leading evangelist, and after about twenty-five years, thousands had been baptized, with over thirty churches planted in the area.

With her ministry rooted in this rural, communal setting, Moon found herself teaching men along with women and children. "She solved the dilemma [of the prohibition of women teaching men] by stirring up enough interest in her women's meetings to rouse the men's curiosity to the point that they could not resist coming to hear. But she made it clear that her 'preaching' was to the women. How could she help it if 'the men crowded silently behind them and studied along with them.... Even Paul would not have objected'" (Tucker 1987, 303–4[4]).

As the work in Pingtu expanded, Moon saw the need for more missionaries. In 1887, she suggested that Southern Baptist women organize a fundraising group that would take an offering at Christmastime that would support women missionaries in Pingtu. Women caught her vision, raised funds, and sent new recruits. This initial challenge, which in 1918 became the Lottie Moon Christmas Offering, has raised billions of dollars for missions.

---

4. Tucker cites Irwin Hyatt, *Our Ordered Lives Confess: Three Nineteenth-Century American Missionaries in East Shantung* (Cambridge, Mass.: Harvard Univ. Press, 1976), 135–37.

Lottie Moon—a symbol of true womanhood and of what women could accomplish for missions.
(Ruth Tucker)

From 1890 until her death in 1912, Moon evangelized in the village, trained missionaries, and counseled Chinese Christians. She maintained correspondence with churches in America, earning their respect and exercising tremendous influence for missions. "Although she returned home on furloughs and occasionally spoke before large audiences," Tucker writes, "it was chiefly her pen that stirred the hearts of Baptist women in the South" (Tucker 2004, 297).

Moon was so dedicated to the Chinese church and the works in Tengchow and Pingtu that she refused to leave the country during the Russo-Japanese War (1904–5) and the Chinese Revolution (1911). During those times of crisis, she housed and cared for the poor and needy.

In 1912, Moon became malnourished, partially because she gave her share of food to others. Physical and emotional stress took a dramatic toll on Moon's health. Local physicians advised her to return to America for better care. Moon took their advice but did not survive the voyage. She died on Christmas Eve, 1912, on a ship bound for America.

Moon's influence extended far beyond the rural areas where she poured herself out in ministry. Tucker writes, "For Southern Baptist women, she had become a symbol of true womanhood and of what women could accomplish for missions" (Tucker 2004, 298). She exemplifies true servanthood and what one can achieve when one is fully devoted to sharing the love of Christ.

KEY PERSONALITY: SAMUEL CROWTHER

By the end of the nineteenth century, missions began to move away from a strict paternalistic approach. This began the move toward ordination of nationals, and by the end of the First World War, "in a large number of missions of every conceivable ecclesiastical complexion, the number of ordained nationals far exceeded the number of ordained foreigners" (Neill 1986, 219).

Samuel Crowther was a Nigerian national born in 1807. At thirteen, he was captured by raiders and sold to Portuguese slave traders. His slave ship, however, was intercepted by the British at Sierra Leone. There he was baptized in the Anglican Church at age eighteen. In Sierra Leone, Crowther was educated to a collegiate level. He studied the Yoruba (Nigeria) and Temne (Sierra Leone) languages while working as schoolmaster and evangelist in schools for newly "liberated Africans"—former slaves who, like Crowther, were freed by British naval interceptors.

In 1841, Crowther was invited to serve as interpreter and helper for Europeans on a missionary expedition along the Niger River. After this expedition, Crowther studied in England and was ordained in the Anglican Church. He then worked in a mission effort in Abeokuta, Yorubaland, with others from the Anglican Church Mission Society. In his work alongside the European missionaries on the translation of the Bible into Yoruba, he insisted that markings indicating the tones of the language be included. According to Walls, Crowther was "the first native speaker able to judge and act on an equal footing with the European" (1994, 135).

On Crowther's second Niger expedition in 1854, he began a mission at Onitsha, Igboland, and went on to evangelize among the Nupe and Hausa peoples. Crowther effectively evangelized the Muslims in this area, engaging them in dialogue, seeking common ground between the Qur'an and the Bible, and responding to questions with Scripture. His work "represents the first sustained missionary engagement with African Islam in modern times" (Walls 1994, 136).

In 1864, Crowther was consecrated bishop of "the countries of Western Africa beyond the limits of the Queen's dominion." The young slave boy grew to be a man of great influence. This humble and devout man, who possessed a faith that was "essentially African and essentially missionary," was ahead of his time, becoming the first "representation of the indigenous church principle" (Walls 1994, 137).

While the church in foreign lands was expanding rapidly during the colonial period, Christianity in Europe was declining. Despite a revival in the nineteenth century, the continent was largely secularized by the middle of the twentieth century. Christianity, however, was growing in hundreds of cultures on other continents. "Once again, Christianity had been saved for the world by its diffusion across cultural lines" (Walls 1996, 22).

Global Embracing (1900–present)

During the past century, a new spirit has emerged in missions: the "old sending churches" increasingly recognize the importance of partnering with the global church. Mission is no longer "us" going to "them" but God's people working together to bring the gospel to those who have not yet been reached.

In 1910, John R. Mott organized and chaired the first World Missionary Conference in Edinburgh, Scotland. This conference gave birth in 1921 to the International Missionary Council, which became part of the World Council of Churches in 1961 (Neill 1986, 557). Albert Nevins says that "in the missionary conference of Edinburgh in 1910 the foundations for modern ecumenism and the WCC were set in place" (1971, 530). Through 2005, this movement had held thirteen major conferences, and Edinburgh hosted a centennial celebration of the movement in June 2010 (Günther and Cook 1997, 502–9; WCC 2009).

These world missionary conferences were primarily held in the context of the ecumenical movement (Günther and Cook 1997, 502). Roman Catholics and evangelical Christians had little impact on these conferences. Some evangelicals, such as Donald McGavran, distanced themselves, believing that the theological liberalism in some of the participating churches produced ambiguity about the primary task of Christian mission. Evangelicals held their own conferences, such as those at Lausanne (1974), Manila (Lausanne II, 1989),[5] and Cape Town (Lausanne III, 2010).

In the twentieth century, both Catholic and Protestant churches made strides toward indigenous leadership. The Catholic Church consecrated its first six Chinese bishops in 1926. By 1962, there were sixty-nine indigenous Catholic bishops, as well as a number of cardinals, from "mission" countries (Neill 1986, 523–24). Protestants' progress was slower (Latourette 1945, 24). However, in recent years they have made good progress in raising up indigenous leadership.

Other significant developments that have taken place since 1910 include the appearance of Pentecostal churches, with their fire for mission and their impact on Christianity, in underdeveloped nations. Former mission fields have become sending countries. For example, North America, now a major sender of missionaries, was once considered a mission field. The same is true for Asia, Africa, and Latin America. The twentieth century also saw nondenominational mission

5. Lausanne Occasional Papers from these and other meetings in the Lausanne tradition are available online at *www.lausanne.org*.

agencies, such as African Inland Mission,[6] SIM,[7] OMF,[8] and Frontiers,[9] emerge as the primary mechanism for missionaries.

Many have exerted great influence in the development of missions in the twentieth century. We will look more closely at Donald McGavran, David Bosch, Lesslie Newbigin, Paul Hiebert, and Ralph Winter.

KEY PERSONALITY: DONALD MCGAVRAN

Donald Anderson McGavran was born in Damoh, India, on December 15, 1897, and later became a third-generation missionary of the Christian Church (Disciples of Christ). He received his higher education in the United States, completing his Ph.D. at Columbia University following two terms in India (Hunter 1992, 158). He established the Institute of Church Growth at Northwest Christian College in Eugene, Oregon, in 1961, and the School of World Mission at Fuller Theological Seminary in Pasadena, California, in 1965. McGavran died on July 10, 1990, about three months after the death of Mary, his wife of sixty-seven years.

McGavran is best known as the father of the "church growth movement," but this distinction came later in life. In other writings, I have described how his missionary experiences shaped this perspective.

> McGavran's Church Growth perspectives were formed while ministering from 1923 – 1955 within the context of India, where colonial missionaries felt the need to not only Christianize but also civilize. Mission compounds were established as enclaves of the new civilization. Replicating the Western culture with which they were familiar and developing Christian ministries in these Western enclaves provided a sense of security for missionaries with little preparation for significant cultural adaptation. . . .
>
> Within this context McGavran challenged the missions community to shift from maintenance to ministry. He believed that the missions stations should be given to national church leaders to control and maintain. Missionaries should focus on evangelizing the lost and incorporating them into local churches. These missionaries (and the national leaders they train) should look upon themselves as identificational, incarnational ministers. The end result of this thinking was a massive

---

6. *www.aimint.org/usa* (Accessed March 24, 2013).
7. *www.sim.org/index.php/content/sim-history* (Accessed March 24, 2013).
8. *www.omf.org* (Accessed March 24, 2013).
9. *http://frontiers.org* (Accessed March 24, 2013).

> repositioning of personnel and resources into personalized forms of direct evangelism and church planting. (Van Rheenen 2004, 170 – 71)

McGavran reminded the church that its mandate was not to get "decisions for Christ" but to make disciples, which, in his view, required incorporating believers into churches. To McGavran, church growth was a measure of faithfulness to the Great Commission. In order to maximize church growth, McGavran stressed the use of thorough research and strategic planning.

Prior to 1968, McGavran participated in the ecumenical missionary councils. He then had a radical change in his thinking. Reading preparatory documents for the Uppsala conference, he concluded that "the World Council of Churches and all its member denominations would be turning away from mission as Christianization to mission as humanization. Instead of seeking to disciple *panta ta ethne* [all peoples], winning them to Christian faith, and multiplying churches among them, the effort would be to spread brotherhood, peace, and justice among all people regardless of what religion or ideology they espoused" (McGavran 1986, 54).

McGavran believed strongly that reconciliation with God is the primary goal of mission. He engaged in social ministries but maintained that good works "must never replace the essential task of mission, discipling the peoples of earth. Indeed, all these good deeds must help in its accomplishment" (McGavran 1986, 54).

McGavran encouraged missionaries to remove barriers inhibiting people from becoming Christians, except for the "stumbling block" of the gospel itself. He felt that "people like to become Christians without crossing racial, linguistic, or class barriers" (1990, 163). Churches therefore would be composed of "homogenous units" of people. Critics say that McGavran's "homogenous unit principle" leads to segregated churches rather than demonstrating unity among people of different races or social classes. The concept, however, is still highly influential in contemporary missions. Hunter points out that although the "term has largely been dropped, in favor of 'people groups' or 'peoples,' … in these current forms the concept has experienced an extensive impact" (1992, 160).[10]

10. Ralph Winter coined the term "unreached people groups" in his plenary address at the 1974 Lausanne Congress (Lausanne Movement 2010).

I am deeply indebted to Donald McGavran. Throughout the years my wife and I spent in Africa, he read our mission reports and occasionally sent personal replies and suggestions. I have always felt that his affinity stemmed from sharing a common heritage in the Restoration Movement[11] and from his intense desire to see churches grow among all peoples of the earth. As our team saw local church leaders maturing, and therefore contemplated phasing out of our work, he wrote, "Your ministry has demonstrated such receptivity that it is not time to retreat but to amplify forces. Instead of pulling missionaries out, you should amplify forces to win the winnable while they are winnable" (McGavran 1985). His message demonstrated not only his personal concern for us, but also his urgency for growth as the major criterion for missions effectiveness.

KEY PERSONALITY: DAVID BOSCH

One of the most important transitions taking place in global Christianity is the growing role of churches from the global south and east. David Bosch's personal journey reflects this shift.

Bosch was born in 1929 to South African parents who were loyal members of the Dutch Reformed Church. He received a "Christian nationalist" education and in his early years did not question the assumptions of apartheid. Bosch, however, experienced a "conversion of sorts" when, as a university student, he organized a worship service for black laborers on his family farm (Livingston 1999, 26). His rejection of paternalistic methods is evident when he later wrote that "as [missionaries] work with national churches, it is in a fraternal, side-by-side role instead of the paternal, I-lead-you-follow role of ages past" (Bosch 1991, 365).

Sensing a call to ministry, Bosch pursued a doctorate under Oscar Cullman at the University of Basel in Switzerland. After returning to South Africa, he worked for nine years among the Xhosa people of Transkei before a back injury forced him to leave this rugged rural labor. During his years in Transkei, Bosch strived to "integrate his experience ... with the scholarly insights of various anthropologists, theologians, and missiologists" (Livingston 1999, 27).

11. The Restoration Movement, frequently called the Stone-Campbell Movement, developed on the American frontier and is inclusive of three different streams: Churches of Christ, Christian Church (Churches of Christ), and the Disciples of Christ. McGavran was an evangelically oriented Disciple of Christ.

When he returned to Europe in 1959, Newbigin observed a timid church whose distinct message had been silenced by the Western scientific worldview.
(Michael Goheen)

In 1972, Bosch became professor of missiology at the University of South Africa in Pretoria and later served as dean of the faculty of theology there. He worked as an agent of reconciliation between the denominational and theological groups. Bosch participated in both the ecumenical and evangelical missions movements and attended most of their international gatherings. His book *Transforming Mission* (1991) is the most comprehensive and thorough study of Christian mission in the twentieth century.

KEY PERSONALITY: LESSLIE NEWBIGIN

Twentieth-century missionary and theologian Lesslie Newbigin left a lasting legacy by calling Western Christianity to rediscover its missionary identity. Born in 1909, he entered Cambridge University as an agnostic. Newbigin, influenced by an older, believing student, volunteered at a Quaker service center for unemployed miners in South Wales. While there, "he saw a vision of the cross touching, as it were, heaven and earth. The cross embraced the whole world and the whole of life" (Shenk 1998, 3).

Newbigin's conversion experience led him to begin serving in 1936 as a missionary in India with the Church of Scotland. In India, "he modeled what it means to contextualize Christian witness by immersing oneself in the language and culture of a particular people" (Shenk 1998, 3). Newbigin recognized that when the gospel is proclaimed in the cultural categories of its hearers, it also challenges culture. It is, at once, "at home" and "at odds" with the culture (Goheen 2004). His identification with the people and understanding of their culture led to his being named bishop of the Church of South India.

In 1959, Newbigin returned to Europe, where he served on ecumenical and mission bodies in London and Geneva for six years. He then returned to India as Bishop of Madras from 1965 to 1974. Upon his return to Britain, he ministered, taught, and wrote for the remaining twenty-four years of his life. Newbigin died on January 30, 1998 (Robinson 1998, 2).

In Britain, Newbigin observed a timid church whose distinct message had been silenced by the Western scientific worldview (Goheen 2004). Christianity had lost its place as "public truth" and had been relegated to the category of "private opinion." Cultural relativism brought into question the legitimacy of mission. Although "the culture of modernity" had its roots in Christian thought, it had "developed powerful defenses against the thrust of the gospel" (Newbigin 1998, 99).

Newbigin's vision of a cross that embraced the whole world and touched every area of life no doubt motivated his desire to help the church recover its voice in Western culture. Newbigin believed that mission is not merely a legitimate concern of the church; it defines the very nature of the church. He understood that "the church was instituted by Jesus Christ to be a sign of God's reign throughout the world. The church that refuses to accept its missionary purpose is a deformed church" (Shenk 1998, 6). Christian truth is public truth, not private opinion. As such, it makes a claim on people's lives.

> So the logic of mission is this: the true meaning of the human story has been disclosed. Because it is the truth, it must be shared universally. It cannot be private opinion. When we share it with all peoples, we give them the opportunity to know the truth about themselves, to know who they are because they can know the true story of which their lives are a part.... Thereafter the situation can never be the same. (Newbigin 1989, 125)

Newbigin applied his missionary insight directly to the Western church. What would "a genuinely missionary encounter between the gospel and this modern Western culture" look like? How could the experience of missionaries and the work of theologians be brought together to address the ineffectiveness of Western Christianity? (Newbigin 1986, 3).

Michael Goheen, who wrote his doctoral thesis on Newbigin's missionary ecclesiology (Goheen 2000), summarizes Newbigin's understanding of such a missionary encounter as "the recovery of three things: the public truth of the gospel, the missional nature of the church, and a missional analysis of Western culture" (2013).

In Europe, Newbigin was active in the Gospel and Our Culture movement. This movement inspired a parallel network in North America, which has provided much of the theological impetus for the contemporary missional church movement. Leaders in this network have acknowledged their debt to Newbigin. George Hunsberger notes, "The publication in 1986 of Lesslie Newbigin's book *Foolishness to the*

> I am deeply indebted to the writings of Lesslie Newbigin. I used his book *The Gospel in Pluralistic Society* in my graduate course at Abilene Christian University. Our ministry through Mission Alive has its seeds in his reflections that the church must once again take the gospel to a post-Christian Western culture, which is becoming not merely a secular society without gods but a pagan society with false gods.

Greeks, loosed a new wave of his influence among pastoral issues in the USA" (1998, 10). Contributors to *The Missional Church* acknowledge that "Bishop Newbigin and others have helped us to see that God's mission is calling and sending us, the church of Jesus Christ, to be a missionary church in our own societies, in the cultures in which we find ourselves" (Guder 1998, 5).

Lesslie Newbigin's influence on the church in Europe and North America illustrates the contribution that global missions makes to the universal church. Newbigin himself wrote, "It is now widely accepted that missions in the modern world must be multidirectional, that every church has a responsibility for world mission, and that there is a mission field in every land" (Newbigin 1998, 99).

Shortly after Newbigin's death, Martin Robinson wrote, "Few can match his astonishing contribution to the world of ecumenism and mission. His offerings include his writings, but beyond the written page his unceasing energies as a teacher, pastor and ecumenical statesman mark him as one that matched a keen mind with personal kindness and zealous conviction" (1998, 2).

KEY PERSONALITY: PAUL HIEBERT

Paul Hiebert (1932 – 2007) was born in India to second-generation Mennonite Brethren missionaries. He inherited his family's commitment to mission as well as the high value they placed on education. After completing his theological education at Mennonite Brethren Biblical Seminary (Fresno, California), Hiebert, like many other missionaries, studied anthropology. His field research and six years of missionary service in India led him to question the validity of colonial-era models of mission (Priest 2007). His search for more culturally appropriate yet biblical models dominated his lifelong dedication to a "trialogue" between theology, anthropology, and missions (Frykenberg 2007, 129; Cathcart and Nichols 2009, 209).

Hiebert intended to return to India after a one-year teaching assignment at the University of Kansas. That proved impossible, however, because of his wife's health. He then taught missions at a Mennonite Brethren seminary, and anthropology at the Universities of Kansas and Washington. Hiebert, however, "was unable to connect his professional achievements with his sense of calling ... struggling to link the free moments of his life to what really mattered, missions. For years he kept telling people that he and Fran would someday return to India as missionaries, only gradually acknowledging even to himself that this would not happen" (Priest 2007).

Hiebert was able to reconcile these roles when he joined the faculty of the Fuller School of World Mission in 1977. For the next thirty years, Hiebert successfully wedded his dual roles into a singular vocation as a missionary anthropologist (Frykenberg 2007, 128). In 1990, he moved to Trinity Evangelical Divinity School to provide leadership for the Ph.D. program in intercultural studies. After his wife's death, Hiebert modeled his home after the Indian "ashram," or spiritual hermitage, where students lived with him in community (Priest 2007).

Hiebert's themes of the "excluded middle," the "fourth self," and "critical contextualization" have been significant in missiology.

The Excluded Middle

During his time in India, Hiebert realized that traditional Western missions failed to provide solutions to the spiritual concerns that dominated the Indians' daily lives. Western theology addressed issues of ultimate reality, and Western scientific pragmatism dealt with the functional, mechanical issues of the world. Yet Western culture largely ignored "the middle level of *supernatural but this-worldly* beings and forces" or what Hiebert labeled "the excluded middle" (Hiebert 1982, 43, emphasis added).

In this middle level, "one finds the questions of the uncertainty of the future, the crises of present life and the unknowns of the past." People seek answers to questions such as, "How can one's future safety and prosperity be guaranteed?" "How can one cope during a crisis?" "Who is responsible for tragedies?" or "Who is guilty of crimes?" Because their theology failed to provide answers to such common questions, Western

> Paul Hiebert was my teacher, mentor, and catalyst. His course Phenomenology and Institutions of Animism, through Fuller Theological Seminary, was a catalyst to my own studies, leading to the writing of *Communicating Christ in Animistic Contexts* (Van Rheenen, 1991). He helped me understand the move from theology to practice, as reflected in chapter 3 of this book.

missionaries to India found themselves unprepared to understand and speak to practitioners of folk religions, which do address these everyday issues (Hiebert 1982, 43 – 45).

Hiebert taught missionaries to provide "a holistic theology [which] includes a theology of God in human history: in the affairs of nations, of peoples and of individuals. This must include a theology of divine guidance, provision and healing; of ancestors, spirits and invisible powers of this world; and of suffering, misfortune and death" (1982, 46). Those answers must, however, recognize the sovereignty of God and never reduce the power of God to a magical power that can be manipulated. "In religion, we want the will of God, for we trust in his omniscience. In magic, we seek our own wills, confident that we know what is best for ourselves" (Hiebert 1982, 46).

The Fourth Self

Mission agencies have long accepted the "three-self" model of the indigenous church, first enunciated by Rufus Anderson and Henry Venn in the 1860s. Young churches, according to this model, become independent when they are self-propagating, self-supporting, and self-governing. Hiebert, however, challenged the sufficiency of this model. To be truly independent, Hiebert asserted, a church must also become self-theologizing (Hiebert 1985).

Hiebert suggested a distinction between "Theology" and "theologies." Theology is ultimate truth as God perceives it, whereas theologies are local, partial, culturally bound, yet valid expressions of truth. He wrote, "We all see through a glass darkly.... But the fact that we are humans and see through a glass darkly does not mean that we do not see at all. We can read the Scriptures and understand them" (1985, 198).

Young churches must be allowed, even encouraged, to develop local theologies, "and if — for fear that they will leave the truth — we do not allow them to do so, we condemn them to spiritual infancy and early death" (Hiebert 1985, 208). New theologies answer new questions, address new cultural categories, and critique existing and developing worldviews (1985, 210 – 12).

Hiebert argued not merely for contextual theologies but for the development of a transcultural theology. Such a theology is necessary "to build a worldwide fellowship of believers,... to share in the mission of the church,... to help us see more clearly the cultural biases in our theologies and help us avoid the syncretisms that emerge when we contextualize our theologies uncritically" (1985, 219).

Critical Contextualization

Hiebert encouraged local theologies while recognizing that "uncritical contextualization" could open the door for syncretism. Hiebert contended that critical contextualization begins with *exegesis of the culture*. "The purpose here is to understand the old ways, not to judge them" (Hiebert 1987, 109). This is followed by *exegesis of Scripture*, in which "the pastor or missionary leads the church in a study of Scripture related to the question at hand." "This step is crucial," said Hiebert, "for if the people do not clearly grasp the biblical message as originally intended, they will have a distorted view of the gospel" (1987, 109 – 10). Christians who properly exegete both Scripture and their own cultures, as well as formulate a *critical response* to the unique questions raised by their own context, produce biblically faithful contextual theologies. Bringing these together, they evaluate local customs based on their new biblical understandings in order to determine the stance that they, as followers of Jesus, should take toward their traditions (Hiebert 1987, 110).

The editor of *Missiology*, which first published Hiebert's essay titled "Critical Contextualization," proposed that the article "has been employed as a theoretical framework in more missiology Ph.D. dissertations in the last twenty years than any other single missiological contribution" (Priest 2007).

KEY PERSONALITY: RALPH D. WINTER

Ralph Winter (1924 – 2009) helped shape the direction of cross-cultural missions when, at the International Conference on World Evangelization (Lausanne I), he called for the Western church to overcome its "people blindness" and see the world's unreached people groups. *Time* magazine recognized him as one of America's Top 25 most influential evangelicals. They said, "With his impassioned call in 1974 for Christians to serve the world's 'unreached peoples' by looking beyond national borders, Ralph Winter revolutionized what remains (even today) the true lifeblood of Evangelicals — missionary work overseas" (*Time* staff 2005).

Winter, who studied civil engineering (California Institute of Technology), structural linguistics (Ph.D., Cornell University), and theology (B.D., Princeton Theological Seminary), turned down a faculty position at Massachusetts Institute of Technology to serve among the Mam people of Guatemala. Reflecting years later on that decision, Winter said simply, "Between academics and mission, I chose the latter" (Winter 1995).

In Guatemala, Winter realized that Western theological training was inadequate for local church leaders. When the missionary establishment resisted his plan to provide medical as well as theological training, he started seventeen businesses to provide support for missions and churches. He also became a key architect of Theological Education by Extension (TEE), which was discussed in chapter 6 (Winter 1995; Pierson 2009, 196).

Winter's innovations in mission funding and theological education were the result of an inquisitive spirit. Paul Pierson wrote, "From the beginning [Winter] was asking new questions about the missionary enterprise in ways that combined his training in engineering, anthropology, linguistics, and theology" (Pierson 2009, 196).

After his service in Guatemala, Winter joined the faculty of the School of World Mission at Fuller Theological Seminary in 1966 and established William Carey Library in 1968. During that period, he was instrumental in forming the American Society of Missiology. In 1976, two years after his landmark address at Lausanne, he left Fuller to establish the U.S. Center for World Mission *(www.uscwm.org)*. Winter also created the course Perspectives on the World Christian Movement, which is taught around the world to educate believers about and call them to participate in the full scope of biblical missions.

The attention that Winter drew to unreached peoples at the 1974 Lausanne conference left a lasting impact on Christian missions. Pierson calls this Winter's "greatest contribution" (2009, 197). It has been hailed as "one of the milestone events of missiology" (Lausanne Movement 2010). Winter himself wrote, "The world has never known a more significant transition than we see in the period between the 1974 bombshell of the International Conference on World Evangelization held in Lausanne, Switzerland, and the end of the century" (Winter and Hawthorne 2009, xviii).

At Lausanne, Winter took issue with the increasingly popular idea that the task of Christian missions was complete since each of the world's nation-states had some sort of Christian presence.

> I'm afraid that all our exultation about the fact that every *country* of the world has been penetrated has allowed many to suppose that every *culture* has by now been penetrated.... Let us call it "people blindness," that is, blindness to the existence of separate *peoples* within *countries*....
>
> "People blindness" is what prevents us from noticing the sub-groups within a country which are significant to development of effective evangelistic strategy. (Winter 1975, 221)

Winter argued that though there were Christians in most countries, they often were culturally distant from their non-Christian neighbors and therefore unable to reach them through traditional evangelistic methods (1975, 213).

To facilitate a discussion of cultural distance as it relates to evangelism, Winter proposed a three-point scale (E – 1, E – 2, E – 3) which measures cultural distance between Christians and people they hope to reach with the gospel. E – 1, or "near neighbor," evangelism may be preferable and more effective, but Winter argued that "E – 1 evangelism is literally *impossible* where there are no witnesses within a given language or cultural group" (Winter 1975, 220).[12]

Where there are few or no Christians who can communicate the gospel in their context, Winter believed that cross-cultural evangelism (E – 3) was "our highest priority" (1975, 221). Twenty-five years later, John Scott emphasized the continuing importance of this commitment.

> In his landmark speech, Dr. Winter warned that it will take "radically new efforts of cross-cultural evangelism in order to effectively witness to these 2387 million [almost 2.4 billion] people." Today God is doing remarkable things among some of these peoples through such radically new efforts in cross-cultural evangelism — in places like India and China, and across Africa. Yet this forgotten fourth still make up over 28% of the world's population. (Scott 2010)

12. Winter's E-scale is explained more fully in chapter 10.

Conclusion

In a very real sense, this chapter is a continuation of the biblical story of a "missionary God" described in chapter 1. God, who created the world, who walked in the Garden of Eden seeking the man and woman who had sinned against him, who made a covenant with the people of Israel to have them be a light to the nations, who came to the earth in the person of his Son Jesus Christ, who formed another covenant people called to him by the proclamation of reconciliation with God in the person of Jesus Christ, *is the same God* whose Spirit ignited a Jewish movement on the day of Pentecost, who helped the early church survive catastrophic persecution to become a mighty movement shaking the very foundation of Roman idolatry and emperor veneration, who worked through monks and missionaries to spread the faith as the Roman Empire crumbled, who spread the gospel of peace in spite of the violent means of its messengers during the Crusades, who inspired missionaries to stand against the injustices of the colonial powers under whose flags they sailed, who opened eyes of understanding to other cultures, who called (and calls) his messengers regardless of gender or ethnicity to proclaim his sovereign power and grace to the nations, who continues to awaken his church through thought-shaping leaders, and who most often uses nameless, faithful servants to make his glory known.

In this chapter, we see the touch of God's hand on all of human history. It is a story of people in relationship to God, sometimes in harmony, sometimes in rebellion, frequently struggling to live faithfully under God.

REFLECTION AND APPLICATION

Questions

1. How did Christianity's move from a minority religion to the official religion of the Roman Empire affect its theology? Its role in society? Its global mission?
2. How did the monastic movement contribute to the spread of Christianity during the Middle Ages?
3. What examples from church history demonstrate the importance of communicating the gospel in local vernacular languages?
4. What were the positive and negative effects of the Crusades on Christian mission?
5. What theological reasons explain early Protestantism's hesitancy to engage in missions? What convictions led to overcoming these barriers?
6. What can missionaries from Western or developed nations learn from the story of Samuel Crowther about working with Christians from less developed regions?
7. How did Lesslie Newbigin's reflections on missions as a missionary in India enable him to lay the foundations of missional thinking in both Europe and North America?
8. Explain Hiebert's three-step process of critical contextualization. How would this process help you and a community of believers evaluate and make decisions concerning a certain custom in your own culture or in another culture where you currently minister?

Application

1. In what ways has persecution hindered Christian mission? In what ways has it served its advance?
2. With which of the key personalities discussed in this chapter do you most identify? Give at least two reasons why you are drawn to this missionary leader.

Personal Inventory

How has God spoken to you through this chapter? What is God calling you to do about it?

chapter 9

Becoming Incarnational

Illustrations of Incarnational Ministry

Beginning Illustrations

PRISON MINISTRY IN ASIA

A doctor and nurse in Asia wanted to treat patients in a notorious prison hospital. They finally got permission but were forbidden to share the gospel. When they arrived, the smell was unbearable. The toilets and ward were filthy. They could only stay one hour. They decided on their next visit to clean the toilets and ward. They asked a local church to help. Cleaning supplies, gloves, gowns and masks were assembled. Everything was scrubbed clean, even the toilets. The gospel was not proclaimed in words. The authorities were overwhelmed. They now allow the volunteers to treat the prisoners anytime, with complete freedom to speak of Christ. (Moffitt 2006, 13)

RELATIONAL MINISTRY IN INDONESIA

Robert, a pastor in Indonesia, hired an elderly lady to help around his house and to help him learn the native language. She was very slow in her work. But she was not hired just for her labor, but for her soul. She was strong in her Muslim faith and often tried to convert Robert. Daily they prayed and ate and worked together. When Robert didn't receive his support for three months, this helper found ways to provide for his family. She saw Robert deal with a difficult adoptive daughter. She saw him give generously to those in greater need than himself. After two years of living with Robert and his family, this woman became a follower of Jesus. Now she has been equipped as a missionary to her own village. After three weeks, fifteen of her friends and relatives desired to be baptized. Now there are over one hundred believers in her village. (Lausanne Committee 2005, 10)

CHURCH PLANTING IN UGANDA

As part of my research for a master's thesis, I interviewed leaders of various religious groups in Uganda for the purpose of correlating their philosophies of ministry with the growth of their movements (Van Rheenen 1976). In this research I discovered the tendency for missionaries to create foreign institutions through which they attracted Ugandans into their movements. Missionaries felt extremely uncomfortable ministering where they did not know the language and culture of the peoples, and they therefore created training schools to teach the Bible in the missionaries' language and culture. I termed this method of pulling people out of their cultures and into the missionaries' arena *extraction*.

Few missionaries choose the difficult process of learning the local language and culture, personally teaching people the way of God, nurturing them to minister effectively within a body of Christ, and training them as Christian leaders. I began to call this process *identification* and later *incarnation*. As I compared extraction and identification as approaches to mission, I always found a direct correlation between the growth of religious movements and the personal relationship of their leaders with specific national peoples.

Beyond Identification to Incarnation

A DEFINITION OF IDENTIFICATION

Missionary identification is empathy between communicants involving a compassionate, interpersonal, reciprocal sharing of feelings and concepts. Empathy means that the missionary understands the local culture and feels the people's struggles, triumphs, defeats, and temptations. Christian

In their Introduction to Missions class, Jim and Julie were asked to respond to the question, "What does it mean for us to live like Jesus?" They pondered the motivations and incarnation of Jesus after reading Philippians 2:3–8:

> Do nothing out of selfish ambition or vain conceit. Rather, in humility value others above yourselves, not looking to your own interests but each of you to the interests of the others. In your relationships with one another, have the same mindset as Christ Jesus: Who, being in very nature God, did not consider equality with God something to be used to his own advantage; rather, he made himself nothing by taking the very nature of a servant, being made in human likeness. And being found in appearance as a man, he humbled himself by becoming obedient to death—even death on a cross!

"What does it mean to live 'in humility'?" they asked. "How do we think and minister with the 'mindset' of Christ? How does Christ's incarnation shape our personal ministry?"

empathy, however, is not the blind acceptance of the local culture. Christian missionaries must approach a new culture knowing that God must be sovereign over every facet of culture even though Satan has distorted significant elements. Although missionaries are frequently called to introduce radical changes in worldview, they do so with empathy and love for the people.

> Empathy means that I understand why my people are what they are no matter what they are.... Without approving polygamy the missionary must understand why his people are polygamists, and without tolerating fetishness or promiscuity he must understand why his people venerate fetishes and are promiscuous.... Although empathy is internal, it is nonetheless clearly perceptible to the local people, and it is a prerequisite for genuine apostolic identification. (Luzbetak 1970, 96–97)

Missionaries therefore feel the struggles of people as they grapple with Christian teachings, and rejoice with them as they make Jesus a part of their culture.

Identification is characterized by *sharing*, which Nida defines as an active "participation in the lives of people, not as benefactors but as co-workers" (1990, 230). It necessitates standing *with* new Christians, not standing *over* them. Evangelists who identify with the people learn to build a traditional house by participating in the building. They learn about death by ministering to the dying and to their families. They learn the significance of a rite of passage by witnessing the event and conversing with participants about its function in society.

During my thirteen years of working with the Kipsigis tribe in Kenya, I developed empathy with Samuel arap Koske and his wife, Mary. We walked together as they were unable to conceive a child and later suffered together as we buried their stillborn baby in the corner of our yard. Together we prayed seemingly unanswered prayers, sought to understand, and asked God for even greater faith. Sharing these struggles with Samuel and Mary opened a whole new realm of cultural understanding concerning procreation in an African setting. Personal identification opens the door to cultural understanding.

INNER AND OUTER IDENTIFICATION

Identification is more than physical conformity. One can live among a people — eating their food, living in their houses, and making a living as they do — without truly identifying. For example, a European construction worker and his family lived among the Banyoro people of Uganda for economic reasons, in order to save money, but they never learned to communicate with their neighbors. They even ridiculed Banyoro customs and lifestyle. Missionaries can mimic a lifestyle without understanding the people they are living among. Physical conformity, sometimes called "outer identification," should not therefore be equated with "inner identification," the heartfelt empathy discussed in this chapter.

Sometimes, however, outer identification does enhance inner identification. After one of our children began to crawl, we bought a large rug for our living room floor. Many Kipsigis visitors, accustomed only to bare floors, walked around the edges of the room and jumped to a chair so that they would not step on the rug. We soon replaced the large rug with a smaller one that we could easily take up when visitors came.

Another mission team in a remote area spent their first four years building houses and a compound. During a political campaign, the opposition party accused them of being spies. As evidence, the accusers pointed to the missionaries' "luxury homes," their radio towers, diesel generators, four-wheel-drive vehicles, and the absence of any visible evangelistic or church-planting activity.

This mission team was shocked, sometimes refuting these charges and sometimes attributing the attack to Satan. One introspective team member, however, confessed, "It is possible that we have been accused of being CIA agents because people perceive us as rich, selfish, impatient white Americans rather than as ambassadors of Christ."

It is wise for Western missionaries ministering in poorer areas of Asia, Africa, Latin America, and Eastern Europe to have simple (or modest) lifestyles. This is fitting for Christians who are dedicating their resources to Christian ministry, and it minimizes the economic gap between them and the people they are ministering among. In Kenya, we lived in a cement block house with a concrete floor and tile roof. The house had both running water and electricity. Although it was substantially better than the thatch-roofed, mud-walled houses of most Kipsigis, the house portrayed neither excessive affluence nor cultural separation.[1] If a missionary's house is of such luxury that local people feel uncomfortable visiting, or if unusual elements of the house dominate conversation when nationals come, some changes should be made. In many parts of today's world, it would be naive for missionaries to live in thatch-roofed houses when people around them are saving money to build houses roofed with tiles or corrugated iron.

INCARNATIONAL MINISTRY: REDEMPTIVE IDENTIFICATION

Christian missionaries, however, must strive to go beyond identification to incarnation. Incarnation is redemptive identification, expressed through empathetic relationships used by God to transform the heart, the mind, and the soul. Not only must missionaries identify with, and minister in terms of, the local culture; they must do so as God's ambassadors, his representatives in that particular culture.

It is possible to identify without being incarnational. In 1966, a year after Vincent Donovan joined the Roman Catholic mission established among the Maasai of Kenya, he wrote a letter to his bishop explaining the state of the work there. By Donovan's account, the mission priests had identified with the local culture. They established strong friendships with the local people; they visited and even slept in their homes. They drank their traditional drinks of milk and honey beer and attended the Maasai circumcision ceremonies.

1. In this discussion, I have only briefly dealt with the relationship between inner and outer psychological identification. For further consideration, read Grigg (2004) and Bonk (1990).

Despite their commitment to identification, however, the mission priests were failing to embody the gospel. Donovan wrote,

> But never, or almost never, is religion mentioned on any of these visits. The best way to describe realistically the state of this Christian mission is the number zero. As of this month, in the seventh year of the mission's existence, there are no adult Masai practicing Christians from Loliondo mission....
>
> That zero is a real number, because up until this date no Catholic child, on leaving school, has continued to practice his religion, and there is no indication that any of the present students will do so. (Donovan 1978, 15)

Donovan proceeded to discredit the prevailing assumption that adult Maasai communities could not be taught and converted directly. He began to offer extensive teaching to adults in Maasai villages. Often, as he concluded his times of teaching, many people would make collective decisions to accept the message, be baptized, and form communities of believers.

Incarnational missionaries identify with their hosts because they are committed to God's work of redemption among them. They develop deep relationships because God is relational. They communicate in people's heart languages — ones learned from birth — so they can give verbal witness to the good news of Jesus. Incarnational ministry is identification that extends the redemptive purposes of God.

JESUS CHRIST: THE INCARNATION OF OUR MISSIONARY GOD

God, in the person of his Son, Jesus, came into the world in the ultimate demonstration of his missionary heart. Jesus Christ is the perfect example of incarnational ministry. His very name, Immanuel, "God with us" (Isa. 7:14; Matt. 1:23), reveals that the man Jesus is the incarnation of divinity. Christ existed in the form of God but set aside his transcendence[2] in order to identify with humanity. He humbled himself by becoming human and dying in a human way for human sins (Phil. 2:5 – 8). Christ — God himself, the one and only Son — the Word, "became flesh and made his dwelling among us" (John 1:14). He became

2. God is both "transcendent" and "immanent." In his transcendence, he is unique, holy, and exalted. In his immanence, he draws near to humans for our redemption.

human in order to reveal God to humanity. By becoming human, Jesus Christ became the presence of God among his people *and* the supreme example of how Christians relate to the world.

The "enfleshing" of God is so radical and total that it is the bedrock upon which rests all subsequent acts of God in his world.
(Michael Frost and Alan Hirsch)

Qualities of Incarnational Ministry

Christians are called to imitate the character of God (Eph. 5:1). God tells his people, "Be holy, because I am holy" (Lev. 11:44 – 45; 19:2; 20:7; 1 Peter 1:15 – 16). Through the incarnation, Jesus Christ revealed the nature of God in tangible, cultural forms. Incarnational missionaries strive to accomplish this same purpose. Though humans are imperfect, God uses these "jars of clay" to transmit his message, demonstrating that the "all-surpassing power is from God and not from us" (2 Cor. 4:7).

Incarnation is much more than a method or strategy. It defines the missionary's existence in the world. Michael Frost and Alan Hirsch, in *The Shaping of Things to Come*, say,

> When we talk of the Incarnation with a capital *I*, we refer to that act of sublime love and humility whereby God took it upon himself to enter into the depths of our world, our life, and our reality in order that the reconciliation and consequent union between God and humanity may be brought about. The "enfleshing" of God is so radical and total that it is the bedrock upon which rests all subsequent acts of God in his world. A halfway house on the way to God would not do for a lost humanity, and so God had to come down to man, not halfway but the whole way. (2003, 35)

Hugh Halter and Matt Smay insist that "becoming incarnational is not so much about our direction; it's more about how we go, what we do as we go, and how we are postured in the culture God calls us to engage. Incarnation is the personality of our proclamation" (2010, 56). Missionaries strive, through the power of the Holy Spirit, to display many facets of the character of God. This section will discuss some of the most important for cross-cultural ministry.

COMPASSION LEADING TO INTIMATE RELATIONSHIPS

The compassion of God is central to incarnational ministry. The word *compassion* literally means "feeling or suffering with" another. In the same way that God wept over the sin of Israel and expressed his love for her (Hosea 11:1 – 8), incarnational missionaries who have internalized God's love cry over the brokenness and alienation of this sinful world.

Jesus' ministry demonstrated the compassion of God. He was continually "*moved* [or *yearned*] with compassion" (Matt. 9:36 NKJV, emphasis added) when he saw that the multitudes were "harassed and helpless, like sheep without a shepherd" (Matt. 9:36). This compassion led him to touch the untouchable leper (Mark 1:40 – 42 NKJV), feed the hungry multitude (Matt. 15:32), and give sight to two pleading blind men (Matt. 20:29 – 34).

Jesus came to *serve*, not to *be served* (Matt. 20:28). He existed in "the form of God" but took on "the form of a servant" (Phil. 2:5 – 7 ESV). When we adopt this attitude and serve in the name of Jesus, we embody God's presence in the world.

Compassionate love characterized Jesus' interpersonal relationships with the family of Lazarus. Jesus loved Lazarus and his family (John 11:5). When Lazarus died, Jesus saw his sister Mary and her friends weeping. Feeling the pain of people he loved, Jesus was "deeply moved in spirit and troubled" (v. 33), and he also wept (v. 35). Jesus was not weeping because Lazarus had died; he had just acknowledged himself to be the "the resurrection and the life" (v. 25). He was empathetically feeling the pain of those he loved.

The love of Jesus Christ is demonstrated in his incarnation. Jesus gave up life in holy heaven to dwell on sinful earth (John 1:14), relating with humanity. He came as the Great Physician, healing the sick and ministering to the poor and outcast. He defined his ministry by quoting Isaiah:

> *The Spirit of the Lord is on me,*
> *because he has anointed me*
> *to proclaim good news to the poor.*
> *He has sent me to proclaim freedom for the prisoners*
> *and recovery of sight for the blind,*
> *to set the oppressed free,*
> *to proclaim the year of the Lord's favor.*
>
> (Luke 4:18 – 19)

It is difficult for humans to fathom divine compassion. God so loved the world that he entered into the human arena of sin and brokenness. He became the Savior who dared to enter a burning house and rescue his children. By his love, his children have been saved!

Fielden Allison, my coworker for thirteen years, epitomizes such compassionate love in his life. Kipsigis Christians knew they could call on him to carry their dead from the hospital to their compound for burial. They knew he wanted to pray with and minister to their sick. They knew he would help them with their livestock and crops. They knew he would accept them as guests in his home. They knew he would love them even if they strayed from their faith. They knew his life was committed to helping them in the love of God. To the Kipsigis, this life of compassion was more important than his skills as a teacher or missionary strategist.

One great measure of incarnation is the degree to which missionaries compassionately enter into the suffering of their people. Such redemptive identification is not an external facade designed to create artificial congeniality; it is the heart of God incarnate in the missionary.

INTERPERSONAL RAPPORT

A second characteristic of incarnational ministry is interpersonal rapport. God's revelation of his Trinitarian nature teaches us that intimate relationship exists in the very being of God. The Father, the Son, and the Holy Spirit, although distinct, dwell together in perfect unity. Jesus therefore prays to the Father, saying, "You are in me and I am in you," and we, living within their fellowship, must dwell together in "complete unity" (John 17:20 – 23). As people made in God's image, we are intended for relationship. As God's representatives in the world, incarnational missionaries demonstrate God's nature by building and ministering through authentic relationships.

This was evident as Jesus participated in his apostles' day-to-day life. His three-year ministry included personally helping twelve men, as diverse as a tax collector and a Zealot, understand the true nature of the kingdom of God as they participated in his ministry to the masses. The effect of such personal engagement is seen in the transformation of Andrew, Peter, and John.

When Andrew and another disciple heard from John the Baptist that Jesus was the "Lamb of God," they followed him. They asked Jesus, "Teacher, where are you staying?" He answered, "Come, and you will see." That evening they stayed with Jesus, who was willing to give his time to sharing life with these two men. Andrew wanted to tell others about his newfound friend. He located his brother Simon and brought him to Jesus. Jesus immediately began a dialogue with Simon about his name, thus establishing a personal bond between them (John 1:35 – 42).

When they first met, Jesus renamed Simon "Cephas," or "Peter," which means "rock" (John 1:41 – 42). Yet the Gospels frequently portray Peter as rash, confused, impetuous — anything but a rock. After acknowledging Jesus as the Son of God, Peter took him aside to rebuke him for saying that the Messiah should die (Matt. 16:13 – 23). He denied Jesus three times during his trial (Matt. 26:69 – 75). Following the crucifixion, Peter returned to fishing (John 21:3), but Jesus called him back to apostolic ministry and exhorted him to "feed [his] sheep" (vv. 15 – 17). Under the hand of the Divine Potter, this struggling fisherman became the rock of the early Christian church and was given the keys of the kingdom of heaven (Matt. 16:18 – 19). Simon's life was transformed by Jesus.

The transforming influence of Christ's incarnational ministry can also be seen in John, who was changed from a "[son] of thunder" (Mark 3:17) to the "apostle of love." For example, John and his brother wanted to call down fire from heaven to destroy Samaritans who would not receive Jesus (Luke 9:51 – 55). John, however, became "the disciple whom Jesus loved" (John 13:23). In later life, John's writings reflect the love that had invaded him. He grasped, perhaps more clearly than others, that God's essential nature is love (1 John 4:7 – 8).

Though Paul was not one of the original twelve apostles, his personal investment in others reflects the practice of Jesus. Paul's personal relationship with specific churches and individuals is illustrated by the numerous greetings found, for example, at the end of his letter to the Romans. Paul included personal greetings to twenty-five individuals, three churches, and two households (Rom. 16:3 – 16). He also conveyed the greetings of eight brothers working with him (vv. 21 – 24). In many of his letters, he recorded prayers for churches and individuals (Rom. 1:8 – 10; 1 Cor. 1:4 – 9; Eph. 1:15 – 23; 3:14 – 21; Phil. 1:3 – 5; 1:9 – 11; Col. 1:3 – 8; 1 Thess. 1:2 – 4; 2:13; 2 Thess. 1:3; 2:13; 2 Tim. 1:3). These prayers show Paul's intense concern for people and his desire to maintain long-term relationships with them.

Paul, like Jesus, trained leaders interpersonally. Training seems to have occurred within the context of a community of evangelists traveling and ministering together. At times, Paul had seven (Acts 20:4) or eight (Col. 4:7 – 14) traveling with him, ministering with him, and learning from him. John Mark (Acts 13:5) and Timothy (16:1 – 3) were two such missionary apprentices. These evangelists were then left behind at newly established churches.

RECIPROCITY

In addition to compassion and interpersonal rapport, incarnational ministry also implies reciprocity. Reciprocity is mutual respect, mutual sharing, and mutual giving. God's relationship with humanity takes place in the context of a reciprocal covenant typified by the theme, "I will be your God, and you will be my people" (cf. Ex. 6:7; 19:5 – 6; Lev. 26:12; 1 Peter 2:9 – 10). Jesus Christ interacted with people in authentically human ways. He asked the Samaritan woman for a drink, and when she provided it, he reciprocated by offering her living water (John 4:7, 10). This relationship is described in "one another" passages in Scripture, such as "Be kind and compassionate to one another, forgiving each other, just as in Christ God forgave you" (Eph. 4:32).

Incarnational missionaries realize that people will respond to them in the way that they respond to others. They must learn in order to teach, appreciate in order to be appreciated, love in order to be loved, and forgive in order to be forgiven. They must share their own joy in order for others to share their joy (Phil. 2:17 – 18).

Reciprocity requires transparency — an opening of one's life and personality. Reticence to openly portray inner feelings, struggles, hopes, and temptations hinders identification. At the Inter-Varsity Missionary Convention in 1961, Anglican bishop of Uganda Festo Kivengere said, "How can I open my 'box' when the missionary's 'box' is not only closed, but has a lock on it?" (Kivengere 1962, 27 – 29). When communicants open their souls to one another, tremendous power is unleashed. People who share — though different in culture and background — become one in heart and soul (Acts 4:32). For example, the Great Revival in East Africa began after missionaries and nationals began confessing their faults to one another (Van Rheenen 1976, 64).

In the very early stages of our work in Kenya, while I was still learning the language and trying to understand new cultural perceptions, I shared my frustrations with a group I was teaching. They were from the Luo tribe but were working in the Kipsigis tribal area. As I told of my struggles, these Luo brothers began to express the temptations and problems they faced while living away from home and working in a different tribal area. This time of fellowship and sharing created an empathy that drew the Christian community together.

These three characteristics — compassion, interpersonal rapport, and reciprocity — define incarnational ministry. An incarnational approach enables missionaries to enter empathetically into human relationships, guided by God and attuned to his purposes. Like Jesus Christ, the living Word in flesh, we do not separate ourselves from people by means of impersonal programs and institutions. Rather, as God's ambassadors, we must become the Word in flesh dwelling in the midst of people.

Contrasting Incarnation and Extraction

How did Jesus relate to people? To me, the answer is found in the distinctive way in which God in Christ entered the world. Michael Frost and Alan Hirsch, in *The Shaping of Things to Come*, write,

> For us the Incarnation is an absolutely fundamental doctrine, not just as an irreducible part of the Christian confession, but also as a theological prism through which we view our entire missional task in the world. So when we talk of incarnational mission, we hope to, in some real way, directly draw inspiration and motivation from the unique act whereby God entered into our world and into the human condition in the person of Jesus Christ. (2003, 35)

The two approaches to ministry presented in this chapter, incarnation and extraction, are general frameworks devised to enable Christian ministers to examine how they relate to unbelievers within their communities.[3] They are analytical categories to help Christian ministers evaluate present evangelistic ministries and plan future ones. *Few*

3. Current writings frequently contrast the incarnational and attractional approaches of missions. However, since God's gospel by its very nature *is* attractive, as light shining in darkness, *extractional* seems a more appropriate term.

missionaries or missionary programs are exclusively incarnational or extractional. Rather these descriptions are extremes on a continuum bound by redemptive identification at one end and extraction at the other. The approaches of incarnation and extraction will be contrasted in five different areas.

Incarnational missionaries humbly go to the field as learners. Extractional missionaries expect to be teachers without prioritizing learning.

1. PERSPECTIVE ON LEARNING

Recognizing that they know only their own culture, incarnational missionaries enter a new ministry environment humbly, taking the role of learners. They understand that they must be learners before they can be teachers. Extractional missionaries, on the other hand, expect to be teachers without first learning. They assume that their university education qualifies them for ministry. They enter the new culture thinking they have the answers, when in reality they do not yet know the questions.

2. PERSPECTIVE ON RELATING TO PEOPLE

Incarnational missionaries regard the local people as equals and have reciprocal relationships with them. Not only do they eat their food, sleep in their homes, and understand local problems; incarnational missionaries also welcome nationals into their homes and their lives. In contrast, extractional missionaries prefer that the local people learn in the missionary's own environment, where he feels at home and in control. They rarely, if ever, eat local food, sleep in homes of local people, or perceive local problems. On the other hand, as Erwin McManus observes, "Jesus did not come into this world and live His life on a mountaintop isolated from human suffering. He walked among us, ate with us, and shared in our humanity. He did not heal lepers from a distance, but touched them into wholeness" (2003, 111). Halter and Smay, recognizing that church planters in North America often find themselves in cross-cultural situations, suggest that incarnation is closely tied to context. They write, "Context takes time to develop and unpack. And that's why you must learn to engage the culture with the primary motivation of becoming friends, weaving a web of relationships across a region of a city" (2010, 56).

3. PERSPECTIVE ON LANGUAGE

Incarnational missionaries learn the language of the local people. They know that culture is communicated by verbal symbols and consider language learning the most important tool of culture learning. Extractional missionaries, however, feel little need to learn the local language but assume that they can adequately communicate the gospel through translators or by teaching nationals who know English. They assume that these English speakers will become Christian leaders and eventually launch the Christian movement. They sometimes rationalize, "All world cultures are learning English and becoming like ours anyway." Consequently, they expect their students to know their language, or they use a translator.

4. PERSPECTIVE ON USE OF INDIGENOUS THOUGHT FORMS

Incarnational missionaries teach in ways people can understand. Realizing that cultures conceive reality differently, they use indigenous categories of thought. They struggle to adjust their teaching methodologies to fit local patterns of learning and reasoning. Extractional missionaries fail to perceive differences in cultures and continue to use Western thought categories. They assume that people can understand them if they teach exactly as they do in their own culture. They seldom perceive cultural dilemmas, because they have shunned intimate relationships with nationals, who could have become their culture tutors.

5. PERSPECTIVE ON MINISTRY

Incarnational missionaries personalize their ministry. Language learning and cultural understandings enable them to develop personal relationships with local people. They are not against institutions, but they believe that national leaders should help organize and oversee these institutions. Extractional missionaries, because of linguistic and cultural limitations, relate to nationals *only* through institutions. These institutions either provide translators to help missionaries bridge language and culture barriers or express the expectation that, as a prerequisite to study, nationals must speak the language and know

Figure 9.1 Incarnational vs. Extractional Missionary

Incarnational Missionary	Extractional Missionary
• Humbly goes to the field as learner.	• Expects to be a teacher without first learning.
• Empathetically goes to the people.	• Expects people to come to him.
• Learns the language of the local people.	• Expects others to learn his language or uses a translator.
• Teaches in ways people can understand. Uses indigenous categories of thought.	• Teaches in ways foreign to the people. Uses Western categories of thought.
• Personalizes his ministry.	• Relates to the people through institutions.

the culture of the missionary. Extractional missionaries are unable to study the Scripture personally with nationals in the people's native language or work with local Christians to implement appropriate programs and institutions for their environment. Consequently, they superimpose their own cultural perspectives and organizational programs on local people.

The Nature of Extractional Thinking

Extractional missionaries generally *assume that all people are alike.* They wrongly assume that people who wear Western clothes and speak English are just like them. They deduce that similar externals correlate to similar internals. In other words, they assume that all people think as *they* think, feel as *they* feel, and communicate as *they* communicate.

Quite often, new or short-term missionaries express the belief that people all over the world are basically alike. They see a child's fascination with balloons, a mother's tender care for her baby, or a man wearing Western styles of clothing and quickly judge that people everywhere are similar. They may initially write home to their friends, "People are people are people! We can use English here, and everyone knows what we are talking about." These new missionaries fail to understand that *locals are forced to identify with them!* And they are able to reach only people who have the formal education and/or international contact to use English effectively and understand foreign categories of thought!

Extractional approaches to missions *seldom focus on specific audiences.* In tribal societies, extractional missionaries do not distinguish between specific ethnic entities. Local people are identified as Kenyans or Ugandans rather than as Kikuyu, Kipsigis, Luo, and Kamba (peoples of Kenya) or the Acholi, Baganda, Ankole, and Bachiga (peoples of Uganda). Kenya has forty such ethnicities, Uganda twenty-two. In Africa, countries south of the Sahara have a mosaic of ethnic identities, with an emerging national culture developing in urban centers.

People of India are divided into castes. Castes are hierarchical rankings of people based on purity and pollution, two "pivotal concepts of South Asian thought" (Kluck 1985, 219–37). *Brahmans* are at the top of the scale because of their purity and abstinence from pollution. They must remain ritually pure in order to intercede with the gods on behalf of all the people. *Untouchables* are at the bottom because they have been born into castes that do polluting tasks. Numerous locally defined castes exist between the upper and lower ends of the scale. Lower castes perform more polluting tasks than do higher castes. Maintaining purity of caste and family is central to social relations in the Indian subcontinent. This social arrangement is the unifying feature of Indian society; it "transcends religious, linguistic, and regional boundaries" (Kluck 1985, 221). Extractional missionaries tend to see all types of people in this country as Indians and fail to recognize caste differences.[4]

The multicultural nature of most world-class cities makes them difficult to understand. In Singapore, socioeconomic status adds another layer of diversity to ethnic differences. Chinese make up about three-fourths of the population of this city, with Malays and Indians being principal minorities. Although Malays are traditionally Muslim and usually face strong family opposition upon conversion, receptivity to the gospel among Chinese and Indians depends more on socioeconomic class and education than on ethnicity (Hinton 1985; cf. Hall 1986, 2).

4. Recognizing the existence and importance of ethnic and caste distinctions does not mean that missionaries are unconcerned with the bias and injustice that are often perpetuated through such institutions. At times, living incarnationally involves modeling a Christian stance against the unjust attitudes, structures, and institutions of society.

North American cities are undergoing radical social transition. Once American cities, like American culture in general, were great melting pots where people of various national and ethnic heritages slowly merged into the mainstream American culture. Until the end of World War II, cities were the domain of the white middle class. After the war, affluent whites began moving to the suburbs as Southern blacks migrated to the cities. These blacks and destitute whites remaining in the city were soon joined by immigrants from throughout the world. These new immigrants, however, tended to live in enclaves and retained their own languages and cultures. As early as 1983, the Population Reference Bureau saw the United States developing into "a multicultural society, which while still predominantly English speaking, would tolerate and even accept other languages and cultures." New York, for example, became "a patchwork of thriving ethnic pockets ... with the arrival of thousands of Haitians, Jamaicans, Vietnamese, Koreans, Indians and others. Nearly 1 in 4 New Yorkers ... is foreign born." A Dallas journalist described how he could "walk four blocks and move through five cultures — upscale white, low-income white, black, Hispanic and Asian" (Chaze 1983, 49 – 51). By 2010, 33 percent of New York City residents were white, 26 percent Hispanic, 26 percent black, and 13 percent Asian.[5] Almost 40 million people, or 13 percent of the total population of the United States, were foreign born (Grieco 2012, 1 – 2). Eighty-five percent of these families spoke a language other than English at home (Grieco 2012, 15).

Since extractional missionaries do not typically differentiate between types of people, they are not equipped to focus on specific cultural problems. They consider all people within their host context to be "peas out of the same pod" rather than distinctive types of people.

Extractional approaches to missions *almost invariably create national churches and institutions dependent on outside sources for support and guidance.* Typical of Western-sponsored mission enterprises in the developing world is the mission compound. Mission compounds are initiated when missionaries select an area and enclose it for privacy. They build Western houses for their accommodations and construct

5. The Furman Center for Real Estate Urban Policy, "The Changing Racial and Ethnic Makeup of New York City Neighborhoods," *http://furmancenter.org/files/publications/The_Changing_Racial_and_Ethnic_Makeup_of_New_York_City_Neighborhoods_11.pdf.*

hospitals and schools to serve the community. Typically, the missionaries' houses are separated from the rest of the mission station by a hedge or a fence. Almost all contact with nationals occurs within the mission compound. The missionaries train leaders by bringing nationals to the compound for formal schooling and attempt to evangelize by sending compound-trained leaders back to their villages. Naturally, leadership training is limited to people who are able to speak the missionaries' language and understand their cultural framework. The cost of maintaining the compound makes it very difficult to turn the mission enterprise over to the national church without continued financial subsidy. The mission compound is an arena where the missionary can feel at home in the midst of a foreign culture.

This mission compound approach was first used by early missionaries who knew little about the indigenous people they had come to minister among. No pre-field training and orientation was available. They knew little about the new culture or the best way to reach the people with the gospel. Early missionaries therefore created environments that provided them with cultural and physical security in a foreign environment. Later missionaries frequently adopted this method of ministering and training and failed to consider more incarnational options.

Extractional approaches to missions tend to secularize non-Western societies. Though they want to bring greater Christian influence to societies, extractional missionaries lack the language skills and cultural understandings to meaningfully communicate a Christian view of reality and to contrast sovereign God with the people's traditional allegiances. Since communication is on a merely functional level, there is a vast disparity between what the missionaries intend to communicate and what they actually communicate.

For example, although medical missionaries intend to display the caring love of God, they may inadvertently convey the idea that spiritual beings (including God) have only limited power to overcome disease. Giving pills and therapy without prayer leads people to trust in medicine rather than in the Great Physician. Extractional missionaries (and other secularizing forces) thus unconsciously undercut spiritual concepts that could be directed toward faith in God's working through Jesus Christ. For medical missions to be holistic, missionary doctors and nurses must integrate teaching and prayer ministry with medical practice.

Likewise, Western schools, both church-related and non-church-related, frequently instruct students in the physical causes of ecological phenomena, such as rain, drought, and earthquakes. They fail, however, to teach about the Giver of rain and the One who holds the ecological system together (Col. 1:17; Heb. 1:3). This may lead to the belief that humans, with their scientific understanding, are self-sufficient, able to handle all obstacles in life, and therefore do not need God.

Extractional approaches *require a high degree of indoctrination and a long period of dependence on the missionary, because the frame of reference is foreign to the locals.* Christian concepts appear foreign because they are encased in unfamiliar illustrations and language and cannot be quickly integrated into past experience. Extractional missionaries believe that lengthy indoctrination is necessary because the people have been rooted in paganism for many years. They fail to grasp the life-changing power of the gospel that led Ephesian Christians to burn their books of magic (Acts 19:18 – 20) and motivated the Thessalonians to turn "from idols to serve the living and true God" (1 Thess. 1:9 – 10). Many years of indoctrination are necessary when locals are required to believe and act in the missionaries' accustomed ways. Missionaries must be willing to train locals to think for themselves and to answer theological questions on their own.

Conclusion

Incarnational missions is the most demanding yet most rewarding type of ministry. It is demanding because it requires missionaries to learn new languages, communicate the gospel through metaphors and parables understood by local peoples, and personally relate with people where they live, rather than expecting them to come to the missionaries. It is most rewarding because interpersonal relationships with Christians of other cultures enrich spiritual perceptions and broaden horizons. Above all, incarnational missions plants Christianity in such a way that the kingdom of God spreads organically and naturally within its recipient environment — not in a foreign language, a foreign place, with foreign metaphors. Paul writes,

> *Though I am free and belong to no one, I have made myself a slave to everyone, to win as many as possible. To the Jews I*

became like a Jew, to win the Jews. To those under the law I became like one under the law (though I myself am not under the law), so as to win those under the law. To those not having the law I became like one not having the law (though I am not free from God's law but am under Christ's law), so as to win those not having the law. To the weak I became weak, to win the weak. I have become all things to all people so that by all possible means I might save some. I do all this for the sake of the gospel, that I may share in its blessings.

(1 Corinthians 9:19 – 23)

REFLECTION AND APPLICATION

Questions

1. Define the term *identification*. Why is empathy important to identificational missions?
2. Discuss the relative importance of both *inner identification* and *outer identification* to missionary life.
3. Explain how the practice of *incarnation* goes beyond *identification*.
4. Describe the life of Jesus as the great illustration of incarnational ministry.
5. Describe the role of compassion in incarnational missions.
6. Describe how Jesus used interpersonal rapport in his ministry. Give an example.
7. Describe five general characteristics of extractional thinking, according to this chapter.
8. How have extractional approaches to missions led to secularization of cultures in various parts of the world? Be specific.
9. What is the *unifying feature* of Indian society? Into what types of groups are the people of India divided?
10. Briefly describe the current change in North American cities.
11. Define the term *mission compound*. Why were mission compounds originally created?

Application

From your experience, describe a domestic or foreign missionary whom you consider incarnational.

Personal Inventory

How has God spoken to you through this chapter? What is God calling you to do about it?

Case Study

Make a chart contrasting the approaches of the two missionaries who have gone to minister in the country of Zinzin. Each interchange illustrates one major contrast.

Missionary 1: When I went to Zinzin, I knew that I had much to learn. I wondered, "How will God use me as a Bible teacher and as a nurse?" I praise God that he gave me Basuben as my language and culture teacher. After a short time, he became not only my teacher, but also my brother in Christ. God has been teaching me so much, especially through Basuben.

Missionary 2: I came to Zinzin to be a medical missionary. Shortly after arriving, I found this man called Basuben. I hired him as my translator. Since I was trained as a teacher and a nurse, I opened my clinic to make contacts and then asked all contacts to come for Bible studies in the evenings. It is great to be a teacher!

Missionary 1: I have enjoyed visiting Basuben's house and talking and eating with his family. At first, the food and surroundings seemed strange, but now I am getting used to them. Eating with chopsticks has been especially difficult to learn. My family and I have decided to live with Basuben and his family for a month to learn their culture. Of course, I find that I cannot stay there without teaching people who do not know the gospel and treating any who are sick. It is also a joy to involve my family. I guess you could say that life has become ministry.

Missionary 2: Generally, I feel it is best for people interested in the gospel to come to visit me in my clinic and Bible study center. I like to separate my work time and my personal family time. Otherwise, these people will consume all my time and energy. We must not lose our privacy. I have instructed my children not to eat the food, and I will not eat it except on special occasions. My surroundings are very primitive, and I am frightened for the health and well-being of my family.

Missionary 1: The most difficult task for me is learning the local language. You see, I am not good at learning a language. However, I am thankful that my wife and children are gifted. Basuben has also been an exceptional teacher. While teaching us the language, he has also taught us how people think. I have discovered a most amazing fact: the words we use and how we think are intimately related! I am learning the Zinzini culture by learning their language!

Missionary 2: There is no need for me to learn the Zinzini language. Their young people are learning English, and English is the language of the future! Also, time is so limited. Should I delay working for a year and learn this language, when they are learning mine?

Missionary 1: I am attempting to teach the people of Zinzin in ways that they can understand. Because they believe in a number of gods and evil spirits, I am teaching them that Christ has defeated the evil powers on the cross; he has put them to open shame! Colossians 2:15 has become a significant verse in my teaching. I still have much to learn, but my new brothers and sisters in Christ have become my teachers. How could I possibly minister without them?

Missionary 2: People are people are people. What has amazed me is how similar people are around the world. I am teaching basically as I have always taught in the United States, and people seem to understand what I am saying. So Basuben says.

Missionary 1: The way I minister among the Zinzini is very simple. I am developing friendships, showing compassion through ministering to the sick, and teaching the gospel to people who have become my friends. Then they take me to their friends. I have more teaching opportunities than I can handle. However, Basuben and others are quickly becoming teachers themselves. They will soon be better teachers than I am.

Missionary 2: I have come to Zinzin to be a medical missionary. I have first established my clinic in the town. Constructing the building and getting licensed with the government has taken a considerable amount of time. My next project is the construction of a Bible study center to train church leaders next to the clinic. Maybe Basuben and others might even become preachers. Basuben sure is a good translator and might even become a Christian with some encouragement. I guess I need to study with him sometime.

chapter 10

Entering a New Culture

Learning to Be Learners Where Worldviews and Customs Are Different

Jim and Julie rejoiced because God was working powerfully through their youth ministry. They began to realize, however, that almost all the people in their youth community were upper-middle-class white students who liked basketball and football but had less interest in soccer.

What would it be like, Jim and Julie wondered, to be Christ to people of the other cultures within their school — those of African American, Asian, and Latino ethnicity or Muslim and Hindu heritage? The cultural distance between the students was evident within the school as well as within the broader culture. Could youth ministry provide an entree to all the people of their city, enabling their church to become multicultural — to be Christ to the whole community?

Jim and Julie enrolled in a Missionary Anthology class in the seminary where they were studying. They were pleased that the course not only helped them understand cultural diversity, but also provided ways to listen to and discern customs and worldviews that others hold. They began to perceive how peoples of other cultures hear the eternal gospel through different grids, through different stories and illustrations. They began to perceive that becoming multicultural would enrich not only them but also their entire church. Above all, the gospel would be preached to the nations — right here at home!

HUMAN BEINGS — whether they are Kipsigis of Kenya, Kalingas of the Philippines, urbanites of Caracas, or middle-class suburbanites of Kalamazoo — are influenced and shaped by their culture both before and after they come into a relationship with God. Missionaries

Defining culture in terms of diversity allows us to overcome the tendency to interpret all understandings of reality in terms of our own.

must therefore understand the concept of culture and how to minister in terms of, and frequently in opposition to, human customs and worldviews. This chapter helps equip the missionary to understand the nature of culture.

The Character of Culture

Cultures may be defined as *different perceptions of reality*. Defining culture in terms of diversity allows us to overcome the tendency to interpret all understandings of reality in terms of our own. This definition helps ease the mental rigidity of assuming that all people interpret the world as we do.

Nonverbal aspects of culture illustrate this cultural diversity. Different cultures frequently use the same form of nonverbal expression to convey two entirely different messages. For example, it is very common in Africa to see two men or two women holding hands. Visitors to Africa might interpret this custom through American eyes as a sign of homosexuality.

Two Americans who had both recently arrived in Kenya responded to this custom in totally different ways. One saw a national leader holding my hand and inquired, "What are you doing!" I attempted to describe the African meaning: "Holding hands has an entirely different meaning here. It means friendship or personal communication with a confidant." His spontaneous retort sprang out of his own cultural limitations: "Well, if a man holds my hand, I'll hit him!" The other American also saw men holding hands with men, and women holding hands with women, but asked, "What does this mean? Does holding hands have the same meaning here as in the United States?" His questions reflected his expectation that cultures are different and demonstrated that he was ready to enter the culture as a learner.

A gesture instinctively used by an American within his own cultural milieu may be an insult to a person of another culture. In the United States, curling one's index finger upward and toward oneself is used to invite another person to come closer. In Thailand, this is used only to summon animals. A person is called by placing the palm down and bringing the fingers to touch the palm (Cox 1999, 1–2). In American culture, sitting with one's legs crossed is a way to relax or to deal with a cramped seating space. In West Africa, it indicates one's status. Only an important person, such as a chief, sits with his legs crossed. When Westerners adopt this posture, locals see it as consistent with their status as important people, but it may communicate a sense of superiority that missionaries do not intend (Burk 2011). When missionaries saw the Makua people of Mozambique shrug their shoulders, look away to the side, raise their eyebrows, and say, "Eeeee," they interpreted this as meaning, "I don't know." Later they discovered that it simply means, "No" (Westerholm 2011).

Greeting rituals also vary widely. My former teammate Fielden Allison has compiled many examples from across Africa. Sudanese, for example, greet by first shaking hands, followed by hitting each other's shoulders several times. Women from the Sabaot tribe of Kenya place their right hand on the left shoulder of another woman in greeting. Some Nigerians greet by slapping the back of their hands three times before the traditional handshake. In parts of Uganda, women get on their knees to serve or greet people. In Malawi, women bow before their husbands, with the idea that if they cannot be humble before their husbands, then they cannot be humble before anyone.

Languages also reflect cultural diversity. Languages are composed of arbitrary symbols. While a set of symbols represents a particular idea in one language, in another language the same set of symbols may have a totally different meaning. For example, when Americans see the word *anyone*, they understand it to be an indefinite pronoun meaning "no person in particular." Kipsigis, however, pronounce *anyone* as *ah-nyo-nay*, and interpret it to mean, "I am coming." The combination of symbols (or letters) is the same, but the meaning and pronunciation are different.

The Kipsigis of Kenya frequently tell a story about a white farmer who owned land in the tribal area during colonial days. Because he and his sons spoke only English and their field laborers spoke only Kipsigis, the farmer hired an educated local man to serve as assistant farm manager. His job was to translate the owner's orders for the day and see that all assignments were carried out. One day, the Kipsigis manager was ill and could not come to work. The farmer himself was forced to give orders. He walked to where the Kipsigis were waiting for their work assignments and began with the words, "I want *six boys*." The farmhands heard the Kipsigis words *siks bois*, which literally meant, "kick the old men." Offended, the Kipsigis workers left, thinking, *That is just like white people! They have no respect for old people!* The colonial farmer, on the other hand, thought, *That is just like Africans! If there is work to do, they run away!* The colonial farmer and the Kipsigis workers reacted differently because they had different perceptions (interpretations) of the same reality (the arrangement of sounds to make words).

A Kipsigis man invited a new missionary, who was struggling to learn the Kipsigis language, to visit his home. While the missionary and the host were waiting for a meal to be served, others from the village came to greet the visitor. After exchanging greetings with the villagers, the missionary repeatedly heard remarks using the word *tondet*, or "visitor." Very sensitive to his inability to hear the words, he thought they were saying the English words "tone deaf." His response was, "I am not tone deaf; I am just beginning to learn the language!"

Ideas of personal *body space* vary between cultures. North American visitors to Latin American countries have misunderstood why nationals stand so close to the person they are conversing with. After a short-term mission trip to Honduras, a student remarked,

> When I was in Honduras this past summer, I was made aware that there was a difference with relationship to space in conversation. I was not aware that it was a cultural difference. I merely thought that the people were standing close to me in order to hear my broken Spanish over the roar of the passing vehicles. Naturally, I spoke a little louder, hoping that they would back away, but they did not. (Heard 1988, 1)

In many cultures, people learn to tolerate cramped conditions simply because they have no other choice. In Mozambique, passengers in taxi vans, called *chapas*, have coined a Portugese-based word, *sardinhar*, which roughly means, "to cram in like sardines" (Westerholm 2011). While Westerners would use a similar expression, they would be less likely to tolerate such conditions. Mozambicans accept the cramped situation because they value affordable transportation more than they value protecting their personal body space.

Physical objects are also understood differently. Two gourds hang on the wall in our kitchen—souvenirs of Kenya, mere wall decorations. In Africa, such gourds are used to store milk, beer, and porridge. They also have spiritual uses. Gourds are used by numerous medicine men and witch doctors. Some traditionalists think spirits are trapped in these gourds, and the witch doctors and medicine men call on these spiritual powers to solve villagers' problems. An African friend told me in his language that while he was visiting the medicine man, he had "seen a gourd talk." People holding Western, naturalistic perceptions would think this man was "out of his gourd"! A vast gulf exists between the secular beliefs of America and some animistic beliefs of traditional Africa.

A general comparison of *home life* illustrates that cultures represent different perceptions of reality. First, styles of eating are different. Americans believe that each person must have his own spoon, fork, cup, and plate. It is unhealthy for two people to eat off the same plate or with the same utensil. Many Africans, on the other hand, share food from a common bowl or basket. Eating is a time of fellowship and sharing. If one is guided by the germ theory of disease, the American way is better. If one emphasizes fellowship, the traditional African way is better.

Second, sleeping arrangements are different. American married couples expect to sleep together. Children have their own beds, usually in another room. Wives and mothers in most traditional African contexts, on the other hand, sleep with their children. The children feel secure because mother is near. Some African friends, when first visiting our house, assumed that the room with the double bed was for the mother and children, and they were surprised that we would force our children to sleep away from their mother. The American way is better if the relationship between man and wife is paramount; the traditional African way is superior if the security of the children is emphasized.

The American sleeping arrangement also reflects the value attached to the independence of individuals — particularly the goal that children learn to function independently of their parents. Other cultures attach a greater value to interdependence. A failure to recognize these differing values can bring confusion and even insult. An American missionary to Thailand reported,

> We had a birthday party for one of the Thai students at our church. We had a time of blessing for the birthday girl. One of the American interns complimented the girl for many things and concluded by saying the girl was strong and independent. I could see how hurt the girl was by the reaction on her face. She did not let the intern know at the time because she would have lost face. However, after the party she told her how her comments had offended her. In America, telling someone that they are independent is a great compliment. In Thailand,

> independence, in most contexts, is not a virtue because of the communal nature of the people. (Reese 2004, 5)

Third, family relationship patterns are different. American families are *independent* and *nuclear.* They are independent because the newly married couple live apart from both parental families and are not subject to tight parental control; they are nuclear because only husband, wife, and children make up a typical household. Many African families, on the other hand, are *patrilocal* and *extended.* Newlyweds in patrilocal families take up residence on the land of the husband's parents, and families are extended in that a number of close relatives live in proximity on family land. The preferred eating pattern in a traditional American family is for all members of the nuclear family to eat together, although sometimes family life is today so fragmented that families "eat on the go" without a common time and place for eating. Within many African extended families, however, men eat with other men, and women and children eat separately or later. American nuclear families emphasize a personal relationship between husband and wife; extended families in some traditional African cultures emphasize personal relationships among family members of the same sex. In traditional African culture, a man's wife may be a cook, housekeeper, and mother, but he goes to a brother or cousin for advice or when he wants a companion for a social event. American couples marry and begin "new families"; marriage in patrilocal cultures of Africa implies that wives become an extension of their husbands' families. The American family organization is logical to an American because the American culture stresses independence. The extended family is logical to a Kipsigis, who believes that economic and emotional security is provided by families.

Even the *sounds* we ascribe to animals illustrate cultural diversity. For example, American toddlers are taught that cows "moo" and roosters "cock-a-doodle-doo." Kipsigis youngsters imitate a cow by saying "maw" (with the vowel sound extended), and a rooster with "kukuruku" (koo-koo-roo-koo).

Music also reflects cultural diversity. American music is based on an eight-note scale and primarily uses major keys. Many Africans traditionally have five notes in their scale and prefer their songs to repeat short rhythmic combinations. Before serving with her family as missionaries to Italy, Alicia Little Walls, now an orchestra director, spent a year working with the church in Serbia. Reflecting on her experiences there, Walls observes,

> During my time in Serbia, I first became aware that emotional responses to major and minor keys are often perceived differently from one culture to the next. Granted, it does not seem like much of a revelation now, but since I was young and did not have a lot of exposure to other people and places before that time, it made an impression on me. American folk music has a predominantly major-key feel, with the proportionally few songs of a minor-key orientation in our folk literature being perceived as "sad songs." The use of minor keys is even less frequent in American hymnody than in folk music. In Serbia, as in many places in Eastern Europe, minor keys (or what would be perceived as slight variations on minor tonalities) are employed much more frequently than in cultures from an Anglo/Germanic tradition. People in Eastern European cultures do not necessarily experience the same subconscious reaction of "major = happy, minor = sad" which pervades much of our Western musical heritage. Music of a minor-key disposition is extremely frequent in folk music and hymns in Serbia. While a minor tonality could express sorrow or nostalgia, it could also just as easily evoke joyful emotions. (Walls 2010)

Culture is the integrated system of learned patterns of ideas, values, behavior, products, and institutions characteristic of a society.

Missionaries without cultural training tend to conclude that people all over the world are more alike than different. The preceding discussion, however, has demonstrated that cultures are both diverse and similar and that different perceptions of reality may be equally valid or invalid.

Defining culture as "a people's perception of reality" is helpful as a beginning tool for understanding the diversity of world cultures. This definition, however, does not adequately define the concept. *Culture is the integrated system of learned patterns of ideas, values, behavior, products, and institutions characteristic of a society* (adapted from Hiebert 1983, 25).

Culture is *integrated* because its components "function as an interrelated whole" (Haviland 1987, 37). Culture is *learned* when children are enculturated by family and peers to understand their environment. Culture is not a hodgepodge of miscellaneous traits without rhyme or reason but is patterned and systematic. Culture is composed of five elements:

1. *Ideas,* mental images through which people perceive reality
2. *Values,* the worth, importance, and ethical input of ideas
3. *Behavior,* the observable ways of doing things in culture

4. *Products* or artifacts that make up visible, material culture
5. *Institutions,* the organizational structure of a culture

Culture is formulated within a specific *society.* The word *society* refers to the people who use the customs of a culture and hold to its beliefs. Culture is the road map followed by a society while traveling through life.

Cultural Validity

Cultural validity, from a Christian viewpoint, is the anthropological perspective that cultures are essentially equal to one another but are ultimately judged by God. Missionaries therefore should never imply that their own cultures are superior or that others' are inferior. All cultures have strengths and weaknesses. Compared with tribal societies, Western peoples have strong technologies and economies. Because of their superiority in these areas, Westerners who do not recognize their own weaknesses might be convinced that their culture is superior to other cultures. Tribal societies are characterized by strong social cohesion, emphasizing family, lineage, and clan relationships. Tribal peoples, critical of Westerners' intense individualism and lack of respect for elders, might perceive their own culture as superior.

All cultures simultaneously demonstrate the original goodness of creation and the satanic brokenness resulting from its fall. Cultures exhibit both a proclivity toward sin, which alienates them from God, and attributes of goodness, reflecting divine presence. Africans who follow traditional religion believe in a Creator God but continue to seek guidance from various personal spiritual beings and impersonal forces. Unfortunately, they perceive God to be distant and removed from the everyday concerns of humanity. Westerners of an Enlightenment[1] heritage believe that the world is closed to spiritual influences and controlled

1. "Enlightenment" refers to a philosophical and cultural movement that gained popularity in mid-eighteenth-century Europe (though its roots were much earlier). It placed supreme value on the human intellect, science, and reason and minimized the truth claims of "superstition" and religion. Enlightenment philosophers believed that with their intellectual developments, humanity had finally come of age. Though no longer the dominant worldview of most philosophers, Enlightenment thinking continues to have a profound impact on Western society.

only by "laws of nature." God is excluded from the world he created. Yet these same Westerners view time as linear and have a strong sense of justice, reflecting a Christian heritage. All cultures therefore reflect the influence of both God and Satan in their own ways.

Some missionary anthropologists, borrowing from sociology and social anthropology, have adopted the expression *cultural relativity* to express the perspective that cultures have various strengths and weaknesses and should not be quickly judged by outsiders (Grunlan and Mayers 1979, 26). The term implies that cultures must be "evaluated according to [their] own standards, and those alone" (Haviland 1987, 45; cf. Grunlan and Mayers 1979, 26). From a biblical perspective, however, God often brings nations under judgment, even when cultural insiders believe that things are going well. "When they measure themselves by themselves and compare themselves with themselves, they are not wise" (2 Cor. 10:12). Cultural participants are never wise to judge themselves by their own standards. Although cultures are both valid and invalid because of divine and satanic influences, God is their ultimate judge.

Cultural Distance

Cultures vary in how they see themselves similar to or different from one another. People of similar cultures tend to relate to one another more naturally. Ralph Winter[2] described types of evangelism according to the cultural distance between teachers and people being taught (Winter 1999a, 339 – 55). These designations refer to *cultural* rather than *geographic* distance.

E – 1 evangelism occurs among people who speak the same general language as the missionary and have a similar cultural heritage. When believing Americans teach other Americans of a similar heritage, or Kipsigis teach Kipsigis, or Chinese teach Chinese, E – 1 evangelism is taking place. These missionaries do not have to learn a new language and comprehend a new set of thought patterns. Cultural sensitivity and adaptation, however, are required in E – 1 evangelism, since a significant cultural gap remains between Christians and non-Christians because of vastly different worldviews.

2. The role of Ralph Winter in world missions is described in more detail in chapter 8.

E–2 evangelism is an intermediate category between E–1 and E–3 evangelism, describing Christian outreach to cultures that have some type of general similarity to that of the evangelist. Learning a new language and a somewhat different worldview, however, is necessary. This type of evangelism occurs when Anglo-American Christians teach first-generation Spanish-speaking Hispanics in the United States, Latinos in Central and South America, or Germanic-speaking people in Europe. These languages and cultures have some similarity with American language and culture and are not as culturally distant as those of Africa and Asia. E–2 evangelism also takes place when Ghanaian or Kenyan evangelists travel to unreached areas in Africa to bring the gospel to other Africans not of their immediate ethnic heritage. These African missionaries would have to learn other languages and new patterns of cultural thought to communicate the gospel effectively to the people of these tribes. Yet the cultural jump would not be as great as for Americans or Asians evangelizing in these contexts.

E–3 evangelism occurs when missionaries teach people of a significantly different language and culture. Examples of E–3 evangelism include Kipsigis teaching people of Asian or European heritages, Anglo-Americans teaching Hopi Indians in the Hopi language, and North Americans proclaiming the gospel in Asia and Africa. E–3 evangelism is taking place when Kipsigis Christians teach American secularists or when American Christians teach people of an African ethnic group who are Islamic or hold to traditional African religion. In E–3 evangelism, the cultural gap is wide.

E–0 evangelism (not designated by Winter) is Christian proclamation to nominal Christians who attend our churches but have not embraced Jesus as Lord. They may have accepted Christianity as a type of superior culture or as good ethical training for themselves and their family. Some nominal believers have merely ascribed to the faith of their parents.

Understanding these designations enables the missions community to communicate the task of world evangelism. In the majority of situations, evangelism is most effectively carried out on the E–1 level. The purpose of E–2 and E–3 evangelism is *to bridge cultural barriers to establish responsible, vigorous churches that are effectively reproducing in their contexts.* E–3 missionaries cannot evangelize the world by themselves. They must think of themselves as soldiers going into battle to form beachheads of the gospel in hostile, Satan-held territories. As the newly established churches mature, E–1 leaders are nurtured so that they can lead their people to live under the reign of Christ.

Missionaries wanting to enter E–2 and E–3 contexts must go through a period of extensive learning before they are able to minister effectively in their new cultural contexts. They must learn their adopted people's language and cultural ways of thinking. E–2 and E–3 missionaries must learn to communicate God's message with appropriate metaphors and illustrations without losing its core essence. They must learn how to personally relate to people of their new host cultures. For example, they must learn how to give and receive gifts, how to express hospitality, and how to show respect, in order to minister in cultural contexts that are foreign to them.

The need to understand and appreciate other cultures is relevant to both Western and non-Western missionaries. African Christian College in Manzini, Swaziland, draws students from throughout southern Africa. Part of their training includes evangelizing among the local Swazi population. Because they do not know the Swazi language or culture, however, many have trouble communicating and may be rejected by the local population (Allison 2011).

Some who read this section may express the popularly held belief that because these language and culture gaps exist, it would be better to support locals and bypass missionaries altogether. In fact, K. P. Yohannan calls Western support of locals the "third wave" in world missions. He argues that since Western missionaries are rarely effective in Asia, Western churches need to provide prayers and finances for only *local* evangelists (2009). His mission agency, Gospel for Asia, based in Dallas, Texas, raises millions of dollars for the support of local evangelists.

Many dangers, however, are involved in this approach. Often, these local evangelists are preachers for local churches rather than church planters in unreached areas. In other words, the American church begins to subsidize local leadership doing E–1 evangelism rather than supporting new movements in other ethnic areas. If the local evangelist is not accountable to strong local leadership, Americans risk giving to causes "that really are little more than private enterprises for raising money for the promoter and his family" and "whose ministry is either grossly exaggerated or even non-existent" (Hedlund 1990, 275).

The greatest danger for American churches that support only local evangelists is the tendency to believe that sending their money is sufficient. There is no need to send their sons and daughters.

D. Preman Niles (2004, 81 – 83) highlights several reasons why the international exchange of missionaries is important to the universal church. One reason is that it demonstrates the global nature of the church, that sending and receiving churches are all part of one body. A second reason, Niles says, is that "missionary exchange today can demonstrate in a tangible way what partnership in mission is all about if the power of money does not control the sharing of personnel" (2004, 81). In addition, crossing new frontiers and boundaries has always been essential to the expansion of the church. Missionaries are, by definition, people who cross those frontiers. Today's frontiers, however, are not only geographic, "but also ideological, political, economic, religious, racial, and so on" (2004, 82), requiring the equipping of both domestic and foreign missionaries.

The greatest danger for American churches that support only local evangelists is the tendency to believe that sending their money is sufficient. There is no need to send their sons and daughters. Coggins says that without *personal* involvement in world missions, the entire mission enterprise in Western churches will be dead within a generation (1988, 204). Although partnerships with local churches are desirable, Western churches must never cease preparing, sending, and supporting their own missionaries.

In some cases, people closest to home are the least likely to convert adjoining cultures or people within their own culture. The Christian minority of Pakistan has little contact with the 97 percent of the population who consider themselves Muslim. They are also the least likely people to be accepted by the Muslim majority (Winter 1999a, 340). Although Kipsigis are geographical neighbors of the Kisii, Luo, and Maasai of Kenya, they are ill equipped to teach them the gospel. Incessant intertribal feuds, cattle raids, and competing political alliances within the country have created such animosities that many Kisii, Luo, and Maasai would not accept a Kipsigis evangelist in their midst. American missionaries working as E – 3 evangelists are more effective than Kipsigis as E – 2 evangelists in these contexts. Also, in contexts where the culture of the sending church is idealized by the host culture, E – 2 and E – 3 evangelists might be allowed to communicate the gospel in ways not open to local leaders. This has been particularly true in urban contexts such as Manila, Singapore, and Nairobi, cities accommodating to Western ways. In areas where no vibrant local church exists, cross-cultural evangelists must be trained to carry God's message.

The church of Jesus Christ needs each type of evangelist. E–0 evangelists are needed to revive nominal churches and nominal Christians within vibrant churches. Thousands of E–1 evangelists are needed to initiate new churches in their own culture. The church focusing on domestic missions, however, must not neglect God's mission to the world. E–2 and E–3 evangelists are used by God as bridges into other cultures to initiate new church movements. Their cross-cultural work tends to also broaden the cultural and spiritual horizons of their sending churches.

The principle of cultural distance is important in understanding not only the challenges of international missions, but also the increasingly cross-cultural nature of Christian mission in North America and other Western cultures. Alan Hirsch, an Australian observer of the American religious scene, has adapted Winter's E-scale to create his m-scale, which measures barriers that hinder the communication of the gospel (2006, 56–57). Hirsch describes mission in Western contexts as occurring on a continuum ranging from m0 to m4. On Hirsch's scale, each number constitutes "one significant barrier to the meaningful communication of the gospel" (Hirsch 2006, 57). Possible barriers include language, culture, and race — the kinds of barriers encountered in international missions. In North America, the growing number of subcultures represents not only immigrant groups, but also lifestyles (e.g., gay and lesbian communities), music (e.g., hip-hop), social groupings (e.g., gangs), and others.

Hirsch describes people who fall between m0 and m1 on the scale as having some understanding of Christianity and sharing similar interests, nationality, and perhaps even social class with Christians in their community. People falling between m1 and m2 may be suspicious of Christianity, which may stem from bad experiences with church or Christians. People at m2 to m3 on the scale are probably antagonistic to Christianity, though their knowledge is sketchy, and may "include people marginalized by WASPy Christianity, e.g., the gay community" (Hirsch 2006, 57). M3 to m4 represents people who are highly resistant to the gospel, such as "ethnic and religious groups like Muslims and Jews," whose cultural background presents "many roadblocks to meaningful communication of the gospel" (Hirsch 2006, 57).

In the past, most people whom Christians encountered fell into the m0 to m1 category. Communicating the gospel to this group was fairly straightforward, since non-Christians shared the same cultural assumptions as their Christian neighbors. Through an extractional model, or what Hirsch calls "*outreach* and *in-drag*," the church reached many of these people (2006, 61). Today, however, the proportion of non-Christians who fall into this group is rapidly decreasing. Christians find fewer people around them who share their cultural assumptions and worldview. Thus, communicating Christ in North America and in other Western cultures is becoming more and more cross-cultural.

Cultural Adaptation

Anyone moving from one part of the United States to another has experienced cultural adaptation. Southern culture is very different from that in New England or California. Moving from New York to Texas requires an adjustment of ideas and lifestyle. However, after living in Texas for an extended time, New Yorkers become comfortable with cowboy boots, Tex-Mex cuisine, rodeos, and other aspects of life in Texas. They become acculturated.

Acculturation is defined as the process by which adults acquire the knowledge, skills, attitudes, values, and behaviors that enable them to become functioning participants of a new host culture (Grunlan and Mayers 1979, 85). When individuals make aspects of another culture their own, they are acculturating.

Acculturation is for adults what *enculturation* is for children. Enculturation is the process by which children become functioning members of their own society (Grunlan and Mayers 1979, 76).

Both acculturation and enculturation involve learning new cultures. Children, however, are enculturated into their first culture more completely than adults are able to acculturate into a second culture. It is comparatively easy for children to adapt, because they have no previous cultural behaviors that need to be adjusted. Acculturating adults automatically compare their new culture with the one in which they have been enculturated, and frequently project the ideas of their original culture into the new culture. This makes acculturation much more difficult than enculturation.

CULTURE SHOCK

Frequently, people moving from one cultural context to another experience disorientation. They no longer know how to act appropriately in social situations. Familiar cultural props are gone, and a feeling of confusion arises. Kalvero Oberg coined the term *culture shock* to describe this feeling of disequilibrium. He wrote that culture shock is

> precipitated by the anxiety that results from losing all our familiar signs and symbols of social intercourse.... When an individual enters a strange culture, all or most of these familiar cues are removed.... No matter how broadminded or full of good will you may be, a series of props have been knocked from under you, followed by a feeling of frustration and anxiety. (1960, 177)

American missionaries are greeted with bear hugs and kisses rather than handshakes. American women are shocked by the aggressive nature of Latin men. Products have no firm price but are sold by bargaining. Eating customs, walking customs, pointing customs are all new. Americans may be uncomfortable having to eat with their fingers or with chopsticks. Language learning amplifies this pressure: missionaries struggle to voice new sounds that represent new cultural realities. A student who spent a year overseas describes her culture shock:

> It's the little things—not being able to work this funny foreign washer, not knowing what temperature to bake cookies on, not knowing how to answer the telephone, celebrating New Year instead of Christmas, not knowing how to respond to a kiss on the cheek, and the constant confusion with the language; just confusion—not unhappiness, but just confusion. It tends to magnify emotions. It's easy to swing back and forth from excitement to depression. (Little 1988)

American missionaries in culture shock are often preoccupied with cleanliness and health precautions. They may invest valuable time and energy making sure that water is boiled for the specified time and that all vegetables are sterilized. Fear of germs or parasites may cause them to forbid their children to go barefoot or play in certain areas. Their focus on efficiency and time management may lead to outbursts of anger over delays or other minor frustrations. This may significantly affect their influence in areas of the world where anger is considered a major sin. Their understanding of fairness may lead many of them to feel that they are always being cheated. They may fixate on the difficulty or the primitiveness of the language. They long for home and become nostalgic for anything American. They commonly think in terms of "us-them," comparing *our* ways to *their* ways.

> **Although Christian love is able to lead missionaries to respect and interrelate with the people, Christian love does not exempt missionaries from the effects of culture shock.**

Although Christian love is able to lead missionaries to respect and interrelate with the people, it does not exempt them from the effects of culture shock. Missionaries with little or no cross-cultural interaction are especially susceptible to culture shock. After hearing the material in this section, one ex-missionary said, "You must have gone with us and recorded everything we felt and said. Our performance was a classic case of not being prepared to enter another culture." Fortunately, effective training often reduces culture shock to culture stress and helps facilitate effective cultural adaptation.

STAGES OF THE MISSIONARY ACCULTURATION PROCESS

As monocultural missionaries strive to become cross-cultural, they typically go through three stages: (1) the glamor stage, (2) the rejection stage, and (3) the identification stage.

Glamor Stage

During this stage (also called the *honeymoon* or *fascination* stage), missionaries glamorize the superficial elements in the new culture. The land is beautiful. The thatch-roofed mud houses are quaint. Eating corn mush with one's fingers and drinking clabbered milk is considered proof that one is adapting. Missionaries tend to idealize the work among the people, making it more than it really is. Even having malaria can be an achievement of some importance! New missionaries are awed by everything they see. Statements such as, "Look at that lady carry that basket on her head!" "How can she carry all that firewood?" "Isn't it great that these people have all this time to sit under trees and talk like this?" illustrate fascination with the new culture. Urban missionaries may idealize the size of their city and its historical significance. Their optimistic proclamation that "God will become Lord of this city!" may fail to recognize the reality of the satanic principalities and powers that stand behind the laws, rules, and government of the metropolis.

Cross-cultural communication is limited during this stage. Since missionaries do not know the local language, they rely on English-speaking locals to translate what is said in the local language. These translations, however, typically filter out indigenous concepts.

Idealizing a culture without truly understanding it is naive. As cultural horizons expand, missionaries begin to realize that their idealized pictures of the culture are ill defined. Their translators or mentors have given only partial pictures of reality. They feel cheated! The psychological pendulum begins to swing from idealization to rejection.

Rejection Stage

Learning a new language and culture—operating in an unfamiliar arena—coupled with ignorance of the unknown, creates a high level of stress. This stress causes the pendulum to swing from glamorizing to rejecting the culture. The *rejection* or *fear* stage is characterized by anxiety. This anxiety is generated by the growing realization of how vastly different the new culture is, friction between conflicting ideologies, disappointment of learning the true motivations of some "friends," and fear of what is not yet known about the culture. Missionaries begin to experience the full sense of being in a foreign country, among people who are of a different culture.

During this stage, missionaries experience culture shock. They may feel that everyone is taking advantage of them and become unduly discouraged by the difficulty of language learning. Missionaries begin to talk of *us* and *them*, and nothing in the new culture is as good as things "back home." This idealization of their home culture might lead them to label their host culture with terms such as "primitive," "prideful," or "degenerate." Missionaries find themselves irritated by the inconveniences of shopping, driving, banking, and paying bills in their host culture. This frustration of trying to adapt to another culture may result in angry outbursts.

Training in cross-cultural communication prepares a person for the struggles involved in working in another culture. If the missionary enters the field believing that all people are basically alike, that language learning is not important, and that programs from home fit anywhere in the world, the psychological pendulum swing from idealism to rejection will be intense. If, on the other hand, the missionary has learned that cultures are diverse, that language is a key to understanding culture, and that the message must be presented in a manner that will be understood locally, both the initial glamor and the resulting rejection will be less pronounced. Pre-field preparation serves as a shock absorber — a buffer against culture shock.

Obviously, missionaries must find ways to cope with the anxieties they are experiencing. Coping strategies vary according to the psychological makeup and missiological background of the missionaries. A first reaction, when confronted with the realities of evangelistic work in a different culture, may be to *go home*, as John Mark did (Acts 13:13). This may be the best solution for people who recognize their own insufficiencies and accept them. Not all have the gift of cross-cultural missions. Some will become effective missionaries with more adequate preparation. Going home is not necessarily a negative reaction. Although John Mark returned home and Paul refused to take him on the second missionary journey (Acts 15:36 – 41), Paul later recognized John Mark as one who was helpful to him in his ministry (2 Tim. 4:11).

A second, more typical reaction to extreme cultural anxiety is to *withdraw.* Missionaries may seclude themselves in mission compounds or in their homes and offices and develop impersonal programs to help them avoid relating directly with their host people. By withdrawing, missionaries reject the participation in the lives of the people that is so necessary for effective communication. For example, one missionary spent hours in his apartment watching Western television programs. Another spent almost as much time traveling as he spent in his target city. Still another missionary built a high fence around his home, hired local Christians to screen visitors, and paid numerous local Christians as his evangelists. When he was made aware that many of these "evangelists" were relatives and friends and that very little church growth had occurred, the missionary humbly wrote that he was "dismayed and discouraged," admitting that he did not know what was taking place in his own area.

Other missionaries built a training institute in an urban center before local churches were initiated, chose students to be trained, paid the cost of their education, and after graduation provided them with a generous salary to start churches in their home areas. Small, scattered churches were planted, but no sustained growth took place in any one area. When a change of government brought anti-Christian forces to power and this particular church was banned, Christians melted into non-banned religious communities. These churches did not have the spiritual vitality to live faithfully under God during a time of persecution.

The missionaries who initiated the school did not learn local languages or immerse themselves in any one culture. Instead they withdrew from the people into a more familiar institutional setting. They required people to come into their comfort zone — Western environment, Western language, Western concepts and perspectives. Is it surprising that such an approach could not grow indigenous roots?

Withdrawal is as much psychological as it is physical. As the missionary retreats into his own "shell of culturally acquired beliefs, attitudes, and behavior; he becomes more and more unflinching in his determination to remain at all times a true blue-blooded American" (Luzbetak 1970, 99).

Withdrawal shows itself both in feelings that the local culture is primitive and in nostalgia for the home culture. The missionaries judge the local language to be inadequate to convey Christian truths. They reject traditional rites of passage as pagan or anti-Christian without understanding their function in society. They believe that the elderly, being steeped in tradition, are beyond hope, but with education the young might be redeemed. As these missionaries become more resentful of the local people, they grow more nostalgic for their home country.

A third method of coping with cultural anxiety is to *go native*. This is the process of abandoning the values of one's own culture and blindly accepting the values of a host culture. Luzbetak defines going native as "a neurotic longing for security and an exaggerated hunger for belonging" in a foreign culture (1970, 99). This blind acceptance of foreign values sometimes stems from a feeling of rejection and insecurity in one's own culture. Christian identification is necessary in order to teach eternal Christian values, but people who go native seek a new identity. Luzbetak contrasts Christian identification with going native: "While going native is selfish, apostolic identification is selfless, altruistic. While going native is a blind and indiscriminate reaction to cultural tensions, apostolic identification is positively willed, discriminating" (1970, 99).

The missionary who withdraws rejects the host culture and glamorizes his own culture; the missionary going native rejects his own culture

One element of effective adaptation is *learning to read the culture with the eyes of God.*

and glamorizes the host culture. Both are extreme reactions to cultural stress. Both accept one culture and reject another, failing to see the strengths and weaknesses of each.

Identification Stage

Rather than going home, withdrawing, or going native when confronted with cultural stress, the new missionary may make a conscious decision to *adapt*. Unlike the first three responses, adapting is not a blind reaction to the perceived perfection of one culture or hopeless imperfection of another. The new missionary struggling to adapt strives to see culture as it really is — with its strengths and weaknesses, its divine and satanic influences.

This adaptation leads missionaries to eventually enter the identification stage. In this stage, they feel at home in their host culture. They have become relatively fluent in the language so that they can be understood. They increasingly understand the cultural categories through which the people view reality. Their ministries of teaching, nurturing, and training have been defined while realizing that they will continue to change and develop. The missionaries are able carry out the tasks to which God has called them. Missionary families picture where they live as *home*. They have friends within the culture and know how to extend and receive hospitality.

How do missionaries adapt so they are able to identify with the local people and culture?

One element of effective adaptation is *learning to read the culture with the eyes of God*. This involves *personal identification* of the missionary family with local people. This learning of culture is a primary but difficult task for both domestic and international missionaries! Missionaries struggling to adapt realize that they bear the burden of identification. Rather than expecting the local people to identify with their way of life, they must learn the language and culture of the host society. *To be effective incarnations of Christ, they first become learners of culture.*

Several things are involved in this personal identification. First, missionaries must truly know themselves. For missionaries to identify, they must be comfortable with who they are as servants of God. Their ego is not on the line. They have nothing to prove. They are not servants

> Wine is an important part of the culture in the Republic of Georgia. Georgians have elaborate meals, an important part of which are toasts. These toasts may continue for several hours and take on religious significance. Because moral issues (such as drunkenness) and theological issues (such as toasting a saint) are involved, missionaries must discern how they will participate, if at all, in this important part of Georgian culture (Diles 1993). Do they completely reject such feasts as anti-Christian? Or is there a Christian way to toast with expressions of love and demonstrations of holiness? What will missionaries do when they are invited to a Georgian meal?

of a mission but servants of the Most High God. Second, learning of culture must become specific. For example, when missionaries are learning about kinship, culture mentors help them develop a chart that maps out the names for all kin relationships in the new language that the missionary is learning. When missionaries are learning about life cycle, these mentors describe each stage of life and the rites of transition (birth, coming of age, elder initiation, funerals) that might occur at various stages. In a focused, disciplined way, members of the missionary family become culture learners. Third, missionaries should practice the principle of reciprocity—as they come to know the people, they must also be willing to be known by them. In this learning, missionaries participate as coworkers in the lives of the people. In summary, personal identification involves honest love for the people. They become our teachers as we gradually learn to speak into their lives. Remember: Jesus spent thirty years on earth before launching his official ministry in his hometown synagogue (Luke 4:14–21).

A second element of effective adaptation is *continual self-evaluation*. Effective adaptation takes place only when new missionaries critically evaluate their reactions to the people and their culture. They must neither uncritically accept nor uncritically reject every new concept they learn. An American missionary who married a woman from his host country defended himself against charges of going native. Jokingly he gave this example: “My fiancée eats fish heads. I do not eat fish heads. It’s gross and I’ve told her so.” Fifteen years later, this couple has four beautiful children and are thriving as missionaries.

Missionaries must evaluate new cultural conceptions in light of God’s revelation in the Scriptures. They will learn great spiritual truths that they would never have grasped in their own culture. They will also realize, as their understanding of local culture increases, the great revolutions that

Figure 10.1 The Acculturation Process

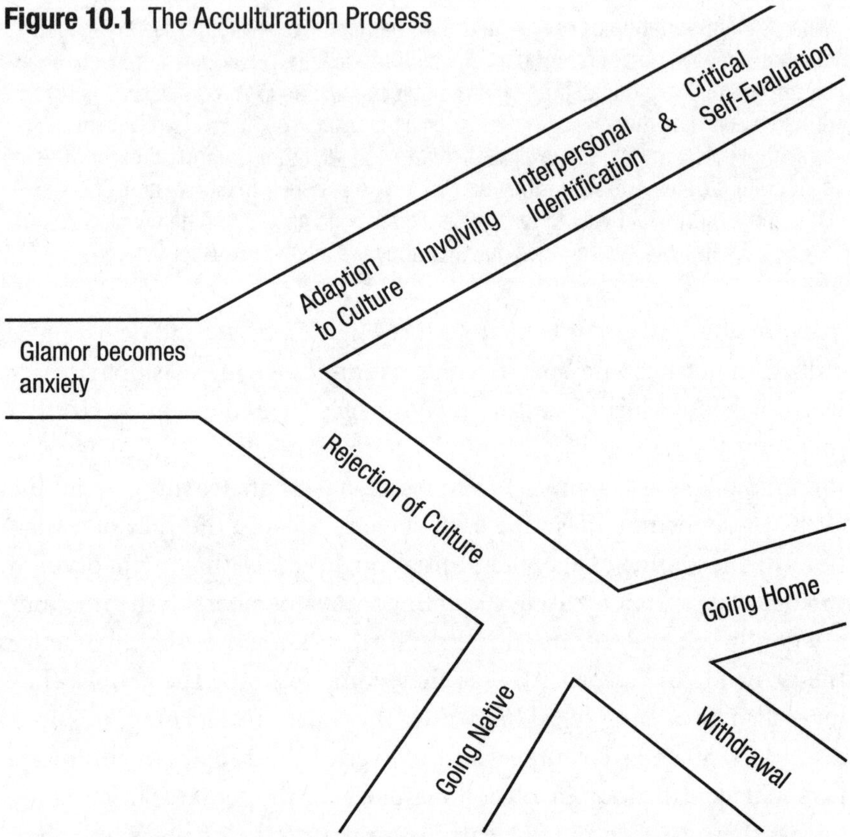

must take place in order for people of the host culture to be truly Christian. Effective adaptation can take place only when the new missionary attempts to perceive culture as it really is, rather than reacting to new cultural perceptions out of past personal or cultural biases.

The diagram above depicts the adaptation process. Initial glamor turns into anxiety as new missionaries realize their inability to communicate in the new culture or to conceive new perceptions of reality. At this point, they may reject the new culture by going home, withdrawing, or going native. On the other hand, they may decide to adapt to the new culture by personally identifying with it and critically evaluating their own reactions to it. It is important to note that the lower fork in this road is a two-way street. Missionaries who find that they are proceeding down the path of rejection may, through prayer and the power of the Spirit, reverse course and move toward the path of adaptation.

Conclusion

This chapter introduces the *culture concept*, which enables missionaries to more effectively learn a new culture. Learning that cultures reflect *different perceptions of reality* reduces the mental rigidity that hampers culture learning. Understanding *cultural validity* helps the missionary realize that all cultures have strengths and weaknesses and are ultimately judged by God. An awareness of *cultural distance* enables missionaries entering cross-cultural contexts to understand the need for adequate training. This awareness also awakens them to the necessity of nurturing new Christians so that they become E – 1 evangelists. This chapter describes how a missionary's fascination with a culture may turn into rejection. Missionaries learn that self-evaluation and personal identification will help them overcome culture shock and enable them to minister effectively in a cross-cultural context. The concepts of this chapter are foundations on which other concepts of missions are based.

REFLECTION AND APPLICATION

Questions

1. On a popular level, *cultures* have been defined as "different perceptions of reality" in order to prepare missionaries for cultural diversity. Give examples of cultural diversity that you have experienced.
2. Define *cultural validity*. Contrast the meanings of *cultural validity* and *cultural relativity*. How does understanding cultural validity equip future missionaries who will live and minister in other cultures?
3. Compare and contrast E–1, E–2, E–3, and E–0 evangelism and give brief yet specific examples of each.
4. How do these categories (as given in question 3) clarify the task of world evangelization? Describe specifically the major goal of E–2 and E–3 evangelism.
5. What is meant by the phrase *culture shock*? Give an example of it from your own experience if possible, or from this book.
6. Briefly describe the three stages of the missionary acculturation process.

7. Describe the psychological *pendulum swing* that occurs between the first and second stages of the missionary acculturation process. Then describe four possible ways to adjust to the anxieties of the second stage of this process.

Case Studies

As long as my husband and I stay in the town of Gboxikon, we have no time off. The work, ministry, and culture differences are constantly upon us. Living in this country is difficult and very different from living in the States. I am now more sympathetic to missionaries who retreat into their homes trying to escape culture stress. Like them, I am also tempted to withdraw into my private "America." I strive to create a comfortable house where we can retreat but also strive to be out with the people. My husband and I stay in the homes of local Christians during teaching trips once or twice a week, and we frequently walk uptown (instead of driving) to greet people along the way.

1. Which stage(s) of the missionary acculturation process are described in this scenario?
2. Describe the culture shock or stress that the missionary is undergoing. How well is she coping?

In the following cases, what type of evangelism (E–1, E–2, or E–3) is occurring in the work of each person?

"My name is Benjamin Koske. I live and work in Nairobi, Kenya, an international city of over three million. I once lived in the rural areas of western Kenya but have lived in Nairobi for twenty years. When I first moved to Nairobi, I was intimidated by the big city. I felt overwhelmed by the hundreds of people that I did not know and who passed by me without a greeting. In my local church, I was amazed by Amos Odia, who grew up in the city, knew its ways, and effectively preached there. Later Amos began teaching Sudanese refugees who have fled their country and settled in Nairobi. The founder of our congregation is a missionary from the United States who can speak to me and other first-generation people in Nairobi in Swahili."

1. Benjamin Koske:
2. Amos Odia:
3. The American missionary:

"My name is Tan Bock Hai. I am a Malaysian Christian who came to study in the United States. I was educated in a Chinese-speaking school and raised in a traditional family. In addition to Mandarin Chinese, I speak both Malay and English. While in the United States, I frequently share the gospel with those from mainland China whose first language is Mandarin Chinese. I feel more comfortable with my Chinese friends than with typical Americans."

1. Tan Bock Hai:

"My name is Miguel Gutierrez. I am a Latino Christian from Guatemala City evangelizing the Quiche Indians in the hill country of Guatemala. My first language is Spanish, the official language of Guatemala. My coworker is an American who has learned both Spanish and Quiche. Both the Latin and Quiche cultures have mingled cultural beliefs of both the Old and New Worlds."

1. Miguel Gutierrez:
2. The American missionary:

Personal Inventory

How has God spoken to you through this chapter? What is God calling you to do about it?

chapter 11

Becoming Multicultural

Overcoming Feelings of Superiority

Jim and Julie's study of missions at the seminary raised many questions about their roles as youth ministers within their local church. They noted that while the demographics around their church building were changing, the church was still predominately upper-middle-class Caucasian.

They felt that God was calling them to reach out to the neighborhood around the church building. They intuitively knew that youth ministry could give access to the Hispanic, Indian, and Arabic people who were moving into nearby houses and apartment complexes. Their young people were already in contact with these families through community activities, especially in the local schools.

They asked, "Is our church ready to welcome people of other cultural heritages? What about feelings toward new immigrants who do not yet know English? What attitudes and habits would have to change for us to become a multicultural fellowship?" They felt the ramifications of the words of Paul: "In Christ Jesus you are all children of God through faith, for all of you who were baptized into Christ have clothed yourselves with Christ. There is neither Jew nor Gentile, neither slave nor free, nor is there male and female, for you are all one in Christ Jesus. If you belong to Christ, then you are Abraham's seed, and heirs according to the promise" (Gal. 3:26–29).

Monocultural and Ethnocentric Tendencies of Missionaries

MEANING OF MONOCULTURALISM AND ETHNOCENTRISM

People who know only one culture and language are *monocultural.* Having limited cultural experience, they are largely unaware of the diversity of cultures in the world. They speak only their own language and think only in the conceptual categories of their culture. Monoculturalists generally project their own perception of reality onto people of other cultures and into other cultural milieus. Monoculturalism therefore is *the assumption that all other people are like "us," resulting in the tendency to judge other people's actions and attitudes on the basis of "ours."*

New missionaries, even those who have read and studied other cultures, are frequently monocultural. They have not learned to speak the language of their host people or communicate in those people's thought categories. Can long-term missionaries also be monocultural? Yes! In fact, monoculturalism can and often does continue after missionaries arrive on the mission field. This occurs when missionaries are isolated from their host culture, communicate with local people only through translators, and think of them as "developing Westerners."

In other words, monoculturalists who live or work in cross-cultural settings interpret reality through their own cultural assumptions. They presume that their ways are superior and thus arrogantly reject new perceptions of reality. This cultural pride, or *ethnocentrism*, may be compared with egotism. Egotism says, "My way is better than your way." Ethnocentrism says, "My culture is better than your culture." Egocentrism on the personal level is parallel to ethnocentrism on the cultural level (Kraft 1996, 70). Ethnocentrism is an extension of monoculturalism and the basis for racism, tribalism, and nationalism. It was at the root of the urban riots that inflamed America's cities during the 1960s and could recur anytime racial tensions increase.

Monoculturalism, in and of itself, is not bad. It is the result of growing up in one culture and knowing only that culture's perspectives. Monoculturalists have narrow horizons because their exposure is limited. Unlike ethnocentrism, simple monoculturalism does not involve the ego. Monoculturalists are simply unaware that the whole world does not operate according to the rules they know. However, because the terms *ethnocentric* and *monocultural* are very close in meaning, they are often used interchangeably.

Many American missionaries arrive on the field proud of the American way of life. Many also hold to a naturalistic worldview. They believe that the world operates according to natural laws, and they question all unseen powers. Missionaries from the United States tend to be individualistic. They assume that all individuals have unalienable rights, and special interest groups seek their "rights" without regard to the ultimate good of society. They believe that democracy is always the best form of government — even though the American form of democratic government is only about two hundred years old. Often, they see capitalism as the only effective way to organize an economy. They cannot conceive that these truths might not be self-evident to people of other cultures.

If missionaries are to identify with a new culture, they must first acknowledge their own tendency to be monocultural. While studying the local language and culture, they may then begin perceiving alternative ways of looking at reality. The purposes of this chapter, then, are threefold: (1) to help missionaries see their own monoculturalism, (2) to make them aware of their ethnocentricity, and (3) to provide them with tools and understandings to enable them to become multicultural.

ILLUSTRATIONS OF MONOCULTURALISM AND ETHNOCENTRISM

The following illustrate how monoculturalism and ethnocentrism affect the interpretation of events.

> Trayvon Martin was an unarmed seventeen-year-old Florida high school student who was fatally shot by George Zimmerman, a self-appointed neighborhood watchman claiming that the African American youth looked intoxicated. He saw the teenager cut through his neighborhood on a sidewalk between two townhouses and decided to give chase. In a dispatch to police, Zimmerman said that he was following a suspicious guy who "looks like he is up to no good or he is on drugs or something.... These a**holes, they always get away." Trayvon Martin's dad reflected, "I don't think he would be followed if he were a white kid."[1]

> During the short war with Iraq in 1991, President George Herbert Bush called for a National Day of Prayer. He declared, "At this very moment, America, the finest, most loving nation on Earth, is at war. At war against the oldest enemy of the human spirit — evil that threatens world peace." (Bush 1991)

> A professor at a Christian university claimed, "In the United States the Judeo-Christian ideals have reached their heights."

1. *http://abcnews.go.com/US/fbi-justice-department-investigate-trayvon-martin-killing/story?id=15955985.*

> A missionary periodical, *Russian Good News*, called for a lecturer to go to Russia to "show the American culture as it is influenced by the Word of God" (1990, 4). The front cover of that issue showed hands holding a Bible flanked by the American and Russian flags (1990, 1). If this symbolizes two countries being nurtured by the Word of God, that brotherhood exists under God, then this represents a Christian perspective. If, on the other hand, the symbol implies that the United States or Russia have Christian truths embedded in their fabric, its meaning is both ethnocentric and ill informed.

Ethnocentrism, of course, is not limited to one culture; people in most cultures are ethnocentric. While visiting a Kipsigis home and examining a Kipsigis artifact, I casually commented, "This looks like a Luo [another Kenyan tribe] object." Everyone looked stunned, embarrassed. Then a friend told me quietly, "That's an insult in Kipsigis. You see, Luo are like children. They are uncircumcised. To say something looks Luo is ridiculing what is Kipsigis."

A traditional Kipsigis proverb says, "One does not steal cattle from *people*" (Orchardson 1961, 41). The word *people* in the proverb refers to other Kipsigis. The proverb means that it is permissible to steal from others, such as the Maasai, Kisii, or Luo, but never from a fellow tribesman.

When an American in what is now the Czech Republic asked a priest if racism existed in Prague, the priest said, "No." Then the American asked, "What about the way people feel about gypsies?" The priest replied, "Oh, that's different. Gypsies are lazy and dirty" (Diles 1993).

Charles Kraft relates the following story.

> The fact that westerners are not the only ones who are ethnocentric came to me quite forcefully a few years ago when talking to a student from Vietnam. About halfway through the anthropology course, he said to me, "Now I realize that we Vietnamese are not supposed to make those mountain people into Vietnamese." I chuckled, because behind his statement lay the fact that the American missionaries working in his area had tried to make him into an American. He had rejected that, saying he wanted to be a Christian Vietnamese, but when he went as a missionary to the mountain people of Vietnam, he started trying to convert them to his Vietnamese culture. (Kraft 1996, 73)

Scripture indicates that ethnocentrism has always existed. In Joseph's day, Egyptians did not eat with Hebrews, because such table fellowship was "detestable to Egyptians" (Gen. 43:32). Agrarian Egyptians also considered shepherds detestable (Gen. 46:34). Jonah did not want God's compassion for his people's enemies; he wanted instead that they experience calamity (Jonah 1:3; 4:1 – 2). Jesus asked a Samaritan woman for water though Jews did not typically associate with Samaritans (John 4:9). Peter, likewise, acknowledged that it was "against [Jewish] law for a Jew to associate with or visit a Gentile." God, however, had shown him that he "should not call anyone impure or unclean" (Acts 10:28). When Jewish believers heard that Peter had visited in a Gentile home, they criticized him because he "went into the house of uncircumcised men and ate with them" (Acts 11:3). The Philippians were proud of their Roman heritage and blamed the Philippian riot on the Jews, who were "throwing [the] city into an uproar by advocating customs unlawful for ... Romans to accept or practice" (Acts 16:19 – 21). When Alexander spoke during the Ephesian riot, the mob, recognizing that he was a Jew, yelled for two hours, "Great is Artemis of the Ephesians!" (Acts 19:33 – 34). The Jewish mob in Jerusalem listened to Paul *until* he described how God had sent him to the Gentiles. Then they declared, "Rid the earth of him! He's not fit to live!" (Acts 22:21 – 22). Although God used Peter to open the mission to the Gentiles, he later "began to draw back" from fellowshiping with Gentiles, because of Jewish Christians who came to Antioch from Jerusalem (Gal. 2:11 – 14).

CHARACTERISTICS OF THE MONOCULTURAL/ ETHNOCENTRIC SYNDROME

The all-inclusive but cumbersome term *monocultural/ethnocentric syndrome* connects cultural pride to the narrow horizons behind it. In this discussion, "monoculturalists" refers to people who exhibit the monocultural/ethnocentric syndrome.

Monoculturalists equate their own perceptions of reality with reality itself. They make no allowances for different perceptions of reality. They believe that their views are the only true views. For example, secular Americans find it hard to accept the African view that anger takes upon itself an impersonal force of its own and can kill. Hitting with a stick hurts only the physical body. Hitting with anger hurts both body and soul. To most North Americans, anger is merely an emotion;

Monoculturalists equate their own perceptions of reality with reality itself. They make no allowances for different perceptions of reality.

it has no power of its own. Their cultural myth says, "Sticks and stones may break my bones, but words can never hurt me." To many Africans, witchcraft is an extension of anger: anger is able to generate an awful power that can kill or maim the people it is directed toward. Thus anger is a terrible sin because of its social consequences. The African belief that illegitimate babies usually are born dead, are deformed, or die at an early age is also illogical to secularists. They see few cause-effect relationships between sin and life.[2]

Secular Americans, along with many Christians, view dreams as the exercise of the unconscious mind during sleep; the mind plays as the body sleeps. Many Africans, on the other hand, believe that when people dream, their bodies remain behind while their spirits journey. Dreams are understood to be real life. People who do not believe that spirits of the dead even exist have great difficulty accepting the African belief that evil spirits are ancestors who have been neglected and have returned for revenge. Many African Christians believe that James 5:15 – 16 shows that some sickness is caused by sin, but American Christians generally believe that sickness is caused by germs or some malfunction of the body. Typically, the American naturalizes what the African spiritualizes. On a continuum with animism at one end and secularism at the other, these views on dreams, spirits, and sickness are polar opposites, yet each culture believes that its own perceptions are valid (Van Rheenen 1991, 95 – 102).

Monoculturalists assume that their beliefs were accepted because they are superior. Their forefathers, they suppose, looked at all the alternatives and selected only the best. Inferior ways were all rejected. Democracy, a relatively new form of government, is superior because it took the best from other governments and meshed them together. Some Americans believe that God led us to our worldview, our form of government, our economic system, and our social system. These Americans therefore relate Christianity and free enterprise and might consider the socialistic tendencies of the early Christian church as situational. Americans do not understand why an individualistic economic system will not work in a group-oriented society such as that of Japan. Production is the goal

2. Though many Americans do perceive a social relationship between sin and life, these perceptions are not typically spiritualized as in the African worldview.

of Western economic systems, but among many non-Western peoples, social interaction on the job is equally important. A monoculturalist fails to realize that there are numerous economic, political, and social alternatives from which the world's peoples might select.

Monoculturalists lack respect for other cultures or subcultures. This is reflected in terminology that monoculturalists use in reference to other peoples: their culture is *heathen*, ours is *Christian*; their language is *primitive*, ours is *advanced*; their beliefs are *superstitious*, ours are *religious*; they have *myths*, we have *history*; they are *underdeveloped*, we are *developed*; they are *childlike*, we are *mature*. Monoculturalists look down on other languages as primitive, other customs as heathen, and other people as crude, childish, pagan.

JUSTIFICATIONS OF AMERICAN ETHNOCENTRISM

Following are some specific devices that Americans use to justify their feelings of superiority.

Technological justification. Some Americans justify their feelings of cultural superiority by alleging that since their technology is superior, their culture is also superior. They say, "What other nation has put a man on the moon? Are there any other superpowers since the demise of the Soviet Union? Are we not the protector of the world?" We think, "Look at the poverty of the developing world in comparison to our wealth!"

Educational justification. Other Americans assert that their greatness lies in the superiority of American education. This thinking says, "Do not hundreds of international students study in the United States? Look at the percentage of Americans who complete graduate degrees. Compare the equipment and facilities of our schools to those of Russia, Latin America, or Africa."

These first two arguments for cultural superiority critique all of culture on the basis of one aspect. If judged by one of its weak points, American culture could easily be described as inferior. For example, what if cultures were to be judged by the social cohesion within their nuclear and extended families? If family cohesion became the measuring rod of cultural superiority, tribal societies with well-developed kinship patterns would be chosen as superior.

American culture is not singularly blessed with divine guidance. All nations stand equal under the sovereignty of God.

Cultural justification. Still others intuitively presume that all cultures are moving to become like America, because it is the most civilized nation in the world. Are not all peoples gravitating toward borrowing our systems of free economies and democracy? This practice of calling one's own culture civilized and others uncivilized is common. Most early anthropologists and sociologists perceived the world from a developmental model: cultures develop, according to this model, from states of savagery to barbarism to civilization. These social scientists placed their own cultures in the elevated category of civilization, and the rest of the world in various categories of savagery and barbarism.

Theological justification. American Christians often feel that their culture is superior because of its Christian heritage. People promoting this justification ask, "Was not this country founded on godly principles? Have not these principles promoted justice, equality, and compassion for people in the midst of calamity?" In response, it is apparent that Christianity has significantly impacted American culture. Godly attributes — such as justice, equality, and compassion — have Christian roots. Satan, however, has also been working in America to thwart the purposes of God. American culture is not singularly blessed with divine guidance. All nations stand equal under the sovereignty of God. God is working through people of other cultural heritages as well.

Theologians subtly hold this form of ethnocentrism when they unduly focus on Western formulations of Christianity. Theology, the study of God, is a global discipline, not a distinctively Western one.

Jim and Julie invited their friends Brian and Jackie to join them as they ministered to newly arrived Asian refugees whose children were studying in one of the local high schools. Most had spent fifteen years living in refugee camps before arriving in the United States and knew only minimal English. Brian and Jackie decided to embrace this new adventure but quickly became frustrated. How could they help people who could not understand their questions and responses? Every time Brian and Jackie visited, the refugees offered them food and insisted that Brian and Jackie eat with them. Why could they not take "no" for an answer? Besides, this food, whatever it was, smelled gross. Jim and Julie sensed their friends' frustration and were not surprised when Brian and Jackie said they couldn't help anymore. Jim and Julie were, however, disappointed and discouraged. Could others in their church relate to these refugees? Could their church ever become multicultural?

TYPES OF MONOCULTURAL POSITIONS

Charles Kraft has discussed various monocultural positions typical in North American contexts (Kraft 1996, 73–74). These positions — eclectic, reactionary, and "one world" monoculturalism — will be discussed in this section.

Eclectic monoculturalism. Eclectic monoculturalists believe that they have creatively selected the best customs from throughout the world in order to formulate a superior culture. They acknowledge good in other cultures but imply that they are better than others in borrowing from other cultures, assimilating the good and rejecting the bad. The emphasis in this model is on effective borrowing and assimilation.

Frequently, the borrowed items are only superficial — on the surface of a culture — rather than integral to its worldview. Eating various foods borrowed from other world cultures does not make one superior. It is always easier to borrow the artifacts and technologies of other cultures than their perspectives on reality.

Customs from one culture are not neatly plugged into another. Borrowed customs are almost always given new meanings within their new cultural settings. For example, the word *karma* has some negative connotations within its original Indian context. It might be translated as "fate" or "destiny," implying that people's actions in this life determine their future existences. The burden of karma prevents humans from breaking out of the cycle of deaths and rebirths and merging with cosmic consciousness. In New Age contexts, however, karma provides hope because humans are understood to be evolving to new levels of consciousness. In China, acupuncture is thought to realign the flow of energy through the body to promote healing. Many Westerners, however, look on acupuncture as a secular discipline dealing with pressure points and nerve endings. When borrowing occurs, there is almost always a reinterpretation of the meaning of the borrowed items to make them fit the overall worldview of the borrowing culture.

Reactionary monoculturalism. Reactionary monoculturalists ridicule their own cultures but idealize their host cultures. They consider their culture to be *bad* and their new host culture *good.* For some, it is this rejection of their own cultures that has driven them into cross-cultural contexts. For others, this rejection is caused by overidentifying with their host culture. Claude Lévi-Strauss, in a classic quote, reflects on how this reactionary thinking describes many anthropologists:

> Why does he (the anthropologist) decide to disdain (his own society), reserving for societies distant and different from his own the patience and devotion which he has deliberately withheld from his fellow-citizens? . . . At home the anthropologist may be a natural subversive, a convinced opponent of traditional usage; but no sooner has he in focus a society different from his own than he becomes respectful of even the most conservative practices. (1964, 381)

The reactionary monocultural perspective is common among young people from developing nations who attend Western educational institutions. These students become convinced through their studies that their own culture is inferior and seek to become part of a seemingly superior Western culture. Their adoption of Western culture, however, is often very superficial. Western clothes, hairstyles, and music do not make a person Western. An Argentine student studying at Abilene Christian University wrote that she had become "ethnocentric about the United States. I saw America as the best country and judged attitudes and beliefs according to American culture." After she had been in the United States several months, her emotional pendulum swung from idealization to rejection. She began to criticize the culture that she had once idealized.

People who never leave their homelands can also fall victim to reactionary monoculturalism. Kraft observes,

> Many nonwestern people have been intimidated by westernization into believing that western culture is good and the customs of their fathers and grandfathers inferior or bad. Such people are often reaching out to become more and more western with very little respect for their traditional cultures or for the traditional people within their cultures who have not westernized. . . .
>
> A lot of problems can come along with this attitude, including psychological problems for those who can no longer feel at home within their own societies yet, in spite of their best efforts, never quite become totally accepted as westerners, either. (Kraft 1996, 74)

Western missionaries can also fall into reactionary monoculturalism, which becomes a type of reverse ethnocentrism. After growing to appreciate their host cultures and recognizing that many in their home cultures are monocultural, missionaries may react by developing an unhealthy disdain for their home cultures. They become hypercritical of people who have not experienced what they have. Members of the home culture often interpret this criticism as arrogance. This can be especially acute for missionaries on home assignment or during cross-cultural reentry.

"One world" monoculturalism. Many believe that all nations are headed in the same direction: accommodation to Western thoughts and ideals. This ethnocentric perspective is called "one world" monoculturalism. What would the Japanese, Chinese, or French say if the news media were to broadcast a public statement suggesting that all nations are slowly becoming American? They would probably be offended, maybe even outraged! All world cultures are *not* becoming Western. To be sure, they borrow from and reshape one another, but each retains its own character.

Becoming Cross-Cultural

DEFINITION OF CROSS-CULTURALISM

Cross-culturalism refers to *the learned skill of relating to people of other cultures within the contexts of their cultures*. Becoming cross-cultural can be compared to learning to ride a bicycle. It is impossible to learn the skill by reading a book and learning how all the parts of the vehicle work together to make it move. The book may even tell how to ride the bike. But learning *about* riding and learning *to* ride are very different. Children who want to learn to ride a bicycle get on, concentrate hard on turning the pedals and steering, lose their balance and fall, pick themselves up, and try again. Each time they get on their bikes, they become more adept. Soon they ride their bikes without thinking about all that goes into it.

For example, I learned Kipsigis culture by immersing my life in the lives of local people. I remember one important lesson I learned: New missionaries learning languages and cultures hear and see things that do not fit their conceptions of reality. When there is such confusion, the new missionary should ask questions and seek answers in culturally appropriate ways.

When I was first learning the Kipsigis language, I heard an old lady greet a young boy and call him "Grandfather." I asked the Christian with whom I was evangelizing, "Did I hear right? Did the old lady call the young boy 'Grandfather'?"

"Yes," he replied, "but she just does not understand." At this point, I was perplexed not only by the old lady's greeting, but also by the Christian's response. The next day, I was visiting a Christian who wanted me to thoroughly know Kipsigis customs. I explained what had happened.

He laughed and said, "Let me tell you about the Kipsigis' *Kurenet* rite." This rite takes place soon after a baby is born, to discern which ancestral spirit has embodied the new child. An old woman will ask, "Are you Arap Tonui?" The women gathered for this rite will wait for some time for the child to sneeze, thus signifying the affirmative. If the child does not sneeze, other names are proposed until the child responds by sneezing.

That night I picked up my copy of Orchardson's ethnography of the Kipsigis and reread this description of the *Kurenet*:

> So firmly is it believed that the child really has the spirit of the *Kurenet*, and is in fact the same person, that his or her mother, when using terms of endearment, will address the child for many years by the *Kurenet's* name." (Orchardson 1961, 45)

I had read this, but had not internalized it by merely reading about it in a book. I learned that the old lady called the boy "Grandfather" because she felt that the spirit of her grandfather had come to live in the body of the young child. The Christian I had consulted was embarrassed that I heard traditional conceptions typically hidden from outsiders.

Becoming cross-cultural, like riding a bike, is thus a learned skill. Missionaries must enter their contexts as learners. They ask questions, listen carefully, ask more questions, and learn to participate in the life of the local people. It is more than reading ethnographies describing the culture.

CHARACTERISTICS OF CROSS-CULTURALISM

The above definition and example imply several characteristics of cross-cultural missionaries. They *have gone through a process of culture and language learning to become cross-cultural.* Becoming cross-cultural requires many hours of listening, speaking, observing, asking, and experiencing — all within the local cultural context.

Cross-culturalists perceive that cultures have both strengths and weaknesses, and take other cultures as seriously as their own. They recognize cultural strengths and weaknesses, empathizing with the people rather than criticizing their culture.

Cross-culturalists perceive that cultures have both strengths and weaknesses, and take other cultures as seriously as their own.

Cross-cultural missionaries model their cultural adaptation after that of Christ. Their ministries reflect the incarnation of Christ. Jesus lived among the people he ministered to. He spoke their language, ate their food, slept in their homes, shared their joys and sorrows. Likewise, cross-cultural missionaries must participate in the lives of the people they minister among, speaking their language and sharing their struggles and triumphs.

Cross-cultural missionaries treat people of other cultures as equals, just as they would people of their own culture. "Respond to others as you want them to respond to you" could be called the Golden Rule for cross-culturalists. For example, if missionaries extend hospitality through food or lodging to visitors from their own culture, should they not also extend hospitality to visitors from their host culture (while respecting their hospitality customs)? If missionaries give financial help to people of their culture, should they not do the same, in culturally relevant ways, to those of another culture? Just as God "does not show favoritism" (Acts 10:34), missionaries should accept people of other cultures as equals.

Christ provides the power to transform monocultural myopia (nearsightedness) into cross-cultural openness. Jesus is "our peace, who has made the two groups one and has destroyed the barrier, the dividing wall of hostility" (Eph. 2:14). Therefore people in Christ "are no longer foreigners and strangers, but fellow citizens" (v. 19). Jesus makes it possible for people of diverse cultures to "be devoted to one another in love" and to "honor one another above [them]selves" (Rom. 12:10).

Crossing Cultural Barriers: From Jew to Gentile (a Biblical Case Study)

THE JEWISH NATURE OF THE EARLY CHRISTIAN CHURCH

The early church was clothed in the cultural garb of Judaism. Early Christians worshiped at the temple (Acts 2:46; 3:1), circumcised their children (15:1; 21:20 – 21), and observed Jewish feasts (20:6). James and other elders of the Jerusalem church describe them as "zealous for the law" (21:20). The church was tied so closely to Judaism that as late as AD 52 – 53, Gallio, the Roman proconsul of Achaia, could not differentiate between Christians and Jews. He believed that the problem between Paul and the Jews was merely a matter of Jewish law (18:12 – 17; note esp. vv. 14 – 16).

During this early period, the cultural pride of the Christian community sometimes reflected that of the larger Jewish community. Jews would not associate with Samaritans (John 4:9). In fact, Jews traveling between Galilee and Judea would take a Transjordan route around Samaria rather than pass through an "unclean" land. Perhaps this is why it was a Hellenistic Jew, Philip, and not a Hebraic Jew, who first took the gospel to the Samaritans, and why it was important for the apostles to participate personally in the coming of the Holy Spirit on the first Samaritan believers (Acts 8:5 – 17).

Later, Peter testified to Gentiles in Cornelius's house, saying, "It is against our law for a Jew to associate with or visit a Gentile" (10:28). After Peter broke this cultural rule, the Jerusalem believers accused him of going into "the house of uncircumcised men and [eating] with them" (11:3).

With such bias, how could Jewish Christians ever teach Gentiles? From a human standpoint, the barrier was insurmountable. But Luke's answer in the book of Acts is that *God broke down the barrier!* God chose as his cross-cultural agent an imperfect man who had little contact with Gentiles (Acts 10:28) and who was tempted at times to separate from them (Gal. 2:11 – 14). By intentionally acting and revealing his actions to us, God communicated his acceptance of all peoples and made known the conditions for their coming into his kingdom.

ACTS 10:1–11:18: DOES GOD ACCEPT ALL WHO COME TO HIM?

In Acts 10, God acted decisively to affirm his acceptance of the Gentiles and to bring them into full fellowship with Jewish Christians. God worked through three mighty interventions: (1) an angel of God directed Cornelius to send for Peter (vv. 1 – 8); (2) through a vision, God told Peter, "Do not call anything impure that God has made clean" (vv. 9 – 16); and (3) the Holy Spirit came upon the people gathered to hear Peter at Cornelius's house (10:44 – 48; 11:15 – 17). When Jerusalem Christians confronted Peter for fellowshiping with Gentiles (11:1 – 3), he recounted God's three miracles (vv. 4 – 17), and the Jews concluded that "even to Gentiles God has granted repentance that leads to life" (v. 18). This intervention of God demonstrated that "God does not show favoritism but accepts from every nation the one who fears him and does what is right" (10:34 – 35). The conversion of Cornelius and his household resolved the issue of *God's acceptance of the Gentiles*.

ACTS 15: SHOULD CONVERTED GENTILES FOLLOW JEWISH CUSTOMS?

Issues of *fellowship*, however, were not fully resolved with the conversion of Cornelius and his family. After Paul and Barnabas began their mission to the Gentiles in Asia Minor, questions arose about the nature of fellowship: How were Gentiles to live in the kingdom of God? Should they follow the Jewish law? Must they be circumcised in order to be saved? These questions set the stage for the Jerusalem conference in Acts 15. This meeting dealt with the cultural demands placed on a newly emerging church by a Christian community in a different culture. Must new believers embrace the culture of the sending church in order to come to Christ?

Luke records three speeches delivered at the Jerusalem conference. Peter spoke from *history*. He declared that God had made a choice to accept the Gentiles. God made no distinction between Jew and Gentile but saved both by grace, not by law. Peter pointedly asked, "Now then, why do you try to test God by putting on the necks of Gentiles a yoke that neither we nor our ancestors have been able to bear?" (vv. 6 – 11).

Paul and Barnabas argued from *ministry*. The miraculous signs and wonders that God performed among the Gentiles confirmed that he accepted them without their following the law (v. 12).

James spoke from *Scripture*. Amos had prophesied that "David's fallen shelter" would be restored and that both the remnant and "the nations that bear [God's] name" would be welcomed (Amos 9:11 – 12). James then made a proposal, which all the Christians accepted: "It is my judgment, therefore, that we should not make it difficult for the Gentiles who are turning to God" (Acts 15:19). The council decided that new believers should not be compelled to adopt the cultural patterns of the sending culture.

The Jerusalem conference established a precedent for the relationships between sending churches and churches established in mission areas.

However, to facilitate fellowship as one body, the Gentiles were given certain restrictions (vv.20 – 21). This was necessary because Gentile Christians came into contact with Jews in the synagogues (v. 21). The restrictions about meat offered to idols, according to Paul's writings, were not binding in all cases (Rom. 14:13 – 23; 1 Cor. 8:7 – 13). Paul said that eating meat offered to idols was wrong only if the act caused a brother or sister in Christ to stumble. All cultures have practices that, if insisted upon, would disrupt fellowship with another culture (or other cultures). These must be eliminated so that they don't cause fellow believers to stumble.

The Jerusalem conference established a precedent for relationships between sending churches and churches established in mission areas. People receiving the gospel cross-culturally were not required to adopt the culture of the sending church in order to be received into Christian fellowship. Specifically, Gentiles were not obligated to undergo circumcision, and thus become full-fledged Jews, in order to be saved. Establishing fellowship between Christians of different cultures demanded some give-and-take on nonuniversal matters. For example, Gentiles were not to eat meat offered to idols, because this could be a stumbling block to Jewish-Gentile fellowship.

ACTS 21:17 – 26: SHOULD DISPERSION JEWS CONTINUE TO KEEP THE LAW?

By the time Paul returned to Jerusalem after his third missionary journey, the acceptance of Gentiles into Christian fellowship was no longer an issue. Hundreds of Gentile churches had been established, and thousands of Gentiles reconciled to God, by the saving grace of Jesus Christ. Jewish Christians no longer required Gentiles to be circumcised and keep Jewish customs. At this point, the issue had become, *Should dispersion Jews, living among the Gentiles, continue to keep the Mosaic law?* This issue, discussed in Acts 21:17 – 26, illustrates how sending churches are eventually impacted by influences from the mission field.

When Paul, Luke, and others visited the Jerusalem elders, Paul related what God had done among the Gentiles through his ministry (vv. 18 – 19). The Jerusalem elders glorified God for this work. They then stated that thousands of Jews had also accepted Jesus Christ but were "zealous for the law" (v. 20). They informed Paul of a rumor that had spread through the Jerusalem church: Paul was teaching Jews of the dispersion to forsake Jewish customs (v. 21). To counter this rumor, the elders asked Paul to purify himself, along with four others, to demonstrate that he was "living in obedience to the law" (v. 24), though they did not dispute Paul's teaching that Gentiles were not bound by the law. Paul concurred with the elders' suggestion and in the temple purified himself along with four Jewish believers (v. 26).

This passage shows the Jewish Christians' concern that their churches might lose their identity because of Paul's influence in mission churches. The Jerusalem elders therefore wanted to establish the principle that Jewish Christians should continue to be Jews even in mission contexts where they lived as minorities within Christian communities composed largely of Gentiles. They also wanted to confirm that even Paul, God's appointed messenger to the Gentiles, must continue to live as a Jew. Perceptions of Christianity worked out on the mission field will eventually shape perceptions of sending churches.

Two final what-if questions will help missionaries think through the implications of this biblical case study.

1. *What if* Jewish leaders had refused to accept Peter's testimony that God had intervened to bring Gentiles, such as Cornelius, into the kingdom of God (Acts 11:1 – 18)?
2. *What if* Jewish leaders at the Jerusalem conference had determined that Gentiles had to be circumcised and follow the Mosaic law in order to be saved?

In each case, the cross-cultural spread of Christianity would have been severely impeded!

In the book of Acts, Luke demonstrated that God does not view people as "circumcised or unclean," but as creatures made in his image, regardless of their cultures.

Conclusion

Extractional approaches to missions, described in some detail in chapter 9, are largely founded on monocultural and ethnocentric feelings. When missionaries equate their own perceptions of reality with reality itself and assume that their beliefs have been accepted because they are superior, they intuitively set up programs that espouse these perceptions. Cultural pride is thus the source of many missionary mistakes. This chapter suggests that missionaries must become learners of their host culture to overcome these feelings of superiority, and that God is working in his people to overcome earthly pride.

REFLECTION AND APPLICATION

Questions

1. Briefly define and contrast the terms *monocultural* and *ethnocentric*. Then give one example of ethnocentrism as recorded in Scripture.
2. Using the sections titled "Characteristics of the Monocultural/Ethnocentric Syndrome" (pp. 263–65) and "Characteristics of Cross-Culturalism" (pp. 270–71), make a chart comparing monoculturalism and cross-culturalism.
3. Which of the following terms would you consider *ethnocentric*? What inferences make them ethnocentric?
   - Coworker
   - Inferior
   - Evangelical
   - Underdeveloped
   - Superior
   - Empathetic
4. Briefly define the following four ways in which people justify their superiority.
   a. Technological justification
   b. Educational justification
   c. Cultural justification
   d. Theological justification
5. Describe the process of becoming cross-cultural, using the analogy of learning to ride a bicycle.
6. Why might one say that the early church was clothed in the cultural garb of Judaism? Describe the Jewish character of the early Christian church.
7. According to the book of Acts, how was the seemingly insurmountable cultural barrier separating Jew and Gentile breached?

8. Briefly describe God's decisive interventions in Acts 10. What missiological lessons can be learned from that chapter?
9. What was decided at the Jerusalem conference in Acts 15? What lessons for missions can be learned from Luke's account of this conference?
10. What did some Jewish believers accuse Paul of in Acts 21:17–26? What lesson(s) can current missionaries learn from this passage?

Personal Inventory

How has God spoken to you through this chapter? What is God calling you to do about it?

chapter 12

The Nature of Cross-Cultural Communication

Encoding and Decoding God's Eternal Message

Jim and Julie enjoyed meeting high school students from Central Asia who had recently arrived from refugee camps in Nepal and India. As they got to know these students and their families, they asked, "What is God calling us to do in this refugee community?" They realized that these new immigrants needed to quickly learn to function in American culture by learning English, finding immediate resources for living, and developing suitable employment. Above all, they wanted these new friends to know the way of God in Jesus Christ.

Jim and Julie and the high school group began a very simple Bible study with these refugees, working through the gospel of Mark. During their second meeting, while they were still in the first chapter of Mark, one story especially captured the refugees' attention—the story of Jesus casting out an impure spirit.

The refugees began to whisper among themselves in their own language. After some time, they switched to English to tell Jim and Julie and the other students in the Bible study about a twelve-year-old girl in their community who had begun acting very strangely. At times she appeared normal, but sometimes her eyes would roll back in her head and she would begin talking in a different voice. She would utter foul curses against members of the community. No one knew what to do. Some had suggested that they send her back to their home country or to one of the refugee camps in Nepal, where there were traditional practitioners who knew how to deal with such problems.

Jim and Julie's initial thought was that the girl had some type of mental illness and would need to be under the care of a psychiatrist, who through medication and therapy would be able to alleviate the symptoms.

The refugees, however, believed that this girl was under the control of an evil spirit. Now they had learned that Jesus had authority over evil spirits. Jim and Julie were followers of this Jesus, were they not? Could they come pray for this girl and command the evil spirit to leave?

Jim and Julie wondered, "Could this really be demon possession? If so, how do we respond?" They were amazed at how these refugees from Nepal were reading the Bible differently out of the background of their culture.

DAVID HESSELGRAVE HAS CONTRASTED the perceptions of Rudyard Kipling concerning East-West dialogue with those of Sir Rabindranath Tagore. Kipling, in "The Ballad of East and West" (1924, 268–72), writes,

> *East is East and West is West*
> *And never the twain shall meet.*

On the other hand, Tagore asserts that the most significant occurrence of the twentieth century is that "the East and West *have met*" (Hesselgrave 1978, 204). This process has been amplified during the information age of the twenty-first century.

To what degree are these contrasting perspectives true? Kipling penned his words during an age of very little intercultural contact. Human understanding of other cultures was limited. Nevertheless, Kipling's words continue to echo whenever Easterners and Westerners attempt to understand each other's perspective.

Tagore was commenting on the increasing interdependence of peoples of the world. International communication and transportation networks have linked the world. Global meetings are held to discuss ecological, political, technological, and religious issues. Never before have human cultures been brought together through such interconnecting forums. The world is becoming a global village.

Perhaps the following statement by Hesselgrave accurately captures the essence of intercultural relationships in our contemporary world: *"The East and West are ever meeting, but the East and West have never met"* (1978, 204). This "ever meeting, yet never meeting" expresses the nature of communication in the current world. Too many missionaries merely dabble at true cross-cultural relationships. They are like characters on *Star Trek*, who are beamed into an unknown world to do a designated job and then beamed back aboard their own starship. In their forays into other cultures, short-term missionaries are "ever meeting" new people and new situations, but often they are "never meeting" the people within the framework of their culture and language. Hesselgrave writes,

> There is a real danger that as our technology advances and enables us to cross geographical and national boundaries with ease and increasing frequency we forget that cultural barriers are real and formidable. The gap between our technological advances and our communication skills is perhaps one of the most challenging aspects of modern civilization. (1978, 615)

This chapter introduces the fundamentals of cross-cultural communication so that missionaries may be better equipped to speak God's eternal message in cross-cultural contexts.

Layers of Communicational Complexity: A Three-Culture Model of Missionary Communication

Communicating Christ in E – 2 or E – 3 contexts involves three cultures.[1] First, missionaries must understand their own culture. If missionaries do not know themselves in their own culture, how can they sort out who they are in the context of other cultures? Second, missionaries must seek to understand biblical meanings as they were communicated within biblical contexts. Scripture was not written in a cultural vacuum. Each book of the Bible was directed toward and written about people in specific cultural contexts. Third, missionaries must learn the cultures in which they wish to communicate. To be heard best, the Christian message must be communicated in the heart language of the local people. This message must attract, impact, and revolutionize the host culture while maintaining its eternal essence.

A ONE-CULTURE MODEL OF MISSIONARY COMMUNICATION

Before cross-cultural (or multicultural) evangelists can understand the process of communicating Christ in other cultures, they must discern

1. See the discussion of cultural distance in chapter 10.

Figure 12.1 A One-Culture Model of Missionary Communication

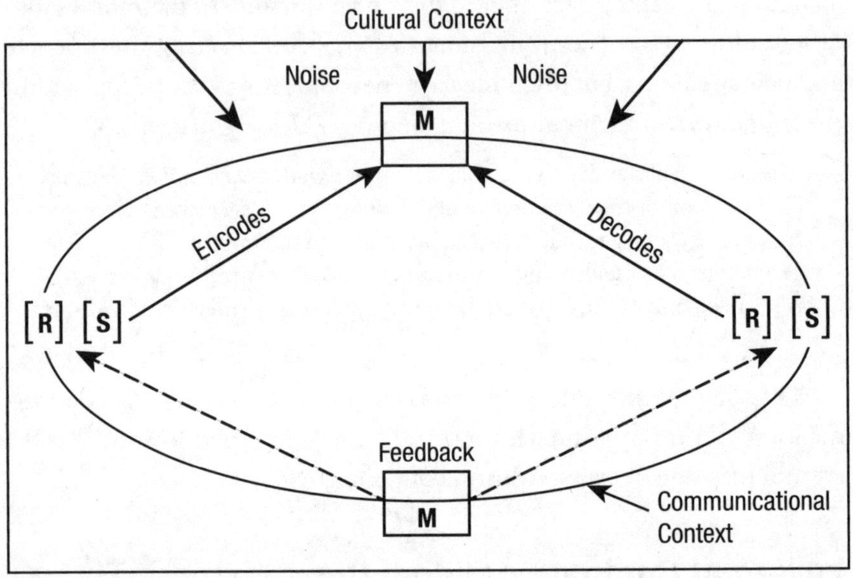

the nature of communication within a one-culture context. For example, what occurs when American Christians communicate the gospel with other Americans of a similar culture?

Figure 12.1 illustrates a one-culture model of missionary communication.[2] Some Christian is the *source (S)* who encodes the *message (M)* of the gospel, and the person hearing the story, parable, or testimony is the *receptor (R)*. The receptor never decodes the message exactly as the source intended. However, precise vocabulary and appropriate illustrations can minimize misunderstandings.

The receptor, however, becomes the source of a message by reflecting on what has been originally encoded. The *feedback*, whether verbal or nonverbal, personal or impersonal, enables the source to know how his message has been decoded and how he is in turn transformed by what has been said. If the receptor asks the meaning of a word or phrase, the source knows that something needs to be clarified. When giving

2. Eugene Nida's discussion "The Structure of Communication" in *Mission and Message* (1990, 37–55) has been formative in this chapter. Rather than diagramming communication as a dialogical (and therefore cyclical) encounter, Nida depicts it as a linear process.

feedback, the receptor *(R)* thus becomes the source *(S)*, and the original source *(S)* becomes the receptor *(R)*.

Noise is any disruption in the communication event. A blaring television, a child asking to be fed, and a receptor thinking about problems at work are all examples of noise.

The communication event takes place within a *cultural context* (designated in the diagram by the rectangle enclosing the entire communication event), which shapes the process. In this case, we will say that *S* and *R* share English as their first language and think in the same general cultural categories. Increased commonality within the cultural context heightens the effectiveness of communication. The use of one's cultural heritage in communicating is diagrammed by placing the outline of the culture (in this case, a rectangle) on the individual. However, because individuals live in distinctive local circumstances and have varying background experiences, differences within the culture must be taken into account. The message itself is even influenced by the culture. For example, the message might reflect the individualism of American culture by emphasizing what a person must do to come into a relationship with God rather than focusing on the activities of God. The impact of the culture on the message is diagrammed by placing the outline of the culture (in this case, a rectangle) on the message.

The immediate *context* (designated by an ellipsis in the diagram) also impacts the communication process. A Bible study or reflection on one's spiritual journey may take place in the receptor's home, at a coffee shop, or at a contact center downtown. A context may be biased for or against the message. In one situation, a mother was so biased against Christianity that it became impossible for her son to hear the gospel over his mother's objections at home. When taught in the home of the Christian, however, the son eagerly heard and accepted the message of Jesus.

We see examples of this communication process in the Bible. Jesus encoded the message that he was the Son of God, the King of the Jews. When Caiaphas heard Jesus claim to be the Son of God, he considered it blasphemy, a challenge to his position, and commanded that Jesus be put to death (Matt. 26:57 – 68). Peter, after hearing Jesus speak with wisdom and seeing God's mighty acts, affirmed that Jesus was "the Messiah, the Son of the living God" (16:16). The same message therefore can be decoded in different ways. The Jewish leaders decoded Jesus' message as sacrilege, and Jesus' followers decoded it as the words of life (John 6:68 – 69).

When Paul healed the lame man in Lystra, the people decoded it as a miracle of healing and deduced that Barnabas and Paul were gods in human form. The priests of Zeus responded with visual feedback by bringing sacrifices to them. Barnabas and Paul, however, hearing the meaning of the intended sacrifice, encoded a message proclaiming that they were not gods as the people supposed. They too were humans. The man had been healed by the power of Creator God. The people were to worship this God, not worthless idols (Acts 14:8 – 18).

Communication in a one-culture setting is a complicated process, allowing much room for misunderstanding. Misconceptions occur because what is encoded by the source is not perfectly decoded by the receptor and because noise interferes with the act of communication. Missionaries therefore must learn to communicate within their own language and culture before attempting the even more complicated process of communicating cross-culturally. Knowing oneself and how to relate to others within one's own culture is a prerequisite to, though not a guarantee of, effective cross-cultural communication.

A TWO-CULTURE MODEL OF MISSIONARY COMMUNICATION

Each book of the Bible is an encoding of God's message for a specific people at a particular time. Paul wrote to the Galatians concerning new Christians who were tempted to forsake the gospel of grace and return to legalistic customs of Judaizing teachers. These teachers were instructing new Christians that they must be circumcised according to the law of Moses in order to be saved. A reader today must understand something of the historical and religious context of the book of Galatians in order to make sense of many parts of it.

A cultural gap separates contemporary societies from the ancient Near East. Concepts such as sacrifice, covenant, circumcision, and principalities and powers, as well as metaphorical statements such as "seated ... in the heavenly realms" (Eph. 1:20; 2:6), may be foreign to many listeners today. Interpreters must cross time and culture to uncover the intended message of the biblical text. Then they must apply it to contemporary times and issues. This twofold bridging to understand biblical

Figure 12.2 A Two-Culture Model of Missionary Communication

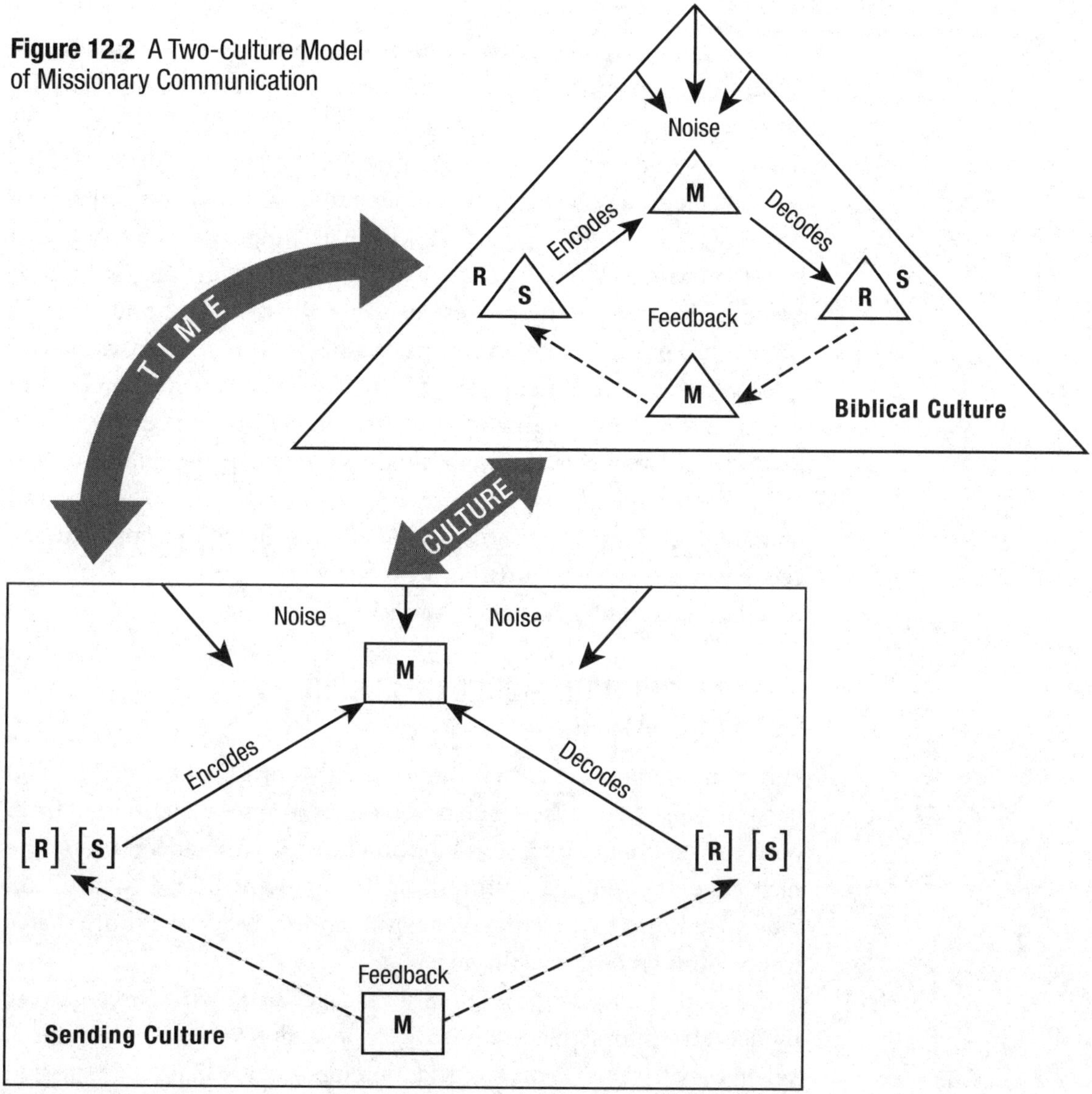

concepts and discern God's meanings is implied by the arrows between *biblical culture* and *sending culture* in the two-culture model of missionary communication. The worldview differences are diagrammed above by outlining biblical cultures as a large triangle. This diagram is limited because the Bible spans many centuries and was written in the context of not just one, but many cultures.

Two issues are clarified by the two-culture model of missionary communication. First, Christian communicators must learn to faithfully interpret Scripture. Most people intuitively interpret the Bible, assuming that their worldview and that of the original audience are identical. This intuitive approach leads to misunderstandings of Scripture because people fail to interpret the text within its linguistic, cultural, and historical setting. All Christians must therefore learn proper biblical exegesis. Exegesis is the process of using the historical and cultural context of a passage to determine its original meaning. Effective biblical interpretation leads missionaries to rise above their own fallen culture and to move closer to an absolute, eternal, God-ordained worldview. Second, Christian communicators must apply the inspired meanings to real issues of contemporary culture. The gospel was meant to be lived and taught, observed in the process of life, not just heard in informational, classroom settings. A Christian worldview must practically shape the morals, ethics, and behaviors of society.

A THREE-CULTURE MODEL OF MISSIONARY COMMUNICATION

When missionaries enter a host culture, this process of encoding and decoding also takes place. The host culture, of course, is different from both the sending culture and biblical cultures. In the diagram on the next page, the sending culture is again represented by a square, and biblical cultures by a triangle. The oval represents a host culture that is just beginning to receive the gospel.

Two other communication issues are clarified by the three-culture model. First, missionaries must learn to adapt to their new culture. When they first arrive on the field, missionaries are like square pegs in round holes. They have been taught to think like squares but have come to minister where people perceive reality as round. As they learn their new language and culture, their squareness is rounded off. Unless this basic learning occurs, the message communicated and lifestyle modeled will not adequately reflect the Christian meanings that the missionaries want to communicate.

Second, the process of interpreting Scripture and applying it to life also occurs in the third culture. The developing Christian leaders in the host

Figure 12.3 A Three-Culture Model of Missionary Communication

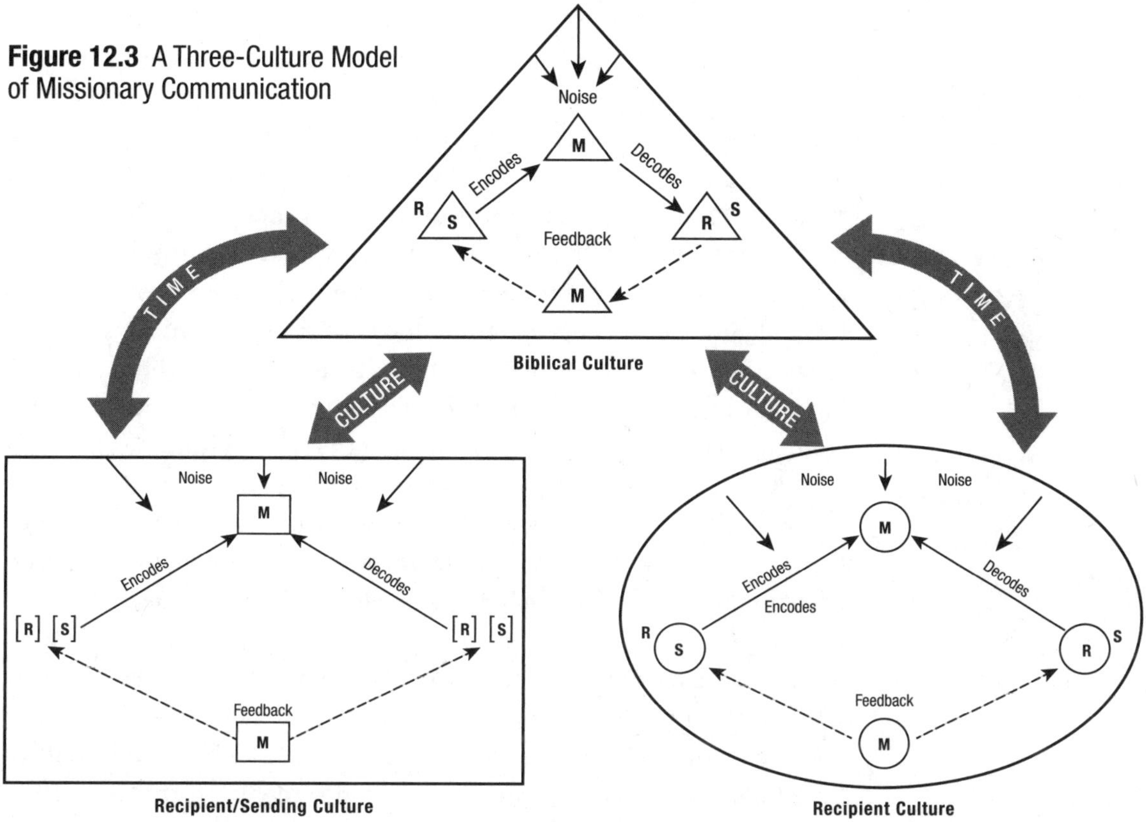

culture must learn to interpret the Bible and apply its meanings to their culture just as Christians in the missionaries' home culture do. Missionaries must become master teachers equipping the church to accomplish these functions. This perspective assumes that the missionaries believe that the people can learn to interpret the message for themselves and make divine applications to contemporary issues. As missionaries communicate the message and model the Christian life, they must serve as *mentors of movements* rather than fathers or founders. Mentoring implies equality; fathering or founding denotes paternalism. Missionaries must walk alongside local leaders rather than stand over them.

Church-planting missionaries frequently become resource people for developing Christian fellowships. New believers ask missionaries how people in Christ become adults, marry, become elders, and die or bury their dead. What is the role of the church and the family in each of these aspects of life's cycle? Missionaries are tempted to give their own

Missionaries must serve as *mentors of movements* rather than fathers or founders. Mentoring implies equality; fathering or founding denotes paternalism. Missionaries must walk alongside local leaders rather than stand over them.

cultural answers to the new fellowship because it is easier to borrow than to innovate. Sensitive missionaries, however, will give the new church the freedom to innovate rites under the guiding hand of God's Spirit so that rites from the sending culture will not be incorporated superficially into the host culture as *Christian* rites.

Communicating the message of Christ across cultures requires asking many significant theological questions. For example, what is the biblical concept of time? A Hindu looks at time as cyclical: the dead are reincarnated into life in numerous rebirths. On the other hand, the biblical perspective is linear: at death, the physical body perishes and "returns to the ground it came from, and the spirit returns to God who gave it" (Eccl. 12:7). God, although eternal, began time with creation and will ultimately bring it to culmination with the second coming of Christ. Time is in the hand of God; as the great sovereign over time, he determines the length of each person's life as well as the time for Christ's return (Matt. 24:36).

Missionaries must also ask, "How do human cultures classify reality?" Western culture divides reality into two large slices — the secular and the spiritual — and thereby separates God from his world. Neither Scripture nor non-Western cultures divides reality in this way. How should decisions be made? Western culture is highly individualistic; biblical cultures are moderately group oriented, and African cultures are extremely group oriented. Who or what are the principalities and powers (Rom. 8:38; Eph. 6:12)? Westerners generally believe that spiritual powers do not exist but are merely myths of primitive peoples. Scripture and most world cultures, however, recognize the presence and activity of spiritual powers and forces.

These illustrations emphasize that cultural decisions and theology cannot be separated. Missionaries must help the people of their host culture develop theologically sound perceptions of reality.

> We don't always communicate what we desire, especially when communicating cross-culturally.
>
> I was preaching one of my first lessons in the Kipsigis language. "For *all* have sinned and fallen short of the glory of God," I proclaimed. To emphasize universal human sinfulness, I asked, "How many of you have sinned?" All was quiet for a few moments. I could detect uneasiness in the audience — a feeling of disagreement.

Finally, the old man in whose house we were meeting responded, "I have not sinned!" (literally, "I have not done *tengekto*"). I was stunned! Adding insult to injury, all in the room, following the old man's lead, testified that they also had never sinned! I had preached this sermon in both English and Swahili in various East African contexts, and the audience had always responded, "We have all sinned."

Feeling confused and a little hurt that my lesson was not accepted, I asked, "What is sin (*tengekto*)?"

The old man, proud to assume the role of teacher, said, "*Tengekto* means four things. Stealing from a Kipsigis is *tengekto.*"

"What about stealing from a Kisii or a Maasai [other tribes in Kenya]?" I interjected.

He hesitated, knowing that I was not a Kipsigis and might not understand his logic. "We would not classify stealing from the Kisii or Maasai as sin but as war," he sheepishly replied. I was puzzled. Did the Kipsigis believe that sin occurs only in their own cultural group?

"Killing a Kipsigis is also a *tengekto,*" the old man continued.

"But killing a Kisii or a Maasai is not *tengekto*?" I asked, testing my hypothesis. He responded indignantly, "Of course not! That's also war! We sin against Kipsigis; we make war with the enemy." Pausing only briefly, he continued, "*Tengekto* encompasses two other things: immorality and bewitching. Bewitching is the worst of sins, because it is malevolently directed against the living."

"Sin is understood as an action in this context," I deduced. "And the same action may not be sin in a different situation."

New words! New categories! New definitions! What an eye-opener! I realized that all peoples have their own understanding of sin and corresponding beliefs about salvation from sin. Missionaries, as cultural outsiders, must learn the local, or indigenous, words for concepts such as "sin" or "salvation" before they can effectively communicate the Christian message.

I soon learned that the Kipsigis language has four distinct words for sin: (1) *lelutiet*, a broad, general category of faults which might easily be translated into English as "mistake"; (2) *kwekyenet*, willful, premeditated sin which one does even when one knows it is wrong (Heb. 10:26); (3) *sogornatet*, the most hideous type of sin, such as incest and witchcraft (used in 1 Cor. 5:13); and (4) *tengekto.*

Which of these was our Christian community to use as the primary term for "sin" in Christian proclamation? *Lelutiet* was too general and lacked the strength to convict of guilt; to say that "people have made mistakes" would not lead to conversion. *Kwekyenet*, on the other hand, was too strong, and *sogornatet* too specific. The only alternative was to use *tengekto* (or the synonymous term *chalwokto*) and broaden its meaning by redefinition and application.

Missionaries must always partner with developing Christian leaders in learning how to teach in another culture (Van Rheenen 1991, 275–77).

A Practical Case of a Three-Culture Model of Missionary Communication

What practical problems arise when evangelists of one culture seek to Christianize people of a second culture by presenting a message that was initially proclaimed in still a third culture in yet another age? More specifically, how do American evangelists present Christianity to Africans living south of the Sahara? As in the matter of Jewish relations with Gentiles in the early Christian church, cultural frictions are inevitable. In a preliminary way, this section presents an American cultural worldview, contrasts it with an African worldview, and then delineates the process of rethinking and theologizing that occurs as Americans attempt to communicate God's message in Africa. This case study will demonstrate a three-culture transmission of the Christian message.

AMERICAN CULTURAL PERSPECTIVES

The worldview of most Americans is (1) naturalistic, (2) individualistic, (3) optimistic, and (4) present oriented and linear. These cultural characteristics have so permeated American Christianity that they are seldom questioned. American Christians tend to accept these dominant cultural values even when they conflict with Christian truths. At the same time, Christianity does influence American culture. For example, the belief in the possibility of progress is feasible only if time is linear, as in a biblical worldview, instead of cyclical, as most Eastern views hold.

Americans are *naturalistic*. They make a distinction between the natural and the supernatural, between the physical and the spiritual.

In this view, God, angels, and demons, if they exist, are supernatural and are not part of normal life. People in the natural realm — the tangible, physical world — can perceive the activities of these beings only through miracles and visions. This physical world is thought to be guided by laws of nature, studied by experimentation, and understood by scientific analysis. Everything within this world can be perceived through the five senses. People act by knowledge of the natural. Miracles are generally questioned, and the spiritual world is thought to have little direct contact with the physical. God, however, may *intervene*, like an intruder, in this world. Some Americans even deny all spiritual

Figure 12.4 Segmentations of Reality in American Culture

SUPERNATURAL REALM	Angels Demons	Perceived by miracles and visions People act by faith
NATURAL REALM	Man The Church Science The World	Perceived by sight and experience People act by knowledge

Adapted from Paul Hiebert, "Phenomenology and Institutions of Animism," classroom notes, Fuller Theological Seminary, Pasadena, CA, 1983. Used by permission.

powers because they cannot be perceived. The world — paradoxically, even for many Christians — is a "closed universe." Christianity deistically aligns itself with the spirit of the age.

The American perception of disease further illustrates this point. Americans seek natural causes of disease. They do not generally believe in spiritual causes: sin does not induce sickness, angry ancestors cannot accost their descendants, and Satan does not tempt the living by causing illness. Rather sickness is caused by germs or some malfunction of the body. No spiritual reasons stand behind these physical causes. Americans, expecting some natural explanation, ask *what* caused the illness; they do not designate personal or spiritual causes by asking *who* caused the disease or *why* one has become sick.[3]

Americans are *individualistic.* They generally believe that the individual is more important than the group. At an early age, children learn to distinguish between "my things" and "your things." As adults, they differentiate "my rights" from "your rights." Nuclear families mirror

3. The wall between the natural and supernatural is now beginning to fall among two types of people in the American population. Bible-believing Christians are challenging the secularism that denies the work of God in the world he created. The God of the Bible is a personal, working God (John 5:17) who wants to relate to his people (Hos. 11:1 – 5). In addition, the New Age movement influenced Western postmodernism, which is now a dominant worldview. Followers of the New Age movement make no distinction between the natural and the supernatural. They believe that the physical and spiritual worlds are "interrelated, interdependent, and interpenetrating" (Groothuis 1986, 18). For example, one New Age therapist uses crystals for healing purposes because "physical problems are manifestations of spiritual problems" (Friedrich 1987, 64). As the naturalistic influences of secular American culture wane, an impending battle, between Christian and New Age ideologies, is emerging for the hearts of the American people.

the culture as a whole; each nuclear family does its own thing, independently of the extended family. Also, the intense individualism of the nuclear family erodes parental respect and leads members of the family to do their own thing. Democracy stands as the cultural ideal; each individual has an equal voice in government, regardless of his understanding of the issues involved. Praise and honor are given to the individual who achieves above his peers; certificates of achievement decorating the walls testify to a person's success. Team sports are individualized, with detailed statistics — the number of strikeouts, home runs, and stolen bases or field goals, free throws, assists, and rebounds — kept on each player. Star players are often given more attention than the team that wins. Americans feel that people must make their own way, without reliance on groups or outside help.

The intense individualism of American culture has become destructive. Families are fragmenting. Culture is losing its cohesion. Special-interest groups meet their own felt needs without considering others. Let us pray that the sovereign hand of God will mobilize the church to become a cohesive, distinct people in a fragmented, lonesome society.

Americans are *optimistic*. Most Americans, despite the recent economic recession, are filled with confidence that they can succeed. Because the world is orderly and humans are rational, they can chart their own course to success. This optimism is rooted in the belief that opportunities are continually expanding. There are always new frontiers to conquer: undeveloped lands to the west, space beyond the stratosphere, or more advanced computer and telecommunications technologies. One person's success does not necessarily come at another person's expense. Even the common person can succeed. Only in America, they feel, can one go from a log cabin to the White House.[4]

Americans are *present oriented and view time as linear.* A shift from a future orientation to a present orientation is one of the most significant changes in American culture in this generation. The traditional, future-oriented attitude was expressed by religious billboards and tracts

4. This optimism was tempered by the failure to achieve military victory in Vietnam, reemerged with initial success in the Persian Gulf, was shattered by the destruction of the Twin Towers in New York City on 9/11, was frustrated by an unwinnable and naively planned "war on terror," and was traumatized by a great recession and the subsequent polarization of political parties.

exhorting the sinner, "Prepare to meet your Maker," but now sermons are seldom heard on such topics as the second coming of Christ, heaven and hell, and the future hope of Christians. In the past, the accepted philosophy was to work hard now in preparation for the future. Today, instead of saving for the future, Americans live for the present. Individuals — and the government — buy goods on credit so they can have now and pay later. This shift in time perspective has undermined our country and secularized our churches.

The American perspective of time is also linear. Americans generally believe that life begins at birth and ends at death. Unlike people whose cultures have a cyclical orientation of time, Americans view children as being born with a clean slate, having no previous heritage. Many traditional Western psychological therapies are based on this presupposition: early imprinting is the basis of a person's psychological makeup, because a child has no previous impressions written on his personality.[5]

American secularists conclude that since people have only one life to live, they must make the most of it. They deduce that they should eat, drink, and be merry, for the future is unknown. American hedonism, under such glamorous captions as "the playboy philosophy," acclaims this perspective.

AFRICAN CULTURAL PERSPECTIVES

There is still a significant gap between the cultural presuppositions of Americans and those of Africans, despite the global influences readily accessible during this information age.[6] Africans are spiritualistic rather than naturalistic, group oriented rather than individualistic, fatalistic rather than optimistic, past oriented rather than present or future oriented.

Africans are *spiritualistic*. All of life is pervaded by spiritual power. Africans believe in personal spiritual beings — ancestors and ghosts, gods and spirits — who guide their destinies and affect their lives.

---

5. This linear perspective is now being challenged by Eastern and New Age perspectives proclaiming a new type of eternity. There is no such thing as physical death. Human spirits are thought to be reincarnated and live again.

6. Though significant differences exist among African people groups, the generalizations made here hold true for many living in sub-Saharan Africa.

Impersonal spiritual forces — powers that have no personalities and yet impact people — are used to bless friends and family and curse enemies. Africans generally do not give up belief in spiritual powers when they become Christians or Muslims. Christ most frequently is accepted as the Lord who has defeated the principalities and powers. Some Africans blend their Christianity with traditional African religion. They worship God yet depend on their gods and ancestors when they are sick or when catastrophes occur. Many professing Christians continue to believe that ancestral spirits protect them and bring them good fortune. The accumulation of material goods is thought by many to be related to spiritual power. How could one, it is thought, accumulate material goods without spiritual power?

African spirituality is greatly concerned with the cause and cure of disease. Many Christian and non-Christian Africans believe that extended illness is caused by sin. Sins are thought to come back and "eat up" people who commit them. Ancestors are also thought to cause illness. They become angry when they have been forgotten or when their wishes have been violated by the living. Witchcraft and sorcery might also cause serious illness and death. Another cause of disease is spirits, who are free to roam the world. Someone who becomes seriously ill begins looking for the spiritual reason for the illness. Although most Africans will agree that germs and body malfunctions cause illness, they might also consider them only surface causations resulting from the activity of animistic beings and forces.

If the Western dichotomy between the physical and spiritual is accepted, the result is that the people become secular "Christians" who have little faith in the work of any spiritual power, including God. If the dichotomy is rejected, dominant African leaders are apt to split away to initiate independent movements. If the dichotomy problem remains unresolved, there is a continual tension between local Christians who believe in spiritual causation and Western-trained leaders who deny any such cause for illness. Fielden Allison believes that much African syncretism is a result of missionary teaching that has focused on objectionable behaviors — drinking, adultery, polygamy, stealing, lying, cursing — without focusing on heart allegiances. The result, says Allison, is "the pretender or hypocrite who is only a Christian outwardly" (2011).

Africans are *group oriented*. Their lives are tied together by intimate family relationships. They live in extended families in which the father's brothers are also called "fathers," and in many cases the father's co-wives are all called "mothers." First-generation cousins are called "brothers" and "sisters." Disputes are solved and financial decisions made primarily on the extended family level. When young people move to the cities, they are considered the extension of the family there. Family members will attempt to find jobs for others of their family or, if they become influential, may hire family members to work under them to provide finances for the extended family. While the practice of hiring family members for jobs in government and large corporations is considered unethical in an individualistic society, it is a way of life in areas where a person's first responsibility is to his family.

Extended families of the same totem[7] make up a clan. In many ethnic groups, clans live within a concise geographical area, such as a district or a location. In other ethnic groups, clans are dispersed over a wide geographical area, and clan distinctions are used only in determining whom to marry and for settling disputes related to the murder of fellow clan members.

These clans make up tribes. Before the colonial era, tribes were the largest natural grouping of the people. Colonial powers artificially imposed larger boundaries on tribal areas and called them "nations." It is therefore not surprising that many African states have difficulty developing a sense of nationhood and that voting tends to follow the lines of tribal allegiances.

Local villages form another type of group. Village councils frequently serve as problem-solving forums for marriage, land, and personality issues. Disputes in families, clans, and villages are discussed at length until a consensus is achieved. Voting is thought to be divisive because it forces decision makers to take sides.

Within African society, an individual seldom stands against the group. Rather a person's identity is formed by the group. This is indicated in the African theologian John Mbiti's adage "I am because we are" (Mbiti et al. 1980, 11). When men of the Tiv tribe of Nigeria meet,

7. A totem is usually an animal (less frequently a plant or physical feature) that is spiritually linked to the clan to empower it and give it identity.

they seek each other's identity by asking, "U Ngu No?" — literally, "You [singular] are who [plural]?" The answer is the name of a clan (Terpstra 1996). Africans tend to come to Christ in groups rather than as individuals. Family and village groups discuss the implications of the gospel for hours and, through group interaction, come to belief or disbelief. In such contexts, effective missionaries seek to teach people in their natural groups rather than individually.

Africans are *fatalistic*. They believe that people are not in control of their own destinies. They feel the control and entrapment of powerful ancestors and spirits. In certain contexts, social obligations hinder the accumulation of capital, so that economic advance is difficult. Wealth and position are not personal achievements but possessions of the entire family. Kipsigis farmers frequently state their inability to get ahead by saying, *"Matinye kimnatet,"* literally meaning, "I don't have strength." They do not have the power to plow a field for corn, the financial ability to build a house, or monetary strength to begin a business. They are bound by spiritual forces, their family, and their environment. They fatalistically believe that there is no way to escape except through outside financial assistance and education.

Often, this fatalism manifests itself in churches that have had time to become self-governing and self-supporting. Instead of doing so, they declare, "We don't have strength; we need your help." Sometimes Christians who should be free in Christ continue to feel the bondage of spiritual forces. Fortunately, when people give their full allegiance to God, his mighty power can break the fetters of African fatalism.

Africans are *past oriented and may conceive of time as either linear or cyclical*. Mbiti writes that the *tene* period — the ancient times — "is the centre of gravity in [African thought]: people's thinking and understanding of the world are orientated toward this finality — not in the future but in the past." Africans consider history to be moving backward rather than forward (Mbiti 1971, 28). The present is understood in terms of the past. Myths of the past explain the present, and proverbs — the sayings of ancient times — interpret present events. The past is projected into the present. Time is two-dimensional, with a "long 'past,' and a dynamic 'present.'" The perspective of a distant future, however, is virtually nonexistent in African traditional thought

(Mbiti 1971, 24). Modernity, however, is eroding this past orientation, as young people become more and more focused on the present.

Some Africans conceive of time as linear; others conceive of it as cyclical. In linear cultures, ancestors are spiritual beings whose names are remembered and who continue to be part of the family folklore. They are concerned about the family and intervene when forgotten or when decisions are made with which they disagree. Because of their closeness to the living, they might be considered "the living dead." Ghosts, on the other hand, are spiritual beings whose names have been forgotten and who have faded into the realms of the spirits and gods. Because they are more distant from the living, they are called "the dead."

In cyclical cultures, a person's body and spirit are distinct. When someone's body dies, his spirit eventually comes back to live in other bodies. Life is considered good; death is feared and bad. Thus an ancestral spirit's primary goal is to come back into a body and live again. From a traditional African standpoint, human spirits are fluid. Even while a person lives, his spirit is able to depart for short times without his body dying. This happens during dreams and visions. The Kipsigis caution against waking someone quickly, because if his spirit is not in his body, the shock would cause death. The cyclical view of life is illustrated in the Kipsigis' *Kurenet* rite. This rite, as mentioned in the previous chapter, takes place immediately after a child is born, to ascertain which ancestral spirit has embodied the new child (Orchardson 1961, 45).

Western and Christian influences are radically changing African conceptions of time. Secular Western education and contemporary patterns of social life emphasis the "now" without much reflection on the past or the future. Beliefs in ancestors and ghosts are ridiculed, thus forcing traditional beliefs to go underground. Conservative Christian influences teach that God, who created the world, continues to work today and will bring this world to its ultimate conclusion. At Christ's second coming, God will claim his own to live eternally with him, and the church is dedicated to preparing the world for this.

Father God, help us to be holy, loving, and faithful as we live in Christian community. Lead us to see beyond the confines of our own culture to a portion of your Reality as revealed in Scripture and through the leading of your Holy Spirit. And finally, help us, O Father, to broaden our cultural horizons to become bicultural or tricultural, yet distinctively Christian, in order to minister to the nations of the world. In Jesus' name, amen.

Communicating God's Eternal Message in Africa

What significant changes must missionaries go through in order to minister in a considerably different culture? For example, how do American missionaries faithfully represent God in a largely animistic African context? Should American missionaries consider the worldviews of both cultures equally valid within their own contexts? To what degree should these worldviews be accepted or rejected? People who affirm Scripture to be God's particular revelation to humanity believe that the Christian community, whether in America or in Africa, should look to God's revealed message as the ultimate portrayal of reality. Although the American and African cultures are *perceptions* of reality, Scripture reveals actual reality, given in a different time period and directed to problems in specific cultures. Cross-cultural missionaries must allow God's message to shape their own worldview and must seek to communicate this eternal view of reality in both their own culture and the host culture.

How then should cross-cultural evangelists present biblical Christianity to people of an African culture? Effective missionaries go through a concurrent process of (1) reevaluating their own worldview in light of Scripture, (2) seeking God's foundational message for all humanity, and (3) applying this message to their own and to their host culture.

REEVALUATING THEIR OWN WORLDVIEW

American missionaries encountering an African culture will be forced to ask themselves some fundamental questions about life. First, since Africans generally affirm spiritual powers that Americans deny, American missionaries will ask whether there are spiritual powers that cannot be seen. As they reevaluate their own culture, they will find, perhaps surprisingly, that Scripture assumes the reality of spiritual powers. The Old Testament describes them as gods; the Gospels, as demons; and the Pauline epistles, as principalities and powers. Paul's statement in Ephesians 6:12 summarizes this biblical perspective: "Our struggle is not against flesh and blood, but against the rulers, against the authorities, against the powers of this dark world and against the spiritual forces of evil in the heavenly realms."

Second, American missionaries of an Enlightenment tradition must ask whether they fully understand God's sovereignty over the world. Or have they so compartmentalized reality that they virtually exclude God from the world he created? The theme of God working within his world is a thread running through the biblical text. Jesus describes God by saying, "My Father is always at his work to this very day, and I too am working" (John 5:17).

Third, if God is active, what is the role of science and scientific inquiry? Does God work through laws of nature, or does the orderliness of the world reflect the nature of the God who sustains it? The Bible shows God in Christ upholding the physical world. Paul writes that in Christ "all things hold together" (Col. 1:17). The letter to the Hebrews describes Christ as "sustaining all things by his powerful word" (Heb. 1:3). Scientists can never objectively study God, Christ, and other spiritual beings; they can study only what God has made. Paul writes that "God's invisible qualities — his eternal power and divine nature — have been clearly seen, being understood from what has been made" (Rom. 1:20). Therefore Christians who scientifically study the complexity of God's world should stand in awe of its Creator.

Fourth, have we placed too much confidence in human abilities and human ingenuity? All who come to Christ do so by faith, realizing that "the foolishness of God is wiser than human wisdom, and the weakness of God is stronger than human strength" (1 Cor. 1:25). Salvation is ultimately based on submitting to the will of God. Humans are unable to work out their own spiritual dilemmas. Jeremiah rightly says, "People's lives are not their own; it is not for them to direct their steps" (Jer. 10:23).

Fifth, how do we perceive God? God as Sovereign Lord is described by Moses, after Israel's deliverance from Egyptian captivity, as "majestic in holiness, awesome in glory, working wonders" (Ex. 15:11). In the Old Testament, God is characterized by "steadfast love" *(hesed)*. He is "compassionate and gracious … slow to anger, abounding in love and faithfulness" (34:6 – 7; cf. Num. 14:18; Neh. 9:17; Ps. 86:15; 103:8; 145:8; Joel 2:13; Jonah 4:2). In the New Testament, this attribute of love is seen in God sending his divine Son to become flesh and die for sinful humanity (Rom. 5:8). God's eternal nature is love (1 John 4:7 – 8), but he is also holy. The heavenly host proclaims, "Holy, holy, holy is the Lord God Almighty" (Rev. 4:8; cf. Isa. 6:3). Leviticus describes a sacrificial system based on a holy God wanting to reunite sinful people with himself. Therefore God identifies himself as "the LORD, who makes you holy" (Lev. 20:8).

These two attributes define both why and how God relates to humanity. God did not merely create the world and then leave it. He loves the people he created and wants to live in a relationship with us. Yet he wants humans to reflect his nature (1 Peter 1:15; cf. Lev. 11:44 – 45). As a holy God, he feels our sins. He is like a father who tenderly loves his disobedient son (Hos. 11:1 – 11), a husband who devotedly loves his unfaithful wife (Hos. 1 – 3), a husbandman who lovingly shapes and cultivates his unproductive vineyard (Isa. 5:1 – 7), and a physician who compassionately cares for the sick (Matt. 9:12). God loves us in spite of our unholiness.

SEEKING GOD'S FUNDAMENTAL MESSAGE FOR ALL PEOPLE

As American missionaries in Africa reevaluate their own worldview, they must also discover the fundamental message of God that must be taught, modeled, and obeyed in every age and context. The essence of the gospel does not change with the ebb and flow of cultures but is as unchangeable as eternal God.

The essence of the gospel can be discerned from the great speeches of Old Testament prophets, the teachings of Jesus, and the sermons of early Christians. For example, Ezra's praise and confessional statement made in Jerusalem during a time of spiritual revival encapsulates significant elements of the gospel (Neh. 9:6 – 37). God, the righteous One, keeps his promises in spite of Israel's unfaithfulness. His desire to redeem is rooted in his great love. Jesus said, "I am the way and the truth and the life. No one comes to the Father except through me" (John 14:6).

For Paul, the gospel was the death, burial, and resurrection of Christ (1 Cor. 15:1 – 4). Paul proclaimed this message whenever he preached to Jewish audiences. Luke's summary of this message was that "the Messiah had to suffer and rise from the dead," and that this Jesus was the long-awaited Messiah (Acts 17:1 – 3). Christ's incarnation, ministry, death, and resurrection were rooted in the love of God, who sends and saves (John 3:16). Non-Jews, who did not know the Creator God, were also introduced to his sovereignty and attributes (Acts 17:22 – 31; 14:14 – 18). These speeches and sermons reveal eternal themes communicated within cultural contexts by the inspiration of God.

COMMUNICATING GOD'S ETERNAL MESSAGE IN THE AFRICAN CONTEXT

As American missionaries enter African contexts, they must learn to communicate God's message appropriately.

First, at every significant point, the God of the Bible must be compared to, and contrasted with, the African view of God. Creator God, who was traditionally considered distant in African culture, must be presented as approachable, caring, and powerful. An emphasis must be placed on biblical stories and praises describing his creative power (Gen. 1 – 3; Ps. 8; 24), continued work (Neh. 9:5 – 37; Ps. 106), and divine attributes (Ex. 34:6 – 7; Ps. 103:8 – 22; Deut. 31:30 – 32:43). To know God, who is "majestic in holiness, awesome in glory, working wonders" (Ex. 15:11), is the beginning step on the path to conversion. Allegiance to him must displace allegiance to all other spiritual beings, whether they are ancestors, personal spirits, or tribal gods. The Christ of the New Testament is understood through the clear picture of the God revealed in the Old Testament.

Second, Christ must be proclaimed as the only way to God. In America, Christ is typically presented as one who reconciles people whose sin has alienated them from God, or as one who justifies sinners who are guilty before a pure God. Although the metaphors of *reconciliation* and *justification* are understood in Africa, they do not make a particularly strong impact. The metaphor that stirs the heart of the African is that of *liberation*: Christ has defeated the principalities and powers and rescued his people from their dominion. By his death, he "disarmed the powers and authorities" and "made a public spectacle of them" (Col. 2:15). This liberation metaphor is the classic doctrine of the atonement that was reintroduced to Western theology by Gustaf Aulén in *Christus Victor* (2003; originally published in English in 1931). This message has consis-

Africans understand sacrifices to be human efforts to placate, propitiate, and coerce spiritual beings.... The Christian missionary must deal appropriately with this issue and not ignore it.

tently led Africans to forsake spiritual beings and forces, which stand in opposition to God, in order to worship their sovereign Creator (Van Rheenen 1991, 141 – 42).

Third, African concepts of sacrifice must be radically reinterpreted. Africans understand sacrifices to be human efforts to placate, propitiate, and coerce spiritual beings. They ritually offer chickens, sheep, goats, and cattle in traditional ceremonies to appease angry ancestors, spirits, and gods who have brought evil upon humans and to invoke blessings upon social activities such as initiation into adulthood, marriage, and death (Van Rheenen 1991, 292). The Judeo-Christian understanding of sacrifice is based on different presuppositions. Rather than being rooted in human initiative, sacrifices were prescribed by God himself. They were rooted in God's love and compassion — reflecting his desire to reconcile sinners to himself — and were not intended to manipulate or coerce. Christ's death is God's ultimate sacrifice to replace all other sacrifices (Heb. 10:1 – 14). Because sacrifice is prevalent in African culture, the Christian missionary must not ignore this issue but deal with it appropriately.

Fourth, a Christian conception of God's sovereignty over time must radically engage African perspectives. Christianity, like traditional African religion, emphasizes the past. God acted mightily in history by creating the world, choosing Abraham and his descendants to be his people, delivering Israel from Egyptian captivity, giving Israel the land of Canaan, and sending prophets and priests to proclaim his message. Likewise, God's activity in the past establishes his sovereignty in the present. God expected Israel to obey and follow him because of his activities in their lives. God's rationale for giving Israel the Ten Commandments was that he was Yahweh, their God, "who brought [them] out of Egypt" (Ex. 20:2). The biblical accounts are not tribal myths describing human origin and initiative but God-inspired accounts of his claim to sovereignty.

The most radical reorientation of the traditional African concept of time occurs in relation to the future. The God of the Bible not only has worked in the past but also is working in the present and will continue working until the consummation of the world. Anticipating and preparing for the end is integral to a Christian worldview. Thus African Christians must develop an enhanced anticipation of the ultimate reign of

God in Jesus Christ! This expectation leads them to urgently declare the kingdom of God and live righteous lives as participants of this kingdom!

Finally, at every critical point of culture, Christian evangelists must present relevant alternatives to traditional cultural rites.[8] The critical areas include the blessing and naming of children, rites of transition from childhood to adulthood, marriage, transitions to elderhood, and death. During our early years ministering among the Kipsigis of Kenya, for example, Christian leaders struggled with how Christians marry. Traditionally, Kipsigis marriage was sealed through a ceremony called *katunisietab segutiet* ("the wedding of the grass band"). The bride and groom, dressed in traditional skins, stood before an elder of the village. They bound their hands together with a braided band made from crab-grass. The elder then invoked the ancestors' approval on the marriage by words of blessing and the spitting of traditional beer. Should Christians follow such customs? The African Inland Church introduced *katunisietab beteit* ("the wedding of the ring") into Kipsigis, calling it "Christian." Should Kipsigis Christians borrow Western customs and make them their own? The Church of Christ at various times adapted forms of both of the above marriage ceremonies but began to introduce an innovated form called *katunisietab kayanet* ("the wedding of faith"). This form is both Christian and Kipsigis. Marriage is based not on any physical item, such as a grass band or a ring, but on faith in sovereign God. The community is called together to witness a special union of people under God.

This section recounts the process of theological reevaluation that I went through on the mission field. At times, I felt guilty for retrieving my American cultural presuppositions. American ethnocentrism, patriotism, and legalism surfaced as I encouraged African Christians to accept Western options because they appeared Christian. Sometimes I was tempted to go to the opposite extreme, that is, accommodate too fully to traditional African customs. May God forgive me! The process of reevaluating my worldview in light of scriptural truths, seeking God's

8. African culture is rapidly changing. Sometimes traditional customs are displaced by Western ones. Very typically, traditional customs survive just under the surface, hidden from the eyes of outsiders but practiced during times of illness, famine, and death. These customs are not static but always changing—being shaped, sometimes displaced, by Western ones.

Trusting in God and in his almighty working helped me overcome the temptations to idealize the Western way as the Christian way, on one extreme, or to find Christian roots in all African conceptions, on the other.

fundamental Christian message, and learning to communicate God's eternal message in appropriate, relevant, and clear ways occurred without my being aware of it. We followed Paul Hiebert's contextualization process of (1) exegesis of culture, (2) exegesis of Scripture, and (3) critical response (Hiebert 1987, 109 – 10)[9] without knowing it. Trusting in God and in his almighty working helped me overcome the temptations to idealize the Western way as the Christian way, on one extreme, or to find Christian roots in all African conceptions, on the other.

REFLECTION AND APPLICATION

Questions

1. Define the meaning of the words *noise*, *feedback*, *encoding*, and *decoding* in communication theory.
2. Why is it important for missionaries to communicate the gospel within their own language and culture before attempting to communicate cross-culturally?
3. Describe a two-culture model of missionary communication. In other words, discuss the cultural gap that separates the missionaries' sending culture from the culture of the ancient Near East.
4. What specific mission lessons, summarized by the words *interpretation* and *application*, can be learned from a two-culture model of missionary communication?
5. Why, in the three-culture model of missionary communication, might a new missionary be called a square peg in a round hole?
6. What do the arrows extending from the host culture to biblical culture(s) and returning to the host culture designate? Describe the missionary task in terms of the importance of these arrows.
7. Contrast the role of *mentoring* a movement with that of *founding* a movement.
8. Discuss why cultural decisions and theology cannot be separated. In your answer, give an illustration of a non-Western theological dilemma typically encountered by missionaries.
9. Make a chart contrasting American and African worldviews in the following five areas: (1) perceptions of the spiritual world, (2) orientations toward the

9. See "Critical Contextualization" in chapter 8.

individual and the group, (3) perspectives about optimism and fatalism, (4) understandings of time, and (5) beliefs about the causes of illness.

10. Describe a threefold, concurrent process that missionaries must go through in order to communicate God's eternal message to people of other cultures. In your answer, discuss the value of understanding this threefold process. (Use the last paragraph of the chapter as a resource to answer the second part of this question.)
11. Apply this threefold process (see question 10) to some world culture. Use the African illustration in the text if you are new to the study of missions.

Application

Have Christians in your congregation been able to proclaim the gospel across cultural barriers? What has hindered them or aided them in communicating across these barriers? Have you taught someone of another cultural background? What has hindered or aided you in cross-cultural communication?

Personal Inventory

How has God spoken to you through this chapter? What is God calling you to do about it?

chapter 13

The Missional Helix

Developing Practices for God's Mission

"They need to listen to and learn from each other," Jim and Julie concluded. The purpose of the seminary is to serve the church. The church in turn should listen to people from the seminary with years of study and experience. Jim and Julie were learning equally from each environment: they were studying missions and ministry at the local seminary while ministering with youth in their local church.

They noticed disparity in focus, contrasting orientations. People in the seminary focused on biblical and theological formation and the historical development of these theologies. They viewed pastoral and missional ministry as the practice of theology and, though they acknowledged the importance of these ministries, the hands-on aspects were ill-defined. Church leaders, on the other hand, tended to focus on pragmatics—asking about cultural relevance and success. They wanted to draw people to their church, shape the people's lives, and make a major impact on the community.

Jim and Julie had seen how easy it is for church leaders and missionaries, whether domestic or foreign, to make pragmatic plans without theological reflection. They recalled lessons learned earlier in their missions course, about moving from theology to practice in order to minister out of the will of God: "A theology of mission, like the rudder of a ship, guides the mission of God and provides direction," or it is "the engine of a ship, propelling forward the mission of God."[1] They believed that a theology of mission is both a primary and an ongoing activity in missionary practice and remembered their friend Bill. After he had planted a church by seeking to meet the needs of the community, Bill perceived that the church had become more of a vendor of goods and services than a community of the kingdom of God.[2] Jim and Julie concurred that pragmatism without theological reflection threatens the future of the church. They were, however, thankful for ministry within a church

1. Chapter 3, p. 63.

2. Chapter 4, p. 93.

where the Word of God was studied, disciple making was emphasized, and leaders were prayerfully seeking to live like Jesus.

They heard church leaders claim that theologians are ivory tower thinkers unable to connect with the common people and discerned truth in this statement. It is easy for people in the seminary to process intellectually without serving incarnationally. Recognizing this tendency, the organizers of the seminary curriculum asked entering students to read Helmut Thielicke's classic book *A Little Exercise for Young Theologians* (1962) in the class introducing graduate studies. This book describes the cultural dislocation of seminary students who no longer speak the language of the common people. Jim and Julie were pleased, however, that almost all of their professors, especially those in missions and ministry, taught out of their ministries and experiences within local churches.

They realized that they had the best of both worlds: a good seminary where they could learn deeply and a church community genuinely committed to faithfully following the way of God in Jesus Christ!

THIS CHAPTER GIVES an integrative model of learning that brings together the strengths of studying in a seminary with those of ministering in a local church.

The Missional Helix

In ministry formation, neither theology nor strategy stands by itself as a self-contained discipline; they are two strands of an ongoing process involving various elements. Ministry formation can be seen as a spiral. The coils turn round and round, passing the same landmarks, but always at a slightly different level. This spiral, a helix, is descriptive of the process of effective ministry formation.[1] (See Figure 13.1.)

The spiral begins with *theological reflection* on such theologies as the *missio Dei*, the kingdom of God, incarnation, and atonement, which focus and form our perspectives of culture and the practice of ministry. *Cultural analysis* forms the second element of the helix. Cultural awareness enables missionaries and ministers to define types of peoples within a cultural context, to understand the social construction of their

3. The Missional Helix was first described in a Missiological Reflection in Missiology.org in August 2002 *(www.missiology.org/?p=203)* and then applied to church planting in another Missiological Reflection in January 2003 *(www.missiology.org/?p=157)*. This Missional Helix was used to present the reformist view in the book *Evaluating the Church Growth Movement* (McIntosh 2004, 167 – 89).

Figure 13.1 The Missional Helix

TR = Theological Reflection
CA = Cultural Analysis
HP = Historical Perspective
SF = Strategy Formation

reality, to perceive how they are socially related to one another, and to explain how the Christian message intersects with every aspect of culture (birth rites, coming-of-age rituals, weddings, funerals, and so on). The spiral proceeds to consider what has occurred historically in the missional context. *Historical perspective* narrates how things got to be as they are, based on the interrelated stories of the particular nation, tribe, lineage, the church, and God's mission. Finally, *strategy formation* helps shape the practical methodology of ministry. As illustrated by the Missional Helix, contextual strategies draw deeply from cultural and historical understandings to theologically discern what God is saying about the practice of ministry and develop actual practices to implement the strategies. This shaping of ministry takes place within the environment of *spiritual formation* as Christian servants humbly submit their lives to a covenant relationship with God as Father and enthrone Christ as their King.

The Relationship between the Five Elements of Ministry Formation

The Missional Helix is a spiral because the missionary returns time and time again to reflect theologically, culturally, historically, and strategically under the guiding hand of God to develop ministry models

Figure 13.2 The Missional Helix Spiral

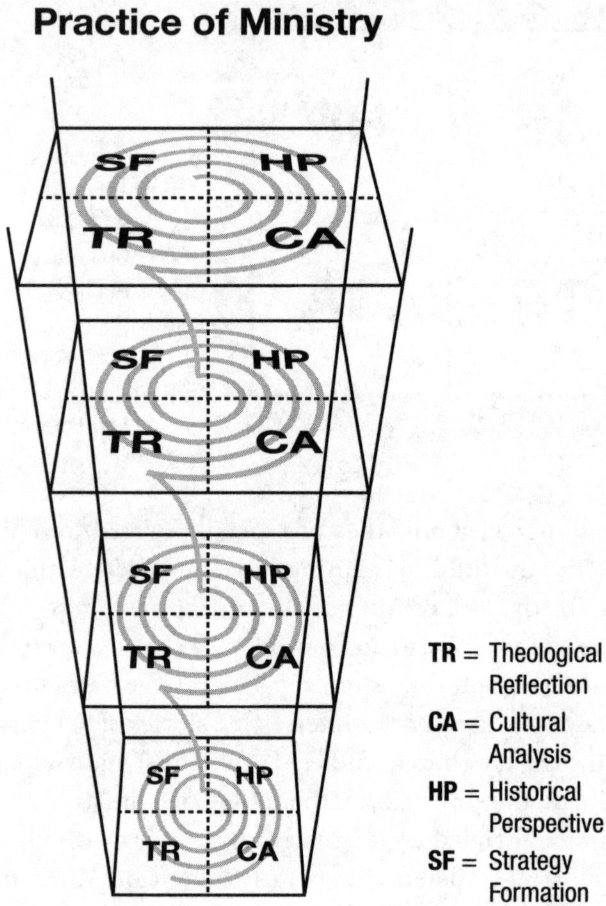

appropriate to the local context. Theology, social understandings, history of missions, and strategy all work together and penetrate each other within this environment of spiritual formation. Thus praxis impacts theology, which in turn shapes the practice of ministry.

In Figure 13.2, the broken lines between the four internal elements of ministry formation demonstrate how each interacts with the others. In this process, God is shaping who Christian leaders are and what they do within an environment of spiritual formation as they humbly and prayerfully submit to him as Father and to each other.

The diagram is a helix because theology, history, culture, and the practice of ministry *build on one another* as the community of faith collectively develops understandings and a vision of God's will within its cultural context. Like a spring, the spiral grows to new heights as ministry understandings and experiences develop. Ideally, the missionary is always learning, growing in the Lord, always spiraling to a new level of understanding and competence.

Ideally, the missionary is always learning, growing in the Lord, always spiraling to a new level of understanding and competence.

The Components of the Missional Helix

Each of these four internal elements of the Missional Helix (theology, culture, history, and strategy) is essential in reflecting on and planning for Christian ministry.

THEOLOGICAL REFLECTION

Theological reflection is the beginning point for ministry formation and the most significant element within the internal structure of the spiral. All missiological decisions must be rooted both implicitly and explicitly in biblical theology in order to mirror the purposes and mind of God.

Too many missionaries, while acknowledging the Bible as the Word of God, allow culture rather than Scripture to shape their core understandings of the church. The Bible is used to proof-text practice rather than to define the church's essence. Without a biblically rooted ecclesiology, the teachings and practices of the church are likely to be shaped either implicitly by the dominant evangelical culture or explicitly by random surveys to ascertain what people want. A biblical understanding of the nature of the church, consequently, enables missionaries to plant and nurture churches that are rooted in the mission of God rather than in presuppositions of popular culture.

The Missional Helix proposes that missionaries use Scripture to form a biblical understanding of the church. Paul, in Ephesians 2:19 – 22, for instance, uses multiple metaphors to describe the nature of the church. The church is a new nation: newly converted Christians are "no longer foreigners and strangers" but "fellow citizens" in a community of faith (v. 19). The church is a family, or God's "household" (v. 19). The church is a holy temple, well constructed, with each part joined together and built around Jesus Christ, the chief cornerstone (vv. 20 – 22). This fellowship comes into existence through conversion: people dead in sin (2:1 – 3) have been made alive with Christ (vv. 4 – 7) by God's grace (vv. 8 – 10). Paul stacks metaphors one on another to illustrate a redeemed fellowship brought together under Christ (1:3 – 11) and existing "for the praise of his glory" (v. 12). These perspectives form an inspired picture of God's divine community.

Theological reflection, however, extends beyond textual study. Missionaries must realize that all readers understand and apply Scripture within their historical traditions, based on their rational systems of thought, and formed by their experience. The missionary therefore must be cognizant of four resources that shape theological reflection: Scripture, tradition, reason, and experience (Stone and Duke 1996, 43 – 54). For example, in rural, face-to-face cultures, Christians tend to perceive the church as a "family"; in modern, industrial contexts, as a "business"; and in postmodern, informational cultures, as a "network," or sometimes as a "community." Missionaries and ministers, as theological "meaning makers," must theologically reflect on the connotation of these metaphors, using all four resources.

CULTURAL ANALYSIS

In addition to theological reflection, missionaries must perform an in-depth analysis of the local culture's worldview. Much too often, this second element of the Missional Helix is excluded. Church planters naively project their worldview on other contexts and interpret reality in terms of their own heritage. This intellectual colonialism results in transplanted theologies, reflecting the missionaries' heritage, rather than contextualized theologies, developed by reflecting on Scripture within the context of local languages, thought categories, and ritual patterns. Transplanted theologies are merely uprooted from one context and transferred to a new one, with the expectation that the meanings will be the same in both cultures. The beginning point of theologizing in a new culture is always a thorough analysis of the culture on a worldview level. With these cultural understandings, trained missionaries are able to be theological brokers to people within the culture and minister alongside them in developing a local, contextualized theology.

Christian ministry does not occur in a cultural vacuum; it occurs in cultural contexts, where rival perspectives of reality vie for human allegiance. Missionaries must therefore become adept at differentiating worldview types and discern how these types influence the host culture. These understandings enable missionaries to communicate God's message so that it interacts with the culture's perspective of reality.

At least four different worldview types are present in world cultures. Stated succinctly, a *secular* worldview divides the world into natural and supernatural realms and focuses almost exclusively on the natural. God is considered to be either nonexistent or irrelevant to human affairs. Secularists tend to be resistant to the gospel until they realize, usually during times of trauma, that humans are unable to "direct their [own] steps" (Jer. 10:23), that the divine and the human are interrelated. An *animistic* perspective of reality believes that personal spiritual beings and impersonal spiritual forces have power over human affairs. During times of disease, death, and drought, animists use divination to discover which beings and forces are impacting them, in order to ward them off or to employ their power. Animists must learn that Creator God is approachable and concerned about human life, and unlike the gods, "majestic in holiness" (Ex. 15:11). Through the death and resurrection of his Son, God has defeated all the principalities and powers (Col. 2:15). A *pantheistic* worldview perceives that an impersonal, all-pervading essence, sometimes defined as "god," fills the universe. As droplets of water merge to become a stream, then a river, and finally an ocean, so individuals can become one with the essence of the universe through meditation, thus achieving a change of consciousness called enlightenment. The pantheist, through living illustrations of Christian meditation, must experience God to be living and personal, full of compassion and having a distinctive holiness. A *theistic* worldview presupposes that God created the heavens and the earth and continues to care for that universe. Some theists follow God's distinctive way of salvation through Jesus Christ, while others focus on submitting to and honoring Allah.

Using these typologies, missionaries and ministers can diagram the intertwining influences of secularism, animism, pantheism, and theism within their host culture. While most cultures emphasize one or two of these types, influences from all four types may be syncretized in various configurations. Understanding the different influences in the culture enables missionaries and ministers to encode the gospel in theological metaphors appropriate to the context.

Worldview analysis is only one of many tools of cultural inquiry. Other tools include study of the epistemological sources forming worldview, the types of cognitive processes, a culture's grid/group orientation, the levels of technology and the resultant strategies for use of money and media, the differing definitions of sin and related conceptions of salvation, and the logico-structural integration of its worldview universals within the culture.

Frequently, church planters analyze bits and pieces of a culture but are unable to make a systematic cultural analysis. Or they effectively analyze culture in broad, general terms, such as premodern, modern, and postmodern, but are not equipped to make localized cultural analysis.

HISTORICAL PERSPECTIVE

Likewise, missionaries must develop ministry based on historical perspective rather than being oblivious of what has previously occurred. Because of their short national history and focus on practical inclinations, many North Americans sense the future without understanding the past. Samuel Escobar believes that North American missiologists tend to negate theory and historical background. In other words, they look at missions as a management task necessitating "a task-oriented sequence of steps to be followed in order to achieve" specified goals. He challenges the North American missions community to expand the horizons of their "managerial missiology" (1992, 13–14; cf. 2000, 109–12).

Historical perspective provides many insights that guide missionaries in developing their practice of ministry. For example, the reading of history greatly helps contemporary evangelists to understand syncretism. Ancient Israelites, like many people coming out of animism, were tempted to follow both God and the gods of the nations. They "bow[ed] down and [swore] by the Lord and ... by Molech" (Zeph. 1:5). Modern Christians have syncretized secularism and theism by negating the Holy Spirit and demythologizing spiritual powers. Postmodern Christians have brought new syncretisms, including pervasive relativism, fascination with spiritual powers, focus on power and neglect of truth, and interpretation of emotions and intuition as the work of the Holy Spirit.

Missionaries will find it difficult to understand the nature of syncretism without historical perspective.

STRATEGY FORMATION

Missions, by its very nature, necessitates strategic planning. Strategy formation, however, should never stand by itself as a self-contained, how-to-do-it prescription. Never should practitioners merely ask the question, "Does it work?" Many strategies that "work" and enable the church to grow for short periods of time do not reflect the qualities and purposes of God. For example, the "health-wealth" gospel produces numerical results, but when God takes away health or wealth, as in the case of Job, the faith of people who have come to Christ to receive his "benefits" will likely prove deficient. A question that better reflects the Missional Helix model is, "Does this model of praxis guide people to become disciples of Jesus and people of his mission within this historical, cultural context?"

A question that reflects the Missional Helix model is, "Does this model of praxis guide people to become disciples of Jesus and people of his mission within this historical, cultural context?"

The foundational understandings of theology and the perspectives developed through cultural analysis and historical views should, then, lead missionaries to critical reflection on praxis. The missionary or minister should return time and time again to reflect theologically, culturally, historically, and strategically, within the context of spiritual formation, in order to develop ministry models that are appropriate to the local context. The four elements work together and interpenetrate each other. With these understandings in mind, we can say that strategy is the practice of model formation for ministry shaped by theological reflection, cultural analysis, and historical perspective and by the continued practice of ministry while being spiritually formed as disciples of Christ.

Currently, missions strategies are undergoing radical transformation as missiologists reflect on the different social contexts of missions and the need for the church to be God's distinct, called-out people. For example, the United States once considered itself to be a Christian nation. Many early immigrants fled Europe seeking religious freedom in the New World. As new towns emerged, churches occupied a central location, reflecting the church's role in shaping cultural customs and values. People moving west were generally receptive to the gospel of Christ. In fact, Christianity flourished on the North American frontier.

The Christian church in the twenty-first century, however, has generally lost this privileged position in the United States, except to some degree in the Bible Belt (the south-central and southeastern areas from Texas to the East Coast). The church is now only one of many influences shaping contemporary culture. Nevertheless, many Christians assume that the USA is still a Christian nation and attempt to promote Christian morals and ethics through public political activity. This has caused outsiders to view the church as sheltered, judgmental, and antihomosexual (Kinnaman 2007).

Returning to England after thirty years of missionary work in India, Lesslie Newbigin, father of the contemporary missional movement, witnessed an even greater decline of Christianity in his country. In *Foolishness to the Greeks*, he asked, "What would be involved in a missionary encounter between the gospel and this whole way of perceiving, thinking, and living that we call 'modern Western culture'?" or in its shortened, more popular form, "Can the West be converted?" (1986, 1). This must also be a guiding question for us in North America during this generation. The church must learn to serve in pre-Constantinian ways as a minority — to survive from the margins rather than from the center of culture. "Missions, which have been accustomed to flowing down the current of world power, are now faced with the necessity of learning for the first time to swim against the current" (Newbigin 1994, 8). Patterns for missional, incarnational church planting and renewal will be discussed more fully in chapter 16.

The Environment of Ministry Formation

From my perspective, the most important sentence in this chapter up to this point is this:

This shaping of ministry takes place within the environment of spiritual formation as Christian servants humbly submit their lives to a covenant relationship with God as Father and enthrone Christ as their King.

DEFINING SPIRITUAL FORMATION

Spiritual formation is walking with God in such a way that we are being "transformed into his image with ever-increasing glory" (2 Cor. 3:18). This glory is embodied in Christ, who brought a new covenant which brings life enlightened by God's Spirit. This glory is contrasted with the fading glory of the old covenant of Moses, which was merely written on "tablets" or "letters" of stone (vv. 3, 7). Paul says, "Will not the ministry of the Spirit be even more glorious? If the ministry that brought condemnation was glorious, how much more glorious is the ministry that brings righteousness!"(vv. 8 – 9).

Paul compares his ministry with that of Moses. Because of the hope embodied in this new covenant, "we are very bold" (v. 12). When Moses came down Mount Sinai, his countenance so reflected the radiance of God that the Israelites could not look at him; Moses, however, put a veil over his face to hide this "fading glory" (v. 7 HCSB). Paul speaks not only of himself but also of all Christians who have "unveiled faces" (v. 18). All who have turned to the Lord are being transformed "into his image" by the Holy Spirit (v. 18). Like light permeating darkness, Paul's message gains credibility because of the spiritual formation that is taking place within the churches.

May we be people of unveiled faces boldly reflecting God's glory as we are transformed into his likeness by the Holy Spirit!

These twin themes of covenant and kingdom reverberate throughout the Bible. Covenant signifies the personal, intimate relationship of God with his people. Kingdom reflects God's rule with authority and power among his people. This shaping of ministry thus takes place within the environment of spiritual formation as Christian servants humbly submit their lives to a covenant relationship with God as Father and enthrone Christ as their King.

THE COVENANT TRIANGLE

Mike Breen describes the covenant by means of a triangle. Jesus reveals his relationship with God the Father and invites us to participate with him in this relationship (Breen 2010, 225). Jesus does only what he sees his Father doing (John 5:19). "In shared identity, common purpose is forged. As his disciples mature in their relationship with him, Jesus

Figure 13.3
The Covenant Triangle

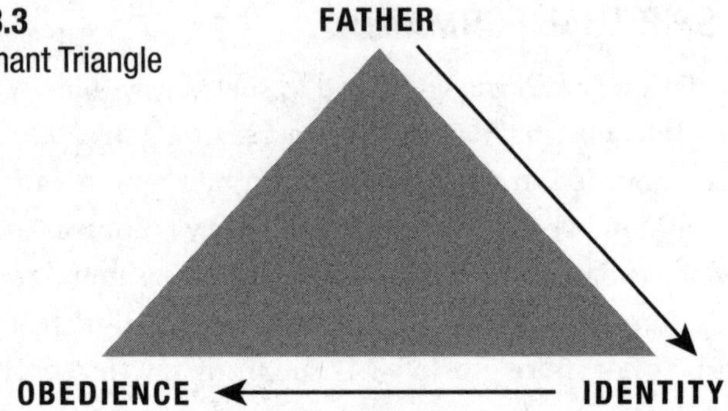

reveals that they will share in a common relationship with the one that he calls Father and that together they will fashion the cords that will hold the Covenant together" (2010, 225). This cord is love. Jesus said, "Anyone who loves me will obey my teaching. My Father will love them, and we will come to them and make our home with them" (John 14:23).

This identity flows from God our Creator, who faithfully redeems by the blood of his Son and indwells us through his Holy Spirit. "We are children of God, born again into a new family, given a new name and a new identity by which we can gain access to all of the resources of our Covenant partner" (Breen 2010, 226). Our participation in the death, burial, and resurrection of Christ in baptism signifies a new life in union with God in Jesus Christ (Rom. 6:3 – 7). The Lord's Supper is a covenant meal celebrated to help remind us whose we are (Luke 22:14 – 22).

We thus obey God because we are his children walking in covenant relationship with him. Jesus said, "If you love me, keep my commands" (John 14:15). The way of God is spiritually formed within our hearts, minds, and souls. We begin to live with "security and confidence" (Breen 2010, 226 – 27) in covenant relationship with the God who formed us. We no longer seek to approach God through obedience; we seek to approach him through "a simple recognition of our identity" (Breen 2010, 227) with God in Christ, led forward by his Holy Spirit.

THE KINGDOM TRIANGLE

Mike Breen also defines the kingdom by means of a triangle. As described in chapter 3, the kingdom of God is a theme woven through

Figure 13.4
The Kingdom Triangle

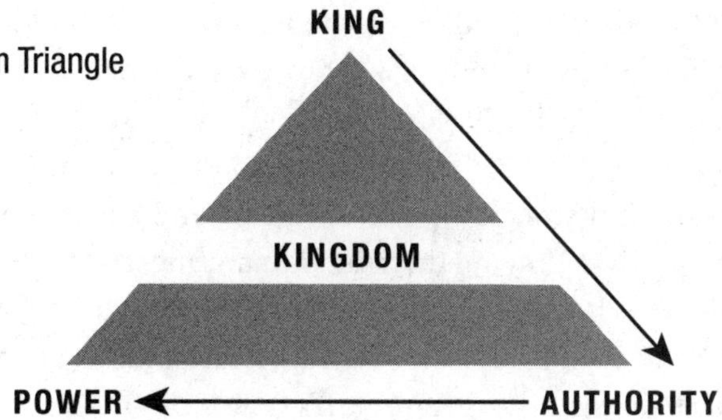

the fabric of the biblical narrative. Jesus began his public ministry by "proclaiming the good news of God," saying, "The kingdom of God has come near. Repent and believe the good news!" (Mark 1:14 – 15). He taught his disciples to pray, "Your kingdom come, your will be done, on earth as it is in heaven" (Matt. 6:10). As servant King, Jesus healed the sick, cast out demons, fed the poor, and forgave the sinful. His parables described the reception, value, and priority of his kingdom.

Most frequently, Jesus' kingdom glory was camouflaged, but occasionally it was revealed in its entire splendor. At his baptism, heaven was opened and God gave his blessing: "This is my Son, whom I love; with him I am well pleased" (Matt. 3:17). On the Mount of Transfiguration, Jesus was enveloped in a cloud that also covered Moses the great lawgiver and Elijah the great prophet, and God said, "This is my Son, whom I love; with him I am well pleased. Listen to him!" (Matt. 17:5). In his ascension, Jesus was taken into heaven before the eyes of the apostles, who then heard two angels promise that he would likewise return (Acts 1:9 – 11).

Jesus as King gives his disciples authority to act for him. They are to represent him as King. Breen writes, "In the gospels, we read of Jesus' amazing authority as he represented God's Kingship. In turn, having followed him and learnt to imitate his life, his disciples chose to receive the authorization to act on his behalf. Disciples choose to give as they have received — giving forgiveness, healing, deliverance and blessing" (2010, 229).

When Jesus sent seventy-two disciples out on the Limited Commission, he commanded them to "heal the sick who are there and tell them, 'The kingdom of God has come near to you'" (Luke 10:9). They returned with joy, saying to Jesus, "Lord, even the demons submit to us in your name" (Luke 10:17). Jesus said, "I saw Satan fall like lightning from heaven" (Luke 10:18). They did not do this by their own power or might; they did it by the delegated authority God had given them. This is not done by power flowing through human fingertips, typifying some human ability; it is done via prayer to God, who has all authority to forgive sin and defeat Satan. This defeat of Satan during Jesus' ministry was a foretaste of his disarming Satan's power on the cross (Col. 2:15).

Breen describes the Kingdom Triangle in simple terms: "The Kingdom begins with the King, who exercises authority through us his representatives, and with that authority, he sends power for us to be able to do all that he wants us to do" (2010, 229).

The Missional Helix thus takes place within the environment of spiritual formation as Christian servants humbly submit their lives to a covenant relationship with God as Father and enthrone Christ as their King.

Functions of the Missional Helix

The Missional Helix is useful in at least two ways. First and foremost, it provides the Christian practitioner with a model of a decision-making process that must become both intentional and instinctive. In other words, the missionary or minister should seek theological understandings, cultural analysis, historical perspective, and strategy formation when developing patterns for ministry. Second, the Missional Helix could be used as a model for theological education. Equipping for ministry should not put high emphasis on some elements and give little consideration to others. Rather it should provide an intentional, integrated model of ministry formation.

REFLECTION AND APPLICATION

Questions

1. What are the benefits of learning in seminary while ministering in a local church?
2. Why is learning illustrated by a spiral or a helix?
3. What is the role of theological reflection in ministry formation?
4. What is the role of cultural analysis in ministry formation?
5. What is the role of historical perspective in ministry formation?
6. How does strategy formation draw from all items of the Missional Helix to define spiritually transformative and contextually appropriate paradigms of ministry?
7. Define *spiritual formation*.
8. How does *covenant* help form our spiritual identity?
9. How does *kingdom* empower us to minister?

Case Study

Paul's letter to Titus illustrates the development of strategy for a specific cultural context. Titus was ministering in a demoralized culture where no central government existed, the economy had disintegrated, and insolence and arrogance reigned. A local prophet, quoted by Paul, characterized his own people as "liars, evil brutes, lazy gluttons" (Titus 1:12). Even the Christians on Crete were described as "rebellious people, full of meaningless talk and deception," who were "teaching things they ought not to teach" (vv. 10–11). Paul suggested to Titus an appropriate strategy for working in this culture. He directed Titus not to handle all the problems of the Cretan church by himself and to avoid petty arguments because they were "unprofitable and useless" (3:9). Rather he was to appoint elders in every town, who would then determine God-ordained solutions to Cretan dilemmas. Throughout the process, Titus was to remember that conversion is of God and that all believers were once foolish and disobedient, enslaved by passions and desires, but had been saved by God's mercy (vv. 3–7). Titus was to "stress these things, so that those who have trusted in God may be careful to devote themselves to doing what is good" (v. 8). Because of the demands of the gospel and the demoralized cultural milieu, Paul called Titus to a focused ministry of mentoring, training, and ordaining Cretan leaders.

1. How did historical and cultural understandings help Paul suggest a strategy to Titus?
2. How did theology shape Paul's suggested practices?
3. What was the role of spiritual formation in this scenario?

Personal Inventory

How has God spoken to you through this chapter? What is God calling you to do about it?

chapter 14

Creative Strategies for Planting, Nurturing, and Training

Practical Ways of Implementing God's Purposes

DEVELOPING A STRONG MOVEMENT OF GOD in a new city or ethnic area requires the accomplishment of three essential tasks. First, initial evangelism must lead to planting new churches. Second, Christians must be nurtured to maturity within these churches. Third, leaders must be trained to evangelize and to plant other churches, to pastor and shepherd the community of believers, and to train still other leaders. This chapter surveys various strategies for accomplishing these primary mission tasks. While secondary mission tasks may amplify them, a strong movement of God cannot come into being without intentional focus on these three central tasks.

Jim and Julie began to dream about what God might do during the next stage of their lives. Was it possible that God would use them to develop a church-planting movement, either domestically or in some receptive overseas context? What would this look like? What are the basic tasks of beginning a church-planting movement? This chapter, used in their class on church planting and development, helped them understand three major ministry tasks in church planting.

Planting New Churches

The theological and strategic foundations on which churches are planted greatly affect their ability to grow and mature. Paul encourages the church planter to "build with care" (1 Cor. 3:10). At some point, every builder's work will be tested with fire. Those who build with incombustible materials (gold, silver, and costly stones) will receive a reward, but those who build with combustible materials (wood, hay, and straw) will experience loss (vv. 10 – 15).

DEFINITION OF CHURCH PLANTING

Church planting may be defined as *initiating reproducing fellowships that reflect the kingdom of God in the world*. This definition reflects several characteristics of church planting.

1. Church Planting Is Aimed at the Creation of Fellowships

The church is the family of God, the body of Christ (Eph. 1:22 – 23), a "chosen people" who are "God's special possession" (1 Peter 2:9). These biblical metaphors indicate that the church must become a cohesive body reflecting the qualities of God in an alien world (1 Peter 2:11 – 12). Evangelism should focus on producing bodies of believers rather than scattered individual converts. Matayo Lang'at, an early convert in God's movement among the Kipsigis in Kenya, often used a farming metaphor to illustrate why new Christians must work together to become part of a functioning fellowship.

> Here in Africa, one person cannot cultivate with oxen by himself. There must be people in the field to guide the oxen on each side as well as one who holds the plow. Likewise, one cannot be the church by himself. He must call others who are in Christ to work together with him. (Translation from sermon, 1976)

Donald McGavran, the father of the church growth movement,[1] concurs: "Would-be disciples must be joyfully built into his body — they must not wander alone in the wilderness" (1990, 7). Short evangelistic events often leave a few new Christians to fend for themselves.

1. Dr. Donald McGavran's role in world mission is described in chapter 8.

Workers often leave before a fellowship of believers has come into existence. These few Christians face the grave danger of abandoning their newfound faith, because they were never incorporated into communities that could mold and guide them in their spiritual journey.

2. Effective Church Planting Focuses on Cultivating Fellowships That Reproduce

Some churches are established without the expectation that new converts will teach others. These churches are like seedless grapes, delightful to taste but lacking reproductive power. They are like the fig tree that Jesus caused to wither because it did not bear fruit (Matt. 21:18 – 19).

Wendell Broom, my teacher and mentor,[2] many years ago described such churches as "terminal" (Broom 1976, 88 – 89). Terminal churches may have spiritual vitality but can reproduce only arithmetically (2, 4, 6, 8, 10, 12, and so on). Missionaries teach others but do not train new Christians to reproduce; they initiate churches but do not prepare leaders to plant other churches.

The author of Hebrews described terminal churches when he wrote, "Though by this time you ought to be teachers, you need someone to teach you the elementary truths of God's word all over again. You need milk, not solid food!" (5:12).

Germinal churches, on the other hand, grow exponentially (2, 4, 8, 16, 32, 64, 128, 256, 512, and so on). They reproduce like rabbits in Australia, bananas in Bermuda, and papayas in fertile areas of tropical Africa. They are like starfish, which multiply when cut into pieces. It is within the nature of each part to reproduce.[3]

Exponential church growth can be illustrated by strawberry plants or Bermuda grass, which send out runners in many directions. These runners then develop their own root systems and send out still new runners until the field is covered. The roots each represent a new church or cell group planted in a new village or new area of the city. Once the Christian community develops sufficient roots, it is able to plant still

2. Wendell Broom taught missions and Bible at Abilene Christian University for many years. I had the great opportunity to succeed him as a teacher of missions at this university.
3. Broom compares terminal churches, on the other hand, to mules. They do a lot of valuable work but are limited by their inability to reproduce.

other fellowships. Paul urged Timothy to encourage his converts to use germinal principles in church leadership: "The things you have heard me say in the presence of many witnesses [first generation] entrust to reliable people [second generation] who will also be qualified to teach others [third generation]" (2 Tim. 2:2).

Broom describes the potential effects of germinal multiplication.

> Ten missionaries can each plant one church each year. If the churches they plant have *terminal* life, after ten years their field will have 100 churches. If the missionaries die or return home, the number of churches remains static, for they do not plant other churches. The same ten missionaries, by planting churches that have *germinal* life, will in ten years have 5,110 churches in their field. If the missionaries die or return home, the churches will continue to multiply, because they have germinal life. (Broom 1976, 88)

My past student Andrew Johnson (2010) has described the germinal growth of the kingdom among the Dagara people of Burkina Faso in West Africa. Johnson is part of a missionary team who learned the French language before arriving in Burkina Faso in 2002, then devoted almost a year and a half to learning the local language and understanding the culture before starting to teach in two villages. About two months later, the first believers were baptized. The missionaries encouraged them to meet together on Sunday, while they continued to teach during the week. The missionaries then began evangelism in two more villages. A new church was planted in one of these villages within five months.

Less than a year after the planting of the first two churches, Christians from these villages co-planted, working with the missionaries, two more churches. Over the next year, more churches were planted by missionaries and Dagara Christians working together. Two years after the first churches were planted, a Dagara evangelist planted a church with no missionary assistance. About two years later, Johnson says,

> Evangelism done by the Dagara really took off, and they stopped even telling us when they were doing it, much less asking for our help — they just did it. This was a period of fast growth. We missionaries roamed around, visiting lots of churches doing a lot of church development, given that we were no longer needed in the evangelism game (teaching on things like Christian living, elders, Godly families, holiness, etc.) ... although we each continued at least one church plant at all times because ... once that gets in your blood, it's hard to resist it! (2010)

By 2009, five and a half years after the first churches were planted, Dagara Christians were independently planning regional meetings and planting churches among other people groups. New mission personnel started a physical development ministry, focusing initially on repairing nonfunctioning water wells.[4]

By 2012, over forty Dagara villages had functioning churches, with a total of about five thousand baptized believers — and more churches are being planted! Development initiatives extended to a collaborative effort by missionaries and nationals to supply milk to Dagara orphans under two years of age, as well as a literacy program (Johnson 2012).

The Dagara work demonstrates that germinal growth occurs best when missionaries equip local believers, then release them to minister in the power of the Holy Spirit. Johnson notes that most of the "failed" church-planting attempts among the Dagara were initiated by expatriate missionaries (2010). It also illustrates that germinal church planting often begins more slowly than other approaches but usually produces churches that are more sustainable and less dependent on foreign assistance.

Certain theological commitments provide special impetus to germinal growth. Anticipation of and preparation for the second coming of Christ is an example. When Christians perceive that they stand between the first and second comings of Christ, it motivates them to teach people around them to prepare for his return. The reality that this present world is temporary — that a believer's real identity is not of this world but in Christ — propels disciples of Christ to speak of eternal truths.

The understanding that God is active and is convicting the world of sin through the Holy Spirit (John 16:7 – 11) also fosters germinal church planting. Christians who believe in God's mighty acts will be ready, when the Holy Spirit touches them, to teach a Cornelius or an Ethiopian. Their lives are attuned to God's reality rather than to secular "realities" that deny the active working of God. Greg Newton, reflecting on the great church growth among the Sukuma people of Tanzania, said, "We praise God for the Spirit which is moving to inspire

4. Note that, in this case, physical development ministry was begun after a local church-planting movement was firmly established. While other circumstances may require missionaries to address physical conditions sooner, it is better if development ministries are conducted in partnership with strong national churches.

Christians to evangelize" (1994, 1). Recognition of the temporary nature of this world, and faith in the working of the Holy Spirit, are two beliefs foundational to germinal growth.

3. Church Planting Is More than Creating Social Communities

These fellowships must accept God as their sovereign Lord and strive to reflect his nature. Thus church planting is *initiating reproducing fellowships that reflect the kingdom of God in the world*. The term *fellowship* expresses the horizontal relationships among Christians within the body; the phrase *that reflect the kingdom of God in the world* expresses the vertical relationship between God and the fellowship over which he reigns. This distinction is vital because a church fellowship can divorce itself from the divine and become a social fraternity, much like the local Kiwanis or Rotary clubs. This type of fellowship lacks the divine impetus to germinate.

4. Effective Church Planting Requires Nurturing

In effective church planting, bodies of believers are not planted and then left but are nurtured until they reflect the kingdom of God in the world. The term *initiating* in the definition of church planting implies that something must follow the planting of the church.

GUIDELINES FOR PLANTING NEW CHURCHES

While specifics of church planting vary, four general guidelines are fundamental in every context. First, church planters must view their work as a spiritual activity. They must pray and fast both for the city or ethnic group in which God has placed them and for God's empowerment in the task of evangelizing. They must realize that these people are not yet followers of God, because they are still under the dominion of Satan. Christ, however, came "to destroy the devil's work" (1 John 3:8). Church planters must therefore pray for wisdom and power from God, knowing that evangelization is ultimately reclaiming for the kingdom of God territory that is currently held by Satan. Prayer demonstrates recognition of God's role, acknowledging that only God in Jesus Christ can deliver people from the grip of sin and the clutches of the Evil One. Evangelizing unbelievers and nurturing them to grow in Christ is not primarily a human endeavor but the work of God through his people.

Second, church planters must guide new converts to visualize what God's church should look like within their culture and to implement this vision. The church must reflect the presence of God in its own culture because it is *the distinctive people of God called by him through his mission and set aside for his mission*.[5] Therefore the forms of church — language, worship, decision making, and so on — vary from culture to culture. Must a Russian church speak English in worship services and rely on American models of the church? Should their songs reflect the rhythms and harmonies of Western music? Are decisions made by foreigners or by locals? How are decisions made — by voting or by consensus? Christian meanings must be communicated in indigenous forms. The local population should perceive the church not as a foreign religion but as part of their own society. This does not mean syncretism with non-Christian religious elements, that is, the mingling of Christian perspectives with pagan or secular understandings from popular culture. It means the communication of Christian beliefs in terms acceptable and meaningful to the culture in which the church is planted. Like a banana plant in the Bahamas,[6] the church thrives within the culture because it allows God to use its resources rather than superficially borrowing cultural forms from a foreign source.

Third, church planters must learn to communicate God's eternal message within the plausibility structures of the culture. They should take into account the worldview of the people and present the gospel in a way that makes sense to them. Church-planting missionaries enter a new culture as learners seeking to understand how to communicate God's message and initiate a church that reflects the kingdom of God

---

5. Chapter 4 offers a more complete theology of the church.

6. One day while traveling in Canada, I noticed banana plants in front of a house. I inquired how banana plants could grow in Canada and learned that they must have special care. During cold periods, the plants were uprooted and taken indoors to be replanted during warm summer periods. The plants had also never produced fruit! Like transplanted banana plants, American churches planted in foreign lands need special care just to survive and are not able to reproduce.

within that context. For example, proclaiming that Christ has defeated the principalities and powers (Col. 2:15) makes little impact on secular Americans who have limited understanding of spiritual powers. This concept of Christ, the triumphant one who has defeated the spirits, however, stirs the heart of animists and brings them to the foot of the cross (Van Rheenen 1991, 141–42). Deliverance from the fear and control of the satanic realm is found only in Christ.

Fourth, church planters must study the webs of relationships that tie people of the culture together.[7] Kinship is the dominant web relationship, especially in rural societies. In Africa, Asia, and Latin America,

> the web counts tremendously. Every man has, knows and is intimate not merely with brothers, sisters, and grandparents, but also with cousins, uncles, aunts, great-uncles, sisters-in-law, mothers-in-law ... and many others.... Members of other clans or families can become Christian and he remains unmoved; but let "one of us" become Christian and he is deeply stirred. (McGavran 1990, 243–44)

The Kipsigis of Kenya live in patriarchal extended families. Fielden Allison's research shows that, in the early stages of the church-planting movement among them, 87 percent of all churches were initiated through kinship contacts, and the strongest churches had many interwoven kinship relationships. An older brother teaching a younger sibling was the most effective teaching relationship (1983, 56–67).

In urban contexts, relationships become more complex. Occupational and associational ties vie with kinship relationships for people's time and allegiance. Mr. Chun, a Christian banker, leads a cell group of financial leaders in Seoul, Korea. The group meets weekly in the nonthreatening atmosphere of a restaurant and has a yearly goal of bringing two professional colleagues to know Jesus. These new believers are then nurtured toward Christian maturity within their small group. This type of evangelism follows occupational networks.

The church-planting missionary must map out the web relationships that connect people to people. The gospel travels along these relational pathways.

---

7. Web relationships are the kinship and associational ties that connect people of a culture with one another.

Nurturing New Christians

The second major task of missions is to nurture new Christians to maturity. The Kipsigis say, *"Magisiche lagok si kebagach"* — "We cannot give birth to children and then leave them." It is relatively easy for Western Christians to travel to another land, preach through translators for a few days, convert a few souls hungry to know God (and sometimes hungry to know foreigners), and leave them without basic understandings of the Christian faith and without the ability to work out this faith in their everyday lives. A major challenge of missions is not *conversion* of unbelievers to following Christ but *reversion* of new believers from following him.

DEFINITION OF NURTURING

Nurturing stems from the very heart of God. God is a vinedresser who devotedly tends his vineyard (Isa. 5:1 – 7), a physician who tenderly nurses his patients (Matt. 9:12), and a parent who lovingly teaches his child to walk (Hos. 11:1, 3). These metaphors reflect God's desire to relate personally to Israel, his chosen people. God is portrayed in Scripture as the ever-present, compassionate Lord who sends his messengers to nurture his people so they will come into relationship with him. Thus when we nurture new Christians to maturity, we are reflecting God's heart.

In his letter to the Ephesians, Paul had much to say about nurturing. He described the church as the body that, although living on the earth, dwells in the heavenly realms with the resurrected Christ. This body has been transformed from death to life by the extension of God's grace in Jesus Christ (Eph. 1:18 – 2:10). People of Christ's body — both Jewish believers and Gentile believers — must grow together to become one. They should no longer be "foreigners and strangers" but "fellow citizens with God's people and also members of his household" (2:11 – 22, esp. v. 19). This unity is based on God's four-dimensional love described by Paul:

> *I pray that you, being rooted and established in love, may have power, together with all the Lord's holy people, to grasp how wide and long and high and deep is the love of Christ, and to know*

Nurturing prepares new believers to withstand the fire of Satan's persecution by walking personally with older Christians to experience listening to God and responding to him in obedience.

> *this love that surpasses knowledge — that you may be filled to the measure of all the fullness of God.*
> (EPHESIANS 3:17 – 19)

The gifts present in the body are to be joined together so that the work of each part contributes to the strengthening of the whole. When this occurs, the body becomes mature in Christ. Members are no longer like "infants, tossed back and forth by the waves, and blown here and there by every wind of teaching" (Eph. 4:14; see vv. 7 – 16).

Nurturing, then, is *the process of bringing individual Christians and the Christian community as a whole to maturity.* It is building up the body of Christ so that each part uses its gift for the good of the whole. In this process, young Christians, "like newborn babies, crave pure spiritual milk, so that by it [they] may grow up in [their] salvation, now that [they] have tasted that the Lord is good" (1 Peter 2:2 – 3). Nurturing prepares new believers to withstand the fire of Satan's persecution by walking personally with older Christians to experience listening to God and responding to him in obedience.

GUIDELINES FOR NURTURING

Nurturing, like church planting, varies greatly, depending on the philosophy of missionaries and church leaders and the context in which they are working. However, there are certain general guidelines that apply to all situations.

First, nurturing is most effectively done in the context of a loving, caring community of believers. The Christian life was never meant to be a solitary journey; it was meant to be a pilgrimage of disciples committed to the kingdom of God. Discipleship takes place within the context of Christian fellowship. New Christians are guided to know God and find their gifts and ministries within the context of intimate fellowship within the body of Christ.

> *They devoted themselves to the apostles' teaching and to fellowship, to the breaking of bread and to prayer. . . . Every day they continued to meet together in the temple courts. They broke bread in their homes and ate together with glad and sincere hearts, praising God and enjoying the favor of all the people.*
> (ACTS 2:42, 46 – 47)

Second, nurturing leads new Christians to visualize specifically what God wants them to become. Because they do not understand the transforming grace of God, Christians who have not been properly discipled are frequently overwhelmed by their own sins and inadequacies. They must grow to know the radical nature of conversion and how to live as distinctive and pure people in the kingdom of God. Conversion therefore is a radical *turning of self to God*. New believers turn from darkness to light, from death to life, from the dominion of Satan to the kingdom of God (Acts 26:18). They become new creatures who have been spiritually elevated into the heavenly realms to dwell with Christ (Eph. 2:6). As new Christians begin to understand their new identity, they also recognize that they can become holy as God is holy (1 Peter 1:15). They imagine themselves standing with the heavenly host proclaiming, "Holy, holy, holy is the Lord God Almighty" (Rev. 4:8; cf. Isa. 6:3). The love of God consumes them so that they love their enemies in the midst of suffering, forgiving as Christ forgave the people who crucified him.

Third, nurturing involves modeling the Christian disciplines. New Christians must be taught to turn their hearts and wills to God in *prayer*, humble themselves before God in *fasting*, acknowledge through *worship* that God is sovereign, seek God's truth through *Bible study*, and reflect on God's Word and his work in their lives through *meditation*. Without mentoring and modeling, people tend to embrace the forms of Christianity without growing spiritually through the Christian disciplines.

Fourth, nurturing is an ongoing process; otherwise the church grows stale and dies. One generation teaches the next generation, which in turn teaches the third.

> *... he commanded our ancestors*
> *to teach their children,*
> *so the next generation would know [his laws],*
> *even the children yet to be born,*
> *and they in turn would tell their children.*
> (Psalm 78:5–6)

Nurturing allows the baton of faith to be passed from generation to generation. Without it, the evangelist's work becomes terminal instead of germinal.

Training Leaders

The third major task of missions is training leaders. In rapidly maturing Christian movements, leaders are seldom selected; they are discovered. God raises them up while the whole church is being nurtured so that members can perform various ministries within the body. Congregational nurturing therefore always precedes or is coupled with leadership training. In the midst of this congregational nurturing, God raises up leaders and places them in the body "just as he [wants] them to be" (1 Cor. 12:18). Once these leaders rise to the surface, they should be specifically trained.

DEFINITION OF LEADERSHIP TRAINING

Christian leadership training is *the equipping of God's people "for works of service, so that the body of Christ may be built up"* (Eph. 4:12). Christ is the prime mover of leadership development because he has provided, by his grace, specific gifts to the body (vv. 7 – 8, 10; cf. 3:7). Christ himself prepares leaders (apostles, prophets, evangelists, pastors, and teachers) to nurture the body (4:11). *Equipping* implies a process of growing to maturity: Paul describes the separated becoming unified, infants growing to maturity, the empty attaining to the "fullness of Christ," and people blown about by worldly winds or "tossed back and forth" by non-Christian cultural currents becoming anchored in Christ (vv. 13 – 14).

The result is truth speaking that leads to *equipping of equippers*. Christians *grow up* in Christ! They know who they are not: Paul writes, "We will no longer be infants, tossed back and forth by the waves, and blown here and there by every wind of teaching and by the cunning and craftiness of people in their deceitful scheming" (v. 14). They also know who they will grow to become: Paul comments, "Instead, speaking the truth in love, we will grow to become in every respect the mature body of him who is the head, that is, Christ" (v. 15). A mature church body, then, is one in which all parts are related to the head, Christ, and joined to each other. Within this mature body, the church "builds itself up in love, as each part does its work" (v. 16). In our ministry among the Kipsigis people of Kenya, we used this passage as a description of a mature church: Equipping of leaders occurs within a community of faith in which the body "builds itself up in love, as each part does its work"!

Leadership is frequently defined as the *process of influence* (Elliston 1992, 21; Clinton 1988, 245). This definition, while having aspects of truth, has its dangers. When influence is understood as power to control and manipulate, it stands in contrast to biblical metaphors of leadership.

Blending servant, shepherd, and steward produces the distinctive hue of leadership intended by God.

Three metaphors of leadership are evident in Scripture (Elliston 1992, 23 – 24). First, Christian leaders are *servants* who voluntarily submit themselves to the lordship of Christ and the sovereignty of God. Thus the typical view of "leader" is inverted: the mighty become servants of the weak. Christ "did not come to be served, but to serve, and to give his life as a ransom for many" (Mark 10:45). As divinity serves humanity, people who are "great" in this world must become servants (v. 43). Second, Christian leaders are *shepherds* who tenderly care for their flock. This analogy implies that the shepherds feed, protect, and guide their flock. They know the names of their sheep and will even lay down their lives for them (John 10:11 – 15). The true shepherd "gathers the lambs in his arms and carries them close to his heart" (Isa. 40:11). Third, leaders are *stewards* who "are entrusted with the message of the gospel, gifts for ministry, and [God's mission] to perform" (Elliston 1992, 24). Stewards are trustees guarding "what has been entrusted to [their] care" (1 Tim. 6:20). Blending servant, shepherd, and steward produces the distinctive hue of leadership intended by God.

LEVELS OF LEADERSHIP

Vibrant Christian movements require leaders at five levels. These are described in this section.[8]

Level 1, or *grassroots leaders*, serve as beacons of light for the gospel — the frontline soldiers of the kingdom of God. They may be small group leaders, missional community leaders in neighborhoods

8. The writings of Elliston (1992, 26 – 35) and Clinton (1988, 246) have been formative in this discussion. They have built on the initial classification of Donald McGavran, who in 1969, in a lectureship at Columbia Bible College, first described five types of leaders for growing churches, and on Lois McKinney's article "Training Leaders," in *Discipline through Theological Education by Extension*, edited by Virgil Gerber (1980). I have altered their designations from "types" to "levels" of leaders and applied appropriate designations (grassroots, shepherding, and so on) to each type of leader.

and relational networks,[9] Bible class teachers, youth organizers, and committee participants and leaders in specific ministries. They have frequent contact with searchers and, in vibrant, growing churches, are the disciplers and nurturers of new believers.

Level 2, or *shepherding leaders*, are also lay leaders, but with more authority and broader influence than level 1 leaders. These leaders serve as elders and deacons in their churches, supervisors of Sunday school programs, mentors of small group leaders, coaches of congregational missional leaders,[10] and lay counselors. In various mission contexts, especially in the developing world, shepherding leaders may be unpaid evangelists who preach in local churches or work to initiate other churches. Their ministries are direct or face-to-face, like those of level 1 leaders, but their influence, unlike that of level 1 leaders, extends beyond their immediate group.

Level 3, or *formal leaders*, influence their local churches and the communities around them. In Western contexts, they are typically full-time ministers in congregational settings. In the developing world, level 3 leaders are involved in face-to-face ministry but are likely to be bivocational. Most have had some form of theological education or discipleship training that has equipped them to preach, teach, and evangelize. Their influence is generally deep but not broad — significant among people they minister to but not extensive beyond their local area.

Level 4, or *regional leaders*, have an influence much wider than the church or agency in which they work. They serve as leaders of multistaff or multisite churches, within parachurch ministries, or as missionaries planting churches, nurturing new Christians to maturity, and training leaders in a domestic or foreign context. These leaders have completed a formal system of training, and their influence reaches beyond the people they personally relate with (adapted from Elliston 1992, 31).

Level 5, or *apostolic leaders*, are those Christians who, like the New Testament apostles, have national or international influence. These

9. A missional community is "a group of 20 – 50 people forming an extended family on mission together" (Breen 2012, introductory definitions).

10. Coaches of missional leaders use a "huddle" to equip a small group of Christians to form missional communities in neighborhoods and relational networks and model this missional ministry so others can imitate it (just as Christ modeled ministry with his disciples).

highly competent leaders greatly influence the nature of ministry through their writing, teaching, and speaking. They thus provide the philosophical models out of which others minister. Although some of their ministry is indirect, they influence many people. To remain connected to real life, level 4 and 5 leaders must simultaneously function as level 1 and 2 leaders. For example, Peter, an apostle and therefore a level 5 leader, also served as a church elder, or level 2 leader (1 Peter 5:1).

Effective leadership training blends the formal, nonformal, and informal modes of training to equip various types of leaders.

Understanding the different types of leaders enables missionaries and local church leaders to make plans for appropriate training. It is apparent that mature churches need hundreds of level 1 and 2 leaders, since effective evangelism requires that all people in a community must be influenced personally, face-to-face. Elliston says, "The number of people one may ... directly influence at a worldview level may range between ten and twenty." Hence, to reach a community of 100,000 with leaders relating personally to at least ten people, 10,000 grassroots leaders would be needed, plus 1,000 shepherding leaders, 100 formal leaders, 10 regional leaders, and 1 apostolic leader (adapted from Elliston 1992, 31). Level 3, 4, and 5 leaders typically have a broad theological education and therefore understand formal leadership training. Level 1 and 2 leaders, on the other hand, may require different modes of training.

MODES OF LEADERSHIP TRAINING

A study of curriculum theory, especially its three modes of training—formal, nonformal, and informal—is significant in planning to equip leaders (Elliston 1988, 211). Effective leadership training blends these modes to equip various types of leaders.

Formal training generally refers to classroom instruction within an organized institutional setting. Structured online training also falls within this category. This mode is extremely beneficial in conveying information and paradigms of thinking. Applying knowledge and developing communication skills, however, are secondary. Formal education is organized hierarchically: teachers guide the learning process of students through syllabi and tests; teachers in turn are supervised by administrators; and so on. Students are most often trained outside the contexts in which they hope to minister, and upon completing their training, they receive diplomas or certificates attesting to their level of training.

Formal modes of training have long been used by people of the Judeo-Christian heritage. Ezra established synagogues whose purpose was teaching the law. This firm teaching enabled many Jews to retain their identity in Babylon and to believe God's promise to restore his people. Jewish rabbis, especially the Pharisees, embraced this form of training. Hillel wrote, "The more teaching of the law, the more life; the more school, the more wisdom; the more counsel, the more reasonable action. He who gains knowledge of the law gains life in the world to come" (*Aboth* 2.14). Paul received instruction in this mode from the rabbi Gamaliel (Acts 22:3). Origen of Alexandria established a school in Egypt "for elementary instruction in the faith," but this school also became an evangelistic agency when unbelievers began to attend (Green 1970, 204). Centers of formal education have been in the forefront of the mission movement of North America. For example, many mission teams came together, were spiritually nurtured, and were academically equipped while I taught missions and Bible at Abilene Christian University. I have touched and tasted the impact of university seminary education on the preparation of people going into domestic and foreign mission contexts.

Nonformal training is based on the premise that students most effectively learn through designed experiences in a deliberately organized program. This training is both "non-programmatic" and "non-institutional" (Clinton 1988, 251). Edgar Elliston writes that nonformal education is "planned, staffed, and organized, but structured outside the normal school system" (1988, 212).

When I served as professor of missions at Abilene Christian University, we sought to integrate a nonformal dimension with the formal elements of our missionary training. We recognized that formal education alone was not adequate to prepare candidates for the mission of God. In our CARE mentoring program, faculty and resident missionary staff gave personal guidance to students in the areas of *character*, *ability*, their *relationship* with God, and the *experience* of being an active follower of Christ in a local community of believers. This included evangelism, nurturing, and cross-cultural practicums. Mentors assessed students at different points throughout their academic careers in an attempt to determine their suitability for long-term mission work. This program, although tied to a formal educational institution, was an example of nonformal education.

Informal training "uses life-activities as the basis for purposeful training" (Clinton 1988, 244). This type of training is "unstructured in the sense of being controlled and deliberately planned" (Elliston 1988, 212). It is highly relational and participatory. Teachers and students join together in accomplishing the mission of God. As teachers model effective ministry, students learn by observing and doing.

Jesus used informal training with his disciples. He took twelve men, as diverse as a tax collector and a Zealot, revamped their concepts of reality, and molded them into a cohesive group. He appointed these twelve "that they might be with him and that he might send them out to preach and to have authority to drive out demons" (Mark 3:14 – 15).

I was honored to spend two separate years teaching missions at Harding University as a visiting missionary during my time in Africa. Each year, we developed a missions community, at that time, called the Third World Missions Fellowship.[11] During this fellowship, my wife and I worked with missions students to provide nonformal modules of missions training (skits, discussions, cultural blessings, and so on) to both spiritually and practically prepare them for mission. But of greatest importance were the summer internships when our students came to the Kipsigis area of Africa and participated with us and local Christian leaders in actual missions practice. Later, while I was teaching at Abilene Christian University, my wife and I collaborated with students to develop a similar group focused on Africa, called African Missions Fellowship.

Informal training has had a transformational impact in the era of modern missions. According to Peter Wagner, informal training was a major factor in the growth of Pentecostals in Latin American cities (1973, 89 – 100). Jonathan Chao comments that "seminaries in the streets" trained developing Christians for effective ministry. In fact, Christian leaders were required to start a self-supporting church before being ordained. In China, "seminaries of the field" that train itinerant evangelists contributed to the great growth of the church there (Chao 1989, 58).

---

11. The Third World today is typically called the Two-Thirds World, composed of Asia, Africa, and Latin America. During this era, the Western world (Western Europe, the USA, and Canada) made up the First World, and the Communist world (the Soviet Union, including much of Eastern Europe and China) the Second World.

Although the need for training Christian leaders exists in every developing and mature church, modes and methodologies of training vary.

GUIDELINES FOR EFFECTIVE LEADERSHIP TRAINING

This section seeks to apply understandings about the types of leaders and modes of training just discussed. What modes of training best equip different types of leaders? How do training patterns change as a movement matures? Although the need for training Christian leaders exists in every developing and mature church, modes and methodologies of training vary. Four general guidelines, however, are fundamental in every context.

1. Training Should Be Appropriate for Leaders' Ministries and Time Schedules

Level 1 and 2 (grassroots and shepherding) leaders typically require informal training to minister effectively in the body. For example, new small group leaders are formed as they assist experienced leaders; Bible class teachers learn to teach while contributing to Bible classes; lay youth ministers learn to organize activities by participating in youth programs; committee leaders learn the functions of their committees while serving as members; new Christians learn to evangelize by seeing older Christians model evangelism; new Christians learn hospitality, service, kingdom testimony, and expectant prayer while participating in a missional community.[12]

The lay leaders' learning experience, however, can be greatly enhanced by formal and nonformal training. Weeklong or weekend seminars provide lay leaders with the theologies and practices that undergird their ministries. Nonformal learning then provides task-oriented experiences and exercises that add much to what has been learned formally and informally.

Level 3 (formal), 4 (regional), and 5 (apostolic) leaders generally require some level of formal training. Preaching is more effective when the presenter has a deep understanding of the message. Organizing curriculum in a large church is enhanced by knowing the available resources. On the other hand, years of formal training may produce leaders who think conceptually but are unable to apply the concepts to ministry. Many of the disciplines required of level 4 leaders are best

12. Note a description of this model of ministry in chapter 16, where the Diamond of Ministry is discussed.

learned through nonformal learning, and many of the specialties of level 5 leaders through informal learning. Thus these leaders must be engaged in hands-on activities in nonformal and informal settings to learn the actual skills of ministry.

2. Effective Training Integrates Various Modes

While informal training may be very effective in conveying a particular set of knowledge and skills, the nonformal mode may be more appropriate for another set of skills, and formal training is valuable for still others. Thus effective trainers must know when each mode is appropriate and how to integrate the three in the equipping process. Theological Education by Extension (TEE) and obedience-oriented mentoring, described in chapter 6, illustrate this integration of modes. TEE combines formal with nonformal aspects of leadership training, while obedience-oriented mentoring blends informal and nonformal dimensions.[13]

3. Training Modes Vary Based on the Maturity of the Christian Movement

In newly established churches, where little is known about the Christian lifestyle, most training will be done informally. Through effective modeling, new Christians learn to lead prayers, read the Bible, share their faith, and live as Christians in their community. This modeling continues as the churches grow to maturity with their own level 3, 4, and 5 leaders. Intensive courses provide developing Christian leaders with knowledge of Scripture and understanding of practical ministry, in a short period of time. Group study also greatly enhances motivation. Leadership Training by Extension (LTE) can also be employed.[14] As the

---

13. Chapter 15 will describe how our team in Kenya employed all three modes in training leaders to plant new churches among the Kipsigis.

14. Leadership Training by Extension (LTE) is similar to Theological Education by Extension (TEE) but does not seek to confer academic credentials. In this model of instruction, the teacher goes to the students to teach and mentor them where they live rather than have the students come to the teacher. LTE is highly adaptable. Instruction occurs where and when the students are able to study, adapts to their economic and academic levels, and takes cultural differences into consideration. Dr. Ed Mathews suggests that teachers consider themselves *catalysts* creatively employing nonformal models of instruction rather than merely formal models (1976, 123 – 39).

movement matures, locals and missionaries must plan together for the more structured training required for level 3, 4, and 5 leaders, which will give the movement both cohesion and the necessary formal training for developing Christian leaders.

4. A Comprehensive Phaseout Strategy Is Needed

Church-planting missionaries must begin with a comprehensive strategy for phasing out missionary personnel once local leaders have been trained. Steffen writes that strategies often develop piecemeal. New missionaries "focus more on 'phase-in' activities (e.g., evangelism and discipleship) than on 'phase-out' activities (e.g., activities that would empower nationals to develop leadership among themselves with an eye toward ministry that reproduces)" (1993, 3). In a healthy church-planting movement, missionaries move through four periods: learning, growing, collaborating, and phasing out (Van Rheenen 2000a, 36 – 47). Roles change during each stage, for both missionaries and local leaders.

During the learning period, missionaries develop the cultural and linguistic understandings to think missiologically about their cultural context, assuming the role of a learner. During the growth period, missionaries face the challenge of developing an effective paradigm of church planting which is both biblical and reproductive. They serve in multiple roles: evangelists, church planters, maturers of new Christians, and trainers of developing leaders. Missionaries in the collaborative period help the new churches develop structures of continuity that will provide the movement with long-term stability. During this period, they are equippers, encouragers, and advisors. National leaders, who were converts during the learning and growth stages, become colaborers and fellow resource people — full participants in a collaborative process. With these foundations in place, cross-cultural missionaries begin to phase out of the work. They continue to serve as encouragers and advisors through correspondence and occasional visits, perhaps even moving on to repeat the cycle in new, unreached fields.[15]

15. Note a full discussion of this in chapter 7, in the section about missionary service.

Conclusion

Missionaries who fail to prioritize the essential tasks of missions typically leave little behind when they depart.

To untrained missionaries, the purpose of missions is frequently nebulous. Sometimes missionaries who do not understand the long-term strategy are sent to the field to fill an assigned role. Sadly, missionaries who fail to prioritize the essential tasks of missions typically leave little behind when they depart. The goal of church-planting missionaries is to initiate reproducing fellowships that reflect the kingdom of God in the world. They must therefore evaluate such activities as teaching English or literacy, digging water wells, providing medical care, or instructing students in schools or camps as to their effectiveness in developing such churches. Do these strategies express the compassion of God and open doors for gospel proclamation? This chapter has emphasized how the church must prioritize and intentionally carry out the major tasks of missions: planting churches through evangelism, nurturing new Christians to maturity, and training leaders to continue the process. These churches will then holistically glorify God in all that they do. Unless local churches do not have the capacity to respond to an immediate crisis (such as a famine or a hurricane), it is better for compassionate activities to flow from local churches than through foreign parachurch organizations.

One basic guideline applies to formulating plans for each of these three significant missionary tasks. Church leaders must visualize what God desires in each area, set specific goals, and then formulate plans to fulfill these goals.

REFLECTION AND APPLICATION

Questions

1. Briefly describe three primary tasks of missions.
2. After reading the section defining church planting, write the definition of the term and briefly describe the meaning of each significant word of the definition.
3. What theologies give special impetus to germinal growth? Why?
4. What four guidelines for effectively planting new churches are given in the chapter? What other guideline(s) might you add to these?
5. What application does the Kipsigis proverb "We cannot give birth to children and then leave them" (*"Magisiche lagok si kebagach"*) have to missions?
6. What four guidelines for effectively nurturing new Christians are given in this chapter? What additional guideline(s) might you suggest?
7. After reading the section defining leadership training, write the definition of the term and briefly describe the meaning of each significant word of the definition.
8. Contrast leadership as the process of influence with biblical metaphors of leadership. Why is this distinction significant?
9. Describe five levels of leaders present in all vibrant Christian movements.
10. Briefly describe three modes of training.
11. Discuss the mode(s) of training that best equip(s) each of the five types of leaders.
12. What four guidelines for effectively training leaders are given in this chapter? What other guideline(s) might you add to these?

Special Application Question

Many movements stagnate because Christian leaders have not developed the creative capacities for strategic planning. How do Christian movements stagnate because strategies are inadequate or ill-conceived?

Creative Exercises

1. Picture an area of the world (domestic or foreign) where God might use you to plant a new church within the next ten years. Creatively imagine how you might devise a strategy to plant and mature a church (or churches) in this area and the type of strategy this church would have as a mature church.
2. Describe the strategy model of your local church. How will God use you within this body to nurture fellow members and to train leaders for his glory?

Case Study

You have just been hired as the education minister of a major church in Big City, America. The Big City church will soon complete a major building program and would like to use the finances that once went toward their building program for world evangelization. Their total missions budget will likely go from $75,000 this year to $425,000 in five years. Because you have been overseas, graduated with a Bible degree, and have an interest in missions, the elders have asked you to become an adviser to their missions committee. The missions committee has tentatively decided to focus on the nation of Zinzin because other churches in their area have targeted adjoining countries. During December, a committee member joined others on a survey trip to different cities in Zinzin and placed ads for English Bible correspondence courses in Zinzini newspapers. This summer, they want to conduct two weeks of door-to-door evangelism to begin the church in Zinzin. At present, they know little of the country they hope to target.

The missions committee wants to move quickly to evangelize Zinzin before a change of government closes the door. The elders are more cautious because, as executives of large companies, they know how easily business mistakes occur in international contexts. The preacher is interested in missions and is willing to help you. As the new residential *authority* in missions, you have been asked to give guidance to the committee and help them make decisions. How will you advise them? Describe (1) the content of your advice, and (2) the process of advising them.

Personal Inventory

How has God spoken to you through this chapter? What is God calling you to do about it?

chapter 15

Planting, Nurturing, and Training

An Incarnational Model for Tribal Africa

Jim and Julie read with interest the African case study describing a church-planting movement among the Kipsigis people of Kenya. It resonated with their experiences in Haiti. They appreciated the focus on language and culture learning. Above all, they were intrigued by how the church-planting model was developed by applying theological understandings to ministry within a certain culture. They understood Paul's message to the Ephesians in a new and different way. They observed each phase of the church-planting process, from the initial church stage to the established church stage to the independent church stage to the mature church stage. The model showed a respect for the local people, a confidence that equipping local leaders would produce strong new churches. They were excited to think that a church-planting movement could emerge through discipling and equipping local leaders. Could God use them to start such a movement?

MY WIFE, BECKY, AND I served as church-planting missionaries among the Kipsigis people of Kenya from 1973 to 1986. We were part of a missionary team with Fielden and Janet Allison and Richard and Cyndi Chowning. Drawing on our missions training, we searched for an ethnic group with an animistic heritage[1] who were being prepared

1. Animism is "the belief that personal spiritual beings and impersonal spiritual forces have power over human affairs and, consequently, that human beings must discover what beings and forces are influencing them in order to determine future action and, frequently, to manipulate their power" (Van Rheenen 1991, 19–20).

by God to receive his kingdom.[2] We discerned that when the gospel was effectively communicated, certain types of animistic people were very receptive to the message. The book *Church Planting in Uganda* (1976, William Carey Library), my master's thesis through Abilene Christian University, was the foundation for our research. This book, written before political instability forced us to flee Uganda in 1972, described the research we did in choosing an ethnic group among whom to serve. In a sense, God used the Uganda experience as an apprenticeship for what he would do through us in Kenya.

After some time learning the Kipsigis language and culture, we taught our first gospel lessons in the local language. We were amazed that people heard God's message and made decisions to come to Christ. Six people were baptized in a village called Chebongi, across the valley from the small town where we lived. I remember thinking, "We have planted a church!" and then reflecting, "What is a church? What does God desire for a church to be and do?" We felt inept! These questions, however, helped us begin the model of ministry formation described in the Missional Helix of chapter 13: under the guiding hand of God, we were led to reflect theologically, culturally, historically, and strategically as we developed a ministry model appropriate for the Kipsigis context.[3]

After thirteen years of ministry, this movement had grown to 100 churches, and by 2013, to a mature movement with hundreds of leaders in over 450 local congregations.

Planting Kipsigis Churches

Among rural tribal peoples, effective mission endeavors usually target a specific ethnic group, one homogeneous unit, with teaching done in the local language. In our work among the Kipsigis, we first learned Kiswahili, a national intertribal trade language used in portions of East and Central Africa. We soon learned, however, that this language was inadequate for us to understand the local culture and communicate the good news of the kingdom of God. Knowledge of the heart language — the language in which local religious values and assumptions are formed

2. Note the research in chapter 19 about choosing areas for missionary service.
3. Read about this process on page 311.

and articulated during the enculturation of children, the language through which beliefs are passed on from generation to generation—was essential.

Missionaries cannot be effective teachers unless they are first learners.

Some missionaries, passionate about reaching the lost and planting churches, want to bypass the crucial stage of language and culture learning. Missionaries, however, cannot be effective teachers unless they are first learners. Neglecting language and culture learning during the first months on the field reduces missionaries' effectiveness in all other stages, and the resulting movement is often anemic rather than vibrant.

Even during the early learning stage, however, we did not abandon our identity as missionaries, ambassadors for the kingdom of God. We learned the language *as Christians.* Learning a language is inherently a social exercise, and the people with whom we interacted during this process were also the reason for our effort. Language learning provided an arena for building relationships and learning to communicate the essentials of the gospel message, though initially in an elementary way.

We saw six people come to Christ within four months after we arrived in the Kipsigis area. During this period, I was pulled in two directions. I worked with members of the Kipsigis tribe and also ministered to hundreds of workers on area tea estates. Within a year, 150 people from these estates were baptized. We soon realized, however, that the workers on these estates were all "visitors" living outside their tribal area and that establishing a permanent movement where all the people are visitors is very difficult. Although a large number made a profession of faith, many soon reverted to their old ways because they were not surrounded by support from their home community. We came to understand that stable churches grow in areas where believers "live" rather than "stay," a linguistic differentiation made in both the Kiswahili and Kipsigis languages. Thus our model of ministry radically shifted to concentrate on areas where people "lived," that is, their home area, rather than where people "stayed," that is, their workplace.

As our understanding of the culture grew, we learned that the Kipsigis typically live in large extended families and know everyone in their village. They also have relatives and acquaintances in outlying villages. Because of these relational networks, contacts for evangelism and church planting flowed principally along kinship lines. As people came to Christ through the relationships we built, we often did not choose the villages in which to plant churches; the villages, in a sense, chose us. People who had converted in one village would lead us to other villages where their relatives lived. The distance separating new believers, and the expense of travel, made it more practical to establish numerous congregations than to expect people to travel even a few miles to the nearest church (Van Rheenen 2000a).

Nurturing Kipsigis Churches

From the beginning of the work among the Kipsigis, church-planting missionaries were concerned with church nurturing. Our team developed a methodology of maturing churches after an in-depth study of the church as the body of Christ, in the book of Ephesians. In this book, Paul describes the power of Christ in his body. At one time, the Ephesians were under the power of Satan and his principalities and powers (Eph. 1:21; 6:12), but now they dwelt in the heavenly realms, far above the principalities and powers (1:18 – 23).

Paul's writings assume that the people understood these powers but had not been completely freed from their control. Ephesus was a center of cultic activity, where animistic practices and beliefs were flourishing. The city was known for the *Ephesia Grammata*, the "Ephesian letters" that were thought to be laden with magical power to ward off demons and that were employed "either as written amulets or spoken charms" (Arnold 1987, 15 – 16). Artemis was worshiped as a supreme deity with unsurpassed power — a god who descended directly from heaven (Acts 19:35). She was called upon to protect followers from malevolent powers and "to raise the dead, heal the sick, and protect the city" (Arnold 1987, 20 – 22, 39). Demons were thought to exist everywhere and were immensely feared. The book of Ephesians therefore gives Paul's response to converts who had questions and continuing fears about malevolent spiritual forces (Arnold 1987).

The phrase "in the heavenly realms" *(ta epourania)* occurs only in the book of Ephesians (Eph. 1:3, 20; 2:6; 3:10; 6:12) and has the same meaning throughout the book (Lincoln 1973, 469). Note these usages: Christians have been blessed "in the heavenly realms" with every spiritual blessing in Christ (1:3). God has raised Christ from the dead, exalted him to sit at his right hand "in the heavenly realms," and from this vantage point given him authority over the powers of Satan (vv. 20 – 21). We have access to the power of God in his church, "which is his body, the fullness of him who fills everything in every way" (v. 23).[4] Believers in Christ, once subjected to the powers of Satan (2:1 – 3), have now been exalted and enthroned with Christ "in the heavenly realms" (vv. 4 – 6). Christ's own exaltation and enthronement in the heavenlies (1:20) is compared with the believer's exaltation and enthronement (2:6). A radical transition occurs from death (vv. 1 – 3) to life (vv. 4 – 7) by the grace of God (vv. 8 – 10). Those making this transition must not remain "foreigners and strangers" but become "members of [God's] household." They must be united into the body of Christ (vv. 11 – 22).

Thus "living in the heavenly realms" connotes that Christians live as distinctively transformed people — participants in the kingdom of God. The church must not accommodate to the world but have lives transformed by the power of God in Christ.

Paul tells the Ephesians to "stand firm" against the devil's schemes and powers by putting on the full armor of God "in the heavenly realms" (6:10 – 18). In this context, Christians living in the heavenly realms with Christ were tempted to revert to their old ways and live according to the customs of the world. How could Christians who have entered God's heavenly realms return to their old ways? Paul therefore exhorts them to *stand*: "stand against the devil's schemes" (v. 11), "when the day of evil comes ... stand your ground" (v. 13), and "stand firm" with the armor of the Christian faith (v. 14). Paul defines this spiritual armament as the belt of *truth*, the breastplate of *righteousness*, the footwear of *the gospel of peace*, the shield of *faith*, the helmet of *salvation*, and the sword of the Spirit, that is, *the Word of God.* Spiritual warfare therefore is standing with God in prayer and against the principalities and powers to defeat Satan through truth, righteousness, the gospel of peace, faith, salvation, and the Word of God.

---

4. In Ephesians 1:18 – 23, Christ is shown to be "not only a risen, living Savior, but an exalted, reigning Lord who is sovereign over all" (Penner 1983, 18). During the life of Christ, the principalities and powers opposed him, even plotting his death (1 Cor. 2:8). Christ put himself under their power in order to break their power (Powell 1963, 168; MacGregor 1954, 23). He became human in order to break the power of death, which Satan had used to hold humanity in his grasp. He broke "the power of him who holds the power of death — that is, the devil" (Heb. 2:14).

Equipping implies a process of helping new believers _grow up_ in Christ to become mature.

In this battle against the principalities and powers, Christians are advised to stand "shoulder to shoulder" with "shields overlapping." The plural is used throughout the paragraph, signaling that the whole church, as a body, is being called to take up arms against spiritual powers aligned with Satan (Wink 1984, 88).

We see in retrospect how formative this type of theological reflection was in helping us effectively plant churches in the Kipsigis context.

As already described in chapter 14, Ephesians 4:11 – 16 has been an anchor passage in our ministry model. A unified church living in the heavenly realms equips God's people for kingdom service with various roles (apostles, prophets, evangelists, pastors, and teachers) to nurture and lead the body (v. 11). *Equipping* implies a process of helping new believers *grow up* in Christ to become mature. They are "no longer ... infants, tossed back and forth by the waves, and blown here and there by every wind of teaching and by the cunning and craftiness of people in their deceitful scheming. Instead, speaking the truth in love, we will grow to become in every respect the mature body of him who is the head, that is, Christ" (vv. 14 – 15). All parts of the body, according to this metaphor, are related to the head, Christ, and joined to each other. Within this mature body, the church "builds itself up in love, as each part does its work" (v. 16). Among the Kipsigis, as mentioned earlier, we used this passage as a description of a mature church: Equipping leaders occurs within a community of faith in which the body grows to the point that it "builds itself up in love, as each part does its work"!

A Kipsigis proverb, *"Malale kwendet agenge"* ("One piece of firewood does not burn by itself"), describes this process. The fire of one ignites another. The heat of community sustains the fire and increases its intensity. We know that "it only takes a spark to get a fire going. And soon all those around can warm up in the glowing. That's how it is with God's love once you've experienced it."[5] Community building is the foundation of disciple making.

Using these foundations, we worked with local leaders to develop four stages leading to congregational maturity. (The first two stages of this model — the initial church stage and the developing church

5. "Pass It On," *http://filledwithpraise.blogspot.com/2009/06/it-only-takes-spark-to-get-fire-going.html.*

stage — are discussed in this section on nurturing churches. The next two stages — the independent church stage and the mature church stage — are covered in the subsequent section on training leaders.) In this model, the role of the initial church planter, whether missionary or local evangelist, changes, depending on the maturity of the church with which they are working (Van Rheenen 1983a, 79 – 88).

We receive hospitality and extend the grace of God.

THE INITIAL CHURCH STAGE

The initial church stage focuses on introducing a community to the kingdom and covenant of God in Jesus Christ. The stage begins when a searcher or a group of searchers request that we come to their village or neighborhood of a town or city to tell them the story of Jesus. During these visits, we go house to house, greeting the neighbors, drinking more tea than any human should consume, speaking a word from the Lord, and praying blessing and healing on the home. We receive hospitality and extend the grace of God. We do not go alone but with Timothys and Tituses who are learning to minister along with us. Besides, I always need someone to lead songs, pray with me over the sick, and amplify what other brothers and I teach. In actuality, I am training others to be evangelists (2 Tim. 2:2). After a time of ministry, we gather in the home of a searcher, a person of peace who has received us (Luke 10:5 – 6). We follow the example of Jesus, who said, "Heal the sick who are there and tell them, 'The kingdom of God has come near to you'" (Luke 10:9). We know that we have little power except what flows from the Father as we pray to him.

During this initial stage, new converts are like newborn children, unable to walk. Their knowledge is limited; they do not know the names of the books of the Bible or how to pray or how to teach others. But they have declared that God is Creator and that Jesus Christ is Lord, and they have decided to give their lives to the way of God in Jesus Christ. During this stage, the church planter is primarily an *evangelist*, proclaiming the foundational message of the gospel: God has acted to save his people in spite of their sins; God has accomplished this mighty act of reconciliation in Jesus Christ; people, however, must respond to him in faith and obedience. The church planter teaches and builds relationships with the people as a group, because the formation of a vibrant Christian community is essential for the individual believer's spiritual survival. This stage takes up to ten weeks, depending on the people's receptivity to the gospel. Among less receptive people groups, it might take longer. It is important, however, to begin the second stage as soon as possible, in order to incorporate the young Christians into a functioning body. The joy of this initial stage is seeing a congregation born through giving and receiving hospitality, through expectant prayer, and through gospel proclamation.

This initial community must be nurtured to maturity. Otherwise, most of these young Christians, without following mature Christians who know the way of God in Jesus Christ, will fall away from Christ.

THE DEVELOPING CHURCH STAGE

The developing church stage, then, focuses on building a discipling community on mission with God. Those who have come to Christ are exhorted to "rid yourselves of all malice and all deceit, hypocrisy, envy, and slander of every kind. Like newborn babies, crave pure spiritual milk, so that by it you may grow up in your salvation, now that you have tasted that the Lord is good" (1 Peter 2:1 – 3). These new Christians, like hewn "living stones" shaped to fit around Jesus Christ, the chief cornerstone, become God's holy temple (vv. 4 – 5). They are no longer "foreigners and strangers" but grow together as a body to be "fellow citizens with God's people and also members of his household" (Eph. 2:19). During this stage, Christians learn to walk with Jesus as Lord, nurture each other in Christian community, and express to seekers their allegiance to God. They learn to walk by the Spirit and not by the flesh. They learn how to pray, encourage others in their community, and help searchers discover the way of God. The church planter, working with Timothys and Tituses, serves during this stage as a *church maturer.* He models the Christian life by spending one or two days each week visiting from house to house and holding evangelistic and nurturing meetings throughout the village. He reflects Paul's feelings for the new church in Thessalonica:

> *Just as a nursing mother cares for her children, so we cared for you. Because we loved you so much, we were delighted to share with you not only the gospel of God but our lives as well.*
> (1 Thessalonians 2:7 – 8)

During this developing stage, all Christians are spiritually nurtured as a fellowship, allowing godly leaders to naturally emerge. The focus is forming character and competence to reflect God's qualities of love, holiness, and faithfulness, as seen in Jesus Christ. Character formation is the transformation of the inner person to reflect these qualities. Competence is the ability to bear fruit in disciple making and mission as children of the kingdom (Breen 2012, 12 – 18). Because leaders emerge through this process of disciple making, *new Christians in developing mission churches should never be elevated to leadership roles by outsiders.* Leaders should be called by God in the midst of active church life rather than artificially selected before nurturing.

New Christians in developing mission churches should never be elevated to leadership roles by outsiders. Leaders should be called by God in the midst of active church life rather than artificially selected before nurturing.

Training Timothys and Lituses

In our work among the Kipsigis, we most often began by using informal methods to train leaders, but we also integrated formal and nonformal methods. The following account relates how I informally trained two Kipsigis evangelists.

> Each Wednesday, I am presently working with two Christians, Michael Chepkwony and Johanna Lang'at, from the Kapsinendet church in Kipsigis to initiate a new church in a nearby village. Michael works as a night watchman at a nearby tea estate, and Johanna is the overseer of the local cattle dip. I called these two men to minister with me because they both have the God-given gifts to plant churches and nurture new Christians to maturity. They also want to teach relatives and friends in an adjoining village.
>
> Michael, Johanna, and I meet at the village about 12:00 each Wednesday. We first go from house to house visiting those we think might be interested. Later in the day, we have a large meeting in one of the homes of our first contact people. In these home visits and evangelistic meetings, Michael and Johanna learn the fundamental gospel message and how to teach this message to different types of people as they hear me teach. I also gently guide and encourage them as they teach. When the first converts were baptized, I began to teach Michael and Johanna how to nurture new Christians to maturity. We then worked to equip our new brothers and sisters in Christ to teach the first principles of the kingdom of God and the gospel of Christ to their relatives and nurture them in the Christian lifestyle.
>
> I remember that day when the first five people were baptized in Mombwo. I told Michael, "These are your friends who now believe in Christ. It is your responsibility to baptize them." On the way to the river, Michael pulled me off to the side and said, "I have never baptized anyone. Would you show me how?" I then demonstrated to Michael how to baptize.
>
> This training is informal. It is based on the perspective that Christian ministry must be not only taught but also modeled. We have grown to believe that formal and nonformal training without concurrent informal training is inadequate. (Van Rheenen 1983b, 40 – 41)

Church planters ask two significant questions during this developing stage: "Do Christians understand the central truths of the Christian faith?" and "Are they practically living out these truths in their lives?" As part of spiritual discernment, Christians learn the storyline of the Bible and discern from this story how God wants them to live in their current cultural context. Church planters so intimately relate to the new Christians that they not only teach the concepts of the Christian faith but also live them out in practical life. Although I previously published a list of concepts that should be taught during this stage (Van Rheenen 1983a, 81 – 82), I now think it wiser for each church-planting team to develop its own curriculum for teaching and nurturing during each stage. The joy of this stage is seeing new Christians grow into a cohesive body able to stand on its own.

Two extremes must be avoided during this developing stage. If the church planter concentrates on a particular church for too long, it may become dependent on his presence. If, on the other hand, there is not enough concentrated teaching and modeling of Christian life, the church may not internalize basic Christian concepts. This can result in syncretism with non-Christian beliefs and forms or the church's eventual disintegration. Among the Kipsigis, this developing church stage took from six to fifteen months.

Training Leaders in Kipsigis Churches

THE INDEPENDENT CHURCH STAGE

The third period of congregational maturation, the independent church stage, begins when local leaders assume all major leadership roles. The church at this point is able to stand on its own feet, independent of the founding evangelists. Frequently, a rite of transition — a time of commissioning, of laying on of hands to commend the new church to the Lord — occurs as a church enters this stage.

While leaders emerge during the developing church stage, the focus of the independent church stage is to equip these local leaders for the continuation of a church-planting movement. The church planter, with his Timothys and Tituses, becomes a *periodic catalyst to train leaders*. The objective is to train leaders who can guide local Christians to build themselves up in love (Eph. 4:16) and become catalysts of mission in their geographic area. The joy of this stage is seeing such leaders develop.

When leadership training precedes the congregational training of the developing church stage, a sharp distinction develops between clergy and laity. Leaders selected by outsiders and trained before a fellowship is incorporated are rarely respected by local village leaders and therefore are seldom able to initiate new fellowships. It is better for church leaders to be selected from a fellowship that is maturing.

Our ways of training leaders were practical and focused. We believed in taking training to the churches rather than extracting leaders from their local contexts by asking them to come to some central institution. Besides, our churches were planted in clusters, with elders, evangelists, and deacons chosen to minister within these areas. Thus we worked with the early churches to develop localized courses and also used various forms of Theological Education by Extension (TEE).[6]

Localized courses are focused times of Bible study and mission organized and overseen by local churches. When the churches were young, we worked with them in the planning and teaching of the courses. When the churches matured, they continued this custom within their clusters. Food, lodging, and venue are details handled by one of the churches in the cluster. Very typically, food is brought by participating Christians according to requests made by the sponsoring church. Visiting Christians stay in the homes of local Christians or in the local school or church building. In some courses, the daytime hours are periods of organized study, and the evenings are used for evangelistic preaching in homes in the village or town.

As our church movement grew, I developed the rhythm of teaching two localized courses per month (Friday through Sunday) to leaders in different clusters of churches. The leaders would self-select according to calling and roles within the churches. For six months, I might work with Timothys and Tituses to teach the gospel of John or "A Survey of Amos, Jonah, and Micah" or the book of Galatians or a practical course such as "Teaching Searchers to Come to Christ." Fridays and Saturdays would be days of study, reflection, and application, followed by evenings of worship. Sunday would be a capstone day of worship centered on

6. Note discussion of Theological Education by Extension in chapter 6.

what was learned during the preceding two days. In textual courses, we would move from theology to practice, first asking, "What is God saying in these texts?" and then asking, "What are we going to do about it in our churches and personal lives?"

Localized courses have numerous benefits with few of the problems of institutional courses such as preacher training schools. These courses are church oriented. Instead of creating structures separate from the local church, localized courses provide renewal for the church or churches that host them. Since the training occurs in one locality, lessons are taught in the Kipsigis language rather than in Swahili, the trade language, or in English, the language of education and governance. Teachings are also contextualized to fit the needs and issues of the local people. Participants provide their own travel and pay a fee to help cover the cost of food. In other words, there is little cultural dislocation of students. The concept of the localized course is so simple that it can be planned and implemented by local leaders (Van Rheenen 1985, 1 – 2). The dangers are that the courses could shift in another generation from teaching, encouragement, and praising God to decision making.

Theological Equipping by Extension (TEE) was also used for daylong trainings. As mentioned in the previous chapter, I trained leaders from churches in the independent stage to initiate new churches. The following story describes this process leading to the planting of a new church at a place called Chepng'ung'ul.

> Presently, I am working each Thursday for seven weeks with twelve vocational evangelists of the Kamaget and Kipsuter churches in Kipsigis. My purpose in these weeks is to spiritually, theologically, and practically equip these evangelists to initiate and mature a new church in an adjoining rural village. To accomplish this goal, I combine aspects of formal, nonformal, and informal training.
>
> Each Thursday, I arrive at a designated home in Kamaget about 12:00, after an hour-and-a-half trip from my home in Sotik. After a fellowship meal, the evangelists and I discuss and apply the content of a home-study course that they have been studying during the week. The topics covered during the seven weeks are: God — The Source of Mission; Christ — The Message of Mission; The Holy Spirit — The Power of Mission; The Church — God's People in the World; The Church — The Embodiment of God's Mission; Paul — The Preacher; and Nurturing — Preparing New Christians to Live within the Kingdom of God.

An initial planning session was used to help organize the course. During this session, I taught a lesson outlining fundamental Christian motivations for evangelism. These motivations were then discussed at length and compared with earthly, pride-directed motivations. We then prayed as a group for God to spiritually work in our hearts to prepare us as his messengers and help us select a nearby village to initiate a new congregation. After prayer, we selected Chepng'ung'ul as the focus of our seven-week evangelistic effort because there was no organized church there and many people in Chepng'ung'ul have kinship relationships with Christians in Kamaget. Because of the prayers and mutual consent of the Christians, we feel that God guided us in the selection of Chepng'ung'ul.

After the village was selected, we began discussing key people in Chepng'ung'ul who not only would be receptive to the message of Jesus but also could become leaders in a newly forming church. Five names were then written on the blackboard, and prayer was made to God for each of these people. We then selected one older man and his family unit to initially teach and prayed that they might become the host family for the initial evangelism meetings in the village. Evangelists from Kamaget were chosen to go and make plans for the meeting for the following week. Finally, I gave each developing evangelist the first lesson to study before our meeting the following week.

On subsequent Thursdays, we continued to meet at Kamaget for our evangelists' meeting at 12:00. This was our period of interaction about the lesson of the week. About 2:30 p.m., we began our trip to Chepng'ung'ul for our "practicum." As the weeks progressed, new evangelists from Kamaget were learning what spiritual resources God had given them and how to organize a plan of evangelism to initiate and mature a new church. Timothys were trained in action to become Pauls. Disciples were trained to become apostles.

As I write this, we are in the fourth week of training at Kamaget. In our third week, thirty seekers attended a vibrant meeting at Chepng'ung'ul. One evangelist, Edwin Rono, daily teaches people house to house in this village. He also has started a Sunday school for children there. Kamaget evangelists are saying, "We know that God is working through us to start the church at Chepng'ung'ul." (Van Rheenen 1983b, 38–40)

Today one of the strongest churches in this area is at Chepng'ung'ul!

Currently, courses are taught in a more organized way as an extension of Siriat Bible School, and certificates for course completion are given during an official graduation ceremony. This certification and celebration brings discipline to Theological Education by Extension.

The church planter comes periodically to exhort and strengthen the body, but his presence is not needed for the ongoing life of the body.

We praise God for the growth of leaders in these modules of training during the independent church stage.

THE MATURE CHURCH STAGE

After the intense leadership training during the independent church stage, the mature church stage begins with church leaders being selected and ordained. Elders are selected to pastor the flock; deacons are chosen to serve in various ministries; evangelists are set aside to lead the congregation to proclaim God's redemptive message both in the local village and in adjoining areas. Sunday school teachers and other ministry leaders are also selected. The church planter now rejoices in how God has worked to bring this body to maturity. With the ordination of these trained leaders, the founding church planter now assumes the role of *occasional guest*. In other words, the church planter comes periodically to exhort and strengthen the body, but his presence is not needed for the ongoing life of the body. He must overcome the temptation to maintain control over the mature church, thus preventing the church from continuing on its own.

During our years in the Kipsigis area, we classified churches according to their stage of maturity. For example, of the one hundred Kipsigis churches when I left in 1986, twelve were in the initial stage, thirteen in the developing stage, sixty-eight in the independent stage, and seven in the mature stage. We set specific goals each year in terms of church maturation. For example, in 1982, my personal goals were to (1) plant two new churches during the year (one during the first six months of the year and one during the next six months), (2) nurture one initial and one developing church all the way to the independent church stage, and (3) teach ten leadership courses in independent churches on how to use the themes of prophetic literature to strengthen local churches among the Kipsigis.

The following chart depicts the spiritual maturation of a Kipsigis church from its inception to its maturity.

Several key features of this model should be noted. First, it gives explicit priority to making and equipping disciples. Missionaries model discipleship, equip new believers, observe and offer guidance to young churches, and then leave them to continue to grow on the foundation

Figure 15.1 A Nurturing Model for Rural Africa

Stage of Church Maturation	Initial	Developing	Independent	Mature
Primary Objective	Planting of the Church	Disciple Making and Mission	Equipping of Leaders	Continued Disciple Making, Mission, and Equipping of Leaders
Role of the Church Planter	Evangelist	Church Maturer	Leader-Equipper	Guest
Appropriate Teaching	Foundational Gospel and the Response of Faith and Obedience	Christian Truth/ Worldview and Its Practical Applications	How the Body of Christ Is Built Up in Love	Exhortation and Strengthening of the Body

that has been established. In this process, the focus turns quickly from initial evangelism to discipling and equipping leaders. From the earliest stages, the local people lead their own churches. Missionaries serve as advocates of the good news and teachings of Jesus Christ but are not cultural innovators. Instead they guide the local people as they contextualize the biblical message in forms that are most meaningful in their culture.

REFLECTION AND APPLICATION

Questions

1. Why is it important for cross-cultural missionaries to learn the local language?
2. How was a study of the book of Ephesians a pivotal step in developing the Kipsigis model of church planting?
3. Describe each of the stages of church maturation (initial, developing, independent, mature).
4. What is the role of the church planter during each stage?
5. What is the *joy* of each stage?
6. Why is working with Timothys and Tituses during the first three stages significant in developing a church-planting movement?
7. Describe localized courses. What are some of the strengths and limitations of this mode of equipping?

Personal Inventory

What have you learned about missions from this chapter? How has God spoken to you? What is God calling you to do about it?

chapter 16

Planting, Nurturing, and Training

An Incarnational Model for North America

Jim and Julie discerned that they were naturally gifted as evangelists, and this understanding amplified their interest in missions. As youth ministers, they felt the calling of God to begin missional communities, meaning in this case Christian relational networks within schools to help searchers know God and walk with him. With other leaders of their church, they conceived of multiple missional communities, embedded in neighborhoods and relational networks, as extensions of their public worship gathering on Sunday morning. The seeds of the communities were planted when they began to pray with Christian student leaders about their schools and minister with these students during campus activities and in coffeehouses. They were present for many school activities; it was their arena of mission.

Soon Jim and Julie were ministering to a broader group of students who were friends of the core group within the church. They attended many sports events, and the coaches frequently asked them to pray for and minister to struggling students. After a student's death, Jim and Julie were at the school to comfort, counsel, and pray.

Jim and Julie attempted to model Jesus' ministry on earth in their campus environments by teaching, listening, praying, and healing. Reflecting the ministry of Christ, they also prayed diligently for the students from their church who ministered with them. After extended prayer, they selected twelve students, six from each of the two high schools in their area, and invited them into two discipling huddles. The huddles' focus was to help the students grow as disciples of Jesus and to partner with them to be Christ to their campuses. As a result, within a year missional communities of about forty students were ministering in the name of Jesus on each campus and worshiping in the church's public gathering. Mission had gone out of the church building and into the schools and homes of the community.

Our journey as missionaries to North America began in the spring of 2000, when Abilene Christian University granted me a sabbatical to study missions among churches in North America. During this time of reflection, my heart was touched by the great need for North American churches to think of themselves as disciple-making communities on mission with God. Too many were ingrown, plateaued, or dying. They were often lacking the vitality, cohesion, process, and intentionality to build discipling cultures that invite searchers to come to faith and grow to maturity in the Lord. Thinking through the lens of the Missional Helix,[1] we asked, "How can North American churches become spiritually formed to live as people on mission with God?"

During this time of study and reflection, my wife and I were called by God to a ministry of church planting and renewal in North America. We reflected, "How can we be used by God, with all of our finite limitations, to plant new churches and revive existing churches in this highly individualized Western culture?" After studying processes of church planting in North America for three years, I left my position at Abilene Christian University in December 2003 for the uncertainties of beginning a movement. At that time we did not know the learning curve required for such a ministry on our home continent, but we have nevertheless been blessed beyond measure.

We have not walked this journey alone, but with many mentors. The groundbreaking works of Lesslie Newbigin, such as *Foolishness to the Greeks* (1986) and *Gospel in Pluralistic Society* (1989), have been formative.[2] The Gospel and Our Culture Network[3] championed Newbigin's reflections and applied these understandings to North America.[4] Practitioners sought to apply these teachings more specifically to the

1. Note chapter 13.

2. Note the description of the life and ministry of Lesslie Newbigin in chapter 8.

3. *www.gocn.org* (Accessed April 19, 2013).

4. The most influential resources from the Gospel and Our Culture Network have been *Missional Church: A Vision for the Sending of the Church in North America* (1998, Eerdmans), edited by Darrell Guder; *Church between Gospel and Culture: The Emerging Mission in North America* (1996, Eerdmans) by George R. Hunsberger and Craig Van Gelder; *Bearing Witness of the Spirit: Lesslie Newbigin's Theology of Cultural Plurality* (1998, Eerdmans) by George R. Hunsberger; and *Treasure in Jars of Clay: Patterns of Missional Faithfulness* (2004, Eerdmans) by Lois Y. Barrett and others.

renewal of churches in North America.[5] Michael Frost and Alan Hirsch deconstructed the modern church in *The Shaping of Things to Come* (Hendrickson 2003); then Hirsch gave a vision for reconstructing the church for a postmodern age in *The Forgotten Ways* (Brazos Press 2006) and *The Forgotten Ways Handbook* (Brazos Press 2009). Very significant for practical ministry have been *Building a Discipling Culture* (2011, 3DM) by Mike Breen and Steve Cockram, *Multiplying Missional Leaders* (2012, 3DM) by Mike Breen, and *Launching Missional Communities* (2010, 3DM) by Mike Breen and Alex Absalom. It has been a joy to learn from and partner with others on this journey! Tod Vogt, director of ministry operations, and Charles Kiser, director of training, have been invaluable coworkers with us in Mission Alive.

The Cultural Context of North American Missions

During this learning time, I was increasingly struck by the difference between Euro-American contexts and the Two-Thirds World (Asia, Africa, and Latin America). Euro-American culture is characterized by individualism and fragmentation; Two-Thirds World cultures are more cohesive. Among the Kipsigis, for example, sons bring their brides to live on family land and even prefer to be near others of their home area if they move to an urban context. A Kipsigis joke is, "A man became so wealthy that he had no neighbors!" In other words, living alone is feared; people are meant to live in community. Moreover, my neighbor from El Salvador deeply felt this fragmentation of culture when moving to the United States. My wife, Becky, first met him in front of our houses while checking for mail. He asked, "Where are all the people!" In his home country, people lived in community, not isolated behind fences and locked doors.

While visiting Israel, Becky and I chatted with an Arab Christian leader we met in Nazareth. He compared his life with that of his brother

---

5. Seminal writings on church renewal have been *ChurchNext: Quantum Changes in How We Do Ministry* (2000, InterVarsity Press) by Eddie Gibbs; *Emerging Churches: Creating Christian Community in Postmodern Culture* (2005, Baker) by Eddie Gibbs and Ryan K. Bolger; *The Missional Leader: Equipping Your Church to Reach a Changing World* (2006, Josey-Bass) by Alan J. Roxburg and Fred Romanuk; and *Introducing the Missional Church: What It Is, Why It Matters, How to Become One* (2009, Baker) by Alan J. Roxburg and M. Scott Boren.

living in Miami, Florida. He said, "You Americans have no roots. My brother moves every five years. But I live in my father's house, which was his father's house! Our home goes back generations!" Our family is indicative of this fragmentation. Our children and grandchildren live in San Francisco, Atlanta, Houston, and Louisville; we have to board an airplane or travel at least five hours by car to visit any of them.

Bowling Alone (Putman 2000) describes North America's loss of "social capital" beginning around 1960. The book, whose subtitle is *The Collapse and Revival of American Community*, warns that unless North Americans find ways to reconnect with one another, they will experience a deepening impoverishment in their lives and communities. Ray Oldenburg in *The Great Good Place* writes that in suburban North America "a man works in one place, sleeps in another, shops somewhere else, finds pleasure and companionship where he can, and cares about none of these places" (Oldenburg 1999, 4). As we will note later, our churches have also experienced this loss of social capital.

The North American church also suffers from a crisis of leadership. "Our culture, and as part of it the Church, has developed into a management-oriented society. We want to manage growth, manage productivity, and manage human resources" (Breen and Cockram 2011, 115). Our leaders have inadvertently become organizers of ministry rather than makers of disciples in the context of imitative ministry. Dan Kimball suggests changing our focus on the nature of leadership:

> Leadership in the emerging church is no longer about focusing on strategies, core values, and mission statements, or church-growth principles. It is about leaders first becoming disciples of Jesus with prayerful, missional hearts that are broken for the emerging culture. All the rest will follow from this, not the other way around. (2003, 248)

Breen and Cockram prophetically say,

> We need leaders who will step out of "managing church" and make discipling others their primary objective. The time has come to humbly acknowledge before God that we have failed to train men and women to lead in the style of Jesus. Whether through ignorance or fear, we have taken the safe option, training pastors to be theologically sound and effective managers of institutions rather than equipping them with the tools they need to disciple others. (2011, 116)

I am consistently in meetings with leaders who have planted or are leading large churches but prayerfully confess that their churches are not sustainable in a fragmented North American cultural climate and that many of their members have not developed the rhythms of living as disciples of Jesus.

David Kinnaman, in *You Lost Me*, writes,

> We are at a critical point in the life of the North American church; the Christian community must rethink our efforts to make disciples. Many of the assumptions on which we have built our work with young people are rooted in modern, mechanistic, and mass production paradigms. Some (though not all) ministries have taken cues from the assembly line, doing everything possible to streamline the manufacture of shiny new Jesus-followers, fresh from the factory floor. But disciples cannot be mass-produced. Disciples are handmade, one relationship at a time.
>
> We need new architects to design interconnected approaches to faith transference. We need new ecosystems of spiritual and vocational apprenticeship that can support deeper relationships and more vibrant faith formation. We need to recognize the generational shifts from left-brain skills like logic, analysis, and structure to the right-brain aptitudes of creativity, synthesis, and empathy. We need to renew our catechism and confirmations — not because we need new theology, but because their current forms too rarely produce young people of deep abiding faith. (2011, 12 – 13)

Within this fragmented culture, there is a deep yearning for community, especially in the younger generations. Many young adults participated in Christian congregations as teenagers and entered adulthood claiming to be followers of Christ. But soon afterward, they left the church and "placed [their] emotional connection to Christianity on the shelf.... This leads to the sobering finding that the vast majority of outsiders in this country, particularly among young generations, are actually *de*-churched individuals" (Kinnaman 2007, 74). Christian Smith, drawing from his research on the religious and cultural status of young adults, concluded that many of these de-churched individuals find deeper relationships through activities that link belonging and a common goal, such as a sports team. Note this example of a rugby team:

> On the team, everybody's going after the same goal, and it brings people together. At the same time there's a game going on, something that's distracting, so I don't have to carry a conversation, just anything that you thought of could go. I could have said anything, and it wouldn't be

In a missionary movement, disciple making and mission are interconnected and inseparable.

weird while I was just watching or playing the game. (Smith and Snell 2009, 152)

Reflecting on this phenomenon, Breen and Absalom say, "What an incredible description of feeling truly accepted within a community that shares a strong and defining missional focus! This is why linking mission and community is such a potentially powerful and transformative process" (2010, 32). This relationship between community and mission must become the defining essence of church planting and renewal in North America.

It is evident from these understandings why our resurrected Lord mandated that we "go and make disciples" (Matt. 28:19). Disciple making is intrinsic to community building if participants are to reflect the covenant and kingdom of God and thereby become God's light to the nations: this community reflects the nature of a sending God and goes into the world as a missionary people. In a missionary movement, disciple making and mission are interconnected and inseparable. "The future of the Western Church," Jon Tyson says, " ... is a powerful return to Jesus' heart for making disciples, and multiplying them into missionary leaders" (Breen 2012, foreword).

The Purpose of Mission Alive

The purpose of Mission Alive is "Equipping kingdom communities on mission with God" — a purpose carried out in the process of both church planting and church renewal.

EQUIPPING

People called by God have a yearning to grow as disciples of Jesus and be led by him into mission. This thirst for God and for his mission leads to a desire for equipping in both character and competency.

Mike Breen writes, "Discipleship is learning, over the course of our lives, to become people who have both Character and Competency" (2012, 14). Character answers the question, "Are you being faithful?" and competency, "Are you seeing fruit?" Character has to do with *being* faithful to God, reflecting his love, holiness, and faithfulness. Competency focuses on effectively *doing* activities of the kingdom of God —

discipling others and going on mission by hearing and responding to the voice of God (Breen 2012, 14 – 18).

The church should provide the environment for the development of both character and competency — for disciple making and mission. The purpose of Mission Alive is to nurture character and competency in both church planting and renewal.

KINGDOM

Often, we live by our own whims, without divine direction. The kingdom of God, however, challenges our self-sufficiency and teaches us to live within the rule of a gracious, loving, holy God who created us and this world we inhabit.

This kingdom theme is like a scarlet thread woven through the fabric of the biblical testimonies describing how people lived in relationship to God. Israel and Judah, for example, sometimes lived in obedience to God, giving their allegiance to him; sometimes they rebelliously followed the pagan gods of the nations and were consequently punished by catastrophe and exile (2 Kings 17:16 – 18; Jer. 5:19). With the coming of Jesus Christ, the word *kingdom* began to connote God's ultimate reign through his Son. Jesus incisively defines *kingdom* in the Lord's Prayer as giving glory to God so that his will is done on earth as it is in heaven (Matt. 6:9 – 10).[6]

Mission Alive nurtures church planters and church leaders so that they will be spiritually formed, living as representatives of the kingdom of God.

KINGDOM COMMUNITIES

Robert Webber says, "The church's mission is to *show the world what it looks like when a community of people lives under the reign of God*" (2002, 133, italics added). A person being spiritually formed within the kingdom community defines himself as a *disciple of Jesus*. "Kingdom communities" are like God's holy temple: Christians are living stones shaped to fit around Jesus Christ, the chief cornerstone, and growing to become his temple (1 Peter 2:4 – 5). This shaping is illustrated by Jesus,

6. Note the discussion in chapter 4 about the kingdom of God.

> The church's mission is to show the world what it looks like when a community of people lives under the reign of God. (Webber 2002, 133)

who called twelve men, trained them to be his disciples, and then sent them to make disciples (Matt. 28:19).

These kingdom communities typically have *worship gatherings* for inspiration, teaching, and vision; *missional communities* for community and mission in neighborhoods and relational networks; *transformation groups* (embedded within missional communities) for spiritual formation of seekers and new members; *equipping huddles* for leader formation; and *mentoring relationships* for informal, yet personal spiritual direction and ministry focus.[7] (Be mindful that transformation groups and equipping huddles are periodic and not necessarily for everyone.)

ON MISSION WITH GOD

Kingdom communities develop their distinct identity, not only as gathered communities listening to the message of the gospel, but also as *communities on mission with God*. Alan Hirsch describes what he calls the missional-incarnational impulse of "going out" and "going deep." He says, "God continues to send the church *outward* into the world as well as *deeper* into people's lives and contexts, to send and embed the gospel" (Hirsch 2009, 91). Out and deep! Out and deep! This is the nature of kingdom communities on mission with God!

Searchers, for instance, come to Christ, not only by hearing the good news of the kingdom of God, but also by witnessing the kingdom through gracious hospitality, miraculous prayer and blessing, and social justice (ministering at the point of cultural brokenness). Through these activities, they hear about and witness the in-breaking of the kingdom of God.[8] Kingdom habits are both taught and caught in communities that *gather* for teaching and fellowship and *scatter* for ministry and proclamation!

Kingdom communities, like moons reflecting the light of God, establish their rationale for being—their purpose for existing—while on mission with God. Christians grow to understand themselves not as servants of the church (or of the most recent cultural fad of the church), but as servants of the kingdom of God!

---

7. These terms will be defined in the next section.
8. Note the description of the Diamond of Ministry later in this chapter.

Contexts of Imitative Learning

How do we, in fragmented North American culture, equip leaders to renew and plant kingdom communities on mission with God? The task is not easy! Most churches are not organized as disciple-making, missionary churches. This section proposes that the mission of God be carried out in five interconnected relational spaces: (1) equipping huddles, (2) missional communities, (3) worship gatherings, (4) transformation groups (within missional communities) and (5) mentoring relationships.

EQUIPPING HUDDLES: SPACE FOR LEADER FORMATION IN DISCIPLESHIP AND MISSION

The first essential task in church planting and renewal is developing a discipling culture. This model reflects the ministry of Jesus, who equipped apostles and disciples to represent him as his missionaries to transform the world. For transformation to take place in North America's highly individualistic culture, this process must be intentional and structured. In Mission Alive, the process occurs in a group that we call an "equipping huddle." An equipping huddle

- is a group of four to ten people led by an experienced huddle leader.
- has a regular and consistent rhythm of meeting (usually weekly).
- operates in a relaxed and fun environment. Laughter should happen regularly!
- is a forum to train leaders in discipleship and mission to begin a new missional community.
- is a place to give and receive encouragement and accountability.
- gives time to equip leaders to discern the will of God. The basic discipline is listening to God and obeying his desires so that we live and minister out of his will. Transparency and honesty within a congenial environment engender transformation.
- helps develop the rhythms of living as a disciple and imparting these rhythms to others in order to develop a discipling culture. These rhythms are described later in this chapter.

I have been blessed to huddle Fred Liggin, pastor of the Williamsburg Christian Church, and a number of other leaders. Fred has in turn huddled Randy Otis and others in the Williamsburg Church and a sister congregation, in a second-generation huddle. Randy testifies,

> When Fred asked me to be in a huddle that he was leading, I had no idea what to expect. I wasn't sure why he was asking me; as you all know, I'm not an elder, a shepherd, a minister, and at that time not even what I would've considered a leader in the church. But I agreed—with hesitation, but I agreed.
>
> From our very first huddle, Fred has led our group of six through the book *Building a Discipling Culture*, in a way that has opened my eyes and heart, not only to the true meaning of being a Christian, but also to what it takes to be a leader, a disciple. The trust that our group has developed with one another in our huddle is amazing. We have all been able to speak into each other's lives, sharing our troubles and struggles with people who are willing and able to offer words of encouragement and prayer. The huddle has taught me what it means to have deeper relationships and how Jesus lived his life in three ways: Up with his Father, In with his chosen followers, and Out with the hurting world around him.
>
> Fred's deep passion and desire to disciple and to build disciples has been evident to me since the first day I heard him preach, but after being in this huddle with him as the leader, he has shown me what it takes, and the steps that I need to work towards, to be a strong leader, a strong disciple.

- models personal spiritual formation and equipping that church leaders and planters can then imitate to train other leaders within their communities.
- meets for a season, not forever. Participants are asked to commit for nine to twelve months to provide time for them to internalize the rhythms of living as a disciple. (Adapted from Breen 2012, 5–6)

Currently, Mission Alive leads multiple equipping huddles of church leaders and church planters, who are growing as disciples in order to disciple others and, as a result, are learning how to go on mission as Christ's ambassadors. All Mission Alive leaders also participate in huddles as they train others to grow in discipleship and missions. Thus they are simultaneously sheep and shepherds, following and leading, encouraging others to listen to and obey God as they are likewise being encouraged to do.

We in Mission Alive believe, however, that our role in leader equipping goes beyond the structured huddle. It also involves giving leaders access to our lives. Ben Sternke writes,

> Since we know that **imitation** is a key ingredient of discipleship, there needs to be a significant amount of informal time together with those

Figure 16.1 Huddle and Access

> we are discipling.... We need to give them **access** to our lives, so they can observe how we interact with our spouse and kids, how we spend our free time, how we take a day off, how we resolve conflict, how we budget money and structure our days. (Sternke 2012)

In addition, we must give access to our lives as we go on mission in our contexts — the relational networks or neighborhoods where we live.

Huddle is the structured time of leader equipping. Access to life and participation in mission together amplifies and illustrates what is being learned in the equipping huddle.

MISSIONAL COMMUNITIES: SPACE FOR MISSION AND COMMUNITY

The second essential task in church planting and renewal is beginning communities on mission with God in neighborhoods and relational networks. We will call these "missional communities." This task is related to the previous one because, ideally, Christian leaders are trained in equipping huddles to launch missional communities. The Soma Church in Tacoma, Washington, describes a missional community as

> a group of people, about the size of an extended family, who are united through Christian community around a common service and witness to a particular neighborhood or network of relationships. The participants of missional communities find their primary identity of "church" within the missional community, rather than a larger worship service or small group. In essence, this group of people becomes a close-knit spiritual family on mission together. (Soma Church, n.d.)

Breen and Absalom say that "we are hardwired as human beings" to live in community: "We can't help but re-create the extended family" (2010, 42). This impulse has been suppressed in our lonely, fragmented, individualistic Western culture. As a result, we must once again create welcoming cultures—relaxed places of sharing life, easily assessible, where food and drink are available, places where Christians model the distinctive way of living as God's people. The church then grows as Christians become community builders. The extended family community becomes the launching pad for incarnational mission. Using the title of Dietrich Bonhoeffer's classic, it is time for us to learn to do "Life Together." Thus, in all generations and all places where the church grows, Christians become community builders. This is what happened in the early church! The extended family community became the launching pad for mission.

These communities seek to reflect the early church:

> *They devoted themselves to the apostles' teaching and to fellowship, to the breaking of bread and to prayer.... Every day they continued to meet together in the temple courts. They broke bread in their homes and ate together with glad and sincere hearts, praising God and enjoying the favor of all the people. And the Lord added to their number daily those who were being saved.... All the believers were one in heart and mind.* (Acts 2:42, 46–47; 4:32)

This passage provides a model for what God wants the church to be and do. The early Christian church met in public, for teaching people and inviting them into the community, as well as in homes and in other smaller gathering places. They lived in daily connection, eating together, enjoying each other. It was evident that the Lord was working to add to their number as they lived out their Christian way in community. They were a community on mission with God.

> Storyline Christian Community is a network of missional communities in Dallas, Texas (*storylinecommunity.com*). One missional community in that network decided to put its mission focus on a relational network—the Dallas Junior Chamber of Commerce (DJCC). The DJCC is a civic organization for young professionals ages twenty-one to thirty-nine that focuses on professional development, networking, and philanthropy.
>
> Several members of the missional community became members of the DJCC and embedded themselves in its social rhythms: they attended monthly professional development meetings; they mingled with other members at happy hours; they served on steering committees for the organization's signature philanthropic events; some were even elected to serve as board members. In the midst of all this interaction, they simply lived as followers of Jesus, loved the people they were around, and invited them into spiritual community. As a result, several members in the DJCC who were searching for God became part of the life of their missional community.

My reflection on this passage is not intended to overidealize the early Christian church and disparage the contemporary church. We know from the Pauline epistles and John's letter to the seven churches of Asia that these early Christian fellowships were messy: they struggled with legalism, immorality, elitism, identity, and doctrine. We should therefore not be surprised that the issues of the current time are equally emotional and complex. Reading about the early church's struggles helps us deal with our own and overcome our cynicism. "The church this side of heaven is broken and needy of God's grace and peace" (Robinson 2013).

For example, Paul spent much of 1 Corinthians addressing issues related to life within intimate community, such as eating and fellowship around the Lord's Supper, appropriate use of spiritual gifts, the qualities and actions of love, the wrongful use of tongues and the need for edification in the community, and cultural appropriateness (1 Cor. 10 – 14). The contexts of these meetings were extended family house churches, like the missional communities we are discussing in this section. Paul prescribes the relational, interactive tone of these meetings when he says, "When you come together, each of you has a hymn, or a word of

Dietrich Bonhoeffer wrote *Life Together* in 1939 while in a German Nazi prison before he was executed by Adolf Hitler. This quote from his book helps us understand why our experience of Christian community does not always match our expectations:

> Christian brotherhood and sisterhood is threatened most often at the very start ... by the danger of confusing Christian brotherhood and sisterhood with some wishful idea of religious fellowship....
>
> The person who loves their dream of a community more than the Christian community itself becomes a destroyer of the community, even though their personal intentions may be ever so honest and earnest and sacrificial. God hates visionary dreaming: it makes the dreamer proud and pretentious. The person who fashions a visionary ideal of community demands that it be realized by God, by others, and by themselves. They enter the community of Christians with their demands, set up their own law, and judge their brothers and sisters and God Himself accordingly. This person acts as if their dream binds people together. When things do not go their way, they call the effort a failure. When their ideal picture is destroyed, they see the community going to smash. So this person becomes, first an accuser of their brothers and sisters, then an accuser of God, and finally the despairing accuser of themselves.
>
> (*Life Together*, 26–28)

instruction, a revelation, a tongue or an interpretation. Everything must be done so that the church may be built up" (1 Cor. 14:26). These chapters give understanding about the messy struggles and expected tone of church within this social space.

Missional communities help us overcome the cultural fragmentation and individualism of North America and lead Christians to become spiritual mentors and Christian guides to friends and people in their neighborhoods and relational networks. As participants in God's mission, they become community builders, people of hospitality, prayer warriors, justice seekers, and teachers of God's good news where they live, work, and play. Thus missional communities

- have the feel of a social community — high on fun and high on purpose, thus inviting to the outsider. They are not small-group Bible studies, but interactive environments where kingdom life is experienced.
- are the size of extended families (from twenty to fifty people) and are thus "small enough to *care* yet big enough to *dare*." They are therefore more sustainable than traditional, "nuclear family" house churches and have the energy and mission to plant other missional communities.
- are launched by a core team of lay leaders trained via an equipping huddle. Because these missional families are lay led, they must be "lightweight and low maintenance," simple and reproducible.
- focus on a distinct vision for mission in a neighborhood or relational network.
- are the communities in which elders have the most influence in personally shepherding the sheep of the flock.
- develop a name that signifies the identity of their mission. "The imaginative conversations, the prayers and the waiting that are part of the journey towards a name take us right into the reasons that we are setting out on this [mission]" (Adams 2009).
- live UP/IN/OUT, reflecting the life and ministry of Jesus: UP — in relationship to the Father; IN — in relationship with one another in missional community; and OUT — in relationship with searchers in the missional context of the group. Thus they are not like the traditional small groups in many existing

Starting Missional Communities

Imagine a missional community that is firing on all cylinders. The group lives in relatively close proximity, shares an evening meal together once each week, fellowships in the local park or recreational center once a month, babysits each other's children, and above all, prays and helps each other in hundreds of little ways.

They regularly meet for prayer and fellowship each Sunday evening. At times, to learn how the gospel forms and shapes their lives, small groups of new believers or others wanting to grow spiritually meet either before or after these Sunday evening gatherings. During some of these Sunday evening meetings, the entire missional community splits into small groups for spiritual formation. Stories of how God is working are testimonials during the worship gathering (described in the next section) of their community. From the beginning of this missional community, the leader has been investing in a few emerging leaders in a weekly equipping huddle. The missional community has grown from twenty adults and children to sixty adults and children! They are an extended family living in community.

Then, as he often does, God begins to speak into the lives of two huddle participants, a married couple. They hear God's calling and dream of starting a similar community in the Heights, the adjoining neighborhood where they live. Their participation in an equipping huddle has prepared them to imagine what God might do in their neighborhood. The leader encourages them to share this calling and dream with the entire group. They do this at the next gathering, and several members express an interest in joining them. Some live in the same neighborhood. Others have just become Christians and want to help other searchers come to the Lord. Other members, however, ask the leader, "Why do we need to start a new group when this one is going so well?"

The missional community leader brings together all those interested to pray together about the dream. After several weeks of discernment, some change their minds and decide to stay with the original group. But about twenty adults and children decide to be a part of the launch team for ministry in the Heights. Some of these are trained in a weekly equipping huddle for their new ministry.

In a special gathering, the missional community celebrates what God has done in their midst. Several members share stories of how they came to the Lord through the missional community, others of how they have been transformed from pew warmers to disciples on mission. The emerging leaders share how God has called them into mission. The missional community prays together and commissions the launch team for mission in the new neighborhood context.

So God calls servants to continue his mission.

churches that tend to emphasize the UP and IN but are not oriented toward the OUT.
- are committed to forming new small groups within their community that share the vision for ministry.
- have an accountable, trained leader (or leaders) who walks in unity with other leaders of the church in a relationship of *low control and high accountability.*
- meet in whatever place is accommodating to their focus and mission, frequently in inviting homes of leaders or in storefronts pertinent to their mission.[9]

THE WORSHIP GATHERING: SPACE FOR INSPIRATION, TEACHING, AND VISION

It is hard for missional communities (and smaller "nuclear family" house churches) to survive alone as stand-alone entities. Worship gatherings provide a place for the public teaching of God's Word, inspiration from worshiping and celebrating together, and vision casting for discipleship and mission. Mike Breen describes the organized public church, with its worship gathering and related missional communities, as "an aircraft carrier and a battle group."

> If the aircraft carrier is by itself, it's actually not terribly difficult to sink. The same goes with individual ships in the battle group, which may be even easier to sink. But when you have the aircraft carrier *and* the battle group working and inter-relating together ... well, that is very difficult and nearly impossible to defeat. You have the giant guns and the sheer mass of strength of the aircraft carrier, but the deftness and agility of each individual boat in the battle group. (Breen 2010b)

Breen uses a second metaphor to describe the structure and texture of the church.

> In the church, whatever we are growing and building needs the texture of soft tissue wherever it touches the world, but it also needs a strong skeleton that allows the whole Body of Christ to stand up. (Breen 2010b)

9. *http://en.wikipedia.org/wiki/Missional_community* (Accessed 6/24/13); *http://weare3dm.com/mikebreen/we-are – 3dm/5-essential-ingredients-of-a-missional-community* (Accessed 6/24/13); Breen and Absalom 2010, 124 – 25.

Some North Americans are tempted to idealize the "nuclear family" house church as the new way of doing church and to reject traditional, organized church, with its focus on the worship gathering. It is true that house churches are very important where there is immense persecution of Christians.

Searchers in North America, however, are more likely to come into a worship gathering or the larger social space of a missional community to experience Christianity than to come into a small, "nuclear family" house church. Since the home is considered private space, searchers are often uncomfortable having their first experience with the way of God in Jesus Christ in that environment. They find it easier to come into worship gatherings, which provide inspiration, practical teaching, and a vision for living the Christian way and allow them anonymity while searching and discerning their journey. These gatherings are still the most typical environment for interested people to experience the way of God. They then move more readily into communities of disciple making and mission.

We have found that house churches alone are seldom sustainable in North American culture, where home is thought of as a private domain and where ability for mission and service are limited. Momentum for a movement continues to be engendered within worship gatherings and missional communities.

The strong skeleton of an organized church gives the church structure, while missional communities are the soft tissue that touches the world.

These worship gatherings have a unique place in church planting and renewal. They provide a place where

- the Word of God is clearly proclaimed. Hundreds, for example, assemble at the Redeemer Presbyterian Church in New York City to hear Tim Keller and stay afterward for discussion. Many others, like me, listen to his weekly sermons via podcast. We understand from these experiences that we should not underestimate the power of public proclamation of God's Word. Jesus' Sermon on the Mount, Peter's sermon on the day of Pentecost, and Paul's proclamation about "AN UNKNOWN GOD" in the Areopagus in Athens (Acts 17:23) illustrate the significance of public proclamation in early Christian times.
- followers of Christ are inspired by hearing songs of worship, testimonies of transformed lives, and stories of growing missional communities. Inspiration is also drawn from numerous missional communities celebrating together what God has been doing.

- the vision of the church is cast so that missional communities do not lose their orientation and fragment.

Thus the third essential task in church planting and renewal is to begin (church planting) or refocus (church renewal) the worship gathering to reflect these functions of teaching, inspiration, and vision casting.

The church is both *gathered* and *scattered*. Christians gather to hear the Word of God, receive inspiration, and gain vision for continued focus on the mission of God, and they scatter for mission in the neighborhoods and relational networks through various missional communities.

TRANSFORMATION GROUPS: SPACE FOR DISCIPLE FORMATION

Searchers (or Christians) who come into missional communities and worship gatherings must encounter the gospel and how it designs and frames their lives. This happens in small *transformation groups* that are part of the larger missional communities. They tend to meet just before or after missional community gatherings.

These learners need a simple guide or reading pattern to help them live as disciples of Jesus. Over the years, we have used Greg Ogden's *Discipleship Essentials: A Guide for Building Your Life in Christ*, David Watson's Discovery Bible Studies, and Neil Cole's Life Transformation Groups (Cole 2008, 166 – 76; 1999, 63 – 70). Church leaders should examine each of these models of helping new Christians come to maturity and select one that best fits them.

Discipleship Essentials is a topical study plan for helping learners to grow as disciples in three areas: (1) growing up in Christ (focus on the basic spiritual disciplines), (2) understanding the message of Christ, and (3) becoming like Christ.

Discovery Bible Studies help both searchers and Christians learn to read the Bible and apply the Scriptures to their lives. David Watson suggests a very simple three-column process. Participants simply write the key passage being studied word for word in the first column, under the heading "Scripture." Watson says, "When [I] copy a passage word-for-word, [I] actually read it through several (about five to seven) times. It is a form of forced meditation for those of us who can't sit and think about a passage without losing focus. This process also keeps me from skimming familiar passages. When I write it out, I have to think about every word" (Watson 2009c). The second column is labeled "My Own Words." Watson says that he rewrites the passage "like I'm telling a friend about it over a cup of coffee" (Watson 2009c). Describing the passage in his own words forces him to understand and articulate it. Under the third column, entitled "I Will," each participant writes down what God is leading them to do based upon this passage. Watson says,

> I ask God to reveal things I need to add to my life, take away from my life, or change in my life for me to obey this passage. I am very specific. The passage may say that God created the Earth, but I have to decide what that means in my life. How does my life change because I believe that God created the Earth? What do I need to do differently? What can I do in the next 24 to 48 hours to obey this passage? I believe every time we open God's Word, He invites us into relationship. We call His invitation "grace," because we can't do anything to deserve it. Obedience is how we accept His invitation. God lives with those who obey His Word (John 14:23 – 24). When we study God's Word, we have a choice: we choose to obey Him or we choose to disobey Him. It is really that simple. I see this third column as my response to God's invitation. (Watson 2009c)

This inductive Bible study methodology can also be employed orally by having participants read the key passage several times, perhaps in different translations (column 1), having them say what the passage means in their own words (column 2), and then having them testify about what they will do based on what God is saying in the passage (column 3). Watson also describes a simple format for these meetings (2009c), provides key Scriptures to use on various levels of training (Watson, n.d.), and suggests that using Scripture for life transformation and obedience — as in this very simple, portable model — is the driving force of church-planting movements.

The Life Transformation Group (LTG), Neil Cole says, is essential because "we need to get back to the simple yet profound basics when it comes to disciple making" (2008, 175). He says these are the basics:

1. Sin is confessed to one another in mutual accountability.
2. Scripture is read repetitively, in entire context and in community.
3. Souls are prayed for strategically, specifically, and continuously. (2008, 175)

These LTGs

- meet for approximately one hour each week, perhaps either before or after the missional community gatherings,[10]
- are groups of two or three (a fourth person is the beginning of the second group; multiplication is imminent),
- are gender specific,
- need no curriculum, workbook, or training,
- are egalitarian (not leader led).

Cole says, "A simple tool is often very profound. When you are struggling to stay afloat in deep waters, a complicated machine is not what you want. You don't have time to read an operational manual or fumble with batteries. Something that floats is all you want" (2008, 175). Cole believes that the simple LTG is such a vehicle and that "something similar to LTGs has been at the grassroots of some of the greatest revivals," such as the experience of the early church, in which Christians met in private to sustain their faith in a world of persecution, and the class meetings of the Methodist revival in the late 1700s and early 1800s (2008, 176).

Thus the fourth essential task of church planting and renewal is to guide searchers and new members to encounter the gospel and discern how it shapes their lives.

MENTORING RELATIONSHIPS: SPACE FOR SPIRITUAL DIRECTION AND MINISTRY FOCUS

As disciples come to greater spiritual maturity, they perceive in the Holy Spirit others for whom they should provide spiritual direction and ministry focus. Jesus, for example, sometimes gave particular attention to Peter, James, and John. Only these three witnessed the healing of Jairus's daughter, who had died (Mark 5:37 – 42); the Transfiguration, at which Jesus was declared superior to Moses and Elijah, and the voice from heaven declared, "This is my Son, whom I love. Listen to him!" (Mark 9:2 – 12); and Jesus preparing for death by praying in the garden of Gethsemane (Mark 14:32 – 42).

10. This denotes the author's preference. Neil Cole advocates a simple house church model.

Although Peter, James, and John did not fully perceive the meaning and ramification of what they saw, these events were formative in their preparations. Jesus continually spoke into their lives, inviting them to follow him but also challenging them to align their lives with his kingdom. Present-day disciples, following Jesus' example, should take developing leaders under their wings and incorporate them into their lives. This is done organically, personally, heart on heart, in the contexts of the other spaces of Christian community.

Thus, the fifth essential task in church planting and renewal is to focus relationships on the few in order to change the world. This training, like that of Christ, must be personal and imitative. We must humbly say, "Follow me as I try to faithfully follow Christ."

An Anthropological Perpective of Space

In the previous few pages, we have enumerated five spaces of missional ministry: (1) equipping huddles, (2) missional communities, (3) worship gathering, (4) transformation groups, and (5) mentoring relationships. In this section we will give a rationale for these spaces and how they interconnect and amplify each other.

In 1966, anthropologist Edward T. Hall wrote a classic study describing how humans use space to build community. He described four spaces of human interaction:

- *Public space*, where a larger group shares common experiences in a communal gathering, with the speakers or presentations being at least twelve feet away.
- *Social space*, where people meet and greet, get to know each other, and by so doing, develop an affinity for one another.
- *Personal space*, where people develop heart-to-heart relationships with one another and consider themselves close friends or family members.
- *Intimate space*, where "naked truth" (Myers 2003, 50) can be told without shame (Hall 1966, 1003–26; cf. Myers 2003, 39–51; Breen and Absalom 2010, 43).

Jesus ministered in each of these spaces. (See Figure 16.2.) He chose twelve disciples, as different as a tax collector and a Zealot, and called

Figure 16.2 The Ministry of Jesus

Space	The Ministry of Jesus
Public	Jesus proclaiming the kingdom to the multitudes
Social	Jesus and the Seventy-two, parties, weddings, etc.
Personal	Jesus and the Twelve
Intimate	Jesus with Peter, James, and John

Adapted from Breen and Absalom, 2010, 44.

them to follow him. He equipped this group specifically as his servants to lead his mission (personal space). He sent seventy leaders out on the Limited Commission (social space). During all this time, Jesus publicly taught the multitudes who followed him (public space). And finally, Jesus ministered intimately with Peter, James, and John at crucial times during his ministry (intimate space).

In our contemporary model, the spaces (and their purposes) also are aligned with two of our groups (equipping huddles and transformation groups) fitting into "personal space." (See Figure 16.3.)

Figure 16.4 shows the integration of four spaces. The equipping huddle, fitting into the category of personal space, provides leader equipping in discipleship and mission for all the missional spaces. In a sense, it is the engine that moves the church forward. Those who lead transformation groups, missional communities, and worship gatherings are equipped by the huddle. Those formed by the huddle tend to move from being systems managers to being disciple makers on mission with God.

Figure 16.3 Church Space

Space	Church Space	Purpose
Public	Worship gathering	Inspiration, teaching, and vision
Social	Missional communities	Community and mission
Personal	Equipping Huddles Transformation groups	Leader equipping for disciple making and mission Disciple formation
Intimate	Mentoring relationships	Spiritual direction and ministry focus

Figure 16.4 The Four Spaces of Human Interaction

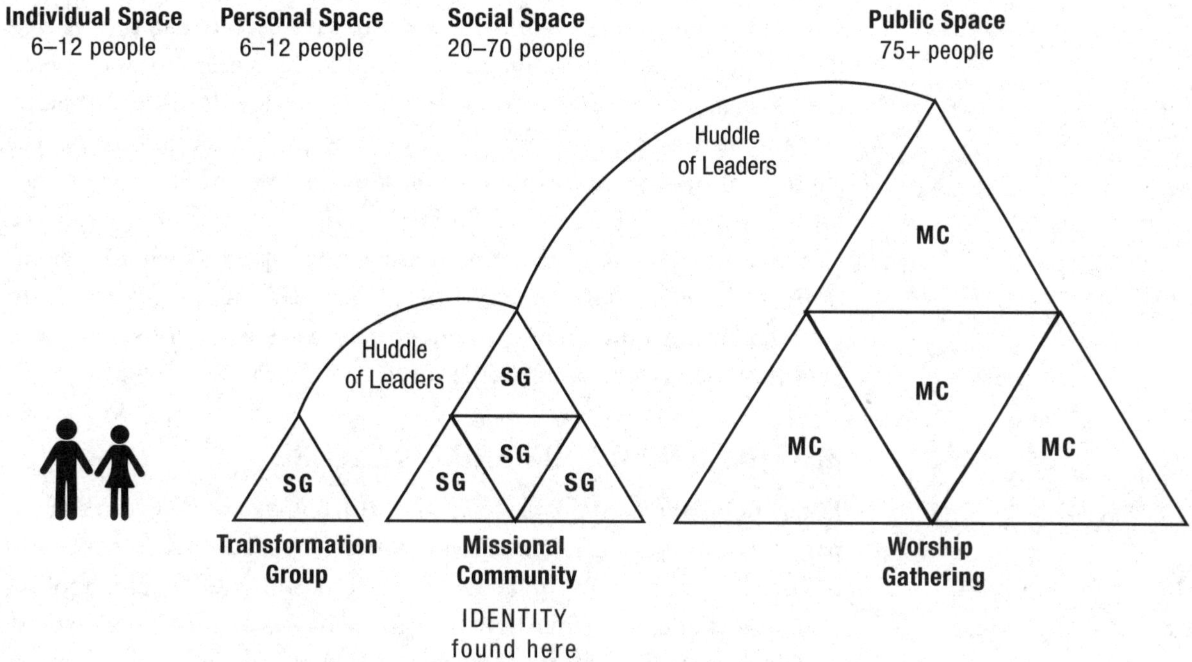

Missional communities, in social space, are the extended families where identity is found—where people of God experience fun, friendship, fellowship, and ministry and invite others to join them. Paradoxically, this community environment is the missing space in North American churches. Many Christians merely "go to church" rather than live as Christian community within their neighborhoods or relational networks. Thus the great task of twenty-first-century North America is rebuilding the community of the church where people live, work, and play, to reflect the light of God to those who are in darkness. Imagine spiritually formed elders shepherding these communities!

Transformation groups, in personal space, meet before or after missional community gatherings for disciple formation—to help searchers or new Christians encounter the gospel and understand how it molds and develops their lives.

Mentoring relationships, in intimate space, provide spiritual direction and ministry focus on a heart-to-heart level.

Rhythms of Disciple Making

God sent Jesus into the world, not only to save us, but also to give us a living illustration of life aligned with God and his mission. As we read the Gospels, we are drawn into the story to follow Jesus and thereby become his disciples. As Jesus' followers, we are called to observe the rhythm of his life and imitate his actions. These rhythms are tangibly described as LifeShapes in *Building a Discipling Culture* (Breen and Cockram 2011). Each LifeShape defines one aspect of what it means to be a disciple. These are rhythms to be both taught and caught in church planting and renewal and nurtured in leaders within Equipping Huddles. This is a brief introduction to a few of the LifeShapes.

RHYTHM 1: INVITATION AND CHALLENGE

Jesus not only *invited* people to follow him, but also *challenged* them, as participants on his mission, to live attuned to God. As disciples becoming disciple makers, we must also learn to both invite people to follow Jesus and challenge them to live transformed lives on mission with God.

Churches with high invitation but little challenge are cozy, consumer churches, joyfully inviting others to follow Jesus in comfortable environ-

Figure 16.5 The Invitation–Challenge Matrix

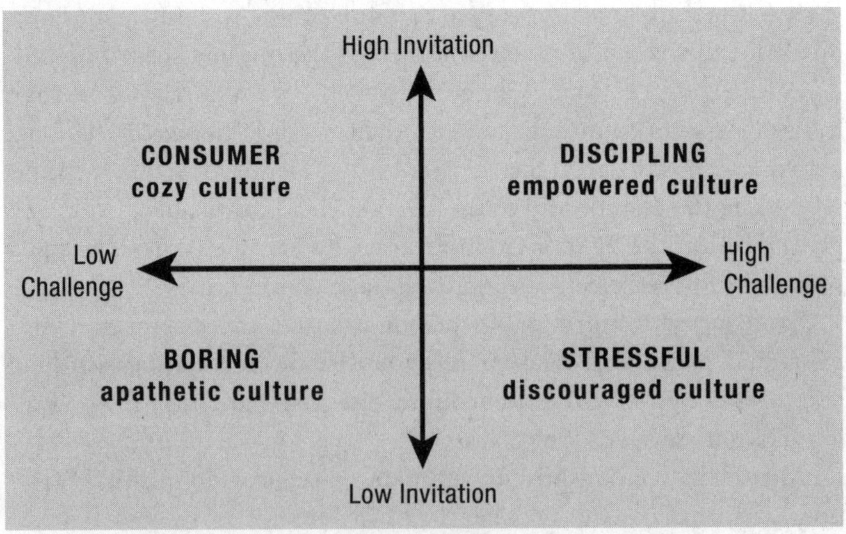

> Building a culture of discipleship is the only way that you will produce the kind of community that Jesus and the New Testament writers would recognize as church. A dynamic living organism with sufficient organization to enable it to function effectively, yet remaining an authentic community that is full of the life of God. A community where hearts are open to the Lord, to one another and to the world in need. (Breen and Cockram 2011, 22)

ments but lacking tangible ways of developing loving, holy, joyous disciples on mission with God. Leaders of these churches are typically shouldering the responsibility for creating the warm consumer environment and therefore are stressed and discouraged (Breen and Cockram 2011, 15 – 22). What a paradox! Leaders are experiencing the stressful quadrant while the majority of members consume what is provided for them!

Churches with high challenge but low invitation are stressful, discouraged churches. Frequently stress comes from the religious rules or expectations projected upon Christians to obey leaders or to hold fast to sectarian ideologies. Sometimes, however, the stress is due to the movement of a church from a consumer culture to a discipling culture as Christians learn to understand themselves as disciples on mission with God. This stress is natural, as some question the transitions being learned and lived out by others.

Churches with low invitation and low challenge continue to exist because of momentum from the past and, without renewal, will die as contemporary generations pass away.

Those becoming disciples are inspired by witnessing the in-breaking of the kingdom of God and become covenant participants in kingdom life. They begin to model the way of Jesus by calibrating invitation and challenge in such a way that they equip others to become disciple makers on mission with God. These rhythms are more easily caught than taught, more easily learned in ministry than through books.

These rhythms are more caught than taught, more easily learned in ministry than learned through books.

RHYTHM 2: LISTENING TO GOD, OBEYING GOD

Jesus was continually attentive to his Father, even to death on the cross. He testified, “The Son can do nothing by himself; he can do only what he sees his Father doing, because whatever the Father does the Son also does” (John 5:19). Jesus, likewise, was attentive to his disciples and to those around him who were ready to hear the good news. Similarly, we as disciples must learn to practice such two-way listening: we must attune their ears both to hear the words of the Father and to listen to those around us seeking to know God. In this process we both listen to God and obey him.

Those of us from secular cultures spawned by the Enlightenment are culturally formed to listen primarily to human voices. However, those of us who become disciples attune our ears to hear the voice of the Father and model this listening for those with whom we minister (Breen and Cockram 2011, 63–77). Jesus concludes the Sermon on the Mount by contrasting the wise and foolish builders: A wise person builds upon a rock by hearing the words of Christ and putting them into practice, but a foolish person builds upon the sand because he or she hears Christ's words yet doesn't put them into practice (Matt. 7:24–27).

RHYTHM 3: LIVING UP, IN, AND OUT

Jesus' lifestyle was thoroughly consistent. He lived UP — in relationship with his Father. He lived IN — in relationship with his chosen followers. He lived OUT — in relationship with the hurting world around him. Jesus modeled this three-dimensional living when he prayed all night before selecting his twelve apostles, brought them into community, and then went out to minister with them (Luke 6:12–19). Likewise, church planting and renewal are intensely relational.

God wants us to live and model this rhythm of UP, IN, OUT (Breen and Cockram 2009, 79–98). The paradox is that living the rhythm of UP, IN, and OUT is not easy. One writer asked, "How do we go OUT to the

Figure 16.6
Living UP, IN, and OUT

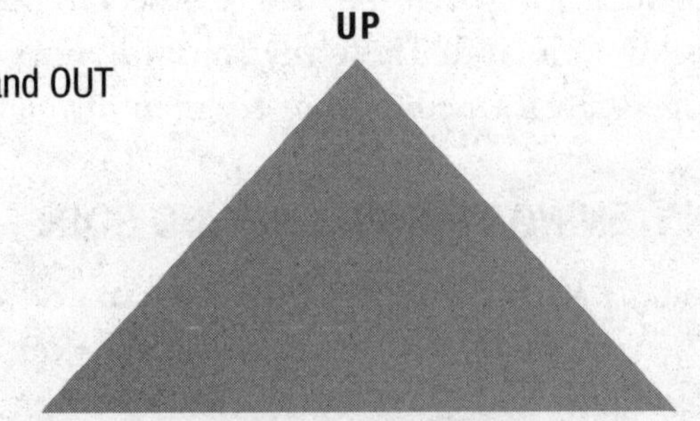

We in Mission Alive were invited to begin walking with Fred Liggin and the Williamsburg Christian Church when he transitioned into his leadership role at WCC in 2010. Fred calls his Mission Alive coach a special mentor, his sounding board and partner, in his personal journey to cast a new vision and lead this church toward spiritual renewal. Fred said, "We came to a crossroads where I realized we needed a partner in the journey. I shared this with the elders, and we invited Mission Alive into our journey."

Theirs is an exceptional story, not just because attendance has doubled and children's ministry has tripled, but also because they have begun to think of themselves as a kingdom community on mission with God. "A church experiences missional renewal," Fred comments, "when she learns how to align herself with God's mission in such a way that each member begins to live on mission with God in everyday ways as everyday people in everyday places" (Mission Alive, 2013).

broken world when inside our community we ourselves are broken?"[11] If all three relationships of the triangle are in rhythm, however, the mission of God goes forward with mighty power.

Think about your life: In which area — the UP, IN, or OUT — are you strongest? In which are you weakest? What is God saying to you?

RHYTHM 4: FROM REST TO WORK, FROM ABIDING TO FRUITFULNESS

Jesus reflected his Father, who worked for six days creating the world, then rested on the seventh. He modeled ministering out of the rhythm of resting in, communing with, and praying to his Father. This rhythm was reflected when he retreated to solitary places to pray (Luke 4:42; 5:15; 6:12); his "usual" custom was to pray in the garden of Gethsemane at the foot of the Mount of Olives (22:39; cf. Matt. 26:36). Jesus then taught his disciples this rhythm (Luke 11:1 – 11).

Jesus describes himself as the true vine and his Father as the gardener. As the branch must remain in the vine to bear fruit, so must we abide in Jesus. He says, "Abide in Me, and I in you. As the branch cannot bear fruit of itself, unless it abides in the vine, so neither *can* you unless you abide in Me" (John 15:4 NASB). As the branches abide in the vine, God prunes them so that they will bear even more fruit (John

11. "Living like Jesus through a Rhythm of UP, IN, & OUT," *http://citystreetchurch.com/living-like-jesus-through-a-rhythm-of-up-in-out/* (Accessed April 18, 2013).

Figure 16.7 The Rhythm of Life

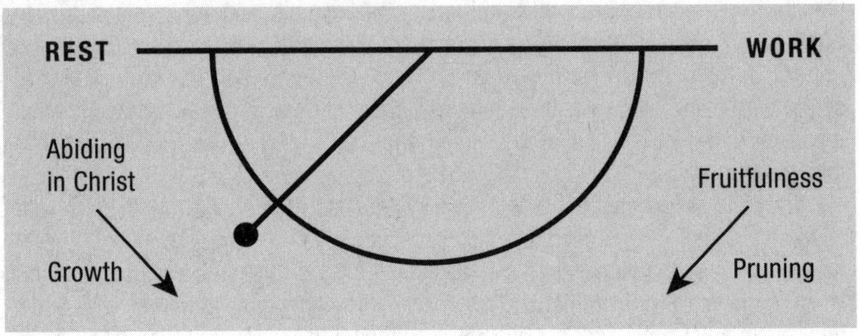

15:2). Thus there is a movement from growing as we abide in Jesus to fruitfulness in ministry because we live in Jesus. We move from times of rest and abiding — times of being shaped by God — to times of fruitful ministry. This is perhaps the most difficult rhythm for many North Americans: Christian ministers tend to be workaholics. We fail to take time to rest and abide in God so that he can shape us to be fruitful.

This LifeShape calls disciples to develop a rhythm of moving from rest to work, from abiding to fruitfulness (Breen and Cockram 2009, 100 – 114).

RHYTHM 5: GROWING AS DISCIPLES, MAKING DISCIPLES

A major rhythm is to grow as disciples while making disciples. We are simultaneously disciples and disciple makers — disciples who follow and leaders who guide — ever growing, ever equipping. Mike Breen and Steve Cockram give four stages of personal discipleship (D1 – 4) and related stages of disciple equipping or leading (L1 – 4). These concurrent stages are illustrated by the four sides of a square (2009, 116 – 32). Their model provides immense wisdom concerning the rhythm of concurrently growing as disciples while helping others become disciples.

Stage One (D1, L1)

When Jesus called disciples to follow him, they were idealistic, like new missionaries.[12] Had Jesus not selected them to follow him?! They were

12. Note the section titled "Stages of the Missionary Acculturation Process" in chapter 10.

naive — *unconsciously incompetent* — confident about the journey, yet lacking understanding and experience. Jesus merely calls them into a relationship with him and leads by example. His mode of leadership is directive: how else could these early disciples learn how to live in covenant relationship within the kingdom of God? Jesus' leadership at this stage is "I do; you watch." Likewise, contemporary leaders must not assume that people coming into their church, even those with a Christian heritage, are already spiritually mature disciples of Jesus. D1 disciples are like infants learning to walk the Christian way; D1 leaders help them take the first steps.

Stage Two (D2, L2)

The initial joy of Jesus' disciples soon turned to consternation and questioning — trying to understand this Jesus whom they were following. They became ambivalent, struggling to understand who this Jesus was, why they should follow him, what he was about, and their places of leadership in his kingdom. They had not expected *this* type of Messiah! They became like missionaries in the rejection or culture shock stage — *consciously incompetent.* Jesus, however, called them to himself, reassuring them: "Do not be afraid, little flock, for your Father has been pleased to give you the kingdom.... For where your treasure is, there your heart will be also" (Luke 12:32, 34). Jesus personally walked with them through this stage of discouragement, graciously giving them a vision of his kingdom. He served as their kingdom coach, their missionary mentor.

Figure 16.8
The Stages of Disciple Formation

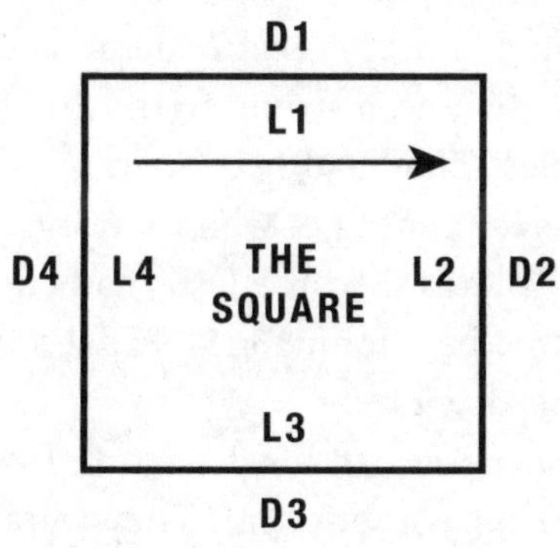

> [God] will always accomplish what he wants done. It is amazing what happens when a leader can take a person or group out of his own striving and into a place of resting in grace. Their confidence begins to grow because they are seeing it is God's work by grace, not their work by their own effort. (Breen and Cockram 2009, 124)

Likewise, contemporary leaders must be extraordinarily sensitive to disciples in this stage. Breen and Cockram say,

> The second stage is the testing point of any leader. During this stage, the leader should clear his or her schedule and spend time down in the pit of the individual or team going through this stage. Leaders need to be there to offer God's grace and encouragement. At this point, there is a ladder the leader can offer to bring his disciples out of the pit. The two rungs on this ladder are *grace* and *vision.* (Breen and Cockram 2009, 123 – 24)

Disciple involvement during this stage grows to "I do; you help." D2 disciples are fearful, hesitant, not sure of next steps. They may slip back to D1 by rejecting the difficult journey of becoming a disciple and by finding a consumer church in which to feel comfortable without going through life change. L2 leaders must give the disciples time, loving words of grace, and vision for what God wants them to be.

Stage Three (D3, L3)

Jesus' disciples grew to the point where he could send them out two by two on the Limited Commission, to places he would soon go (Luke 10:1). As they prepared to leave, Jesus described the harvest, the opposition, how to pray, how to minister, and what to say (Luke 10:2 – 12). At this point the disciples had become *consciously competent*: they could now, if they focused, represent Christ and his mission. Upon return, they joyfully reported, "Lord, even the demons submit to us in your name" (Luke 10:17). By now, a strong friendship had formed between Jesus and his disciples. They had become more than "servants," who follow with little understanding of who they are and what they should do. They were now "friends" because Jesus had taught them everything he learned from the Father (John 15:15). A deep intimacy had formed between Jesus and his disciples.

At this point Jesus described his departure (John 14) and prepared his disciples to minister without him. They were confused, trying to discern what this might mean. Leader involvement had grown to "You do; I help." D3 disciples begin leading in various ways — by discipling others in an equipping huddle to launch a new missional community, by facilitating a transformation group within a missional community, or by organizing a component of the worship gathering. Their developing experience leads them now to minister with increased enthusiasm. L3 equippers provide less direction, high collaboration, and continued times of discussion.

Stage Four (D4, L4)

Jesus' disciples matured so that they understood who he was and began to represent him on his mission. "The continual hearing of Jesus' teaching and putting it into practice sends roots down deep, strengthening the disciples against life's inevitable storms" (Breen and Cockram 2011, 130). At this point, however, Jesus was arrested, tried, and crucified, came back to them as the resurrected Lord, and appeared periodically in the most surprising ways. Then he fully transferred his mission to his disciples by commissioning them to "go and make disciples" (Matt. 28:18 – 20).

Leader involvement during this stage changes to "You do; I watch." Disciples now have the character and competence to lead the mission God has given them. L4 leaders are now low in direction and high on consensus, yet they continue to be high on explanation. The disciple and his equipper become full coworkers in God's mission.

This rhythm of growing as disciples while making disciples helps us discern both where we are as disciples and leaders in various areas of our life and how to coach others to grow as disciples and leaders. In democratic North America there is a tendency to assume that all leaders are at the level of D4 and able to make churchwide decisions. Operating on this assumption, leaders then try to develop a consensus among disciples who are on various levels of understanding, maturity, and experience. The result is almost always ministry and church life dumbed down to a level acceptable to disciples at all levels of maturity. Special attention must be given to those in D2 so that they do not give up ministry or the Christian way of life, because it is hard to die to self and live and minister in a transformed way.

Praying through the Lord's Prayer places God in control of our lives. The prayer nurtures dependence, leads to confession, shapes identity, and comforts our souls. It is the most touching and transforming spiritual discipline that we do.

RHYTHM 6: PRAYING THE MODEL PRAYER

Jesus' disciples saw him pray and requested, "Lord, teach us to pray, just as John taught his disciples" (Luke 11:1). In response, Jesus gave them a very simple prayer, a model prayer to follow (Matt. 6:9 – 13; Luke 11:2 – 4).

The basis of the prayer is described in its first words, "Our Father" (Matt. 6:9). Jesus had just said that his followers should not "keep on babbling like pagans, for they think they will be heard because of their many words" (v. 7). Rather, as God's adopted children, they were to pray, "Our Father. . . ." These first words define the character of the relationship: the disciples were to approach God as his children rather than as workers laboring to prove their worth (vv. 5 – 9; Keller 1995).

This prayer has six elements; each teaches an important truth about the Father.

1. *The Father's character* — "Our Father in heaven, hallowed be your name" (Matt. 6:9). As God's adopted children, we praise God for his love and holiness, which define his nature. Saying this praise helps our hearts open to him.
2. *The Father's kingdom* — "Your kingdom come, your will be done, on earth as it is in heaven" (v. 10). We invite God to rule over our lives.

Figure 16.9 The Lord's Model Prayer

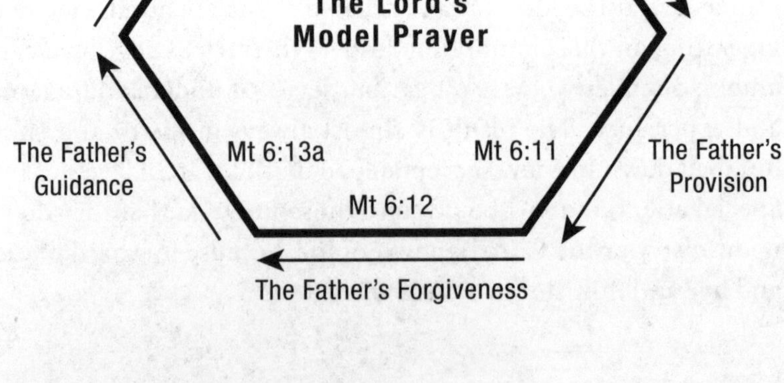

Two themes structure this prayer (6:9–13). First is the plea for the establishment of God's sovereignty over all creation (verse 10). Second is the plea for God's mercy as expressed in provisions for material needs (verse 11), forgiveness of sins (verse 12), and deliverance from spiritual danger (verse 13). (Hamilton et al. 2009, 739)

3. *The Father's provision* — "Give us today our daily bread" (v. 11). We acknowledge that all things ultimately belong to and come from God, and as children, we ask in areas of need.
4. *The Father's forgiveness* — "And forgive us our debts, as we also have forgiven our debtors" (v. 12). Sin has alienated us from God. As children, we ask for God's pardon as we reflect his character by forgiving others.
5. *The Father's guidance* — "And lead us not into temptation" (v. 13a). Because we live in a world of sin, we ask for God's direction and strength.
6. *The Father's protection* — "But deliver us from the evil one" (v. 13b). We pray for God to shield us from Satan, who tries to pull us away from God's love and holiness.

(Breen and Cockram 2009, 155–67)

Learning to pray is one of the most important — and neglected — elements of disciple training. We too often pray as consumers, asking God for what we need and asking him to protect us — for provision and protection. We frequently neglect prayer because of a sense of self-sufficiency, our lack of dependence on God.

If God is moving you to grow in prayer, I suggest two rhythms: During the first week, commit yourself to fervently praying through all elements of the Lord's Prayer in one setting a couple times each day. During the second week, focus on praying through one element of the Lord's Prayer a couple times each day. In this process, discipline yourself to become God's kingdom person, willing to learn the fullness of prayer.

These rhythms and the LifeShapes that illustrate them — invitation and challenge; listening to God, obeying God; living UP, IN, and OUT; from rest to work, from abiding to fruitfulness; growing as disciples, making disciples; praying the model prayer — prepare us to become living illustrations of Christ-formed people as we go on mission with God.

Going on Mission with God

How do disciples being formed by God go on his mission?[13] They acknowledge with Paul that no one "is equal to such a task," but with God's help, they become the aroma of Christ, "speak[ing] ... with sincerity, as those sent from God" (2 Cor. 2:14 – 17). They invite searchers into their lives and share their journey of coming to the Lord and "being transformed into his image" (3:18). Disciples incarnationally walk with searchers as the gospel spreads from person to person, from house to house, from neighborhood to neighborhood. These disciples describe their struggles and growth in the Lord. Searchers, consequently, come to Christ when they touch and taste transformed lives in vibrant relationship with God the Father. God's mission is amplified through these disciples ministering with other believers and searchers within neighborhoods and relational networks as part of missionary communities.

Church leaders and church planters, being formed as disciples, learn to go on mission with God. Paul says, "Christ's love compels us" (5:14) so that we become "Christ's ambassadors ... [imploring people] on Christ's behalf" to "be reconciled to God" (v. 20). That love is embedded in the Spirit who indwells them and leads them forward on his mission.

THE DIAMOND OF MINISTRY

The Diamond of Ministry portrays elements of incarnational ministry. At the core of the diamond is connecting to those described by Jesus as people of peace. Disciples on mission with God enable these people of peace to come to Christ through ministries of gracious hospitality, social justice, expectant prayer, and kingdom witness. Through these activities they hear about and witness the in-breaking of the kingdom of God.

People of Peace

At the heart of the diamond are people of peace. Jesus illustrated this pattern by prayerfully choosing a few disciples to go with him on mission. By being with him, they would learn to preach and minister with

13. Second Corinthians 2:14 – 6:2 is a classic passage answering this question by describing the spiritual formation of Christians to prepare them to go on mission with God.

Figure 16.10 The Diamond of Incarnational Ministry

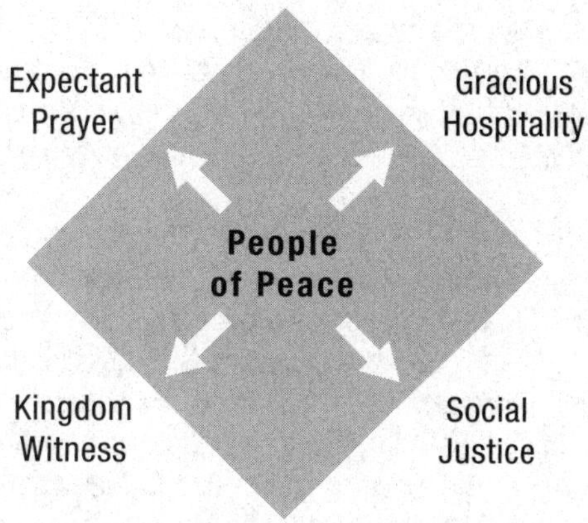

power (Mark 3:14 – 15; Luke 6:12 – 22). These "unschooled, ordinary men" (Acts 4:13) eventually proclaimed the kingdom of God from Jerusalem to Rome and India. They first learned by merely walking with Jesus. Jesus later taught them to imitate his ministry by finding others to teach, mentor, and take on mission. For example, to prepare his disciples for the Limited Commission, Jesus taught them to search for people of peace and minister through them (Luke 10:5 – 6). People of peace have been spiritually prepared to accept the Word of God. They welcome us into their lives, listen to what God is saying through us, and want to serve and support God's mission through us. Gregg Burch says,

> Jesus never pursued anyone. He made himself available to the willing, to those who were sincerely seeking God. In this passage, he is telling us to do the same. This is a wonderfully liberating idea. Jesus tells us to look for persons of peace in our lives. What does that mean? It means God is in the equation. There are certain people who are open to relationship with you. Those are persons of peace. God is at work on the hearts of people all around us. He touches people with His Word, with His Spirit, and through other people.
>
> So if we calibrate our radar, commit to investing ourselves where we have an opening, and work with the willing, we will be following God's plan. Only the Holy Spirit can open a heart to hear the Gospel. When those opportunities arise, we are to be His witness, to tell our story of God's movement in our lives. (Burch, n.d.)

These are people like Lydia and the jailor in Philippi (Acts 16). They welcomed Paul, they heard his teachings, and they invited him

The Story of Dee

We first met Dee when she and her cousin stopped by our house advertising their newly opened dog-walking business. (We just so happened to be their only customers.) We gladly let the two tweens take our active dog, Linus, on walks at least once a week. I'm not sure who walks who, but they all come back happy and thirsty each time.

The next natural step was to invite Dee and her friends to Vacation Bible School, and they came. Not only did she come, but she brought along six of her cousins. After the week of VBS, Dee stopped by regularly just to spend time with me, cuddle our son Judah, and hang out in our backyard. Recently she has begun coming early to missional community each week to help me cook and set up.

In the midst of all these simple opportunities to show Christ's love to Dee, last week she brought her Bible over to our house to read with me. After reading the first fifteen verses of John, Dee decided to begin following Jesus. It was obvious, though, by our conversation that this was not her first encounter with God, Scripture, or faith. Someone has been planting seeds, turning the soil, and encouraging her for quite some time. This just so happened to be harvest time! It was also obvious to me that the words coming out of my mouth were not my own. Evangelism is not my base gifting, but it's certainly becoming an area of growth and stretching right now.

I love this girl; she has a sweet spirit, an intelligent mind, and a servant's heart. God reminded me through her that he's always been using young people to advance his kingdom (think David or Mary!). I can't wait to see how he uses Dee as she grows in him. (Shoemaker 2012)

into their homes and their lives. The first step, then, of developing a missional community is discovering people of peace.

Who might be people of peace in your neighborhood or relational network? Imagine God working through them to plant or expand a new missional community.

Gracious Hospitality

Gracious hospitality is inviting people into our lives to "come and see." John's gospel records the enthralling story of two of John the Baptist's disciples, including Andrew, following Jesus after they hear that he is the Lamb of God. Jesus turns and asks, "What do you want?" Not knowing what to say, these disciples respond, "Teacher ... where are you staying?" Jesus says, "Come ... and you will see," and they spend the day with him (John 1:35 – 39). Immediately afterward, Andrew calls his brother Simon — the man whose name Jesus will change to Cephas, or Peter — to come and see the one he now knows to be the Messiah.

Hospitality is inviting people into our lives to see Jesus.

The next day Jesus invites Philip, "Follow me." Philip, realizing that Jesus is the Messiah, tells Nathanael that he has "found the one Moses wrote about in the Law, and about whom the prophets also wrote — Jesus of Nazareth, the son of Joseph." "Nazareth! Can anything good come from there?" Nathanael asks. Philip simply says, "Come and see." Nathanael comes, hears Jesus describe his character and how Jesus saw him under a fig tree before Philip called him, and declares, "Rabbi, you are the Son of God; you are the king of Israel" (John 1:35 – 51). With power, Jesus invited people into his life to follow him.

"Come and see" is the essence of hospitality. It is inviting people to walk with us in our lives ... to see if this Christ way is the right way. "Come and see" means "Come and think, ... come and examine the evidence, ... come and follow and change your life" (Keller 1998).

Hospitality is inviting people into our lives to see Jesus.

William A. Smalley, in a classic article titled "Proximity or Neighborliness?" describes the difficulty of hospitality in Euro-American contexts.

> In our highly complex society we have built cultural devices for keeping people close by from being neighbors unless for some reason we choose to include them. These barriers provide a protection for us, keep us from having to associate with people who are not compatible, whose race or religion or social status is different from ours. (1967, 302)

A major Christian task in the twenty-first century will be developing in fragmented North American culture an environment that encourages social community to develop naturally. We must relearn how to live in community so that hospitality is the DNA within neighborhoods and relational networks that catalyzes missional community. Gracious hospitality invites people to "come and see" what happens so that people of peace are able to experience living testimonies of the presence of God. However, repositioning small groups focusing on the UP and IN to also include the OUT (the neighborhoods and relational networks in which they live) is the greatest move in missions.

Alan Roxburgh and Scott Boren, in *Introducing the Missional Church*, say,

Bob and Carol are forming a missional community in their new neighborhood. The neighborhood is primarily composed of Hispanic families. When Bob and Carol first moved into the community, they felt awkward: they were a minority, one of only a few Caucasian families there. The children, however, immediately took an interest in them. You see, Bob and Carol inherited a tree house when they moved into their home. The tree house was a place where on any given day you would find kids just hanging out.

Bob and Carol decided to have a back-to-school event for the kids in their community. Several of their friends signed up to bring food items, grills, games, chairs, tables, music, and so on. Everything was set up in Bob and Carol's driveway. The yard was transformed into a place where people could sit and chat, listen to music, play games, or climb up into the tree house and take in the beautiful view. Parents and kids came out to meet the family at whose home their kids were spending so much time. Through such events, parents and children experienced the love that Jesus has for those who desperately need a Savior. Several additional events have been held to encourage the families in the community.

> The task of the local church in our present situation is to reenter our neighborhoods, to dwell with and to listen to the narratives and stories of the people.... It will be in these kinds of relationships that we will hear all the clues about what the Spirit is calling us to do as the church in that place. But this is not a strategy we take *to* a context; it is a way of life we cultivate *in* a place where we belong. (2009, 85)

We must relearn how to live in community. Hospitality is the DNA within neighborhoods and relational networks that catalyzes missional community. Without hospitality, there will be no missional communities; people will continue to live compartmentalized lives, and religion will remain what happens at a church building, rarely connecting with the contexts in which we live, work, and play. Gracious hospitality helps form community; spiritual direction and coaching then lead this gathered people to become Christ's representatives in their neighborhood or relational network.

How is God leading you to become a person of hospitality — in your neighborhood, in your place of work, or in a special niche of culture, such as your children's sports league? Imagine God working through you to gather a missional community through acts of hospitality.

Expectant Prayer

Prayer, like conversion, is a turning to God. This turning to God is very difficult for human-focused, individualistic Euro-Americans and people who have been culturally influenced by the secularism of Western education. How can people who have been taught to rely on themselves rather than on God learn to pray, to turn to God? The answer is, by imitating others who depend on God, modeling their examples.

The early disciples learned to pray by watching Jesus. They watched him go to a solitary place to pray (Luke 4:42). They saw that he "often withdrew" from proclaiming the kingdom of God and healing the sick "to lonely places" to pray (5:15 – 16). They learned that before Jesus selected twelve of them to become his apostles, he "spent the night praying to God" (6:12 – 15). They heard him pray before his death, "Father, the hour has come. Glorify your Son, that your Son may glorify you. For you granted him authority over all people that he might give eternal life to all those you have given him" (John 17:1 – 2).

The journey to his death was not easy. Jesus urged his disciples to pray that they would not "fall into temptation" (Luke 22:39 – 40) and then withdrew "a stone's throw beyond them" and prayed, "Father, if you are willing, take this cup from me; yet not my will, but yours be done" (vv. 41 – 42). Luke says that Jesus prayed so earnestly that "his sweat was like drops of blood falling to the ground" (v. 44). Finally, Jesus died with prayer on his lips — "Father, into your hands I commit my spirit" (Luke 23:46) — believing that God would bring him back from Hades to dwell again with him. Jesus' journey was typified by prayer to his Father and was witnessed by his disciples!

From the Limited Commission to the commissioning of Barnabas and Saul for mission among the Gentiles to the haystack prayers igniting the Student Volunteer Movement,[14] prayer has served as a catalyst to mission. The early Christian church was likewise a praying church. The people devoted themselves not only to the apostles' teaching, fellowship, and the breaking of bread, but also to prayer so that "everyone was filled with awe at the many wonders and signs performed by the apostles" (Acts 2:42 – 43). When undergoing persecution by Jewish leaders, the Christians came together for prayer, seeking for God to intervene, pleading, "Now, Lord, consider their threats and enable your servants to speak your word with great boldness. Stretch out your hand to heal and perform signs and wonders through the name of your holy servant

14. Note this story in chapter 2.

Jesus" (Acts 4:29 – 30). After this prayer, "the place where they were meeting was shaken. And they were all filled with the Holy Spirit and spoke the word of God boldly" (v. 31).

Expectant prayer and worship gathering are catalysts for mission because our God is listening and responding. Imagine praying

- for healing with a sick person in the neighborhood, accompanied by a person of peace who also lives in the neighborhood,
- a blessing over a new baby during a neighborhood celebration of his or her birth,
- a blessing over a new family in the neighborhood (once again with a person of peace who is learning to pray),
- with a family whose child struggles with addictions or has been involved in a crime,
- a blessing over all the children of the neighborhood at a cookout with your missional community, celebrating the beginning of a new school year.

In our missional communities and worship gatherings, we continually celebrate the many times and ways that God has answered prayers.

Because our God is listening and responding, we repeat the praise of Moses:

Who among the gods
is like you, Lord?
Who is like you —
majestic in holiness,
awesome in glory,
working wonders?
(Exodus 15:11)

Social Justice

After being tested by Satan in the desert for forty days, Jesus returned to Galilee in the power of the Spirit and began to teach and minister. Shortly thereafter, he stood up in his hometown synagogue in Nazareth, unrolled the scroll of Isaiah, and read a passage defining his ministry:

The Spirit of the Lord is on me,
because he has anointed me
to proclaim good news to the poor.
He has sent me to proclaim freedom for the prisoners
and recovery of sight for the blind,
to set the oppressed free,
to proclaim the year of the Lord's favor.
(LUKE 4:18 – 19)

These echo the words of the ancient prophets calling the people of Israel and Judah, who had gotten rich by devious business dealings (Micah 6:10 – 12; cf. Amos 5:11 – 15), not to merely make sacrifices and worship the Lord but "to act justly and to love mercy and to walk humbly with your God" (Mic. 6:8). They were encouraged to "stop doing wrong. Learn to do right; seek justice. Defend the oppressed. Take up the cause of the fatherless; plead the case of the widow" (Isa. 1:16 – 17).

Jesus' words express concern for the poor, the prisoners, the blind, and the oppressed. He touched the leper and healed him. He rejected the racism of his day, entering the life of the Samaritan woman and inviting her to be his disciple. In the parable of the sheep and the goats, Jesus poignantly says that he lives within the hungry, the thirsty, and the stranger. Challenging those who ask, "Lord, when did we see you hungry or thirsty or a stranger or needing clothes or sick or in prison, and did not help you?" he replies, "Truly I tell you, whatever you did not do for one of the least of these, you did not do for me" (Matt. 25:44 – 45).

We seek to be like Jesus in our missional communities by ministering at the points of brokenness in our culture. Examples of social justice initiatives include:

- providing sleeping bags to the poor, an initiative of a young man in a new church planting "to give a warm bed to the homeless in Nashville"[15]
- painting a mural reflecting the presence of God in a First Nations Canadian context to symbolically redeem an area where drugs and prostitution once flourished[16]

15. *www.facebook.com/pages/Operation-Sleep-Tight/328419173839164.*
16. *http://gentleroadchurch.files.wordpress.com/2013/06/dove.jpg.*

The Story of Johnnie

Johnnie is a godly man. An educated man, MBA prepared. Johnnie is a strong man, over six feet in stature, with a lean build and a chiseled face. A Vietnam vet who, as a young man, returned from the war with a drug addiction and got a felony. One blot on his record!

For most of his life, Johnnie has been a successful small business owner. Until recently. When the housing bubble burst, his construction company went out of business. He sought work in Nashville. Construction had remained steady there, even though the rest of the country was experiencing a rapid decline. Johnnie arrived in Nashville, lined up some work … and then the 2010 Nashville flood occurred. For the first time in his life, Johnnie found himself homeless.

How does an MBA-prepared, successful business owner find himself homeless? Johnnie is an African American Vietnam vet who once had a drug addiction and has a felony on his record. All this was before Jesus. Johnnie has been clean for thirty years, loves God with all his heart, and even sees his three years of homelessness as a blessing. One that God used to teach Johnnie about contentment, compassion, and simplicity.

So how did our family, church planting in Nashville, meet Johnnie? Through our eight-year-old son's desire to make sure his homeless friends were not cold during the winter. He calls it Operation Sleep Tight. It was Christmas night 2011; we had five bags left to give away. After Christmas dinner, our family headed to the city square. That's where we met Johnnie. He is the kind of man that you respect even before meeting him. He was sitting on the bench reading a book when we asked him if he would like a sleeping bag. That's where our friendship began.

Later we learned that Johnnie volunteers at a local soup kitchen, had adopted a median in the road to clean and landscape, and often donated time to helping the elderly with landscaping needs. Johnnie did all this while he was homeless, because his God called him into the kingdom in spite of his circumstances.

We invited Johnnie into our family, and he invited us into his. Later Johnnie began journeying with Reunion Christian Community, our new church planting. We have been able to share some of his burdens, while he has been able to find some rest. He is a man with wide influence and sees us as a place to invite other people with burdens to come to, and we find ourselves inspired by his faithfulness. What a coworker in God's mission!

(Sergio Rizo, Reunion Christian Community)

- offering a church building to the homeless during the winter months through a temporary winter shelter program[17]
- developing a citywide poverty alleviation process in a highly relational ministry called 3E Restoration "to encourage, equip,

17. *www.williamsburgchristianchurch.org/#/connect/local-mission.*

and empower" friends/families in need to move from homelessness and/or extreme poverty to "self-sufficiency within the context of community and God's sufficiency"[18]
- building affordable houses for the poor[19]
- working with the community to clean up houses on abandoned lots, with all participants eating together in what is commonly called "Weed and Feed"[20]
- using Celebrate Recovery to help people struggling with "hurts, hang-ups, and habits by showing them the loving power of Jesus Christ through a recovery process"[21]

The social justice ministries of relatively new missional communities should be simple and tangible: building a wheelchair ramp for a family in need, helping a family with a chronically ill child or spouse, providing shoes for needy children.

Rick Rusaw says, "Good deeds create good will and out of that we share good news" (class at the 2011 Exponential Conference).

Kingdom Witness

Jesus began his ministry with proclamation: "Repent, for the kingdom of heaven has come near" (Matt. 4:17) — an intriguing theme that what had been was now very near. This proclamation, while nuanced by metaphors and parables, questioning, and intrigue, was both explicit and public. It was so powerful and clear that "the crowds were amazed at his teaching, because he taught as one who had authority" (7:28 – 29). His teaching took place in relationship, embedded in life with his disciples and the people who followed him; they saw his life in relationship to the Father, and he taught out of that relationship.

The early Christians also knew the message. Paul wrote to remind the Corinthians of the gospel, which he preached, which they received, and by which they were saved. This gospel, which Paul passed on to them as being of first importance, was that "Christ died for our sins

---

18. *www.williamsburgchristianchurch.org/#/connect/local-mission.*

19. *http://gentleroadchurch.wordpress.com/2012/12/10/esperanza-development-corporation.*

20. *http://www.missionalive.org/ma/index.php/churchplanting/currentplants/27-current-plantscategory/157-new-river-church – 2#.UtQA0b7nbGw.*

21. *www.celebraterecovery.com.*

according to the Scriptures, that he was buried, that he was raised on the third day according to the Scriptures," as testified to by witnesses who saw the resurrected Messiah (1 Cor. 15:1 – 8). By the power of God, Jesus Christ broke the chains of death, destroying the grip that Satan and sin had on the world. Today we are called to live in relationship with God in Jesus Christ.

The reality, however, is that most of us are hesitant to speak this message to people in Western culture because religion is viewed as a matter of personal conviction and private interpretation. Our culture tends to render us to silence! As Christian ministers, we intuitively know that the good news of the kingdom of God is the cutting edge of church planting and renewal. We believe the words of Paul in Romans 1:16: "I am not ashamed of the gospel, because it is the power of God that brings salvation to everyone who believes."

The Diamond of Ministry illustrates how God raises up people of peace who welcome us, listen to us, and serve us. These searchers become participants of missional communities in which gracious hospitality and compassionate community nurture the soul and shape life. Expectant prayer leads searchers to know and expect the work of God. The deepening relationships of authentic community lead to openness to the gospel.

The next section illustrates a process of kingdom witness within missional communities.

GROWING YOUR MISSIONAL COMMUNITY: OUTREACH INTO NEIGHBORHOODS AND NETWORKS

Charles Kiser, director of training in Mission Alive and planter of Storyline Christian Community, in Dallas, Texas, suggests a dual process of mission. We not only invite searchers to "come and see" what God is doing in our worship gathering and missional communities, but we also "go and find" those who are not yet ready to hear an overt message of the gospel. "Come and see" reflects Jesus inviting the disciples of John the Baptist into his life, and Andrew and Philip inviting Simon Peter and Nathanael to come and see Jesus (John 1:35 – 51). "Go and find" reverses the order, as illustrated by the shepherd in the parable of the lost sheep leaving the ninety-nine to go and find the one that is lost

Figure 16.11 Relational Mission: Plowing, Sowing, Watering, Reaping, Keeping

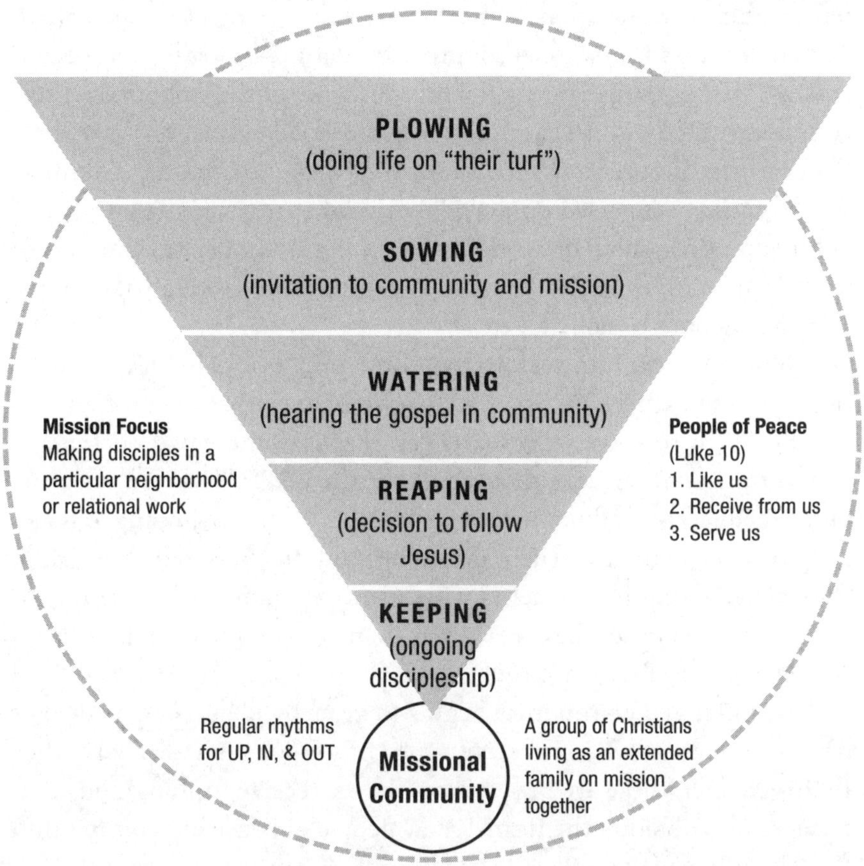

(Luke 15:1 – 7). This occurred in the incarnation: Jesus left his home with his Father in heaven to "go and find" humanity, who had lost its way (Kiser 2013).[22] In a mature church, these two approaches are not mutually exclusive, but complementary, interpenetrating, amplifying one another.

22. The model of incarnational mission overviewed in this section was originally developed by Laurence Singlehurst in *Sowing, Reaping, Keeping* (1995), based on applying the Engel scale to a process of outreach. Mike Breen and Alex Absalom applied the material to outreach through missional communities in *Launching Missional Communities* (2010). Finally, Charles Kiser, director of training in Mission Alive, adapted the material into its present format in a presentation called "Reaching and Discipling Twenty-Somethings" at Pepperdine Bible Lectures (*https://itunes.apple.com/us/itunes-u/pepperdine-bible-lectures/id643020969*) in 2013 with Eric Brown and Matt Dabbs.

This diagram uses an agricultural metaphor to describe how Christians minister incarnationally in the contexts to which they are called. The circle around "missional community" defines its focus on a specific context. Rather than aspiring to make disciples of the whole world, the community focuses on a particular neighborhood or relational network. For example, one missional community in Storyline Christian Community in Dallas is focused on a neighborhood (University Terrace), and another on a relational network (Dallas Junior Chamber of Commerce). Missional community leaders have a calling from God, a passion, for their particular mission context.

These communities seek to live three-dimensionally: UP (in relation with the Father), IN (in relation with one another in community), and OUT (in relation with searchers). Because these are *missionary* communities, however, a major focus is the OUT: "How do we grow our missional community in this context?" Sometimes, hoping to make a significant impact in their neighborhood or relational network, a missional community launches with twenty or more lay leaders on the core team; sometimes the core team is smaller — four to eight lay leaders (Breen and Absalom 2010, 109).

The missional community begins to grow by identifying people of peace — searchers who are receptive to the gospel. As described earlier in this chapter, these are people who like us, receive from us, and want to serve us. All along the funnel, new people of peace are coming into the fellowship as the soil is plowed, sowed, and watered.

The first stage, *plowing*, describes how we find people of peace. We are breaking up the ground so that we can sow the seed. An important understanding is that the group works together to develop community. In a neighborhood we take walks with others from our missional community to get to know the area, go together to the local park, play with our children and meet other parents, invite neighbors for dinner with another family or two from our missional community, go to neighborhood parties, organize a special shopping trip with a few members of the missional community, and invite neighbors for a neighborhood get-together.

In a network such as the Dallas Junior Chamber of Commerce, we do what they do: become members, go to happy hours with others of our missional community, attend professional meetings, perform service

This is a testimony after a hospitality event in our home during the plowing stage.

This morning Becky prayed, "We thank you for all of our guests who came and blessed our home last night." We were indeed blessed! Twenty-four folks from eight families came from our cul-de-sac and the houses behind our home. A great time of neighborhood connection! Jessica, a vivacious lady of Cambodian heritage, was the first to come and the last to leave. She has lived on our cul-de-sac for fourteen years without knowing any of her neighbors. We had simply left a flyer about our "Holiday Open House" at her home, and she in turn called and began a conversation with Becky. In one evening she developed friends—hopefully lifelong, life-changing relationships.

John and Sarah came with their two daughters. We heard about their dating, their marriage, their work, and their connection with Peter and Sarah, our next-door neighbors. Sarah, who works in Human Resources with a local company, remembered a person of the old Meadow Ridge homeowners association who used to organize large community gatherings. Many mentioned our need for further connection.

I also noticed Becky's gift of hospitality—her joy in preparing for the evening and then being with all of the people who gather.

(NAMES HAVE BEEN CHANGED)

projects, and invite others to join us for dinner with another family from our missional community. We hang out and are fully present. They may know that we are Christians, but there is no need to speak about spiritual life at this stage of the relationship unless questions are asked. Plowing is about creating environments where relationships develop easily and naturally.

The next stage, *sowing*, continues to focus on relationship (as in every stage), but with a little more emphasis on spiritual conversation. People of peace are invited to participate in various types of missional community activities, including

- golf with missional community members, with reflection on the nature of life,
- viewing a movie and reflecting on the cultural themes, including spiritual implications,
- serving the homeless or needy in our network or neighborhood, which might include spiritual reflection, perhaps a short Bible study, and prayer,
- a trip to a football, basketball, or baseball game,

- a children's storytime at a local Barnes & Noble, where the books read have spiritual content, with discussion afterward.

Moving from plowing to sowing is determined by the readiness of the people of peace to take steps forward. Our role is to discern where they are and whether we have permission to take them deeper. They must be willing to take the next step on their spiritual journey. Breen and Absalom say, "You don't want to surprise them with spiritual content when they are not expecting there to be any. It is up to you and people in your MC to ask them if they want to go to that place. That bridge represents a bridge of trust that you cannot afford to burn" (2010, 111).

The third stage, *watering*, is a time when searchers hear the gospel fully *"but are not asked to give a response."* The truth of the gospel is allowed to percolate in their minds and hearts and sink into the innermost parts of their being. The change from secular thinking — "I live by my own might and power," so prevalent in Western culture — to "This is God's world; I must live in relationship with him" is so drastic that the ramifications must be allowed to sink into a person's full being. Breen and Absalom speak about a "bridge of trust" spanning the chasm between what we are calling "sowing" and "watering": "People need to know what they are walking into and aren't surprised by the level of spiritual content and have the opportunity to say, 'No'" (2010, 112). Searchers are beginning to belong to a community and are growing to believe.

Watering experiences include

- Communion at a missional community service, where the gospel is fully explained,
- an Easter service in which God's work in Jesus' death, burial, and resurrection are reenacted, with reflections on what this means to us,
- personal conversations that allow searchers to ask questions,
- a neighborhood Vacation Bible School held by the missional community.

These experiences illustrate multiple touch-points of the gospel in the lives of people of peace — personal conversations, events in the missional community, and events in the worship gathering. People are learning in multiple ways within the community of faith (2010, 113).

The *reaping* stage begins when those walking with the people of peace discern that they are ready for an invitation to follow Jesus. There may be several journeying together, sharing their newfound faith and how it ramifies through their lives. They have experienced all the elements of the Diamond of Ministry: they have learned to receive and to give gracious hospitality, have heard the community pray expecting God to respond and then seen answers to prayers, have experienced ministries of social justice, and have heard kingdom testimony. The invitation to follow Jesus may occur in various venues:

- over a cup of coffee with other members of the missional community
- at a missional community retreat full of fun and laughter, teaching and worship, with opportunity for people to respond to what God is saying to them
- in a personal conversation with a member of the missional community

The person of peace, along with others coming to Christ, responds by declaring Jesus as Lord and Savior and participating with Christ's death, burial, and resurrection in baptism, understanding that God's grace made his or her redemption possible.

The *keeping* stage infers continued spiritual growth. Peter describes how new Christians "like newborn babies, [who] crave pure spiritual milk . . . grow up in [their] salvation, now that [they] have tasted that the Lord is good." Consequently, they "rid [themselves] of all malice and all deceit, hypocrisy, envy, and slander of every kind" (1 Peter 2:1 – 3). As my African brothers say, "The road is slippery." Therefore new believers must grow! Growth occurs through personal discipling within the transformation groups of their missional communities, through going on mission with others in their missional community, through continually hearing the Word of God both in the worship gathering and in their missional community, and through growing as a leader in an equipping huddle. Within this environment of nurturing and disciple making, Christians more quickly come to spiritual maturity and become co-ministers in God's kingdom work.

Incarnational Missions Training

Mission Alive has developed Mission Training to guide church planters and church leaders to cultivate the incarnational rhythms of life described in this chapter. Mission Training is a two-year process, consisting of four two-day Equipping Labs that occur every six months. Each Equipping Lab addresses a major move related to planting new churches or renewing existing ones.

CULTIVATE: PERSONAL DISCIPLESHIP

God first wants to do *in* us what he wants to do *through* us. Equipping Lab 1 focuses on the leader's personal spirituality and relationship to God as the foundation of mission. Content includes conversation about Christian identity, theology of spiritual formation, spiritual practices, confession, and the role of mission in personal discipleship. After this lab, participants join equipping huddles, weekly video conference calls that provide ongoing equipping for personal discipleship.

PLANT: MISSIONAL COMMUNITIES

God's mission spreads through the web of relationships found in neighborhoods and relational networks. Equipping Lab 2 focuses on how to

Figure 16.12
Mission Training

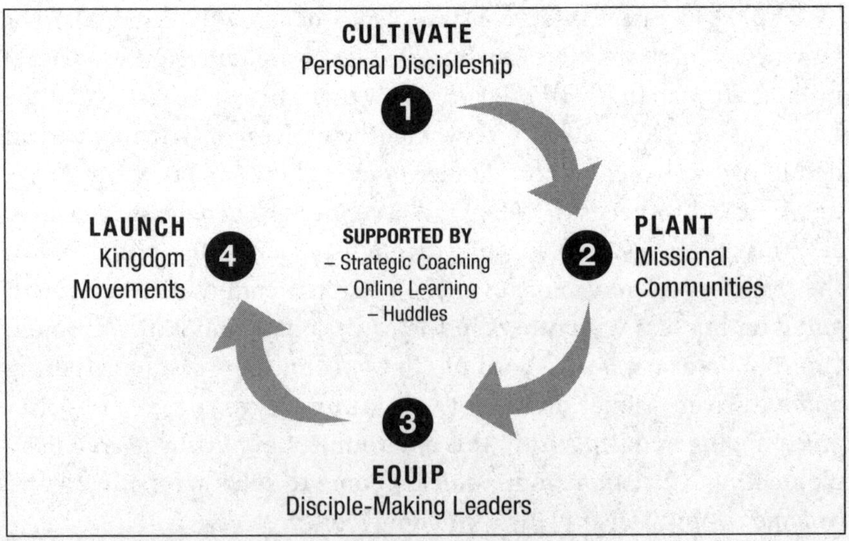

plant missional communities in such contexts. Content includes conversation about theology of incarnation, reading the culture, missional community practices, and strategies for the growth and development of the church.

EQUIP: DISCIPLE-MAKING LEADERS

Missional leaders make disciples who make other disciples. Equipping Lab 3 focuses on multiplying leaders of a missional movement. Content includes conversation about creating a leadership-development process, theology of service, coaching skills, and different types of leaders.

LAUNCH: KINGDOM MOVEMENTS

God uses movements of people to shape culture and impact the world. Equipping Lab 4 focuses on the development of "centers of mission" that serve as hubs for church planting, church renewal, and Mission Training. Content includes conversation about characteristics of movements, developing regional networks, and training network leaders.

Leaders who experience Mission Training will

- grow in their relationship with God,
- learn how to lead searchers to the Lord,
- develop skills for making disciples,
- deepen their theological framework for discipleship and mission,
- be prepared to lead missional communities,
- be prepared to train developing leaders in equipping huddles,
- create a pipeline for developing leaders in their church,
- be equipped to participate in a regional network of discipleship and mission.

Other equipping includes:

- *Supplemental online content.* Our online system guides participants through readings and supplemental content related to each Equipping Lab. Church planters have access to online learning modules that address the nuts and bolts of church planting, from fundraising to developing a prayer team.

- *Regular support and connection.* Between labs, participants receive ongoing personal support in the Mission Training process from certified ministry coaches, from trained spiritual directors, and in a weekly equipping huddle meeting.

Change Dynamic: Processes of Church Planting and Renewal

While the processes of church planting and renewal have a similar essence, the sequencing of tasks is different. Both entail an interconnected, ongoing process of nurturing personal formation, equipping leaders as disciples, and going on mission with God. This is not a step-by-step, linear process, but a concurrent process of maturation — a simultaneous nurture of heart, mind, and soul and the development of missional competence. The role of Mission Alive is to nurture and model this process and develop leaders with focus, motivation, and orientation toward developing church planting and renewal movements in North America.

CHURCH PLANTING

In Mission Alive, church planting begins with the personal spiritual formation of the planters through both Mission Training and equipping huddle led by a trained leader. As church planters gain tools for discipleship and mission, they gather a core team of leaders and equip them in a huddle. With those leaders and their families, they create the UP, IN, and OUT rhythms of a missional community — connecting to God, fellowshiping with one another, and reaching out to searchers.

Huddle serves as the organized way of equipping the core team; the first missional community is the mission expression of this huddle in a specific neighborhood or relational network. It is important during this

> "If you make disciples, you will always get the church. But if you make a church, you rarely get disciples" (Breen and Cochram 2011, 12).
>
> "The future of the Western Church ... is a powerful return to Jesus' heart for making disciples, and multiplying them into missionary leaders" (Tyson in Breen 2012, foreword).

Figure 16.13
The Dynamics of Church Planting and Renewal

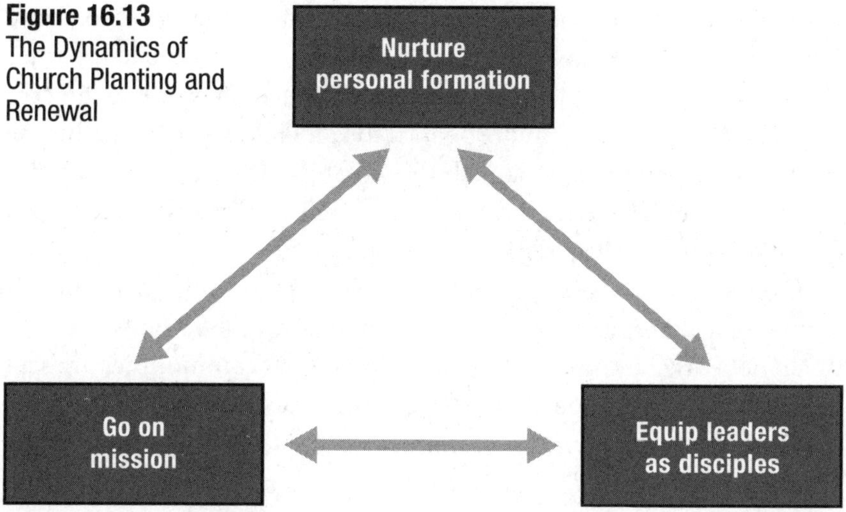

initial phase to allow adequate time to equip the core team as disciples and servants on mission with God who in turn equip others. The goal is not simply to grow by adding new attendees, but to develop a discipling culture on mission with God.

When the time is right, the Holy Spirit[23] will call some within the first missional community to launch a new missional community. This must not be done artificially, from a desire for quick growth. The major focus early in the church movement is developing a discipling culture out of which the mission of God naturally flows. Patience, mixed with wisdom and counsel from those on the journey, is important.

God, through his Holy Spirit, will at some point speak into the church to begin a worship gathering, providing a space for the public teaching of God's Word, inspiration from worshiping and celebrating together, and vision casting for discipleship and mission. There should be at least two healthy, ministering missional communities before the launch of the worship gathering. The frequency of the worship gathering will vary, depending on the number of people who are part of the new church, the time and energy needed to facilitate the gathering, and the logistics of finding an appropriate public space. In some plantings,

23. Throughout the book of Acts, the Holy Spirit is the power of mission (Acts 1:8). The Holy Spirit, for example, spoke within the Antioch church to send Barnabas and Saul on the first missionary journey (Acts 13:1–4).

the worship gathering may begin with a monthly rhythm and evolve to a weekly one, with one week each month dedicated to mission and service in the community. In a few church plantings, there may be enough critical mass (seventy-five or more people) to launch the worship gathering earlier. A temptation is to launch the worship gathering too soon, not allowing enough time for development of a discipling culture in which Christians effectively and urgently go on mission.

Over a period of years, an organized yet organic movement spreads as missional communities are launched in new neighborhoods and relational networks. Eventually, a group of missional communities are sent out with organized leadership to begin another worship gathering closer to where these missional communities are located. This movement is organized and organic, attractional and missional.

CHURCH RENEWAL

Churches going through renewal typically have a worship gathering, a Sunday school, and small groups. They often lack, however, an organized way, such as huddles, to equip leaders as disciple makers and missionaries. They also typically lack "extended family" communities, such as missional communities, practicing the UP, IN, and OUT in neighborhoods and networks.

Ideally, church renewal begins with a decision by core leaders that they want to become a disciple-making[24] church on mission with God. Mission Alive usually meets with leaders at this stage to discuss steps forward and discern if there is a spiritual fit. Like church planting, church renewal begins with the personal spiritual formation of the leaders through both Mission Training and an equipping huddle led by a trained leader. As church leaders gain tools for discipleship and mission, they gather a core team of leaders in a local huddle to launch a prototype of a missional community in one neighborhood. The huddling and launching is called an experiment, a prototype of a community living

24. Disciple making, like any practice, can be and has been misused. One misuse is creating a hierarchical control structure. In Mission Alive, disciple making is spiritually walking with followers of Christ so that they are "transformed into his image" (2 Cor. 3:18); it is helping "newborn babies" in Christ "grow up in [their] salvation" (1 Peter 2:1 – 3); it is part of our missionary mandate: "go and make disciples" (Matt. 28:18 – 20).

together on mission with God in their particular neighborhood. Sometimes small groups, after hearing the stories of outreach in the missionary community, decide to come together once a month for an OUT activity, since small groups usually are better at UP and IN than at OUT.

These groups may at some point decide to come together for fellowship, equipping, and mission to become a new missional community. This decision is not made by the church leaders making changes to the structure; it is made through the gradual concurrence of people in the small groups as they grow in the Lord and in mission. Sometimes one small group will begin to practice the OUT to such a degree that they grow to become a full-fledged missional community. As in church planting, patience is important: the key is developing rhythms of a discipling culture so mission naturally emerges as people begin to live UP, IN, and OUT. There is no magic bullet! Change begins in the heart as Christians give their lives to God and learn to go on mission with him.

The worship gathering will more specifically provide a place for the intertwining practices of teaching God's Word, being inspired by worshiping and celebrating together, and casting vision for discipleship and mission. The teaching of God's Word focuses on the UP, IN, and OUT. Celebration and worship include testimony and praise for what God is doing in mission. The vision for disciple making and mission will become more overt with stories told from the trenches, especially in relationship to the OUT.

At some point, God, through his Holy Spirit, will begin to speak to the church about launching new missional communities. This will likely happen through leaders who are in existing missional communities and/or equipping huddles. New huddles, led by trained leaders, are formed to prepare the team to live out the discipleship rhythms in order to launch the new missional communities. Small groups may also grow to become missional communities by emphasizing not only the UP and IN, but also the OUT.

God, in his time and through his Spirit, will make evident that some missional communities are far from the worship gathering and that another worship gathering is needed. That it is time to begin another one. After prayer and planning, a group of missional communities is sent out with organized leadership to begin another worship gathering closer to where they are located.

Developing and maintaining momentum in disciple making and mission is very important. Momentum is developed as God raises up leaders who, through equipping huddles, develop rhythms of living as disciples on mission with God. Jesus gives two parables describing this movement: *When the kingdom of God authentically spreads, it grows like the mustard seed and is as pervasive as yeast.* Jesus said,

> *The kingdom of heaven is like a mustard seed, which a man took and planted in his field. Though it is the smallest of all seeds, yet when it grows, it is the largest of garden plants and becomes a tree, so that the birds come and perch in its branches.... The kingdom of heaven is like yeast that a woman took and mixed into about sixty pounds of flour until it worked all through the dough.*
>
> (Matthew 13:31 – 33)

The influence of the kingdom is intensive as well as extensive. It affects the whole society with which it comes into contact.

REFLECTION AND APPLICATION

Questions

1. What broad themes emerge from reading the section titled "The Cultural Context of North American Missions"?
2. Describe the purpose of an equipping huddle. Why is this type of space needed for equipping in North American culture?
3. What is a missional community? How is it different from a small group, which is so prevalent in North American churches?
4. Why is it important that the life of Christian community be personalized in neighborhoods and relational networks? Why is it significant for the renewal of the church in North America?
5. What are the purposes of a worship gathering? How does a missional approach shape these purposes?
6. What are the purposes of a transformation group? Where does a transformation group fit within the structure of the church?
7. List the rhythms of discipleship and briefly describe the significance of each.
8. Describe where you are as a disciple and disciple maker (perhaps in various facets of life), using the D1–4 and L1–4 grids.
9. How does the Diamond of Ministry help you personally imagine your life on mission with God?
10. Describe the stages of reaching people of peace, or searchers, as we invite them into our missional communities. To what degree do we speak the gospel into their lives?
11. Specifically describe the process of planting a new church by applying the understandings of this chapter.
12. Specifically describe the process of church renewal by applying the understandings of this chapter.

Personal Inventory

How has God spoken to you through this chapter? What is God calling you to do about it?

chapter 17

Using Money in Missions

The Good, the Bad, and the Ugly

Jim and Julie's friends Dan and Sarah had served on the missions ministry of their church for the past five years and had just returned from a short-term mission trip. During the trip, Dan and Sarah were convicted that God wanted them to commit their lives to missions and serve in this field. Their home church was enthralled. Dan and Sarah would be their missionaries! Jim and Julie were happy for them, remembering how a similar mission trip had significantly changed their lives, but were cautious because of Dan and Sarah's lack of training and the support model their church was using in this particular field. Church leaders felt that Dan and Sarah would help the church by working with them to host short-term teams, following up after the short-termers returned home, and working with local leaders.

Dan and Sarah's congregation had already begun to support three leaders so they could serve the churches in this country. One of these men, a radio preacher for several years, viewed himself as the leader of the two churches in the country. A second man received support to serve as the preaching minister of the larger church in the country. The missions ministry of Dan and Sarah's church, concluding that the best way to establish churches throughout the city was to train preachers, had also built a small preacher training school and hired the first teacher.

Soon after they arrived on the mission field, Dan and Sarah became disillusioned. During the stress of language and culture learning, they were also forced to deal with financial matters. The supported preachers were constantly asking for advances because of emergencies and complaining about their salaries compared with those of pastors from other religious groups. Because Dan and Sarah were from the sending culture, they were assumed to have authority over both the exchange of finances and the amount of salaries. They struggled to discern their role in these financial matters.

Vocational Christian leaders within the two churches were also disillusioned. Some felt that people hired were not the most qualified to lead the church. Many Christians wanted to know how much these preachers were making. They appeared to live at a higher economic level than did their friends and neighbors. Most significant, local Christians felt that foreigners were making church decisions for them.

DAN AND SARAH'S EXPERIENCES represent a common occurrence and illustrate the need for missionaries and mission leaders to reevaluate their perceptions and practices concerning money and missions. This chapter suggests four alternatives for the use of money in missions.

The Personal Support Model

Dan and Sarah and the local Christians where they served were experiencing the personal support model. In this model, foreign churches and individual Christians — and even mission agencies — send money directly to local preachers and evangelists, without collaboration and oversight by mature church leaders on the field. Outsiders make decisions about the use of finances and send them to the field, without a mature body of believers or an agency providing on-the-field planning and accountability. Frequently, this direct support begins when foreigners travel to an area in a mission context and afterward begin supporting the local Christian leader(s) who hosted them.

The abuses of this model stem from the inability of supporters to clearly discern the church situation because of distance and cultural differences. Foreign Christians are seldom able to perceive the motives of the people they support. Those whom visitors see as articulate and capable may lack a deep conviction or God's call, ministering merely to earn income. For example, the executive director of a major denomination in Uganda once told me, "I would jump to another religious group if they paid me more. Currently, I am not making enough to live on the level I desire. Many of the pastors under me feel the same." Many supported leaders, even those who feel God's call, tend to cater to the theologies and methodologies of people who support them financially.

Dependency is often so great that local leaders believe it impossible to initiate new churches without wealthy benefactors. Jealousies between people who do and do not receive support hinder the development of Christian community. Many church leaders go through intense faith dilemmas when their support is terminated and frequently change denominational affiliations or entirely lose their faith. Thus Bishop Zablon Nthamburi of the Methodist Church of Kenya says, "The African Church will not grow into maturity if it continues to be fed by Western partners. It will ever remain an infant who has not learned to walk on his or her own feet" (McQuilkin 1999, 58).

Paradoxically, this model is typically used to support pastoral rather than apostolic ministries. In other words, money from wealthier nations provides salaries for local preaching ministers rather than assisting evangelists or missionaries initiating new church-planting movements. These planted churches, however, should all be self-supporting. In rural areas of the world, where the cultural organization is informally structured and there is more time for ministry, vibrant churches should have numbers of vocational ministers and pastors serving the flock. In urban contexts, where there is a cash economy, growing churches should support their own preaching ministers and pastors.

The personal support model is easy for local churches and Christians in rich lands to implement, because Christians in wealthy nations have only to send money and, if they desire, periodically visit the local leaders they support. Many times, field visits provide only a glamorized picture of the work while offering little understanding of what is actually occurring.

Therefore the personal support model tends to hinder rather than empower missions. Supporters and local church leaders should aim to transition to the partnership model (described later in this chapter) in order to put accountability and decision making into the hands of reputable Christians in the areas where the local evangelists live.

The Indigenous Model

The indigenous model contrasts sharply with the personal support model. In this model, missionaries seek to initiate churches that are self-supporting from their inception. For example, an American, European, or Korean church or agency supports its missionaries so they can plant new churches, nurture young Christians in these churches to maturity, equip local leaders supported by their own people and resources, and then pass the baton of leadership to these developing Christian leaders.

A number of principles guide the self-support orientation of the indigenous model. The dependency created when missionaries, churches, and agencies with great wealth support local preachers living in less wealthy areas of the world ultimately hinders the growth and maturity of the new Christian movement. The support and governance of the mission agencies and sending churches are like scaffolding in the construction of a new building. In some cases, the scaffolding cannot be removed because, paradoxically, it has become the structure holding the fragile building together. Likewise, many anemic mission works are unable to stand without the support of foreign scaffolding (Henry Venn in Beyerhaus 1979, 16 – 17).

Local churches and Christian institutions should generally reflect the economy of their areas. If churches in poor countries are built on the basis of wealthy economies, they will never be able to stand on their own. Frequently, institutions — schools, hospitals, and agricultural ministries — are created via outside finances. These institutions, created in a poor country by using finances from rich countries, seldom become locally supported and supervised. The amount of support (and resulting control) tends to increase, rather than decrease, over the years, resulting in more dependence by local leaders and more control by foreign churches and agencies.

When a preacher or church leader begins receiving support from foreign Christians or an outside agency, it becomes exceptionally difficult to transition to local support. This is particularly true in rural areas, where many people live on a subsistence level. In other words, while they do not have much cash, they do have produce from their farms, which forms the foundation of their economy. These rural churches are generally like a family, informally and interpersonally organized. In these contexts, it is advisable to develop churches with a multiplicity of lay leaders but with very few full-time ministers. Hiring salaried ministers, where there are many lay Christian leaders, frequently creates jealousy and dissension, especially if finances for salaries come from foreign sources.

Should Dan, Sarah, and local church leaders suggest that supporters adopt an indigenous approach? Would currently supported church leaders feel rejected and betrayed? Typically, the indigenous model works well only if the first churches are founded on indigenous principles.

The Partnership Model

The partnership model is significantly different from both the personal support and indigenous models. The partnership perspective recognizes that there are certain contexts in this increasingly connected world where foreign funding, if appropriately used, can empower missions without creating dependency.

This model reflects the growing globalization of the world. In the international business world, for instance, companies become global by exporting products to consuming countries, to be sold by local marketers. Soon these companies set up their own marketing infrastructure to maximize profits. As globalization continues, companies research the new market to determine the needs, and then they develop manufacturing in the new context. The companies also invite their best executives to join them in global decision making and planning. The companies have thus moved through progressive stages to become globalized, simply by expanding their markets. Reflecting this trend, mission agencies and churches in global cities are similarly becoming internationalized.

International partnerships should reflect the foundations of missions seen in the Missional Helix (see chap. 13). Participating leaders recognize that contextual strategies draw deeply from cultural and historical understandings to theologically discern what God is saying about the practice of ministry, which leads to effective church planting, Christian maturation, and social transformation. This shaping of ministry takes place within the environment of spiritual formation, as Christian servants humbly submit their lives to God's covenant and kingdom. Thus people in the partnership are learning and are growing in order to become more effective servants in God's mission. In the partnership, there must be clarity in the practice of ministry, with high expectations for well-defined Christian ministry. Understanding the use of money in missions slowly spirals to new levels as Christian servants grow in their understandings of God's mission.

In the partnership model, Christian leaders mutually decide the duration of the partnership, accountability for the use of money, and methodologies for their specific mission tasks. Without such dialogue, partnership eventually breaks down, because trust erodes and interest wanes. All support should go through a local accountability structure of mature Christian leaders rather than directly to the recipient. Most decisions are made by the leaders closest to the field, but with full consultation and dialogue with outside supporters. Learning from international business leaders helps immensely in developing patterns of accountability and effectiveness.

Two pragmatic factors have led me to consider the need for international partnership. First, it is difficult for church movements to begin from scratch in highly specialized, time-limited, money-driven urban cultures without *initial* financial help. Urban churches planted on the self-support principle seldom survive, because they lack the resources to impact their multicultural context. Those planted using purely indigenous approaches generally become isolated congregations on the periphery of the city.

For example, some Brazilian missionaries who are effectively planting churches in Argentina and Uruguay and as far away as Kenya arrive in their host countries with enough money from Brazilian churches to rent facilities, conduct crusades, print weekly newspapers, and begin a television ministry. Although highly financed in the initial stages, these movements soon become financially self-sufficient. A purely indigenous approach in a city like Buenos Aires (Argentina), Montevideo (Uruguay), or Nairobi (Kenya) would appear naive and shortsighted to these very successful urban evangelists.

Second, mature movements in poor areas of the world require financial assistance to develop structures of continuity that will nurture local churches so that they become missions-sending movements. When missionaries leave before developing "structures of governance, expansion, finance and theological education" (Cox 1999, 217) in collaboration with local leaders, the movement typically disintegrates.

These structures must be organized on both congregational and associational levels. On the congregational level, the community of faith, guided by the Word of God, determines how local churches are organized and how they relate to one another. On the associational level, mature church leaders and missionaries collaborate in developing teaching, equipping, and encouraging structures above the local church level. Local churches bond together to help each other — as did the early churches meeting in Jerusalem. Vocational and full-time local evangelists form teams to complete the evangelization of their area and spread the gospel into both adjoining and distant areas. Training schools, on the associational level, provide forums for creative reflection and equipping leaders and youth for local churches (Van Rheenen 2000b, 43).

Like the indigenous model, the partnership model has many pitfalls. For example, partnership may become another name for paternalism if outsiders control decisions and set agendas. Under the guise of partnership, a subsidy system may be introduced that is, in reality, no more than the personal support model. Partnership is also challenged by cultural differences, which affect the ways that donors and recipients typically make decisions. People tend to idealize partnerships without considering these very significant problems.

Should the churches that Dan and Sarah are working with transition to a partnership model? Are local Christian leaders mature enough to enter into a global partnership? Or would these funds destroy the new church movement?

The Indigenous/Partnership Model

Finally, there may be an integration of the last two models — the indigenous and the partnership approaches — forming an indigenous/partnership model. During the movement's first generation, missionaries work to establish initial beachheads of Christianity by planting the first churches, nurturing new Christians to maturity, and training local leaders. Because the work is self-supporting during these formative years, people come to Christ, not because of financial inducements, but because of faith commitments. In the second generation, when the movement has grown to maturity, churches and agencies that have supported missionaries work through the missionaries to partner with local leaders. This partnership seeks to develop structures of continuity that nurture existing fellowships and train evangelists, enabling this to become a missions-sending movement.

The last three models (indigenous, partnership, and indigenous/partnership) can each be effectively employed in various world contexts. Generally, indigenous and indigenous/partnership perspectives are more appropriate for rural, face-to-face cultures, which do not have a high degree of specialization and do not relate extensively to the international arena. Because urban contexts are more global minded, partnerships there tend to empower the church rather than create dependency and control from the outside.

Missions-sending churches and agencies, however, often operate with no model for the use of money in missions. Their decisions about money and missions are therefore likely to be inconsistent, haphazard, and paternalistic.

Naive use of finances during churches' initial stages has created dilemmas that historically have resulted in division, jealousy, and trauma. Maintaining the status quo relegates the movement to dependence. Church leaders must prayerfully deal with the problem and, considering the context, select the model that will best contribute to the long-term stability and growth of the church.

REFLECTION AND APPLICATION

Questions

1. List and define the four models of using money in missions, as described in this chapter.
2. In what ways can the personal support model be detrimental to churches on the mission field?
3. Why do some sending churches favor the personal support model?
4. What are some limitations of a purely indigenous model?
5. What are some pragmatic reasons for forming constructive partnerships? What theological reasons can you think of that might support such an approach?
6. What are some potential problems that can arise in partnerships?
7. Under what circumstances would a hybrid indigenous/partnership model be preferred?

Case Study

The churches that Dan and Sarah work with, described at the beginning of this chapter, are in a paradoxical situation. Benefactors with good intentions have superimposed a personal support model over the local church. Should support be withdrawn from the local preachers and the teacher in the preacher training school in order to lay an indigenous foundation for the work? Is this church mature enough to transition to a partnership model? What should local Christians and the benefactors now do? How would people who are supported feel if they lost their support? What discussions should take place among supporters, local Christians, and the supported preachers?

Personal Inventory

How has God spoken to you through this chapter? What is God calling you to do about it?

chapter

18

The Benefits and Challenges of Short-Term Missions

How Short-Term Ministry Can Have Long-Term Impact

Because their lives were so profoundly affected by a short-term mission (STM) to Haiti, Jim and Julie were anxious to provide a life-changing, cross-cultural mission experience for their high school group. Jim and Julie were advised by field missionaries with whom they worked to read certain books and articles on short-term missions before beginning their planning. Their discoveries from these sources excited, challenged, and perplexed them.

A CHAPTER TITLE IN AN EXCEPTIONAL BOOK summarizes the theme of this chapter: "Doing Short-Term MISSIONS without Doing Long-Term Harm" (Corbett and Fikkert 2012). North Americans who minister in a Third World culture are spiritually touched and transformed and begin to see the world with new eyes. The recipients of the mission, however, are frequently impacted in negative, though unintentional, ways. Missiologist Miriam Adeney relates a parable told her by an African friend:

North Americans who minister in a Third World culture are spiritually touched and transformed and begin to see the world with new eyes.

> Elephant and Mouse were best friends. One day Elephant said, "Mouse, let's have a party!" Animals gathered from far and near. They ate. They drank. They sang. And they danced. And nobody celebrated more and danced harder than Elephant. After the party was over, Elephant exclaimed, "Mouse, did you ever go to a better party? What a blast!"

> But Mouse did not answer. "Mouse, where are you?" Elephant called. He looked around for his friend, and then shrank back in horror. There at Elephant's feet lay Mouse. His little body was ground into the dirt. He had been smashed by the big feet of his exuberant friend, Elephant. "Sometimes, that is what it is like to do mission with you Americans," the African storyteller commented. "It is like dancing with an Elephant." (2000; cf. Corbett and Fikkert 2012, 151 – 52)

This is the paradox of short-term missions.

Short-term missions have been an exploding phenomenon over the past two decades. There were 120,000 in 1989; 450,000 in 1998; 1,000,000 in 2003; and 2,200,000 in 2006 (Peterson 2007). Participating groups come primarily from Western cultures, as seen by the more than 1.5 million Americans who participated in short-term missions in 2012 (Datema 2012, 14).

STMs, of course, have occurred in various forms since ancient times. God sent Jonah on a short-term evangelistic mission to tell the wicked city of Nineveh that if its people did not repent, the city would be destroyed in forty days. Jesus sent out his disciples two by two on the Limited Commission to prepare the way for the towns and places he was about to visit (Luke 10:1). The church in Philippi sent Epaphroditus on a short-term mission to give aide to Paul (Phil. 4:18).

Like the biblical examples, STMs today vary greatly. Some work with strong churches, others with struggling churches, and still others where no church exists. Some short-term missions take place in developing nations, while others target urban centers. Some focus on evangelism, some on humanitarian and service endeavors. Short-term missions may provide requested help to host missionaries or churches, or they may be initiated by Western organizations to provide spiritual growth or cultural broadening experiences for participants.

This chapter presents a working definition of short-term missions and examines their benefits and challenges. It then proposes some guiding principles for preparing participants.

Definition of Short-Term Missions

In this discussion an STM is defined as *a ministry experience, either domestic or foreign, having an intended duration of less than two years.*

The time frame was chosen because long-term cross-cultural workers require at least two years to become conversant with the local language and culture (Corbett and Fikkert 2012, 152). Thus, a two-year missionary apprentice who is learning the local language and culture is considered to be one type of short-term missionary. Many such apprentices are investing their lives as learners with the likelihood of returning as long-term missionaries. Because short-term missionaries are visitors, they ideally minister under the guidance and wisdom of local leaders. To do otherwise would be presumptuous. Most short-term mission trips last from seven to ten days (Priest et al. 2006, 433).

Benefits of Short-Term Missions

STMs can bring benefit to both participants and recipients. For example, well-planned short-term missions can provide personnel and resources to accomplish tasks or projects that otherwise might go undone (Moreau, Corwin, and McGee 2006, 279). North American Christians often testify to the life-changing impact of STM experiences. They report deeper relationships with God, greater gratitude for their own blessings, more profound commitment to foreign missions, and intense resolution to serve in their home contexts.

GLOBAL PARTNERSHIP

STM trips witness to the universality of the church and build bonds of fellowship that cross geographical, ethnic, and social barriers. Kevin Birth observed the effects of American short-term workers doing manual labor in Trinidad, even though the Trinidadians would have been more competent in performing the work that the Americans were doing. Birth concluded,

> With white American dominance of the world, there seems to be something powerful about seeing such Americans engaged in manual labor serving Trinidadians. Such instances convey three messages of significance: (1) a reversal of the historical master/servant relationship, (2) a demonstration that Americans are not superior to locals, and (3) a manifestation of ways in which Americans are inferior to locals. (2006, 506)

Encouragement provided by an STM benefits local churches and Christians (Wan and Hartt 2008, 83). Many Christians face the challenge of living on the fringe of society. These believers are encouraged by a sense of unity with the universal church. Honza, for example, is the only Christian in his family and school. Any comment he hears about Christianity, in either of these arenas of life, is negative. His church is small, and he is the only high school student. About a dozen college-aged short-term workers came to assist Honza's church. He experienced for the first time how young people live as Christ followers and now has Christian friends with whom he can correspond through email and Facebook.

PROVIDING HUMANITARIAN SERVICE

Organizations and churches that encourage holistic missions often focus their short-term efforts on service projects and humanitarian aid. These projects allow short-term workers to make a positive impact in settings where language and cultural barriers make deep conversation improbable. Humanitarian projects also allow people to use their specific skills (medical, construction, disaster relief, etc.) for the sake of God's kingdom and provide for needs that might otherwise go unmet (Ver Beek 2006, 493). Moreover, service projects allow the visitors to model Christian virtues of sacrifice and service.

MODELING SIMPLE APPROACHES OF OUTREACH AND DISCIPLESHIP

Sometimes STMs, done appropriately, can be effective in evangelistic ministry. Short-term workers are able to spend many hours each day in ministry and to meet and interact with more people than can nationals who must balance jobs and family obligations with ministry. Those workers are sometimes able to offer services that the national Christians cannot, such as teaching English classes using the Bible. A group of short-term workers who are enthusiastic and energetic may spur local Christians to be more evangelistic (Smith 2008, 47; Wan and Hartt 2008, 90). E3 Partners Ministry (*www.e3partners.org*) uses short-termers to provide "on-the-job training in evangelism, discipleship and church planting" by having "North Americans model a simple, biblical, transferable method of multiplying churches using laymen" (Wan and Hartt 2008, 79).

Michael Chung describes the E3 Partners approach as "simple, biblical, [and] transferable," based on a simple inductive Bible study approach similar to the Discovery Bible Study described in chapter 16.[1] On the first day of the trip, campaigners are equipped to teach a simple inductive Bible study, easily replicated by those receiving it. This study focuses on Luke 10:1 – 9 and asks six basic questions. First, the passage is read and participants are asked, "What did you like?" and "What did you not like or find confusing?" After these two questions are discussed, the passage is read again, followed by two new questions: "What does this teach about people?" and "What does this teach about God?" Following this discussion, the passage is read a third time, and two "Live and Tell" questions are asked: "How will you live these out? Be specific," and "Who will you tell about what you have learned? Give a name" (Chung 2013, 84 – 85). Chung comments, "We modeled inductive Bible study for our national partners, helping them to learn, and then teaching new believers how to effectively study the Bible for themselves" (2013, 85).

RECRUITING AND TRAINING FUTURE LONG-TERM WORKERS

Seeing needs and opportunities firsthand also creates excitement and leads to greater involvement in missions (Smith 2008, 35). Many people have considered long-term missions as an option through the exposure of short-term mission trips (Moreau 2008, 18).

Wan and Hartt report that in one church, 16 percent of the people participating in its short-term programs later entered long-term missionary service (2008, 68). Of the 101 long-term missionaries whom Craig Altrock polled, 68 had participated in short-term missions. A large percentage of people with short-term experience ranked it as a "strong" or "essential" influence in their decision to pursue long-term service (Altrock 2009). Short-term mission experiences allow participants to determine their aptitude for long-term cross-cultural ministry (Priest et al. 2006, 435, 437; Moreau et al. 2006, 191; Wan and Hartt 2008, 77 – 78). One student initially viewed her short-term mission as a summer adventure. She began to realize, however, that she was not

1. See pages 380–81.

There simply is no substitute for hands-on ministry when the goal is creating hearts burdened for the task.
(Scott Moreau)

While studying science at a Christian university, Amanda (not her real name) spent two summers in Prague, Czech Republic. After her second short-term mission, the local missionaries invited her to participate in a two-year apprenticeship. Amanda accepted the invitation and returned to Prague after graduation. During the apprenticeship, she did intensive language study, received training in missions principles and biblical studies, observed the missionaries in both home and ministry settings, and participated in ministry. Amanda taught Bible studies, organized various activities, and spent much time developing relationships both with local church members and with non-Christians. As she became more comfortable in her new culture, her ministry skills increased, as did her burden for the Czech people.

At the end of her apprenticeship, Amanda was "promoted" from missionary apprentice to full-fledged member of the mission team. She then spent eight years as a cross-cultural missionary. Health concerns forced Amanda to return to the United States, but her commitment to missions remains strong. She is now pursuing a ministry in missionary care.

homesick and that she liked what she was doing. She concluded that she *could* be a missionary (Diles 2009).

Apprenticeships are also beneficial and provide longer, more in-depth experiences in language learning, relationship building, day-to-day living, and cross-cultural ministry. Thus they also play a role in motivating and preparing participants for long-term missions. Scott Moreau observed, "There simply is no substitute for hands-on ministry when the goal is creating hearts burdened for the task" (Moreau et al. 2006, 247).

PERSONAL SPIRITUAL FORMATION

Many lives are changed by participation in short-term mission activities. In a 2003 survey of people who had attended a Christian high school and university, 25 percent listed a short-term cross-cultural mission trip as the spiritual event that had most influenced their lives (Baker 2003, 40). For college students, short-term cross-cultural experiences have the potential for being one of the most formative and "worldview shaping" pedagogical experiences of their college careers (Johnstone 2006, 528).

STMs often result in spiritual growth for participants, although this is not usually their primary objective. Those from North America often realize that many possessions do not equal happiness, and thus they develop "a new passion and purpose that counters consumeristic culture's influences" (Linhart 2006, 453). Adequate training, well-planned projects, and post-trip debriefing all enhance the long-term impact of these experiences (Ver Beek 2006, 492–93; Johnstone 2006, 524, 528; Blomberg 2008, 598–609).

Church members often become more passionate about their church's long-term mission efforts after participating in short-term missions. Dave Datema, general director of Frontier Mission Fellowship, observes,

> Many churches have gone from "zero to sixty" in a matter of months with regard to mission interest and involvement, solely because of one short-term trip. STMs, at least those done in partnership with a mission agency, help connect churches and agencies, which is crucial for the survival of those agencies. Another part of this is the impact STMs have on those studying for the ministry. One study showed that 51 percent of all M.Div. students reported STM involvement, an encouraging fact when you consider the dearth of mission studies mandatory for future ministers. Having pastors with STM experience is a significant factor, since pastors are a major piece of a church's mission commitment. (2012, 14)

ENTRY INTO OTHERWISE CLOSED AREAS

STMs sometimes provide access to areas otherwise closed to missionaries. This could include medical missions, youth camps, well-drilling projects, or building projects. The work of short-term groups may also lead to the easing of visa restrictions and increasing credibility for long-term workers (Wan and Hartt 2008, 67, 73). In some cases, visa restrictions make it impossible for expatriate missionaries to spend long periods within a country, but missionaries may make short trips to train and encourage local Christians.

Short-term missionaries have played a crucial role in generating and empowering indigenous church-planting movements. In some contexts, Christians from neighboring countries make short-term visits to a restricted-access region to train local church planters, and through this training, an entire region is saturated with a network of small, rapidly reproducing churches.

> Because the province and its people groups included so few Christians, an important church-planting tactic was to use short-term missionaries recruited from other countries. Although they did not speak the predominant language of the province, they were able to speak a shared

There is no question that short-term missions experiences changed the entire direction of my life. When I went to college, my life's goal was to get a business degree and then enter into politics. Many factors contributed to my adjustment of priorities, but two summer mission trips to Australia were the most direct factors in my becoming a long-term missionary. The first trip exposed me for the first time to daily evangelism and dialogue with people of many different faiths. But it was the second trip that caused me to see myself as a potential full-time cross-cultural missionary. Just a few weeks after that trip, I contacted a couple of friends of mine and agreed to join a mission team they were forming. Although that team never actually made it to the mission field, my life's course was set, and I knew I was going to be a missionary. I never looked back and ended up spending twelve years on the foreign mission field.

Because of the impact short-term missions had on me, I have continued to be involved in short-term missions for over twenty years, as participant, host, trainer, intern and apprentice supervisor, and team leader. It has been gratifying to see the impact short-term missions have had both on local churches and on the participants as well.

(Allen Diles)

> language with many people in the county seats. These short-term missionaries came from several different countries. They appeared as if they were from the same general ethnic group as the population, and so did not draw attention to themselves because of their low profile.... There was no temptation to develop dependence on outsiders, because they knew the visitors wouldn't be there that long. (Smith 2012, 7)

Challenges of Short-Term Missions

The tremendous potential of short-term missions requires all involved to recognize the challenges. A Kenyan newspaper, for instance, challenged the need for "slum tourism" in the Kabera area of Nairobi, where STM campaigns come and go with little benefit to its people. Daniel Rickett, reflecting on this story, asks, "What is God's intention through the short-term mission movement? Is it to make us better tourists or better witnesses of his grace?" (2008, 42). "STM is at a tipping point," he says, "and the forces of tourism appear to be winning" (2008, 43). Many of these challenges can be overcome or minimized when participants are adequately prepared, have the humility of learners and servants, and know who they are as Christian ministers.

CLARITY OF PURPOSE

Participants decide to go on STMs for a variety of reasons.[2] Some are fundamental, reflecting God's love and compassion; some are secondary, such as anticipation of seeing a new part of the world or because a friend is going; and some are even deficient, such as to establish self-worth. Prayerful consideration of motives enables people who carry the mission of God to overcome, or at least compensate for, deficient motives while also deepening the foundations of fundamental Christian motivations. The question, "Why are we going?" is thus fundamental.

Therefore, a first major task is helping short-term missionaries understand their identity and how they are to minister as disciples of Christ. Rickett says, "If the short-term movement is the work of God, its purpose is to enable the Church to be the Church in today's global neighborhood. The Church is called to announce Christ, love her neighbors and put God on display" (2008, 43). Robert Reese focuses on the spiritual transformation of campaigners, local Christians in the mission context, and those who have not yet come to Christ by asking, "How can the cross be inserted into STMs? How can STMs become . . . a spiritual exercise?" (2008, 159).

Imagine, for example, an STM team involved in a construction project, the most popular type of short-term mission work[3] (Fann and Taylor 2006, 40; Priest, Wilson, and Johnson 2010, 99). How is God on display? How do all participants serve as cross-formed servants? Clarity of purpose will affect how the STM team

- collaborates with local Christians in making decisions about the mission endeavor,
- fellowships with local Christians in their homes and communities,
- integrates worship and prayer into the daily life of the ministry.

This humanitarian work is distinctive because it is offered in the name of Jesus (Fann and Taylor 2006, 56).

2. These reasons are discussed in more depth in chapter 5, "Motives for Missions."

3. According to the study by Priest, Wilson, and Johnson, however, evangelism and church planting rank a close second (2010, 99).

WHO BENEFITS FROM THE EXPERIENCE

Traditionally, short-term missions were mainly intended to benefit the hosts. Benefits for the participants were a welcome by-product. Today, however, many short-term missions reverse the intentions (Daniels 2008, 152). While most short-term mission trips "involve strengthening and supplementing the witness of local churches," over 80 percent of the resources invested go toward providing transportation, accommodation, food, and sightseeing for the North American travelers (Priest, Wilson, and Johnson 2010, 99).

> Some youth leaders and mission pastors bluntly say that even if STM is of limited value to recipient communities, it is nonetheless worthwhile because of positive benefits to the sending congregation or youth program.... While older models of mission involved more purely altruistic mission expenditures not designed to serve the sending church, STM as a paradigm of mission channels mission funding in ways that serve the interests of the North American sending church as well as (sometimes more than) the interests of those being served. (Priest, Wilson, and Johnson 2010, 100)

Surely, an STM must mutually benefit both hosts and guests for healthy mission to occur and for the mission to reflect the nature of God.

APPEARANCE OF SUPERIORITY

Participants of STMs sometimes project an attitude of superiority to the host culture. Most short-term workers come from affluent societies, thus increasing the possibility of this impression (Moreau et al. 2006, 282). Although this portrayal of cultural superiority may be unintentional, it has negative effects.

This sense of superiority can be conveyed when the short-term team, rather than the national church, sets the agenda for the mission project. It may be portrayed when a group announces that it will be coming (rather than requesting an invitation), dictates the work that short-termers will do, or tries to change the way locals conduct their own church affairs. Even when short-termers request an invitation from a national church, foreign hosts may not feel the freedom to decline, because they fear violating their own cultural norms or endangering their long-term financial support. Visitors may also project a superior attitude by distancing themselves from the nationals, assuming that the "American way" is universally accepted, or refusing to eat local food or use public transportation.

Short-termers must view themselves as servants. They come, not to fix the local missionary or church, but to bless them.

Daniel Rickett advises STMs to "follow the lead of the local host regarding all aspects of engagement such as itineraries, what and how tasks are performed and customs and courtesies" (2008, 45). Short-termers must view themselves as servants. They come, not to fix the local missionary or church, but to bless them, serving in ways that people who know the situation deem best.

DISTRACTION

Another challenge facing short-term missions is the possibility of becoming a distraction to long-term workers. Short-term workers are often unaware of the time and energy expended by the long-term workers in preparing for and hosting them. Short-termers may also be insensitive about planning their trip for a time that is inconvenient for the long-term missionaries (Zehner 2006, 510). Darren Carlson suggests that North American short-term workers should consider the following scenario to better understand their hosts' situation:

> Imagine a team from France calls your church and says they want to visit. They want to put on VBS (which you have done for years), but the material is in French. They have heard about how the U.S. church has struggled and want to help you fix it. They want to send 20 people, half of them youth. Only two of them speak English. They need a place to stay for free, with cheap food and warm showers if possible. During the trip half of the group's energy will be spent on resolving tension between team members. Two people will get sick. They'd like you to arrange some sightseeing for them on their free day. Do you want them to come? (Carlson 2012)

Short-term workers must be sensitive to the additional workload they create for their hosts and strive to distract as little as possible from the hosts' ministry responsibilities. The blessing that they bring should always surpass the added responsibility that comes with hosting a group of visitors.

FAILURE TO RECOGNIZE LIMITATIONS

Participants in short-term missions often feel immediate connection with the local people they are working with in a building project or medical clinic. They may, however, fail to appreciate the day-to-day work done by long-term missionaries, who have learned the local language and culture and whose lives are interconnected with those of the local people. The short-termers' excitement about their "now" experience blurs the vision of God's ongoing mission in the area (Priest et al. 2006, 437).

Sometimes participants in short-term missions overestimate their knowledge of both the area where they have served and missions in general (Smith 2008, 43). Fann and Taylor give an example of a short-termer who, three days after his arrival, assembled local church leaders to enlighten them concerning their congregation's mistakes (2006, 53). Short-termers must realize that it is impossible to adequately understand the host culture after only a short visit and it is very difficult to accurately evaluate a long-term mission work.

UNINTENDED NEGATIVE EFFECTS

Short-term workers may also be guilty of unintentionally deceiving their hosts with promises, either explicit or implied, that cannot be fulfilled. This can be as simple as a flippant promise such as "I'll come back" or "Let's see if I can help." Short-termers may create expectations that the long-term missionaries and local believers are not able to sustain, by providing services, goods, or money. "Maybe" and "I'll try," intended by North Americans as a gentle "no," are heard by their hosts as affirmative promises. They then feel deceived or view the guests as liars.

Even with the best of intentions, short-term missions may create or exacerbate economic difficulties. For example, short-termers performing manual labor may eliminate jobs that could have been done by locals (Ver Beek 2006, 483). Should thousands of dollars be spent to transport Americans to do work that unemployed local workers could do? (Adeney 2008, 136).[4] Donavan Weber and Bill Weber, however, go so

4. As noted earlier in the example from Trinidad, however, finances are only one consideration. Brothers and sisters from different cultures working side by side may have relational benefits that extend beyond the building project itself.

far as to conclude that "national Christian organizations can be just as effective without STM workers regardless of their skill sets.... The most basic form of cost/benefit analysis would question whether [short-term missions] is the most effective way for an organization or community to reach its stated goals" (2012, 209).[5]

Short-termers' advice based on their own cultural perspective can have negative, or even destructive, results. For example, suggesting that a young woman who is unhappy at home should live independently could create serious problems in a culture where it is inappropriate for single women to leave the protection of home.

Arguing with local Christians about theology or church practices is also counterproductive. Short-termers should go to the mission field to serve, not to "straighten out" the locals' understandings of debatable theological issues. They should take care not to introduce theological debates that will divide the church long after they have gone home.

The sheer amount of technology and "stuff" North Americans travel with and their compassionate nature cause them to be seen as agents of Western civilization instead of ambassadors of Christ.

(Robert Reese)

Principles for Short-Term Missions

Adequate preparation helps assure that short-term missions are beneficial to participants, their host missionaries, and local Christians. The following principles should be considered in planning any short-term mission endeavor.

DEVELOP STM AS A SPIRITUAL EXERCISE

The most fundamental question is, "How can STMs become a spiritual, rather than a secular, experience?" Robert Reese writes,

> The sheer amount of technology and "stuff" North Americans travel with and their compassionate nature cause them to be seen as agents of Western civilization instead of ambassadors of Christ. How does this compassion come to be seen as secular? This happens when compassion drives North Americans to try to solve people's problems with American solutions instead of biblical ones. People in developing countries sometimes give Americans near-star status as representatives

5. Weber and Weber cite K. Ver Beek, "Lessons from the Sampling: Review of Quantitative Research on Short-Term Missions," which is a chapter in *Effective Engagement in Short-Term Missions: Doing It Right!* ed. Robert Priest (Pasadena, Calif.: William Carey Library, 2008), 485–86.

> of the sole global superpower; however, this can be a hindrance to a spiritual STM experience. How can the cross be inserted into STMs? (2008, 159)

Spiritual preparation to take up the cross and follow Jesus leads participants to discern "what God hopes to achieve through [the] STM" (Reese 2008, 159 – 60). As described previously, North Americans tend to be naturalistic, individualistic, optimistic, and present focused,[6] and these assumptions form how they do STMs. A Western secular perspective "moves God aside in explaining events" so that these are "explained rationally," assuming that "nature explains" the world (Reese 2008, 160). This secularism shapes how Westerners use time as "a commodity to save, spend or waste," so that the completion of a task is more important than relationships with one another and with God. Problem solving is based on human intelligence rather than on discerning the will of God, and decision making is based on tabulating individual perspectives rather than on lengthy discussion leading to consensus. The source of power is seen to be within us rather than in God through his Holy Spirit (Reese 2008, 160 – 63). Reese concludes,

> For secular-thinking Americans, spirituality is not automatic. Deliberate spiritual preparation can make a great difference in the STM experience.... Our prayer is that learning to do STMs in the way of the cross will create a new style of discipleship which will pervade all aspects of life. Increased Christian spirituality will always give glory to God for whatever it does, because it operates with the real source of power. Our task is not merely a STM project, but to "preach the gospel — not with words of human wisdom, lest the cross be emptied of its power" (1 Cor. 1:17). To God be the glory! (2008, 163)

COOPERATE WITH LOCAL LEADERS

For long-term continuity of the mission of God, STMs must cooperate with local leaders and experienced missionaries. Typically, this takes place when long-term workers invite short-term groups, perhaps from a partnering or supporting church, to work in a specific project that fits into the overall strategy of the local effort. These short-term efforts should not replace long-term works in terms of either personnel or

6. Chapter 12, page 290.

finances. In other words, short-term missions should never be isolated from or in competition with long-term missions.

Working cooperatively with long-term ministries requires trust. Short-termers must recognize that the local leaders and long-term missionaries know the language and culture and will remain after they go home. Therefore they must be learners, deferring to judgment of local Christians and missionaries concerning needs and how best to accomplish the project.

This deference extends to the timing of the mission experience. Since the purpose is to aid the existing work, the timing should be determined mutually by the people who are hosting and the ones who are going. According to Gene Daniels, "It is essential that the needs of the field become the driving factor for when, where and who is sent" (2008, 153).

Chapter 7 introduced the four stages of missionary involvement: the learning stage, the growth stage, the collaborative stage, and the phase-out stage. An understanding of these stages helps clarify how short-term workers can best meet the needs of the field. Participants in STMs can serve as *encouragers* of missionaries during the learning stage. At this stage, the work is young and not yet able to receive a group of short-term workers. Visits of encouragement can be appropriate, if timed to avoid distracting missionaries from developing local relationships and learning language and culture, and to avoid contributing to the homesickness the missionaries may be experiencing. This group would be small, consisting of two or three mature church leaders who are able to listen empathetically, pray, share Scripture, and speak words of encouragement to the missionaries.

As missionaries move through the growth and collaborative stages, short-term missionaries may serve as *participants* with them and with leaders of maturing local churches. Short-termers may help construct a church building for a young church, minister to health and medical needs in a poverty-stricken area, or work with missionaries and local youth to conduct a youth rally or camp.

As missionaries phase out of a work, visitors assume the role of *partners* with the national church, which at this stage is directing its own affairs and planning its own future. Short-term workers should serve at the invitation of local church leaders and under their supervision.

The departure of a foreign missionary should not sever the ties

Many cultures value relationships more highly than accomplishing tasks.

between the national church and former sponsors. Other cultures understand far better than Americans the importance of relationships as a witness to the global, inclusive, and interdependent nature of the body of Christ. As the following section explains, developing these relationships should be an important part of all field visits and short-term mission efforts.

DEVELOP LONG-TERM RELATIONSHIPS

North American short-termers are sometimes criticized for being so focused on their task that they fail to build relationships with local Christians (Zehner 2006, 510). Many cultures, however, value relationships more highly than accomplishing tasks. Ver Beek noted that in one agency, 75 percent of short-term workers failed to stay in touch with their new friends (2006, 487). Although it is common for workers to return from a mission trip reporting all the wonderful relationships they developed, it is much less common for those relationships to be maintained and nurtured.

Short-term workers should therefore interact with local people—worshiping with them, visiting in their homes, eating with them, playing with them. They should also put a priority on maintaining contact after they return home. Technology, including email, Skype, and Facebook, makes staying in touch easier than it used to be.

Repeated visits to the same area tend to increase the effectiveness of mission efforts (Smith 2008, 46, 50). Renewing and deepening long-term relationships has a positive impact on both visitors and locals.

INTEGRATE THE PHYSICAL AND THE SPIRITUAL

Anne-Geri' Fann and Greg Taylor contrast how quick we are to pray for nonbelievers' health when they are sick with how seldom we pray for their souls when they are healthy (2006, 41). In the same way, it is easy to focus entirely on a community's physical needs and to neglect very real spiritual needs. Jesus' ministry, however, was holistic (Matt. 9:35–36). We must imitate Jesus' holistic ministry, attending to both the physical and the spiritual.

STMs lend themselves to ministering to physical needs. They must, however, rather than standing alone, fit into the context of a broader, long-term holistic ministry. In medical ministry in the Two-Thirds World, for instance, it is usually permissible and wise for the doctor or nurse to ask patients how God is working in their lives and then to pray to God for healing. The spiritual and the physical are understood to be intertwined. The Kipsigis of Kenya gave great honor to a Western doctor who would hold the scalpel between uplifted hands, praying for healing, before a surgical procedure.

When short-term workers are unable to communicate in the local language, it is important that someone, ideally a local Christian, be able to explain what motivates them — that they are serving in the name of Jesus — and translate their prayers and testimonies.

BE PREPARED

The increasing role of short-term workers in global missions necessitates that hosts, participants, and senders be well informed and well prepared. Missionaries interviewed by Fann and Taylor reported that "the majority of short-term mission teams do not spend an adequate amount of time learning beforehand about the culture and the spiritual climate of the nation, or preparing themselves spiritually for the challenges ahead" (2006, 52). Adequate preparation can reduce or eliminate the problems discussed above and make the trip more meaningful and helpful to both participants and hosts.

Prior to departure, short-term workers should develop group cohesion. They must cultivate mutual respect and trust and be able to model sacrificial Christian living. They should share their lives, worship together, and work together on projects. Leaders should coach short-termers on how to deal with interpersonal conflicts that might arise on the trip. To avoid culturally inappropriate displays of affection, romantic drama, and distraction from the work, short-term workers are advised not to date other team members, missionaries, or locals during the mission experience.

Sensitivity to the host culture is an extremely important aspect of training for short-term missions. Participants should be taught that their hosts' view of the world is likely different from their own. These differences should be appreciated, not scoffed at. Short-termers must be aware of cultural dos and don'ts, such as whether to remove shoes before entering a house or take photographs during a worship service. They must also be aware of appropriate dress and customs. For example, how do people in the host culture dress for church services? Is it acceptable for men to wear shorts? Is it okay for women to wear slacks? What is the appropriate way to greet someone — a handshake, a hug, a bow, a kiss on the cheek? Adhering to cultural norms demonstrates humility and respect for the hosts. Missionaries hosting short-termers should advise them on these issues well before their arrival.

Karla Ann Koll rightly observes,

> The lists of dos and don'ts to guide the behavior of trip participants should be grounded in an analysis of these power dynamics. For example, why shouldn't trip participants pass out candy to the children that they encounter? Giving candy to children makes them into objects of our giving. But it also objectifies the group members in the eyes of the host community, converting visitors into not only promoters of tooth decay but also ones from whom such gifts are expected. Such apparently innocent, well-intentioned behavior not only guarantees that the group will be mobbed by children wherever they go, but it also inhibits the formation of relationships. (2010, 94)

Language is an important aspect of any culture. Therefore short-termers should be encouraged to learn basic greetings, how to say thank you and goodbye, as well as names of food items and other everyday objects. These simple gestures earn the respect of the local people and make the experience more meaningful for the participant.

Theological and spiritual training should focus on helping short-term participants to include spiritual disciplines such as prayer, Bible study, and meditation in their rhythm of life. It should also guide the participants in how to share the story of Jesus and tell how that story is part of their lives. In other words, short-termers should be prepared to teach both with their actions and with their words.

Flexibility and a servant spirit are very important during short-term mission work (Fann and Taylor 2006, 10 – 16). Because expectations often do not match reality, short-termers must be prepared to adapt and to serve in whatever capacity is needed — even when it is vastly different from what they expected. Rather than saying, "That's not what I came to do," the short-termer accepts the assignment with humility and grace, working "for the Lord, not for human masters" (Col. 3:23). This attitude is a powerful testimony to their hosts.

The Seven Standards of Excellence in Short-Term Missions

1. **God-centeredness.** An excellent short-term mission seeks first God's glory and his kingdom and is expressed through our
   –purpose—centering on God's glory and his ends throughout our entire STM process
   –lives—sound biblical doctrine, persistent prayer, and godliness in all our thoughts, words, and deeds
   –methods—wise, biblical, and culturally appropriate methods that bear spiritual fruit
2. **Empowering partnerships.** An excellent short-term mission establishes healthy, interdependent, ongoing relationships between sending and receiving partners and is expressed by
   –primary focus on intended receptors
   –plans that benefit all participants
   –mutual trust and accountability
3. **Mutual design.** An excellent short-term mission collaboratively plans each specific outreach for the benefit of all participants and is expressed by
   –on-field methods and activities aligned to long-term strategies of the partnership
   –goer-guests' ability to implement their part of the plan
   –host-receivers' ability to implement their part of the plan
4. **Comprehensive administration.** An excellent short-term mission exhibits integrity through reliable setup and thorough administration for all participants and is expressed by
   –truthfulness in promotion, finances, and reporting results
   –appropriate risk management
   –quality program delivery and support logistics
5. **Qualified leadership.** An excellent short-term mission screens, trains, and develops capable leadership for all participants and is expressed by
   –character—spiritually mature servant leadership
   –skills—prepared, competent, organized, and accountable leadership
   –values—empowering and equipping leadership
6. **Appropriate training.** An excellent short-term mission prepares and equips all participants for the mutually designed outreach and is expressed by
   –biblical, appropriate, and timely training
   –ongoing training and equipping (pre-field, on-field, post-field)
   –qualified trainers
7. **Thorough follow-up.** An excellent short-term mission assures debriefing and appropriate follow-up for all participants and is expressed by
   –comprehensive debriefing (pre-field, on-field, post-field)
   –on-field reentry preparation
   –post-field follow-up and evaluation

Participants should be debriefed at every stage of the short-term mission experience.

Short-term workers should understand how their efforts fit into the overall picture of the mission in that locality. Fann and Taylor maintain, "Unless there is some kind of idea of what this mission is all about, all that the trip will be is a feel-good experience, which is not the goal of good mission work" (2006, 44). Realizing that this one-or-two-week endeavor is not a stand-alone affair but one part of a ten-to-twenty-year plan gives lasting importance to participants' time and effort. In other words, short-termers are merely one piece of the puzzle when it comes to God's mission.

In 2001, a group of STM leaders from U.S.-based mission agencies, churches, and Christian colleges sensed that God was leading them to facilitate the formation of a set of standards similar to codes that had been developed in the United Kingdom and Canada. They received input and feedback from five mission networks and more than four hundred mission leaders. Two years of prayer and discussion resulted in a list of seven "best practices" called "U.S. Standards of Excellence in Short-Term Mission." This is a great guide for what mission leaders should expect of STM participants! (U.S. Standards of Excellence in Short-Term Mission, 2011).

CONDUCT THOROUGH FOLLOW-UP

Follow-up is important for both the hosts and the participants of short-term missions. Relationships should be maintained, sometimes through repeat visits. Short-termers, career missionaries, and local Christians should work together to continue to share the gospel with people contacted by visitors, to disciple new converts, and to serve those in extreme physical need.

Participants should be debriefed at every stage of the short-term mission experience — after training, after a language-learning experience, after ministering with local people, and at the conclusion of the mission experience. Debriefing allows them not only to relive their experience, but also to reflect on what they are learning (Johnstone 2006, 524). Post-trip debriefing allows leaders to help participants process both positive and negative experiences, to give affirmation, and to answer any lingering questions.

Even participants in a short mission trip can express significant stress when they reenter their home culture. Participants are changed by these powerful experiences; they are no longer the same people who embarked on the trip. These new people must learn to live in the old society they left, without reverting to their past patterns of living. Group debriefing allows participants to understand that the disequilibrium they may feel is normal and enables them to explore with others how to apply the lessons learned on the trip. God may also use such conversations to help some discern the call to long-term missionary service.

This chapter has demonstrated the possibilities and the challenges presented by short-term missions. People facilitating missions in today's church must see both, strategically embracing short-term missions without diminishing support for long-term efforts.

Holly's Story

A few years ago, Holly engaged in a life-changing short-term mission experience with the World Race (*www.theworldrace.org*). Her story illustrates the role of short-term missions in the spiritual formation of participants.

A single in her mid-thirties, Holly held a corporate job in Dallas, Texas. Although she enjoyed her work, she was not passionate about it. As an active member of her church's missions committee, Holly had visited missionaries in Africa and Asia and had seen the value of long-term missions. She was uncertain, however, as to the opportunities open to a single woman. Through a friend, Holly heard about the World Race, organized by Adventures in Missions. Participants in this program visit eleven countries in eleven months, serving as needed by their local hosts. Holly took a one-year leave of absence from her job and set out on this adventure to see how God would work.

Holly's World Race squad consisted of fifty people, and her team was five other women. Before leaving the United States, the squad participated in a ten-day training camp. They shared group-building experiences, learned about the cultures they would be visiting, discussed logistics of the trip, and lived in rustic conditions. Most important, they prepared spiritually for the adventure. Participants were challenged to lay down their emotional baggage so it would not weigh them down on the race. Holly says that during the first three nights of the camp, she cried a lot. What she had expected to be merely logistical and practical planning for the trip became a time of growth in her relationship to God.

In New Zealand, Holly's team performed hospitality ministry, managing a YWAM facility while the regular staff was away. In Thailand, they worked with children in a rural village that was a source for workers in the sex industry. Their work in the Philippines brought them into direct contact with sex workers who came to the health department for weekly checkups. In Eastern Europe, they tutored people learning English and shared messages of hope with young people.

This experience deeply impacted Holly, challenging and broadening her worldview. Today when she opens a World Vision catalog, she is not calloused to the appeals for help, because she knows that the needs of the people pictured inside are real. Now back in the United States, she is trying to live more simply, to "deaccumulate," so that she is "no longer a slave to the American dream." She finds it difficult, however, because "everything about American life pushes us to pursue this consumer culture," even though Jesus has called us to a different life.

Holly was also stretched by the experience of "relentless community"—sharing life with others around the clock. She lost the privacy and control she was accustomed to. Living in intimate community was "both a blessing and a curse." "I didn't do very well with it," Holly says, "but I did learn a lot."

Holly provided most of the funding for this trip from her personal savings. She has mixed feelings about whether churches should fund short-term missions. It is certainly appropriate, she feels, for Christians to spend their personal vacation budgets encouraging missionaries or helping out in short-term mission efforts. She might personally help someone else go, viewing it as an investment in that person's spiritual formation. Even after the short-term mission experience, however, she believes that long-term missions are more effective in initiating culture-changing movements.

Holly did not return to her corporate job after the World Race. She eventually accepted a position as an administrative coordinator for a church-planting ministry. Holly's experience in the World Race led her to a deeper place with Jesus and created a greater willingness to engage in risk-taking mission and service.

REFLECTION AND APPLICATION

Questions

1. Why are cross-cultural mission experiences lasting two years or less considered "short-term"?
2. If you have participated in a short-term mission effort, which of the benefits did you experience?
3. If you have participated in a short-term mission effort, which of the challenges did you encounter? What other challenges did you face?
4. What positive changes take place in the lives of short-term mission participants?
5. Why should short-term mission workers avoid the temptation to "straighten out" problems they perceive in missionaries and the local churches in which they minister?

6. Why is spiritual preparation important for short-term missionaries?
7. What valuable principles were incorporated into Holly's experience?
8. Based on what you have learned about short-term missions, what advice would you give Jim and Julie about taking their high school students on a mission trip?

Personal Inventory

How has God spoken to you through this chapter? What is God calling you to do about it?

For Additional Reflection

You have been asked by your church's elders to equip short-term workers to help the church's missionary on the field. What modules (topics) of training would you suggest? Describe the content of the training under each of these modules.

chapter

19

Selecting Areas for Cross-Cultural Mission

Intertwining Factors

Jim and Julie began to envision their future as God's missionaries. Where would they serve? Would they serve within their own country among people of similar cultural heritage or perhaps among recently arrived immigrants? Or, should they serve in some other area of the world? Haiti was especially appealing because they had a positive short-term experience and the country was relatively close to home. Their partners could easily visit and observe the work firsthand, even help with it. Jim and Julie knew that the Haitian people would receive them warmly, and the need for the gospel was great. Still, Haiti had already been served by generations of missionaries. Should they go elsewhere—somewhere farther away, perhaps less "friendly," someplace where people had never had the opportunity to hear and respond to the story of Jesus?

"Where is God leading us as missionaries?" Jim and Julie prayed for a Macedonian call. (Acts 16:6–10)

HOW DO MISSIONARIES, sending churches, and mission agencies prioritize and select areas of ministry? The effects of these decisions are far-reaching. Preparation must be tailored to the chosen field. Financial and prayer partners want to know where missionaries intend to serve. Some missionaries thrive on fields where others would languish. Field selection is thus a crucial factor in missions.

Some missionaries thrive on fields where others would languish.

This chapter looks at three criteria used in selecting an area for missionary service. The first criterion considers the extent to which a people group has already had the opportunity to hear and obey the gospel — whether they are reached or unreached. The second criterion looks at the extent to which people are receptive or resistant to the gospel and its messengers. The third, deciding criterion is the leading of God as discerned by missionaries and their senders. The weight given to the first two criteria is determined by the disposition of the missionary, the mission team, and the sending church or organization. There are times when these factors converge — resistant people become highly receptive to the gospel, and God calls missionaries to minister in the once-resistant area.

Unreached Peoples

Researchers of unreached peoples divide the world into three major populations. People who have never heard of the saving power of the blood of Jesus and have no access to the gospel compose *World A*. Those of World A are called "unreached" or "unevangelized." *World B* is made up of people who have heard the message of the gospel but have rejected it. These people are called "evangelized non-Christians." *World C* is composed of people who have accepted the gospel and claim to be Christians. One consideration in prioritizing mission objectives encourages missionaries and mission agencies to focus on the unreached portion of humanity who make up World A, because unreached people "will perish, not because [they have] rejected Christ, but because [they have] no understanding of what Christ has offered" (Barrett 1990, 26; Williard 1993).

Mission resources, according to this perspective, should be directed toward reaching the unreached, but often are not. Christians in World C spend approximately 94 percent of their financial resources on themselves, 5 percent on World B, but only 0.5 percent on reaching the unreached in World A (Culbertson 2011). Bryant Myers writes,

> Too much mission money is spent in that part of the world which already identifies itself as Christian. Far too few human and financial resources are directed at the many people who live in places where it is likely they will never hear the Good News of Jesus Christ unless some-

> one goes to tell them. Too many Christians give where the fields are ready unto harvest, while being unwilling to support taking the gospel where the going is tough. This must change. (1993, 45)

Although World A comprises 24 percent of the world's population, it receives only 1 percent of the world's Christian missionaries. While 33 percent of the world's population lives in World C, fully 90 percent of all missionaries minister there, mostly in newly evangelized parts (Culbertson 2011; Winter and Koch 2009, 543; Williard 1993).

Too many Christians give where the fields are ready unto harvest, while being unwilling to support taking the gospel where the going is tough. This must change.

(Bryant Myers)

DEFINING UNREACHED PEOPLES

The Lausanne Committee for World Evangelization defines an unreached people as "a people group among which there is no indigenous community of believing Christians with adequate numbers and resources to evangelize this people group without requiring outside [cross-cultural] assistance" (Efta 1994, 28). Most mission agencies consider a people group to be reached when 1 or 2 percent of the total population are identified as followers of Jesus. The Joshua Project *(www.joshuaproject.net)*, a service of the U.S. Center for World Mission, provides information concerning people groups around the world. It defines "unreached/least reached peoples" using the dual criteria of "less than 2% Evangelical and less than 5% Christian Adherent" (Joshua Project, n.d.). Others describe unreached peoples as social groupings who have never heard the gospel, have not responded to the gospel, do not have a community of believers within their midst, or do not have a Bible in their mother tongue or readily available for people to read (Efta 1994, 29).

According to the Joshua Project, out of 16,825 people groups in the world, 7,287 (43.3%) of them, comprising 2.91 billion people, are unreached.[1] Using somewhat different definitions, researchers from the International Mission Board (IMB) count 11,263 people groups, 6,601 of whom are unreached. The IMB points out that of these unreached people groups, 2,945 are "unengaged" — there is no active evangelical church-planting strategy in place to reach them.[2]

1. *www.joshuaproject.net* (February 21, 2013).
2. http://*public.imb.org/globalresearch* (December 18, 2013).

Luis Bush makes a technical distinction between the unevangelized and the unreached:

> The *unevangelized* are people who have a minimal knowledge of the gospel, but have had no valid opportunity to respond to it. The *unreached* are the two billion people who have never heard of Jesus as Savior and are not within reach of Christians of their own people. There are, in fact, some 2000 people or nationalities in which there is not yet a vital, indigenous church movement. (n.d., 2)

The terms *unreached* and *unevangelized* are used to define the extent to which people groups are in contact with (or have heard) the gospel — whether they have had the *opportunity* to hear and respond to the gospel, not whether they have actually done so.

Ralph Winter recounts three phases of modern missions. The focus two hundred years ago was on the coastlands of the world. One hundred years ago, the focus shifted to the interiors of the continents, and within the last century, it has switched to the unreached peoples in all areas of the world. Winter advocates that "the purpose of missionaries is to go where the church is not present rather than expand the church where it already exists" (1994, 11).

THE 10/40 WINDOW

At the 1989 Lausanne II Conference in Manila, Luis Bush proposed that if the goal of missions is to reach the unreached, mission finances and personnel must focus on what he called the 10/40 Window. This "window" extends from ten to forty degrees north of the equator and stretches from North Africa through the Middle East to China and Japan. Because this area is largely unreached by Christian missions, it constitutes the "core of the challenge" for world evangelization. Ninety-five percent of the four billion people living in the sixty-nine countries of the 10/40 Window are considered unevangelized (Window International Network 2012).

In addition to being mostly unreached, the 10/40 Window exhibits a number of other characteristics (Bush, n.d., 3 – 8). All three major non-Christian religions — Islam, Hinduism, and Buddhism — originated in the 10/40 Window. Animism, atheism, and Sikhism are also strongly rooted there. Eighty-seven percent of the people are the poorest

Figure 19.1[3] The 10/40 Window

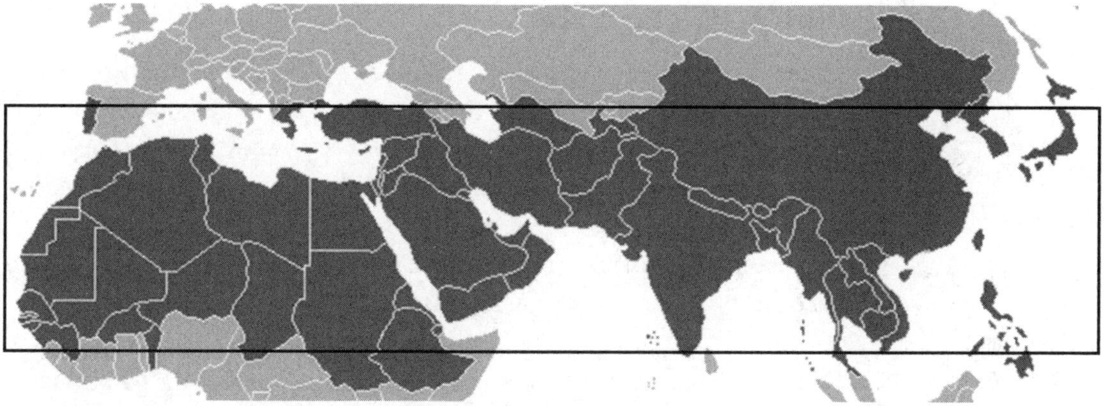

3. See *http://joshuaproject.net/10 – 40-window.php.*

of the poor, living on an average annual income of only $250 per family (Window International Network 2012).

Finally, Satan has a significant stranglehold on this area of the world. Bush writes, "The people living in the 10/40 window not only have suffered hunger and a lower quality of life compared with the rest of humanity, but have also been kept from the transforming, life giving, community changing power of the gospel" (n.d., 7). In the 10/40 Window, the "gospel is veiled" because "the god of this age has blinded the minds of unbelievers, so that they cannot see the light of the gospel that displays the glory of Christ, who is the image of God" (2 Cor. 4:3 – 4). God's people must seek to break these strongholds of Satan. They must reflect the ministry of Christ by proclaiming "good news to the poor" and freedom to the oppressed (Luke 4:18).

All three major non-Christian religions — Islam, Hinduism, and Buddhism — originated in the 10/40 Window and have their greatest strength there.

North India, described by some as "the most spiritually dark place on earth," is an example of an area of unreached peoples. Most missionaries to India work among tribal and outcast groups, leaving the Hindu core of the nation (65% of the population) and the Muslim minority (15%) notably neglected. Beyond the typical obstacles of language and culture, antagonistic religious, political, and caste barriers hinder Christianity's entry into and evangelization of North Indian cultures. Generally, the growth of the church among Hindi people in northern India is "disturbingly slow." People from tribal groups and lower castes are more receptive than those of the middle and upper castes (Winter 1994, 10–14).

STRENGTHS AND LIMITATIONS OF PRIORITIZING UNREACHED PEOPLES

Prioritizing unreached people groups is justified for several reasons. First, this perspective has helped the mission movement focus on areas where Satan's control is greatest. By God's power, these fortresses of Satan must be breached and his strongholds claimed for the kingdom of God.

Second, the vision of reaching the unreached has led many people to become long-term missionaries. Efta writes,

> The logic that led my wife and me to become missionaries went something like this: "We have so many opportunities to hear the gospel on television and radio, in books and magazines, and at many evangelical churches, but because so many other people have little or no exposure to the gospel, we should focus our efforts on those who may never hear it. Work in our country is certainly legitimate and pleasing to God, but we should put more emphasis on those in unreached areas." This logic also influenced our decision about what country we wanted to serve in. We wanted to go to people who had never heard the gospel. (1994, 28)

The frontier mentality — to go where the gospel has not penetrated and to challenge the powers of Satan where he reigns — has drawn adventuresome, dedicated servants into ministry among unreached people.

Third, the desire to reach the unreached has led to the development of special types of missions to break into resistant areas. Vocational missionaries are entering countries where full-time, church-planting missionaries cannot go.[4] Nonresidential missionaries mobilize resources and train personnel for peoples traditionally closed to the gospel, even though they are not allowed to live among them.[5]

For all of these reasons, prioritizing unreached people has made a significant contribution to missions.

Reaching the unreached is important, but several factors compel missionaries to examine other criteria as well. Bush called the 10/40

---

4. See the section titled "Business Missionaries" in chapter 6.

5. David Garrison's book *The Nonresidential Missionary* (MARC 1990) provides a model for opening areas that are either closed or resistant to the gospel. The nonresidential missionary surveys the population group, becomes fluent in their main language, and mobilizes various forms of Christian ministry to the group. The nonresidential missionary concentrates on the priority of initial evangelization and on eliminating gaps or duplications with other mission agencies (Garrison 1990).

Window "the resistant belt" of the world (n.d., 1). In many 10/40 countries, becoming a Christian is a crime punishable by death, and Christians suffer intense persecution. They are frequently beaten and harassed, faced with financial discrimination and job loss, and repudiated and disowned by their families. Even in such places, however, the gospel can take root, grow, and bear fruit with only limited outside missionary involvement. Mission Network News reports that because of the "willingness [of 10/40 Window believers] to take risks, there are hundreds of thousands of believers in Iran" (2012).

God uses varied means, not just Western missionaries, to reach people groups with the gospel. Sometimes he works through missionaries from non-Western nations whose culture is similar to the target culture. Sometimes he uses business-as-mission or nonresidential missionaries. Sometimes it is appropriate to maintain a limited witness while the church continues to pray that God will grant more openness to the heart of the people.

A focus on unreached peoples may result in a narrow concentration on one area of the world. One mission strategist told the European director of an evangelical mission, "All foreign missionaries must leave Europe immediately. They have absolutely no business being there. Europe is evangelized" (McQuilkin 1994, 263). This extreme perspective would negate missions in North and South America and in Europe and in Africa south of the Sahara. The only valid mission work therefore would be within the 10/40 Window.

This, however, is a narrow interpretation of "unreached peoples." Should France be considered reached even though evangelical Christians constitute only 1 percent of the population (Operation World 2012)? Should France be only a launching pad to convert the Berber of North Africa? Should American missionaries retreat from the receptive areas of Africa south of the Sahara as Muslim missionaries flood the area? Should Nairobi be considered only a launching pad to convert Sudanese and Somalians rather than a mission field itself? Instead of focusing on one geographic area, the church must engage unreached people wherever they live in the world.

Nevertheless, Satan's stronghold in the 10/40 Window must be broken. Far greater resources must be focused on reaching the unreached.

Receptivity

Receptivity may be simply defined as *human readiness to receive God's good news.* This second perspective of prioritizing mission fields always influences field selection, either explicitly or implicitly.

THE NATURE OF THE WORLD

The concept of receptivity is rooted in an understanding that the world is dynamic, not static. Consequently, people's receptivity to the gospel message is always changing. Sometimes, hearing the eternal message creates no response. It appears that the people feel no need for the gospel. At other times, the gospel hits home in a society crying over problems and overwhelmed by fears. In a short time, large numbers of people believe the message, are baptized into Christ, organize vibrant fellowships, and revitalize their society through the message of Jesus Christ.

Cultures are like individuals: sometimes they are more receptive than at other times. Young people reared in a Christian home are more receptive at age twelve than at age twenty. If they reach twenty without conversion, they may be inoculated against the Christian message and hardened to it. Individuals are also more receptive when confronted by a crisis. In my own ministry in Kenya, I recall a Kipsigis man who was led to conversion after the death of his father. His heart was stirred, not only by the power of Christ to resurrect and bring to himself those who believe but also by the freedom, given by Christ, from the fear of death. He responded to Christ during a time of brokenness and fear.

The world may be thought of as a vast orchard having many fields. When only some fields are ready for harvest, the farmer continues to care for all the fields because he knows that their harvest will come in due time. Therefore he sends planters and pruners, weed cutters, and insect sprayers to fields not yet ready for harvest. However, to the fields where the fruit is ready he sends numerous laborers. He is concerned that the fruit not fall to the ground and rot before it can be harvested. In this analogy, God is the great farmer, and cultures and cities of the world are the fields. The Lord cares for the entire world and sends workers out to all fields. He is concerned, however, that those he has prepared for the harvest be brought into the harvest. The receptive should be harvested while they are open to the message, and the resistant nurtured until they become receptive.

The relative receptivity of world peoples is more than merely a sociological phenomenon. The ultimate source of receptivity is the mighty acts of God working through the Holy Spirit to convict the world of sin, and working through his messengers who carefully plant the seeds of the gospel in not-yet-fertile soil.

The ultimate source of receptivity is the mighty acts of God working through the Holy Spirit to convict the world of sin.

We may expand our definition of receptivity therefore to *human readiness to receive God's good news and accept his sovereignty.* This definition recognizes that the world is ever-changing and that God is active in it.

BIBLICAL FOUNDATIONS OF RECEPTIVITY

Jesus compassionately described the multitudes as "harassed and helpless, like sheep without a shepherd" (Matt. 9:36). Jesus' description implies that the receptive are seekers: the broken are seeking wholeness; the hungry, food; the sick, a physician; the confused, orientation; the lost, a shepherd. Self-satisfied people, conversely, feel no need for change. Jesus, while seeing these crowds, emphasized harvesting. He told his disciples, "The *harvest* is plentiful but the workers are few. Ask the Lord of the *harvest*, therefore, to send out workers into his *harvest* field" (vv. 37 – 38, emphasis added). Jesus implied that God wants a harvest, and because he is Lord of the harvest, he can provide both the harvesters and the harvest.

Immediately after speaking about harvesting, Jesus called the Twelve together to send them out on the Limited Commission. They were to enter a village, expecting a response: "Whatever town or village you enter, search there for some worthy person and stay at their house until you leave" (Matt. 10:11). If the disciples were not welcomed or if people would not listen to their words, they were to "shake the dust off [their] feet" (v. 14). The unreceptive were to be left in favor of those who wanted to hear.

Paul applied this teaching to his ministry. Although he was concerned with teaching his own people (Rom. 10:1 – 2; 9:1 – 3), Paul turned to the Gentiles when the Jews did not respond in faith. In Antioch of Pisidia Paul and Barnabas taught Jews in their synagogue. But when the Jews became jealous "because the whole city gathered to

Persecution is an attempt by leaders to suppress the social and religious changes they fear — but know that the population may embrace.

hear the word of the Lord," they turned to the Gentiles (Acts 13:44 – 48, 51). In Corinth, Paul preached to the both Jews and God-fearing Greeks in the synagogue until the Jews "became abusive." He then "shook out his clothes in protest" and told them, "From now on I will go to the Gentiles" (18:5 – 6). When the Jews in Rome rejected Paul's message, he announced that "God's salvation has been sent to the Gentiles, and they will listen!" (28:23 – 28).

The response to Paul's preaching in Athens and Corinth demonstrates a contrast between resistance and receptivity. In Athens, Paul met with outspoken hostility and ridicule (17:18, 32), although a few believed (v. 34). His departure for Corinth may have been precipitated by the Athenian court demanding that he leave or by his realization that few would respond to his message in Athens (18:1). In either case, resistance to his message caused Paul to leave suddenly even though he was awaiting the arrival of Silas and Timothy (17:15).

In Corinth, Paul went initially to the Jewish synagogue, where he sought to teach both Jews and Greeks (18:4). When Jews rejected his message, he turned to the Gentiles, even though some Jews were converted. He then moved his preaching from the Jewish synagogue to the house of Titus Justus. During this time, it would have been easy for Paul to give up in despair. But God reassured him in a vision: "Do not be afraid; keep on speaking, do not be silent.... I have many people in this city" (vv. 9 – 10). Paul stayed in Corinth for a year and a half (v. 11), and a local fellowship of believers was established.

Paul could have mistaken persecution for lack of receptivity. Frequently, however, persecution is an attempt by leaders to suppress the social and religious changes they fear — but know that the population may embrace. If Paul had left Corinth because of initial discouragement, he would have missed a great harvest of souls. Likewise, Bible-believing Christians began to reap God's harvest in Bulgaria during the early 1990s, but the leaders of the Orthodox Church forced political leaders to limit the influence of new religious groups. These courageous followers of Jesus, standing against the political pressure of the Orthodox Church, continued to proclaim God's message.

On the other hand, resistant societies such as Athens tend to ridicule new ideologies, not taking them seriously. Paul was sarcastically termed a "babbler" and one who was "advocating foreign gods" (17:18).

Unless missionaries learn how the Christian message connects with the culture's felt needs, societies cynical about the Christian system will remain difficult to penetrate.

In John 4, the woman at the well learned about living water from the anticipated Messiah (vv. 4 – 26). In her urgency she left her water jar at the well to share her new-found secret. She proclaimed in her town, "Come, see a man who told me everything I ever did. Could this be the Messiah?" (vv. 28 – 29). As these people were coming to see Jesus for themselves (v. 30), he spoke to his disciples about harvesting. They need not wait four months for the harvest but could reap where others had sown. He said, "I tell you, open your eyes and look at the fields! They are ripe for harvest" (v. 35). When the Samaritans arrived, Jesus taught them, and they believed in him because of the woman's testimony (vv. 39 – 42). Missions that prioritize receptive areas look for fields that are ripe for harvest.

ILLUSTRATIONS OF RECEPTIVE PEOPLE GROUPS

Following are just a few of many possible examples of receptive peoples coming to Christ over the past several decades.

The Sukuma of Tanzania (1990s)

Bob Bentley, Greg Newton, and their families began work among the Sukuma people of Tanzania in 1991. They chose this large people group (3 – 5 million) because there were few churches among them. While these missionaries were still studying the language, non-Christians would stop them on the road with petitions signed by fifty to seventy people requesting Christian teaching in their village. By November 1994, eighteen churches had been planted and over one thousand Sukuma baptized. The Sukuma people were in a time of transition. They were dissatisfied with fear-laden animistic answers to life's questions and were seeking alternatives (Newton 1994, 1).

Bulgarian Turks (1990s)

Stan Guthrie wrote, "For years, evangelistic efforts among the gospel-resistant Turks have had all the momentum of a glitch-plagued Space Shuttle anchored to its launch pad — potentially a lot of power but no movement" (1992, 1). However, during the Communist rule of Bulgaria, many Bulgarian Turks returned to Turkey to escape suppression. They expected wealthy Arab nations to help with their resettlement, but this assistance never came. Christian organizations, however, offered help, and the Turks from Bulgaria saw God's love in the actions of compassionate Christians. Unemployment in Turkey forced many of these Turks to return to Bulgaria. When Communism was overthrown there in the early 1990s and the Turks began to hear again the gospel story, two thousand became followers of Christ in three years. By contrast, in Turkey only one thousand of a population of 56.5 million were followers of Christ (Guthrie 1992, 4).

Baptist Missions in Uganda (1961–72)

The history of Baptist missions in Uganda also demonstrates a varying degree of receptivity. One Baptist mission, beginning work in Uganda in 1961, concentrated their evangelism in large cities, believing that urban converts would then take the gospel to rural areas. In 1972, their fellowship had grown to seven hundred national Christians in twenty-two churches. Another Baptist group began in 1962 with a similar-sized workforce; they assigned one part of their group the task of urban evangelism while the other part engaged in rural evangelism. In 1972, this group claimed five thousand Christians in 112 churches, with most in rural areas.

Probably neither group realized the transient nature of African cities. William Ochieng' described city dwellers in Africa: "Who is a stranger? A stranger is a guy whose home is elsewhere. That is what most people in Nairobi are—strangers. Give them a holiday and they will be heading for their homes, in the bush" (1981, 6). Some African urbanites refer to their city residences as their "houses," but their residences in rural areas are their "homes." They *stay* in the city but *live* in their village. African cities of the 1960s and 1970s, with their large populations of "strangers," were not as receptive as rural areas. But African cities are changing as new generations are born in the urban context and lose their rural vernacular and parts of their cultural heritage. Cultural perspectives of *home* and the rootedness of people therefore have significant impact on the long-term receptivity.

African Muslims (Twenty-first Century)

The conversion of many African Muslims demonstrates that "unreached" and "receptive" are *not* mutually exclusive categories.

Long characterized as resistant to the gospel, many Muslims around the world are turning to Christ. Most often, these movements are led, not by Western missionaries, but by indigenous evangelists who are committed to multiplying disciples. Outside missionaries, however, may play a role in equipping the early generations of these disciple makers. Cityteam International *(www.cityteam.org)* has documented many such cases, although the details must be obscured for security considerations. Though these movements occur around the world, the following changes were observed in Africa over a seven-year period.

- More than six thousand new churches in eighteen countries have been planted among Muslims.
- Hundreds of former sheikhs and imams, now Christ followers, are boldly leading great movements of Muslims out of Islam.
- More than three thousand new churches have been planted among forty-five "unreached" Muslim-majority people groups who until recently had no access to God's Word.
- Thousands of former Muslims are experiencing the loss of possessions, homes, and loved ones but are continuing to serve Jesus.
- Multiple Muslim communities, seeing the dramatic changes in nearby communities, are insisting that someone bring these changes to them also.
- More than 350 ministries are working together to achieve these outcomes. (Trousdale 2012, 15 – 16)

The conversion of many African Muslims demonstrates that (1) "unreached" and "receptive" are *not* mutually exclusive categories and that (2) "unreached" is not a static category (illustrated also by the Bulgarian Turks). Some unreached people are receptive to a clear, incarnational witness to the gospel. In addition, whole people groups are moving from "unreached" to "reached." Neither can "receptive" be considered a static category. A people group who are receptive today may be unreceptive within a few years. Missionaries should go to areas of known receptivity since the people may not remain receptive without a vibrant, indigenous Christian witness.

The criterion of receptivity does not exclude missions in areas that appear to be unreceptive. The Lord's command to "go into all the world and preach the gospel to all creation" (Mark 16:15) clearly negates such an orientation. No area of the world should be neglected. Donald McGavran believed, however, that those not bearing fruit should be held lightly until signs of a possible harvest are evident. When these signs become evident, workers should be called into the harvest in concentrated numbers (McGavran 1990, 191). Joe Betts, long-term Japanese missionary, expressed this perspective:

> Satan still has this country in his grip, but we keep pecking away with the unchangeable Word and winning a soul now and then. There will come a day when he will have to turn loose and we want to be here to guide the people in God's truth. (1982, 2)

A missionary in the Netherlands wrote to a friend in Africa: "There you plan on establishing eight churches in a year. Here we are glad when we convert about eight people per year." This man is lightly holding his area until it becomes receptive. Mission strategists must be knowledgeable about historical, cultural, and psychological trends so that they recognize which areas should be aggressively harvested and which should be held lightly.

FACTORS AFFECTING RECEPTIVITY

Many factors influence receptivity. Some factors are specific to certain locations, while others are universal. The three universal factors include (1) worldview dissonance, (2) uprooted populations, and (3) competition among Christian groups.

Worldview Dissonance

Worldview dissonance occurs when people no longer accept as plausible the traditional beliefs and assumptions of their culture. In some cases, a new generation arises that does not accept the conceptions of its forefathers; in other circumstances, rapid change induces dissonance during one generation. When traditional gods and magic appear to lose their power, animistic cultures experience worldview dissonance. In secular societies, worldview dissonance develops when the scientific answers do not adequately explain the pain and evil of the world and life after death.

Mission planners must anticipate world changes and prepare evangelists to enter areas that are likely to become receptive.

The introduction of formal education has shattered cultural equilibrium in many parts of the world. Formal education sometimes produces an elite class that challenges traditional authority structures with its desire to create new ways of life aligned with new ways of thinking.

Rapid political and social changes sometimes create worldview dissonance. The fall of the Berlin Wall in 1989 and the demise of Soviet communism shook the plausibility structures in many areas of the world and created ideological vacuums. Areas that were formerly resistant, such as Russia, Ukraine, and Romania, became more receptive to the gospel. Three African countries that formerly had Marxist ideologies — Benin, Mozambique, and Angola — became exceptionally open to the gospel as these beliefs and values changed. Communism's demise also stunned many of Latin America's educated elite for whom Marxism was an alternative to capitalism, thus heightening receptivity in Latin America.

The attack on the World Trade Center on 9/11/2001 and Arab Spring beginning in December 2010 were results of immense worldview dissonance. A competing desire for democracy and Shari'ah law, according to Dudley Woodberry, has led to both "increased resistance and receptivity to the gospel among Muslims, and increased hostility and peacemaking among Christians. It has been the best of times and the worst of times for relations between Christians and Muslims" (Woodberry, 2011). He writes,

> Whenever Muslim governments have adopted a militant type of Islam or have tried to impose a form of Shari'ah law — and where there has been a local example of an alternate, friendly Christian presence — Muslims are attracted to the gospel. But persecution often follows.... Overall, we are seeing Muslims following Jesus as never before in history. (Woodberry 2011)

Receptivity is greatly affected by political and philosophical changes occurring in the world. Mission strategists must prayerfully plan with flexibility, anticipating world changes and preparing Christian ministers to enter areas of anticipated receptivity which might be politically and socially instable.

Uprooted Populations

Because old associations have been broken and new patterns have not yet become fixed, uprooted people are generally receptive to the gospel.

When missionaries from my own fellowship began working among the Kipsigis in Kenya, the greatest response during the early evangelistic period came in newly settled areas. In Latin America, poor peasants, migrating to the cities in hopes of improving their fortunes, have been exceptionally receptive. In North America, many new immigrants learning to adapt to their new culture are receptive to Christianity. In many cases, they had heard and viewed some form of Christianity in their homelands but did not have the opportunity to adequately hear the gospel or experience that nature of Christian fellowship.

Some uprooted peoples, however, are not putting down new, permanent roots. They are transients whose roots are elsewhere. They are strangers in a new area, and they plan to return home. In such contexts, numerous converts may result without a long-term community of believers being formed. In 1973 – 74, I evangelized extensively in the large tea estates of the Kericho district of Kenya. Three small churches were established and 150 adults baptized. Within three years, almost all the converts had returned to their original homes. Initially I felt that as these converts returned to their home areas, they would establish new churches. But the workers were young and had little influence in their extended families. On their return home, they resumed their former life — whether in a Christian church or following traditional religion. Although it would be problematic to say that I should not have reached out to these workers, in retrospect I see that while churches among the Kipsigis became permanent fellowships with their own leaders, the tea estate churches were unable to establish continuity because of the transiency of the population.

Competition among Christian Groups

A third factor affecting receptivity is competition among Christian groups. Non-Christians frequently are unable to differentiate the subtle differences between these groups. A multiplicity of these groups confuses them. In societies where numerous Christian groups are working, churches tend to be smaller, and those that are distinct (often unorthodox) tend to grow faster than the others.

Obviously, evangelizing a receptive people is easier without competition from other Christian groups. This can be illustrated by the Southern Baptists and the Pentecostal Assemblies of God in Uganda. New missions in Uganda typically focused their work in Kampala, the capital city. The city had been the hub of evangelistic activity since the Anglicans (1877) and Catholics (1879) arrived in the country. Between 1960 and 1972, ten new Christian groups began concentrated efforts in this highly Christianized city. Most experienced only minimal growth. The Southern Baptists and Pentecostal Assemblies of God, however, focused their work in relatively untouched societies and became the fastest-growing Christian groups in Uganda (Van Rheenen 1976, 116 – 17). Likewise, our team working in Kenya among the Kipsigis saw more rapid growth in areas that were untouched by other Christian groups or where these groups were relatively weak. Growth occurred where there were vacuums of Christian influence rather than where denominations were strong.

The world is ever dynamic rather than static. Some people groups become more receptive to the gospel, while the receptivity of others fades.

STRENGTHS AND LIMITATIONS OF PRIORITIZING RECEPTIVE PEOPLES

Targeting receptive people groups has a number of strengths. First, this perspective prioritizes those most willing to hear the gospel. Second, it acknowledges the world to be ever dynamic rather than static. Some people groups become more receptive to the gospel, while the receptivity of others fades. Third, this perspective correctly recognizes that God, through his Holy Spirit, convicts the world of sin and thus prepares unbelievers to hear his message. God works unexpectedly, as demonstrated in 1989 by the fall of the wall between East and West Germany. Fourth, because this perspective recognizes that there are different levels of readiness to receive the gospel, mission leaders are able to strategically direct personnel toward areas of greater harvest. Some areas are held lightly while others are aggressively evangelized.

Though everything belongs to God (Deut. 10:14; Ps. 24:1; 1 Cor. 10:26), churches and mission agencies manage finite resources. Wise stewardship demands that those resources — both financial and human — be invested where the greatest harvest can be expected. John Morris recommends that his denomination prioritize unreached, receptive peoples (2010, 157). He advises, “Missionary leaders may decide to engage a group lightly and cautiously that is definitely resistant, but a large investment of evangelistic resources in such a group shows poor stewardship of both financial and human resources" (2010, 151).

This strategy of reaching the receptive while they are still receptive, however, has one major limitation. *God frequently uses missionaries to unreached peoples as the primers to create receptivity.* He uses missionaries from other cultures to sow the seed among unreached peoples, even as he is working through the indigenous people. For example, some of the greatest growth of God's kingdom in our generation is taking place in China. In many parts of China, God is working without the direct influence of any cross-cultural missionaries. But God is also using nonresidential missionaries to help sow the seeds of the kingdom in various areas. Among the eight million Yi people of South China, one nonresidential missionary is recruiting, mentoring, and placing one hundred Christian teachers, doctors, agriculturists, and other professionals to minister vocationally as they also carry the gospel message. In setting priorities, therefore, a balance needs to be established between receptive peoples and unreached peoples. When the unreached are also receptive, such as among many African Muslims, there is an ideal mix.

The Leading of God

Discovering the ideal mix of an unreached yet receptive people group, however, may not indicate the field to which God is calling a missionary. Logistical or health considerations may make it impossible to go to that particular people group. God may be calling the missionary to a people group that meets only one of these criteria. He may be calling him or her to an urban center where multiethnic churches provide the clearest expressions of God's kingdom. Since the world is quickly urbanizing, the Christian missionary movement must urgently seek to win the urban masses.[6] Often, God's calling is less specific, leaving missionaries free to choose among several potential areas of service. How, then, do missionaries discern God's leading, whether general or specific?

6. The urban population swelled to 29.1 percent of the world's population in 1950, 36 percent in 1970, 43 percent in 1990, and 50.6 percent in the year 2010, and it is projected to reach 54.9 percent in 2020 (United Nations 2008).

Sometimes God gives people what many call a *burden* for a specific area or people group. One missionary recruit remarked that she had known for some time that God wanted her family to serve in a Bible translation ministry, but had never felt that it had to be in a specific place, until someone brought a certain province to her attention. She and her husband felt strongly that God had called them to that particular area, and made plans to go there despite the loss of teammates who did not share their call.

God sometimes leads people through *personal relationships with people from a particular field.* During the 1980s, hundreds of Thai students studied at Abilene Christian University and influenced missionary candidates to serve in Thailand. J. M. McCaleb, pioneer Church of Christ missionary to Japan, was influenced by his friendship with Japanese students in the U.S.

Often, personal relationships are formed with missionaries on home assignment who encourage missionary candidates to join their ministries. Several of my students during a 1977 – 78 teaching furlough at Harding University later worked with me as missionary interns and eventually became part of a new team working among related tribes of Kenya. They in turn influenced scores of others to serve in Africa.

God may also lead through *open and closed doors.* In Acts 16, Paul and his companions were "kept by the Holy Spirit" from preaching the gospel in the province of Asia, and the Spirit of Jesus would not allow them to enter Bithynia. While these may have been very frustrating experiences for Paul, the reason eventually became clear when he received "the Macedonian call." Closed doors, together with the Macedonia vision, caused Paul and his companions to conclude "that God had called us to preach the gospel to them" (Acts 16:6 – 10). Throughout the book of Acts, God leads his people to participate with him in accomplishing his mission, the *missio Dei.* Such a conclusion is best discerned over time, through prayer, fasting, and collaboration with the Christian community.

God's specific call is different from *personal likes and dislikes,* but when God's call is less explicit, these may legitimately influence the choice of fields. A family wanting to avoid learning a totally new language may choose to serve in Australia. A great outdoorsman might be attracted to Alaska, or a surfer to Hawaii. The presence of Western conveniences attracts many to the great urban centers of Africa such as Nairobi, Abidjan, and Harare. One team investigated two equally receptive African peoples and selected the area with the healthiest climate. Missionaries should honestly evaluate their reasons for field selection. When God gives a specific call, obedience must take priority over personal preference. God, through his grace, is able to help missionaries overcome, and even change, their own preferences.

Sending churches sometimes discern that God is leading them to an area with *geographic proximity* to them. Some even specify that the work be "within a day's drive of home." This proximity allows partnering churches to be involved in the activities of the mission church. It also allows the sending church to know what is occurring in the mission church and to give encouragement during times of struggle.

Missionaries may also choose to locate in geographical proximity to other missionaries. Soon after a team began ministering among the Fon people of Benin, other teams chose to locate among the neighboring Aja and Watchi peoples of southern Benin and Togo. Within a few years, students who had interned with these mission teams returned to work in northern Togo and Burkina Faso. God worked through relationships and geographical proximity to form a loose network of church-planting mission teams who could support each other strategically and spiritually.

Conclusion

Limited resources prevent mission agencies and churches from immediately sending missionaries to all parts of the world. This is not to imply that certain areas be surrendered to Satan's dominance. Developing priorities is, however, imperative.

How, then, should mission agencies and churches channel their resources for world evangelization? This chapter provides three overlapping and complementary criteria that may be applied — the extent to which a population is unreached, their receptivity to the gospel, and God's specific leading. Although these cannot be evaluated with mathematical or scientific certainty, missionaries may move forward with confidence as they submit their decision-making process to God, discern where he is leading them, and respond to his will.

REFLECTION AND APPLICATION

Questions

1. What is meant by the term *unreached people*? From your reading or personal experience, give an example of an unreached people.
2. Give several characteristics of the 10/40 Window.
3. What are strengths and limitations of prioritizing unreached peoples? Be thorough and specific in your answer.
4. Define the term *receptivity*. In this discussion, how is the world like a vast orchard with many fields? How should laborers cultivate the various fields?
5. Describe receptivity using Jesus' comments in the Limited Commission (Matt. 9:35–10:14).
6. List and describe three general factors affecting receptivity.
7. What are the strengths and limitations of prioritizing receptive peoples? Be thorough and specific in your answer.
8. What are strengths and limitations of using personal preference as a criterion of field selection? Be thorough and specific in your answer. Why does this criterion so frequently determine where missionaries are placed?
9. Identify the strengths and limitations of the following statement: "Since the city is the wave of the future, mission work should focus on the largest world-class cities in the world, then spread to smaller cities, and finally to rural areas."

For Written Reflection

You have recently become the chief executive officer of a small mission agency and want to use your position to partner with local churches and agencies to evangelize the world. You have just read this chapter and have decided to convene a missionary strategy meeting of local church and agency leaders to strategize for world evangelization. What are the major questions to be asked in the strategy conference?

Epilogue

Who Are Jim and Julie?

During the course of reading this book, you have walked with Jim and Julie and learned from them. They have been like a docent in a museum or a guide on a wilderness trek, describing the realities of walking with God, joining him in ministry, and becoming increasingly like him on the journey.

You have learned how the question "Does God want us to become missionaries?" became tangible during their trip to Haiti. To them, the beats of voodoo drums reverberating in the night to ward off evil spirits symbolized the brokenness of a world without Jesus Christ. During this time they made two commitments: to be husband and wife, and more significantly, to look at the world through God's eyes. As developing missionaries, they learned from classes at a Christian seminary while also incarnating these practices as youth ministers in a local church.

You walked with Jim and Julie as they learned to read the ancient stories of the Bible in a new way. The Bible, they realized, is not merely a book of dos and don'ts or a patterned guide to life. It is the story of a loving, holy, faithful God working through his people to accomplish his mission. Jim and Julie learned that this mission did not begin with Jesus or with the journeys of Paul; it began with God, who created the universe. Throughout history, people have been called to enter God's mission, to become participants in God's ongoing story. God was (and is) a missionary God!

Rehearsing the story line of the Bible challenged Jim and Julie and changed their lives. They now recognized that Christianity is a distinctively historical religion and can be understood only through hearing God's ongoing work in human history.

Scripture was shaping their identity and biblical theology was giving them new categories for interpreting the world.

You were there when, being formed by the historical narrative of Scripture, they realized that they could not "become missionaries" by their own might and power. They must learn to rely on God, accept his sovereign reign over their lives, and be "transformed into his image" (2 Cor. 3:18). Like caterpillars crawling on the earth who then undergo metamorphosis to become pollen-carrying butterflies, their lives must be renewed to reflect the love, holiness, and faithfulness of God.

You learned from them as they reflected on the theologies of *missio Dei*, kingdom, incarnation, crucifixion, and resurrection. As Jim and Julie studied these theologies within the context of the biblical narrative, they realized that Scripture was shaping their identity and that biblical theology was giving them new categories for interpreting the world. Like the rudder of a ship, these theologies began to guide them to form practices commensurate with the will of God.

You walked with them as they struggled with the nominalism of the church in North America. Many church fellowships, they believed, were being swept along by culture currents and had begun to look more like social fraternities than communities of disciples on mission with God. You asked with them, "How can the church resist the allure of worldliness while still maintaining a relevant and convincing witness in the world? How do Christians avoid living by the world's standards, yet remain gracious toward and connected with people who do?"

You may have joined Jim and Julie in asking fundamental questions about personal motives for serving as God's missionaries. They asked themselves, "Am I shaped more by *primary* motives that reflect God's love and compassion; by *secondary* motives, like yearning for personal adventure; or by *deficient* motives, like making a name for myself?"

You learned with them that there are different types of missionaries, that one size does not fit all. You asked with them, "What types of missionaries has God called us to become?" and discerned God's calling and the particular gifts that God has put within you.

You learned with them about the missionary cycle — what to expect and how to deal with the issues at each stage.

You heard Jim and Julie share their reflections from their History of Missions course: The story of God's mission did not conclude with the New Testament age, but has continued for two millennia. You heard stories of incredible dedication and sacrifice, of success and failure, and grew to appreciate the claim of Jesus that, in spite of Satan's attacks, the gates of Hades would never prevail against his kingdom. Like them, the more you learned, the more you realized that *you* were part of this ongoing story.

Might God use us to develop a church-planting movement?

You saw them struggle with the nature of missionary identification and incarnation. You heard them ask, "Can we enter a new culture and effectively represent Christ and his mission? How do we think and minister with the 'mindset' of Christ?"

You witnessed how the study of missions led Jim and Julie to look at their youth ministry differently. You heard them ask, "What would it be like to be Christ to people of the other cultures within our schools—those of African American, Asian, and Latino ethnicity or Muslim and Hindu heritage? Would ministry among these students and their families enable our church to become multicultural?"

You saw Jim and Julie meet high school students from Central Asia who had recently arrived from refugee camps in Nepal and India and help them (and their families) to function in American culture by learning English, finding immediate resources for living, and developing suitable employment. You learned how they and their high school group began a very simple Bible study with these refugees, working through the gospel of Mark. You were surprised by the interpretation of the gospel and how it was applied by these new immigrants!

You learned with them how to develop practices of ministry by using the Missional Helix—a progressive spiral of learning that integrates theological reflection, cultural analysis, historical perspective, and strategy formation within the environment of spiritual formation.

You listened as Jim and Julie began to dream about what God might do during the next stage of their lives. "Might God use us to develop a church-planting movement," they wondered, "either domestically or in some receptive overseas context? What would this look like? What are the basic tasks of beginning a church-planting movement?"

You read with Jim and Julie the African case study describing a church-planting movement among the Kipsigis people of Kenya and noticed how it resonated with their experiences in Haiti. You noted that Jim and Julie appreciated the focus on language and culture learning and were intrigued by how the church-planting model was developed by applying theological understandings to ministry within a certain

Who are Jim and Julie? The answer is: You! You ARE a missionary.

culture. The model, you discerned, illustrated a respect for the local people, a confidence that equipping local leaders would produce strong new churches.

You felt their excitement as Jim and Julie began to apply what they were learning in the seminary. You saw how they teamed with students to begin missional communities in two high schools to help searchers know God and walk with him. You noted how they used these missional communities to model Jesus' ministry of teaching, listening, praying, and healing.

You may have been surprised by the many dilemmas concerning the use of money in missions and felt sympathy for the situation in which Jim and Julie's friends found themselves. You realized that the disparity of wealth in the world requires wisdom to plant churches and ministries that are financially self-sustaining.

You saw how short-term missions (STMs) profoundly affected Jim and Julie's spiritual lives and understand why they desire to provide such life-changing experiences for their high school group. You may have been surprised, however, that STMs have both benefits and challenges.

You learned with Jim and Julie about intentional field selection for missions. They were still discerning whether God was leading them to serve in their own country, in Haiti, where they had had positive short-term experience, or in a place where people had never heard the story of Jesus.

You have spent several weeks reading Jim and Julie's story. "Who are Jim and Julie?" you ask. The answer is: You! You are Jim and Julie! Like you, they are both growing as disciples and helping others become disciples. Like you, they are learning to go on mission with God. In a very real sense you are Jim and Julie — learning to grow as God's missionaries!

You ARE a missionary! Whether you live in the United States and serve as a minister for a church or serve as a teacher in a local school, sell cars, or own a small business, or live in a country where you need to learn a new language and culture, you are a missionary! You are a disciple of Jesus who shows others how to be his disciples. May God grow you more and more into the image of Jesus. May he fill you with his love so that it overflows to others. May he give you strength and guidance for the journey. May all the glory be his!

Scripture Versions

Scripture quotations marked ESV are taken from *The Holy Bible, English Standard Version,* copyright © 2001 by Good News Publishers. Used by permission. All rights reserved.

Scripture quotations marked HCSB are taken from the Holman Christian Standard Bible, copyright © 1999, 2000, 2002, 2003, 2009 by Holman Bible Publishers, Nashville Tennessee. All rights reserved.

Scripture quotations marked NASB are taken from the *New American Standard Bible.* Copyright © 1960, 1962, 1963, 1968, 1971, 1972, 1973, 1975, 1977, 1995 by The Lockman Foundation. Used by permission.

Scripture quotations marked NKJV are taken from the New King James Version. Copyright © 1982, by Thomas Nelson, Inc. Used by permission. All rights reserved.

References

Adams, Ian. 2009. *http://inthebellyofthebigfish.blogspot.com/2009/10/ways-into-small-missional-community-8.html.* (Accessed 6/25/13.)

Adeney, Miriam. 2008. "The Myth of the Blank Slate: A Check List for Short-Term Missions." In *Effective Engagement in Short-Term Missions: Doing It Right!* edited by Robert E. Priest, 120–50. Pasadena, Calif.: William Carey Library.

Allen, Catherine B. 1994. "Charlotte (Lottie) Moon, 1840–1912: Demonstrating 'No Greater Love.'" In *Mission Legacies: Biographical Studies of Leaders of the Modern Missionary Movement*, edited by Gerald H. Anderson, Robert T. Coote, Norman A. Horner, and James M. Phillips, 205–15. Maryknoll, N.Y.: Orbis.

Allen, C. Leonard. 2006. *The Cruciform Church: Becoming a Cross-Shaped People in a Secular World*. Revised and expanded edition. Abilene, Tex.: Abilene Christian University Press.

Allison, Fielden. 1983. "The Effects of Kinship on Church Growth in the Kipsigis Churches." In *Church Growth among the Kipsigis of Southwest Kenya*, 56–67. Unpublished document.

———. 2011. Electronic correspondence with Anthony Parker. January 21.

Altrock, Craig. 2009. Survey of long-term missionaries conducted between September 22, 2005, and May 26, 2007. *www.surveymonkey.com/sr.aspx?sm=bmnCVVT57i8vEnni_2fr5y0w_3d_3d.* (Accessed October 15, 2009.)

Ambrozic, Aloysius M. 1972. "The Hidden Kingdom: A Redaction-Critical Study of the References to the Kingdom of God in Mark's Gospel." *Catholic Biblical Quarterly*. Monograph Series 2. Washington, D.C.: Catholic Biblical Association of America.

Araujo, Alex. 1993. "Retooling for the Future." *Evangelical Missions Quarterly* 29 (October): 362–70.

Arnold, Clinton E. 1987. "The 'Exorcism' of Ephesians 6:12 in Recent Research: A Critique of Wesley Carr's View of the Role of Evil Powers in First-Century AD Belief." *Journal for the Study of the New Testament* 30:71–87.

Aulén, Gustaf. 2003. *Christus Victor: An Historical Study of the Three Main Types of the Idea of Atonement*. Eugene, Ore.: Wipf & Stock.

Austin, Clyde N., ed. 1986. *Cross-Cultural Reentry: A Book of Readings*. Abilene, Tex.: Abilene Christian University Press.

Baker, Andrew. 2003. "Spiritual Development in the Harding Community." Unpublished guided research paper, Harding University Graduate School of Religion, Memphis, Tenn.

Bales, Kevin. 2004. *Disposable People: New Slavery in the Global Economy.* Berkeley: University of California Press.

Barnett, Betty J. 2002. *Friend Raising: Building a Missionary Support Team That Lasts.* Edmonds, Wash.: YWAM Publishing.

Barrett, David B. 1986. *World-Class Cities and World Evangelization.* The AD 2000 Series. Birmingham, Ala.: New Hope.

———. 1990. *Our Globe and How to Reach It: Seeing the World Evangelized by AD 2000 and Beyond.* The AD 2000 Series. Birmingham, Ala.: New Hope.

Barrett, Lois Y., ed. 2004. *Treasure in Clay Jars.* Grand Rapids, Mich.: Eerdmans.

Beasley-Murray, G. R. 1986. *Jesus and the Kingdom of God.* Grand Rapids, Mich.: Eerdmans.

Bediako, Kwame. 1995. *Christianity in Africa: The Renewal of a Non-Western Religion.* Maryknoll, N.Y.: Orbis.

Betts, Joe. 1982. Missions newsletter. *The Marcher* 5 (August): 2.

Beyerhaus, Peter. 1979. "The Three Selves Formula: Is It Built on Biblical Foundations?" In *Readings in Dynamic Indigeneity*, edited by Charles Kraft, 15 – 30. Pasadena, Calif.: William Carey Library.

Birth, Kevin. 2006. "What Is Your Mission Here? A Trinidadian Perspective on Visits from the 'Church of Disneyland.'" *Missiology* 34, no. 4: 497–508. *ATLA Religion Database with ATLASerials, EBSCOhost.* (Accessed February 16, 2012.)

Blomberg, Fran. 2008. "From 'Whatever' to Wherever: Enhancing Faith Formation in Young Adults through Short-Term Missions." In *Effective Engagement in Short-Term Missions: Doing It Right!* 590 – 611. Pasadena, Calif.: William Carey Library.

Bonk, Jonathan. 1990. *The Theory and Practice of Missionary Identification (1860 – 1920).* Studies in the History of Mission Series 2. Lewiston, N.Y.: Edwin Mellen.

Bosch, David J. 1991. *Transforming Mission: Paradigm Shifts in Theology of Mission.* Maryknoll, N.Y.: Orbis.

Box, Don. 1999. Personal interview at the Hills Church of Christ. North Richland Hills, Tex.

Breen, Mike. 2010a. *Covenant and Kingdom: The DNA of the Bible.* Pawley's Island, S.C.: 3DM.

———. 2010b. "$$$ / Part 3." http://mikebreen.wordpress.com/2010/04/14/part 3/ (Accessed June 26, 2013.)

———, and Alex Absalom. 2010. *Launching Missional Communities.* Pawley's Island, S.C.: 3DM.

———, and Steve Cockram. 2009, revised 2011. *Building a Discipling Culture.* Pauley's Island, S.C.: 3DM.

———. 2012. *Multiplying Missional Leaders.* Pawley's Island, S.C.: 3DM.

———. 2013. *Leading Missional Communities: Rediscovering the power of living on mission together.* Pawley's Island, S.C.: 3DM.

Broom, Wendell. 1976. "Church Growth Principles." In *Guidelines for World Evangelism*, edited by George Gurganus, 81 – 104. Abilene, Tex.; Biblical Research Press.

Burch Gregg. n.d. "Person of peace." *http://godsfaintpath.com/person-of-peace.* (Accessed July 12, 2013.)

Burk, Aaron. 2009. "A tale of three troups." Posted September 18. *www.aaron burkinafaso.com/2009/09/tale-of-three-groups.html.* (Accessed December 8, 2011.)

———. 2011. Personal e-mail to Anthony Parker. January 9.

Burris, Stephen E. 2012. "Opening the Floodgates: From Everywhere to Everywhere." In *River of God: An Introduction to World Missions*, edited by Doug Priest and Stephen E. Burris, 93 – 107. Eugene, Ore.: Wipf & Stock.

Bush, George H. W. 1991. Radio address to the nation on the National Day of Prayer, February 2. In "Public Papers of the Presidents of the United States." Electronic resource. Washington, D.C.: National Archives and Records Administration. *http://purl.access.gpo.gov/GPO/LPS4752.* Text of radio address at *www.gpo.gov/fdsys/pkg/PPP–1991-book1/html/PPP–1991-book1-doc-pg97.* (Accessed November 5, 2012.)

Bush, Luis. n.d. *Getting to the Core of the Core: The 10/40 Window.* San Jose, Calif.: Partners International.

———. 1994. "Global Consultation on World Evangelization." *Global Church Growth* 21 (Spring): 1 – 8.

Carlson, Darren. 2012. "Why You Should Consider Canceling Your Short-Term Missions Trips." TGC blog. Posted June 18. *http://thegospelcoalition.org /mobile/article/tgc/why-you-should-consider-cancelling-your-short-term -mission-trips.* (Accessed June 21, 2012.)

Cathcart, Rochelle, and Mike Nichols. 2009. "Self Theology, Global Theology, and Missional Theology in the Writings of Paul G. Hiebert." *Trinity Journal* 30, no. 2: 209 – 21. *ATLA Religion Database with ATLASerials*, EBSCO*host.* (Accessed December 29, 2011.)

Chao, Jonathan. 1989. *The China Mission Handbook.* Hong Kong: Chinese Church Research Center.

Chaze, William L. 1983. "Our Big Cities Go Ethnic." *U.S. News & World Report* 94 (March 21), 49 – 53.

Chowning, Richard. 2008. "Unreached People Groups, Last Frontier People Groups, Bibleless People Groups, and Scripture Use … Some Definitions." Posted November 3. *www.africamissions.org/blog/?p=51.* (Accessed February 28, 2012.)

Chung, Michael, with Enzo Saavedra and Mike Jorgensen. 2013. "Church Planting in a Week: Implications for Long-Term Ministry — Bolivia, a Case Study" in *Evangelical Missions Quarterly* 49, no. 1 (January): 82 – 87.

Clinton, J. Robert. 1988. *The Making of a Leader: Recognizing the Lessons and Stages of Leadership Development.* Colorado Springs: NavPress.

Coggins, Wade. 1988. "The risks of sending our dollars only." *Evangelical Missions Quarterly* 24 (July): 204–6.

Cole, Neil. 1999. *Cultivating a Life for God.* St. Charles, IL: ChurchSmart Resources.

———. 2008. *Search & Rescue: Becoming a Disciple Who Makes a Difference.* Grand Rapids, Mich.: Baker.

Corbett, Steve, and Brian Fikkert. 2009, 2012. *When Helping Hurts: How to Alleviate Poverty without Hurting the Poor ... and Yourself.* Chicago: Moody Press.

Cox, Monte. 1999. "'Euthanasia of Mission' or 'Partnership?' An Evaluative Study of the Disengagement Policies of Church of Christ Missionaries in Rural Kenya." Ph.D. dissertation, Trinity Evangelical Divinity School.

Craigie, Peter C. 1983. "Psalms 1 – 50." In *Word Biblical Commentary*, vol. 19, edited by David A. Hubbard and Glenn W. Barker. Waco, Tex.: Word.

Culbertson, Howard. 2011. "Statistics: The 21st Century World." *http://home.snu.edu/~hculbert/world.htm#abc.* (Accessed February 29, 2012.)

Daniels, Gene. 2008. "The Character of Short-Term Mission." *Evangelical Missions Quarterly* 44, no. 2: 150 – 56.

Darrow, Ken, and Brad Palmquist, eds. 1977. *Trans-Cultural Study Guide*. Stanford, Calif.: Volunteers in Asia.

Datema, Dave. 2012. "In Praise of Short-Term Missions." *Mission Frontiers* 34, no. 1 (January – February): 14. *www.missionfrontiers.org/pdfs/34 – 1-Marginalia.pdf.* (Accessed April 10, 2012.)

Davidson, Dave. 2006. "Mission Quotes." *Missiology.org. www.missiology.org/?p=30#prayersmissions.* (Accessed November 7, 2011.)

Dayton, Edward R., and David A. Fraser. 1990. *Planning Strategies for World Evangelization*. Grand Rapids, Mich.: Eerdmans.

Diles, Allen. 1993. Interview by author. May 5.

Diles, M. Laurie. 2009. Interview by R. Allen Diles. November 24.

Donovan, Vincent J. 1978. *Christianity Rediscovered*. Maryknoll, N.Y.: Orbis.

Dougherty, Rose Mary. 2009. *Discernment: A Path to Spiritual Awakening.* Mahwah, N.J.: Paulist Press.

Efta, Damian. 1994. "Who Are the Unreached?" *Evangelical Missions Quarterly* 30, no. 1: 28 – 32.

Elliston, Edgar J. 1988. "Designing leadership education." *Missiology* 16 (April): 203–15.

———. 1992. *Home Grown Leaders*. Pasadena, Calif.: William Carey Library.

Escobar, Samuel. 1992. "The Elements of Style in Crafting New International Mission Leaders." *Evangelical Missions Quarterly* 28 (January): 6 – 15.

———. 2000. "Evangelical Missiology: Peering into the Future at the Turn of the Century." In *Global Missiology for the 21st Century: The Iguassu Dialogue*, edited by William D. Taylor, 101 – 22. Grand Rapids, Mich.: Baker Academic.

Fann, Anne-Geri', and Greg Taylor. 2006. *How to Get Ready for Short-Term Missions: The Ultimate Guide for Sponsors, Parents and Those Who Go*. Nashville: Nelson.

Farris, Sherry. 2009. Electronic correspondence with Anthony Parker. July 29.

Ferguson, Everett. 1989. *The Everlasting Kingdom: The Kingdom of God in Scripture and in Our Lives*. The Way of Life Series. Abilene, Tex.: Abilene Christian University Press.

Friedrich, Otto. 1987. "New Age Harmonies." *Time* (December 7), 62 – 72.

Froese, Vic. 2007. "Paul G. Hiebert: A Selected Bibliography." *Direction* 36, no. 2: 269 – 75. *www.directionjournal.org/article/?1493*. (Accessed December 29, 2011.)

Frost, Michael, and Alan Hirsch. 2003. *The Shaping of Things to Come*. Peabody, Mass.: Hendrickson.

Frykenberg, Robert Eric. 2007. "Paul G. Hiebert 1932 – 2007." *International Bulletin of Missionary Research* (July), 128 – 29. *Academic Search Premier*, EBSCO*host*. (Accessed December 29, 2011.)

Garrison, David. 1990. *The Nonresidential Missionary: A New Strategy and the People It Serves*. Monrovia, Calif.: MARC.

———. 2004. *Church Planting Movements: How God Is Redeeming a Lost World*. Midlothian, Va.: WIGTake Resources.

Gaukroger, Stephan. n.d. "Mission Quotes." *Missiology.org*. *www.missiology.org/?p=30*. (Accessed November 7, 2011.)

Glasser, Arthur F. 2009. "The Apostle Paul and the Missionary Task." In *Perspectives on the World Christian Movement: A Reader*, 4th ed., edited by Ralph D. Winter and Steven C. Hawthorne, 149 – 53. Pasadena, Calif.: William Carey Library.

Goheen, Michael. 2000. " 'As the Father Has Sent Me, I Am Sending You': J. E. Lesslie Newbigin's Missionary Ecclesiology." Doctoral thesis, Utrecht University. *http://igitur-archive.library.uu.nl/dissertations/1947080/full.pdf*. (Accessed March 14, 2013.)

———. 2004. "The Significance of Lesslie Newbigin for Mission in the New Millennium." *Third Millenium* 7, no.3: 88 – 99. *www.newbigin.net/assets/pdf/slnmnm_g.pdf*. (Accessed March 14, 2013.)

———. 2013. "The Lasting Legacy of Lesslie Newbigin: A Missionary Encounter with Western Culture." *www.qideas.org/blog/the-lasting-legacy-of-lesslie-newbigin.aspx*. (Accessed March 14, 2013.)

Gordon, Andrew. 2009. Electronic correspondence with Anthony Parker. July 10.

Green, Michael. 1970. *Evangelism in the Early Church*. Grand Rapids, Mich: Eerdmans.

Grieco, Elizabeth M., et al. 2012. "The Foreign-Born Population in the United States: 2010." American Community Survey Reports. United States Census Bureau. *www.census.gov/prod/2012pubs/acs-19.pdf*. (Accessed July 9, 2012.)

Grigg, Viv. 2004. *Companion to the Poor: Christ in the Urban Slums*. 2nd ed. Waynesboro, Ga.: Authentic Media.

Groothuis, Douglas R. 1986. *Unmasking the New Age*. Downers Grove, Ill.: InterVarsity Press.

Grunlan, Stephen A., and Marvin K. Mayers. 1979. *Cultural Anthropology—A Christian Perspective*. Grand Rapids, Mich.: Zondervan.

Guder, Darrell L., ed. 1998. *Missional Church: A Vision for the Sending of the Church in North America*. Grand Rapids, Mich.: Eerdmans.

Günther, Wolfgang, and Guillermo Cook. 1997. "World Missionary Conferences." In *Dictionary of Mission: Theology, History, Perspectives*, edited by Karl Müller et al., 502 – 9. Maryknoll, N.Y.: Orbis.

Gunton, Colin E. 1991. *The Promise of Trinitarian Theology*. Edinburg: T&T Clark International.

Guthrie, Stan. 1992. "Conversions among Turks Suggest Gospel Lift-Off Near." *World Pulse* 27 (March 6): 1, 4.

———. 1994. "Tentmaking: Putting Down Stakes in Mission Movement." *Christianity Today* (November 13): 80 – 81.

Hall, Arthur. 1986. Book review. *City Watch* 1 (October): 20.

Hall, Edward T. 1966, 1982. *The Hidden Dimension.* New York: Anchor/Doubleday.

Halter, Hugh, and Matt Smay. 2010. *AND: The Gathered and Scattered Church.* Grand Rapids, Mich.: Zondervan.

Hamilton, Mark, ed. 2009. *Transforming Word: One-Volume Commentary on the Bible.* Abilene, Tex.: Abilene Christian University Press.

Harrell, Pat Edwin. 1969. *The Letter of Paul to the Philippians.* The Living Word Commentary. Austin, Tex.: Sweet.

Harris, Randy. 2004. "Imagination." Speech at Mission Alive's church planters' retreat. June 11.

Hauerwas, Stanley, and William H. Willimon. 1989. *Resident Aliens: Life in the Christian Colony.* Nashville: Abingdon.

Haugen, Gary A. 1999. *Good News about Injustice: A Witness of Courage in a Hurting World.* Downers Grove, Ill.: InterVarsity Press.

Haviland, William. 1987. *Cultural Anthropology.* 5th ed. New York: Holt, Rinehart and Winston.

Heard, Renee. 1988. Reading report for missionary anthropology, BMIS 445, Abilene Christian University, September 20.

Hedlund, Roger. 1990. "Cheaper by the dozen? Indigenous missionaries vs. partnership." *Evangelical Missions Quarterly* 26 (July): 274–79.

Herrmann, Steve and Lidia. 1994. *The Hermann Family Newsletter* (November), 1 – 2.

Hesselgrave, David J. 1978a. *Communicating Christ Cross-Culturally.* Grand Rapids, Mich.: Zondervan.

———. 1978b. "Dimensions of cross-cultural communications." In *Readings in Missionary Anthropology II.* Ed. William A. Smalley, 615–26. Pasadena, Calif.: William Carey Library.

Hiebert, Paul G. 1982. "The Flaw of the Excluded Middle." *Missiology* 10, no. 1: 35 – 47. *ATLA Religion Database with ATLASerials*, EBSCO*host*. (Accessed December 29, 2011.)

———. 1983. *Cultural Anthropology.* 2nd ed. Grand Rapids, Mich.: Baker.

———. 1985. "The Fourth Self." In *Anthropological Insights for Missionaries*, 193 – 224. Grand Rapids, Mich.: Baker.

———. 1987. "Critical Contextualization." *International Bulletin of Missionary Research* 11, no. 3: 104 – 12. *ATLA Religion Database with ATLASerials*, EBSCO*host*. (Accessed December 29, 2011.)

———. 1993. "De-theologizing: A response." *Trinity World Forum* 19 (Fall): 4.

Hinton, Keith. 1985. *Growing Churches Singapore Style: Ministry in an Urban Context*. Singapore: Overseas Missionary Fellowship.

Hirsch, Alan. 2006. *The Forgotten Ways: Reactivating the Missional Church*. Grand Rapids, Mich.: Brazos Press.

———, with Darryn Altclass. 2009. *The Forgotten Ways Handbook*. Grand Rapids, Mich.: Brazos Press.

———. 2013. "What Are the Essentials to a Missional Movement?" *www.vergenetwork.org/2013/05/14/what-are-the-essentials-to-a-missional-movement-alan-hirsch*. (Assessed June 30, 2013.)

Howard, David M. 1999. "Student Power in World Missions." In *Perspectives on the World Christian Movement: A Reader*, 3rd ed., edited by Ralph D. Winter and Steven C. Hawthorne, 277–86. Pasadena, Calif.: William Carey Library.

———. 2009. "Student Power in World Missions." In *Perspectives on the World Christian Movement: A Reader*, 4th ed., edited by Ralph D. Winter and Steven C. Hawthorne, 305–11. Pasadena, Calif.: William Carey Library.

Hunsberger, George R. 1996. "Sizing Up the Shape of the Church." In *The Church between Gospel and Culture*, edited by George R. Hunsberger and Craig Van Gelder, 333–46. The Gospel and Our Culture Series. Grand Rapids, Mich.: Eerdmans.

———. 1998a. *Bearing the Witness of the Spirit: Lesslie Newbigin's Theology of Cultural Plurality*. Grand Rapids, Mich.: Eerdmans.

———. 1998b. "Renewing Faith during the Postmodern Transition." In *The Bible in TransMission*, special edition, 10–13. *www.newbigin.net/assets/pdf/trans_full.pdf*. (Accessed March 14, 2013.)

Hunter, George G. III. 1992. "The Legacy of Donald A. McGavran." *International Bulletin of Missionary Research* 16, no. 4: 158–62. *ATLA Religion Database with ATLASerials*, EBSCO*host*. (Accessed March 2, 2010.)

International Association of Missionary Aviation (IAMA). http://www.iama-net.org. (Accessed March 2, 2012.)

International Justice Mission (IJM). 2011. "Injustice Today." *http://ijm.org/our-work/injustice-today*. (Accessed December 9, 2011.)

Johnson, Andrew. 2010. Personal email to Anthony Parker. September 1.

———. 2012. Personal email to Anthony Parker. February 13.

Johnson, Neal, and Steve Rundle. 2006. "Distinctives and Challenges of Business as Mission." In *Business as Mission: From Impoverished to Empowered*, edited by Tom Steffen and Mike Barnett, 19–36. EMIS Series 14. Pasadena, Calif.: William Carey Library.

Johnstone, David M. 2006. "Closing the Loop: Debriefing and the Short-Term College Missions Team." *Missiology: An International Review* 34, no. 4: 523–29.

Johnstone, Patrick. 1986. *Operation World*. Waynesboro, Ga.: STL.

Joshua Project. n.d. "What Is the Joshua Project?" *http://joshuaproject.net/joshua-project.php*. (Accessed March 2, 2012.)

Kallenberg, Brad J. 2002. *Live to Tell: Evangelism for a Postmodern Age*. Grand Rapids, Mich.: Brazos Press.

Keller, Tim. 1995. "Basis of prayer: 'Our Father.'" Sermon. April 23. *http://sermons2.redeemer.com/sermons/basis-prayer-our-father*. (Accessed July 9, 2013.)

———. 1998. "Come and See." Sermon. November 15. *http://sermons2.redeemer.com/sermons/come-and-see*. (Accessed July 12, 2013.)

Kelly, Thomas. 1996. *A Testament of Devotion*. New York: HarperOne.

Kenneson, Philip D. 1999. *Life on the Vine: Cultivating the Fruit of the Spirit in Christian Community*. Downers Grove, Ill.: InterVarsity Press.

Kimball, Dan. 2003. *The Emerging Church*. Grand Rapids, Mich.: Zondervan.

Kinnaman, David. 2007. *UnChristian: What a New Generation Really Thinks about Christianity . . . and Why It Matters*. Grand Rapids, Mich.: Baker.

Kiser, Charles, Eric Brown, and Matt Dabbs. 2013. "Reaching and Discipling Twenty-Somethings." Pepperdine Bible Lectures. May 2. *https://itunes.apple.com/us/itunes-u/pepperdine-bible-lectures/id643020969*.

Kivengere, Festo. 1962. "Personal Revival." In *Commission, Conflict, Commitment*, edited by Eric Fife and Arhur F. Glasser. Chicago, Ill.: InterVarsity Press.

Kluck, P. A. 1985. "Social Systems." In *India: A Country Study*, edited by Richard F. Nyrop, American Handbook Series, 217–72. Washington, D.C.: American University.

Koll, Karla Ann. 2010. "Taking Wolves among Lambs: Some Thoughts on Training for Short-Term Mission Facilitation." *International Bulletin of Missionary Research* 34, no. 2: 93–96. *ATLA Religion Database with ATLASerials*, EBSCO*host*. (Accessed February 14, 2012.)

Kraft, Charles H. 1996. *Anthropology for Christian Witness*. Maryknoll, N.Y.: Orbis.

Lai, Patrick. 2005. *Tentmaking: The Life and Work of Business as Missions*. Colorado Springs: Authentic Media.

Lamascus, R. Scott. 1989. "To understand homeless, minister lives on street." *Christian Chronicle* 46 (August): 1, 10.

Larson, Mildred L. 1998. *Meaning-Based Translation: A Guide to Cross-Language Equivalence*. Lanham, Md.: University Press of America and Summer Institute of Linguistics.

Latourette, Kenneth Scott. 1945. *Advance through the Storm: A.D. 1914 and After, with Concluding Generalizations*. A History of the Expansion of Christianity Series 7. New York: Harper and Brothers.

Lausanne Committee for World Evangelization. 2005. "The Local Church in Mission: Becoming a Missional Congregation in the Twenty-First-Century Global Context and the Opportunities Offered through Tentmaking Ministry." Lausanne Occasional Paper 39. Series edited by David Claydon. *www.lausanne.org/docs/2004forum /LOP39_IG10.pdf*. (Accessed January 16, 2012.)

Lausanne Movement, The. 2010. "About the Lausanne Movement." *www.lausanne.org/about.html*. (Accessed December 15, 2011.)

Lévy-Strauss, Claude. 1964. *Tristes Tropiques*. New York: Atheneum.

Lewis, C. S. 1949. *The Weight of Glory and Other Addresses*. Grand Rapids, Mich.: Eerdmans.

Lightfoot, J. B., and J. R. Harmer, trans. 1989. *The Apostolic Fathers*. 2nd ed. Edited and revised by Michael W. Holmes. Grand Rapids, Mich.: Baker.

Lincoln, A. T. 1973. "A Re-examination of 'the Heavenlies' in Ephesians." *New Testament Studies* 19: 468 – 83.

Lingenfelter, Judith E. and Sherwood G. 2003. *Teaching Cross Culturally: An Incarnational Model for Learning and Teaching*. Grand Rapids, Mich.: Baker Academic.

Linhart, Terence D. 2006. "They Were So Alive! The Spectacle of Self and Youth Group Short-Term Mission Trips." *Missiology: An International Review* 34, no. 4: 451 – 62.

Little, Alicia. 1988. Diary kept in Yugoslavia. February 10.

Livingston, J. Kevin. 1999. "The Legacy of David J. Bosch." *International Bulletin of Missionary Research* 23, no. 1: 26. *ATLASerials, Religion Collection*, EBSCO*host*. (Accessed March 2, 2010.)

Luzbetak, Louis J. 1970. *The Church and Cultures*. Pasadena, Calif.: William Carey Library.

MacGregor, G. H. C. 1954. "Principles and powers: The cosmic background of Paul's thought." *New Testament Studies* 1, (January): 17–28.

Manschreck, Clyde L. 1964. *Readings in the History of the Church from the Reformation to the Present*. A History of Christianity Series 2. Englewood Cliffs, N.J.: Prentice-Hall.

Matthews, Ed. 1976. "Leadership training in missions" in *Guidelines for World Evangelism*, edited by George P. Gurganus. Abilene, Tex.: Biblical Research Press.

Mbiti, John S. 1971. *New Testament Eschatology in an African Background*. London: Oxford University Press.

———, et al. 1980. *The Thailand Report on People of African Traditional Religions*. Wheaton, Ill.: Lausanne Committee for World Evangelization.

McGavran, Donald A. 1986. "My Pilgrimage in Mission." *International Bulletin of Missionary Research* 10, no. 2: 53 – 54. *ATLA Religion Database with ATLASerials*, EBSCO*host*. (Accessed March 6, 2010.)

———. 1985. Personal letter to Gailyn Van Rheenen, July 10.

———. 1990. *Understanding Church Growth*. 3rd ed., revised. Edited by C. Peter Wagner. Grand Rapids, Mich.: Eerdmans.

McIlwain, Trevor. 2005. *Guidelines for Evangelism and Teaching Believers*. Revised ed. Building on Firm Foundations Series 1. Sanford, Fla.: New Tribes Mission.

McIntosh, Gary L., ed. 2004. *Evaluating the Church Growth Movement*. Grand Rapids, Mich.: Zondervan.

McLaren, Brian D. 2004. *A Generous Orthodoxy*. Grand Rapids, Mich.: Zondervan.

McManus, Erwin. 2003. *Uprising: A Revolution of the Soul*. Nashville: Nelson.

McQuilkin, Robertson. 1994. "Six Inflammatory Questions — Part 2." *Evangelical Missions Quarterly* 30, no. 3: 258 – 64.

———. 1999. "Stop Sending Money! Breaking the Cycle of Missions Dependency." *Christianity Today* (March 1): 57 – 59.

McVey, Dan. 2009. Electronic correspondence with Anthony Parker. July 1.

Mission Alive. 2013. *http://missionalchurchplanting.org/2013/04/29/a-revision-churchs-story*. (Accessed July 8, 2013.)

Mission Network News. 2012. "Iran Sees Explosive Church Growth, Sparks of Revival." *Charismanews. www.charismanews.com/world/33002-iran-sees-explosive-church-growth-sparks-of-revival*. (Accessed April 24, 2012.)

Moffitt, Bob, with Karla Tesch. 2006. *If Jesus Were Mayor: How Your Local Church Can Transform Your Community*. Grand Rapids, Mich.: Monarch.

Moltmann, Jürgen. 1981. *The Trinity and the Kingdom*. Translated by Margaret Kohl. Minneapolis, Minn.: Fortress.

Moore, Mark. 2012. "Teach Them to Obey All That I Have Commanded." In *River of God: An Introduction to World Missions*, edited by Doug Priest and Stephen E. Burris, 63 – 77. Eugene, Ore.: Wipf & Stock.

Moreau, A. Scott, Gary R. Corwin, and Gary B. McGee. 2006. *Introducing World Missions: A Biblical, Historical, and Practical Survey*. Grand Rapids, Mich.: Baker.

Moreau, A. Scott. 2008. "Short-Term Missions in the Context of Missions, Inc." In *Effective Engagement in Short-Term Missions: Doing It Right!* edited by Robert J. Priest, 1 – 33. Pasadena, Calif.: William Carey Library.

Morgan, Boyd E. 1967. *Arkansas Angels*. Paragould, Ark.: College Bookstore and Press.

Morgan, Daniel. 2002. *Church Planting Models: Overview of Purpose-Driven Church Planting*. North American Mission Board. *www.churchplantingvillage.net/WorkArea/linkit.aspx?LinkIdentifier=id&ItemID=8589989318*. (Accessed January 21, 2013.)

Morgan, Timothy C., and Tony Carnes. 2005. "Purpose Driven in Rwanda: Rick Warren's Sweeping Plan to Defeat Poverty." *Christianity Today* 49, no. 10: 32 – 36. *ATLA Religion Database with ATLASerials*, EBSCO*host*. (Accessed September 4, 2010.)

Morris, John Michael. 2010. "An Evaluation of Gospel Receptivity with a View toward Prioritizing the Engagement of Groups and Individuals for Evangelism and Church Planting." Ph.D. dissertation, Mid-America Baptist Theological Seminary. *http://gradworks.umi.com/3388877.pdf*. (Accessed April 24, 2012.)

Mulholland, Kenneth. 1999. "Teaching Them … All Things: Three Dots and a Pilgrimage." In *Teaching Them Obedience in All Things: Equipping for the 21st Century*, edited by Edgar J. Elliston, 1 – 15. EMIS Series 7. Pasadena, Calif.: William Carey Library.

Murray, Stuart. 2001. *Church Planting: Laying Foundations*. Scottdale, Pa.: Herald Press.

Myers, Bryant L. 1989. "Where Are the Poor and the Lost?" In *Target Earth*. Pasadena, Calif.: Global Mapping.

———. 1993. *The Changing Shape of World Mission*. Monrovia, Calif.: MARC.

———. 1999. *Walking with the Poor: Principles and Practices of Transformational Development*. Maryknoll, N.Y.: Orbis.

Myers, Joseph R. 2003. *The Search to Belong: Rethinking Intimacy, Community, and Small Groups*. Grand Rapids, Mich.: Zondervan.

Nee, Witness. 1995. *The God-Men*. Anaheim: Living Stream Ministry.

Neill, Stephen. 1986. *A History of Christian Mission*. 2nd ed., revised and edited by Owen Chadwick. The Pelican History of the Church Series 6. New York: Penguin.

Nevins, Albert J. 1971. "Roman Catholic–Protestant Missionary Relationships." In *Concise Dictionary of the Christian World Mission*, edited by Stephen Neill, Gerald H. Anderson, and John Goodwin. Nashville: Abingdon.

Newbigin, Lesslie. 1986. *Foolishness to the Greeks: The Gospel and Western Culture*. Grand Rapids, Mich.: Eerdmans.

———. 1989. *The Gospel in a Pluralist Society*. Grand Rapids, Mich.: Eerdmans.

———. 1998. "Culture of Modernity." In *Dictionary of Mission: Theology, History, Perspectives*, edited by Karl Müller et al., 98–101. Maryknoll, N.Y.: Orbis.

———, and Eleanor Jackson. 1994. *A Word in Season*. Grand Rapids, Mich.: Eerdmans.

Newton, Greg. 1994. "Reaching the Sukuma of Tanzania." Unpublished newsletter.

Nida, Eugene. 1990. *Message and Mission*. Revised ed. Pasadena, Calif.: William Carey Library.

Niles, D. Preman. 2004. *From East and West: Rethinking Christian Mission*. St. Louis: Chalice Press.

Nouwen, Henri. 1995. "From Solitude to Community to Ministry." *Leadership* (Spring), 81 – 87.

Oberg, Kalervo. 1960. "Cultural shock: Adjustment to new culural environments," in *Practical Anthropology* 7 (July–August): 77–82.

Ochieng, William. 1981. "City empties for holiday," in Sunday Nation (December 27): 6.

Oldenburg, Ray. 1999. *The Great Good Place: Cafes, Coffee Shops, Bookstores, Bars, Hair Salons, and Other Hangouts at the Heart of a Community.* New York: Marlowe & Company.

Operation World. 2012. "France." *www.operationworld.org/fran*. (Accessed March 2, 2012.)

Orchardson, Ian Q. 1961. *The Kipsigis*. Nairobi, Kenya: East African Literature Bureau.

Patterson, George. 1980. "A Practical Approach: Theological Education in Honduras." In *Discipling through Theological Education by Extension: A Fresh Approach to Theological Education in the 1980s*, edited by Vergil Gerber, 119 – 36. Chicago: Moody Press.

Paulus, Trina. 1972. *Hope for the Flowers*. Mahwah, N.J.: Paulist Press.

Penner, Erwin. 1983. "The Enthronement of Christ in Ephesians." *Direction* 12 (July): 12 – 19.

Peterson, Roger. 2007. "Short-Term Missions, Long-Term Impact." (Plenary address at a conference cosponsored by Interdenominational Foreign Missions Association and the Evangelical Missiological Society. September 28. Minneapolis.

Petry, Ray C., ed. 1962. *Readings in the History of the Early and Medieval Church*. A History of Christianity Series 1. Englewood Cliffs, N.J.: Prentice-Hall.

Pierson, Paul Everett. 2009. "Ralph Winter, 1924 – 2009." *International Bulletin of Missionary Research* 33, no. 4 (October): 196 – 97. *Oct 2009 Christian Periodical Index*, EBSCO*host*. (Accessed December 29, 2011.)

Piper, John. 2010. *Let the Nations Be Glad! The Supremacy of God in Missions*. 3rd ed. Grand Rapids, Mich.: Baker Academic.

Pirolo, Neal. 2000. *The Reentry Team: Caring for Your Returning Missionaries*. San Diego, Calif.: Emmaus Road International.

Powell, Cyril H. 1963. *The Biblical Concept of Power*. London: Epworth.

Priest, Robert J., Terry Dischinger, Steve Rasmussen, and C. M. Brown. 2006. "Researching the Short-Term Mission Movement." *Missiology: An International Review* 34, no. 4: 431 – 50.

———. 2007. "Paul Hiebert: A Life Remembered." *http://hiebertweb.net/story_library/paul_life_rememb.html*. (Accessed December 29, 2011.)

———, ed. 2008. *Effective Engagement in Short-Term Missions: Doing It Right!* Pasadena, Calif.: William Carey Library.

———, Douglas Wilson, and Adelle Johnson. 2010. "U.S. Megachurches and New Patterns of Global Mission." *International Bulletin of Missionary Research* 34, no. 2: 97 – 102. *ATLA Religion Database with ATLASerials*, EBSCO*host*. (Accessed February 14, 2012.)

Pruett, Greg. 2009. "Transformed Lives through God's Word in Every Language." *Christian Standard* (June 14). *http://christianstandard.com/2009/06/cs_article – 1230*. (Accessed December 9, 2011.)

———. 2012. "Crossing Language Barriers." In *River of God: An Introduction to World Missions*, edited by Doug Priest and Stephen E. Burris, 213 – 27. Eugene, Ore.: Wipf & Stock.

Putman, Robert D. 2000. *Bowling Alone: The Collapse and Revival of American Community*. New York: Simon and Schuster.

Reese, Derran. 2004. Response to *Missions: Biblical Foundations and Contemporary Strategies*. Unpublished paper submitted to author. Abilene Christian University.

Reese, Robert. 2008. "Short-Term Missions as a Spiritual Exercise." *Evangelical Missions Quarterly* 44, no. 2: 158 – 63.

Reppart, Jim. 2006. "The Romance of the Universe." Presentation at a Mission Alive church-planting strategy lab. April 3.

Rickett, Daniel. 2008. "Short-Term Missions for Long-Term Partnership. *Evangelical Missions Quarterly* 44, no. 1: 42 – 46.

Robinson, Jarod. 2007. "Thy Kingdom Come, Thy Will Be Done . . ." Lecture at a Mission Alive theology lab.

———. 2013. Bible class on Dietrich Bonheoffer's *Life Together.* Riverside Church of Christ, Coppell, Tex. June 13.

Robinson, Martin. 1998. "A Passion for Mission." In *The Bible in TransMission*, special edition, 2. *www.newbigin.net/assets/pdf/trans_full.pdf*. (Accessed March 14, 2013.)

Roxburgh, Alan J., and M. Scott Boren. 2009. *Introducing the Missional Church: What It Is, Why It Matters, How to Become One.* Grand Rapids, Mich.: Baker.

Russell, Mark L. 2006. "The Biblical Basis for the Integration of Business and Missions." In *Business as Mission: From Impoverished to Empowered*, edited by Tom Steffen and Mike Barnett, 117 – 31. EMS Series 14. Pasadena, Calif.: William Carey Library.

Russian Good News. 1990. Missionary periodical. Hunter Station Church of Christ, Montgomery, Ala. (May), 4.

Sanneh, Lamin. 2009. *Translating the Message: The Missionary Impact on Culture*. 2nd ed. Maryknoll, N.Y.: Orbis.

Scott, John. 2010. "Can You Imagine No More 'Missing Peoples'?" Posted May 31. *http://conversation.lausanne.org/en/resources/detail/10347*. (Accessed January 9, 2012.)

Searcy, Nelson, and Kerrick Thomas. 2006. *Launch: Starting a New Church from Scratch*. Ventura, Calif.: Regal.

Shenk, William R. 1998. "Lesslie Newbigin's Contribution to the Theology of Mission." In *The Bible in TransMission*, special edition, 3 – 6. *www.newbigin.net/assets/pdf/trans_full.pdf*. (Accessed March 14, 2013.)

Shoemaker, Natalie. 2012. "li'l' PoP." *http://somabuilder.wordpress.com/2012/07/16/lil-pop*. (Accessed July 12, 2013.)

SIL International. 2011. "The Role of Translation Theory." *http://sil.org/translation/TrTheory.htm*. (Accessed December 9, 2011.)

Slack, Jim. 1994. "Baptisms Top 300,000 in 1994, a Banner Missions Year." *The Commission* (March – April), 5.

Smalley, William A. 1967. "Proximity or Neighborliness?" In *Readings in Missionary Anthropology*, 302 – 4. Tarrytown, N.Y.: Practical Anthropology.

Smith, A. Christopher. 1994. "William Carey, 1761 – 1834: Protestant Pioneer of the Modern Mission Era." In *Mission Legacies: Biographical Studies of Leaders of the Modern Missionary Movement*, edited by Gerald H. Anderson, Robert T. Coote, Norman A. Horner, and James M. Phillips, 245 – 54. Maryknoll, N.Y.: Orbis.

Smith, Alex G. 2008. "Evaluating Short-Term Missions: Missiological Questions." In *Effective Engagement in Short-Term Missions: Doing It Right!* edited by Robert J. Priest, 34 – 61. Pasadena, Calif.: William Carey Library.

Smith, Christian, and Patricia Snell. 2009. *Souls in Transition: The Religious and Spiritual Lives of Emerging Adults*. New York: Oxford University Press.

Smith, William Y. 2012. "Can Short-Term Teams Foster Church-Planting Movements? The Greatest Blessing Is to Train Others to Start Churches." *Mission Frontiers* 34, no. 1 (January – February): 6 – 9. *www.missionfrontiers.org/pdfs/34 – 1-Story-of-STM.pdf*. (Accessed April 11, 2012.)

Soma Church. n.d. "Missional Communities." *http://6691c6ac87f7da137980-d7680e578bcc584a601ce20243ad8f67.r3.cf2.rackcdn.com/uploaded/s/0e1118087_soma-life-missional-communities.pdf.* (Accessed January 29, 2013.)

Steffen, Tom A. 1993. *Passing the Baton: Church Planting That Empowers.* La Habre, Calif.: Center for Organizational and Ministry Development.

Sternke, Ben. 2012. "How I Make Disciples: Structure & Spontaneity." *http://bensternke.com/2012/06/how-i-make-disciples-structure-spontaneity.* (Accessed June 22, 2013.)

Stone, Howard W., and James O. Duke. 1996. *How to Think Theologically.* Minneapolis, Minn.: Augsburg Fortress.

Telford, John. 1898. "The Mission to Georgia." In *The Life of John Wesley.* New York: Eaton & Mains; Cincinnati: Jennings and Pye. *http://wesley.nnu.edu/?id=88.* (Accessed December 8, 2011.)

Terpstra, Gerald H. 1996. Personal Interview.

Thielicke, Helmut. 1962. *A Little Exercise for Young Theologians.* Grand Rapids, Mich.: Eerdmans.

Thompson, LaNette W. 1992. "Furlough Meets Reality." *The Commission* (October–November), 52.

Time staff. 2005. "The 25 Most Influential Evangelicals in America." *Time* (February 7). *www.time.com/time/specials/packages/completelist/0,29569,1993235,00.html* and *www.time.com/time/specials/packages/article/0,28804,1993235_1993243_1993320,00.html.* (Accessed January 10, 2012.)

Todd, Richard A. 1977. "Clergy, Bishops, and Pope." In *Eerdman's Handbook to the History of Christianity,* edited by Tim Dowley, 187–95. Grand Rapids, Mich.: Eerdmans.

Trousdale, Jerry. 2012. *Miraculous Movements: How Hundreds of Thousands of Muslims Are Falling in Love with Jesus.* Nashville: Nelson.

Tucker, Ruth A. 1987. *Daughters of the Church.* Grand Rapids, Mich.: Zondervan.

———. 2004. *From Jerusalem to Irian Jaya: A Biographical History of Christian Missions.* 2nd ed. Grand Rapids, Mich.: Zondervan.

United Bible Societies (UBS). 2011. "Bible in Ten More Languages, New Testament in 27." Posted October 3. *www.unitedbiblesocieties.org/news/904-bible-in-ten-more-languages-new-testament-in–27.* (Accessed December 8, 2011.)

United Nations. 2008. "World Population Prospects: The 2006 Revision" and "World Urbanization Prospects: The 2007 Revision." *http://esa.un.org/unup.* (Accessed March 04, 2012.)

U.S. Standards of Excellence in Short-Term Mission. 2013. *www.soe.org/explore/the-7-standards.www.soe.org/explore/wp-content/uploads/2011/09/7-Standards-Brief.pdf.* (Accessed April 21, 2013.)

Van Engen, Charles. 1996. *Mission on the Way: Issues in Mission Theology.* Grand Rapids, Mich.: Baker.

Van Gelder, Craig. 2004. "Gospel and Culture View." In *Evaluating the Church Growth Movement*, edited by Gary McIntosh. Grand Rapids, Mich.: Zondervan.

Van Rheenen, Gailyn. 1976. *Church Planting in Uganda*. Pasadena, Calif.: William Carey Library.

———. 1983a. *Biblically Anchored Missions*. Austin, Tex.: Firm Foundation.

———. 1983b. "Leadership Training." In *Church Growth among the Kipsigis of Southwest Kenya*, 37 – 55. Sotik, Kenya: Printed privately.

———. 1985. "Culturally Appropriate Training." *Kipsigis Kommunique* (July).

———. 1991. *Communicating Christ in Animistic Contexts*. Grand Rapids, Mich.: Baker.

———. 2000a. "Learning ... Growing ... Collaborating ... Phasing Out." *Evangelical Missions Quarterly* 36, no. 1: 36 – 47.

———. 2000b. "Money and Mi$$ion$." Posted February 9. *www.missiology.org/?p=278*. (Accessed April 10, 2012.)

———. 2002. "From Theology to Practice: The Helix Metaphor." Posted December 10. *www.missiology.org/?p=203*. (Accessed April 10, 2013.)

———, and Bob Waldron. 2002. *The Status of Missions: A Nationwide Survey of Churches of Christ*. Abilene, Tex.: Abilene Christian University Press.

———. 2003a. "Missions Process." *www.missiology.org*. (Accessed January 21, 2012.)

———. 2003b. "The Missional Helix: Example of Church Planting." Posted January 19. *www.missiology.org/?p=157*. (Accessed April 10, 2013.)

———. 2004. "The Reformist View of Church Growth." In *Evaluating the Church Growth Movement: 5 Views*, edited by Gary McIntosh, 167 – 89. Grand Rapids, Mich.: Zondervan.

———. 2005. "Unspeakable Pain." Posted February 28. *www.missiology.org/?p=132*. (Accessed November 7, 2011.)

———. 2006. *Contextualization and Syncretism: Navigating Cultural Currents*. Pasadena, Calif.: William Carey Library.

———. 2011. "Contrasting Missional and Church Growth Perspectives." Posted January 17. *www.missiology.org/?p=149*. (Accessed March 15, 2013.)

Ver Beek, Kurt Alan. 2006. "The Impact of Short-Term Missions: A Case Study of House Construction in Honduras after Hurricane Mitch." *Missiology: An International Review* 34, no. 4: 477 – 95.

Vicedom, George F. 1965. *The Mission of God*. Translated by Gilbert A. Thiele and Dennie Hilgendorf. St. Louis: Concordia.

Wagner, C. Peter. 1973. *Look Out! The Pentecostals Are Coming*. Carol Stream, Ill.: Creation.

Walls, Alicia Little. 2010. Electronic correspondence with Anthony Parker. December 21.

Walls, Andrew F. 1994. "Samuel Ajayi Crowther, 1807 – 1891: Foremost African Christian of the Nineteenth Century." In *Mission Legacies: Biographical Studies of Leaders of the Modern Missionary Movement*, edited by Gerald H. Anderson et al., 132 – 39. Maryknoll, N.Y.: Orbis.

———. 1996. *The Missionary Movement in Christian History: Studies in the Transmission of Faith.* Maryknoll, N.Y.: Orbis.

Wan, Enoch, and Geoffrey Hartt. 2008. "Complementary Aspects of Short-Term Missions: Case Studies for a Win-Win Situation." In *Effective Engagement in Short-Term Missions: Doing It Right!* edited by Robert J. Priest, 62–98. Pasadena, Calif.: William Carey Library.

Warren, Rick. 1995. *The Purpose Driven Church: Growth without Compromising Your Message and Mission.* Grand Rapids, Mich.: Zondervan.

Watson, David. 2009a. "Church Planting Movements." Conference, Legacy Church of Christ, North Richland Hills, Tex. May 12–15.

———. 2009b. "Church Planting Movement (CPM) — Our Definition." Posted June 15. *www.davidlwatson.org/2009/06/15/church-planting-movement-cpm-%e2%80%93-our-definition.* (Accessed December 9, 2011.)

———. 2009c. "Inductive Bible Study Process." Posted January 21. *www.cpmtr.org/2009/01/21/inductive-bible-study-process/.* (Accessed July 9, 2013.)

———. n.d. *www.cpmtr.org/resources.* (Assessed July 8, 2013.)

Webber, Robert E. 2002. *The Younger Evangelicals: Facing the Challenges of the New World.* Grand Rapids, Mich.: Baker.

Weber, Donovan, and Bill Weber. 2012. "Short-Term Missions: A Cup of Cold Water in My Name?" In *River of God: An Introduction to World Missions,* edited by Doug Priest and Stephen E. Burris, 201–12. Eugene, Ore.: Wipf & Stock.

Westerholm, Chad. 2011. Email to Anthony Parker. January 9.

Williard, David. 1993. *World A: A World Apart.* Richmond, Va.: Foreign Missions Board of the Southern Baptist Convention.

Wilson, J. Christy. 1979. *Today's Tentmakers.* Wheaton, Ill.: Tyndale House.

Window International Network. 2012. "About the 10/40 Window." *http://win1040.com/about-the-1040-window.php.* (Accessed February 29, 2012.)

Wink, Walter. 1984. *Naming the Powers: The Language of Power in the New Testament.* Philadelphia: Fortress.

Winter, Ralph D. 1975. "The Highest Priority: Cross-Cultural Evangelism." In *Let the Earth Hear His Voice: Official Reference Volume, Papers, and Responses, International Congress on World Evangelization, Lausanne, Switzerland,* edited by J. D. Douglas, 213–25. Minneapolis, Minn.: World Wide.

———. 1994. "India: Is It the Greatest Challenge to Finishing the Task?" *Missions Frontiers* 16: 10–42.

———. 1995. "My Pilgrimage in Mission." *International Bulletin of Missionary Research* 19 (April): 56–68. *Christian Periodical Index,* EBSCO*host.* (Accessed December 29, 2011.)

———. 1996. "The Re-amateurization of Missions." *The Occasional Bulletin of the Evangelical Missiological Society.* Spring. *Evangelical Missiological Society. www.emsweb.org/images/stories/docs/bulletins/winter_reamateurization_2_1996.pdf.* (Accessed May 21, 2012.)

———. 1999a. “The New Macedonia: A Revolutionary New Era in Missions Begins.” In *Perspectives on the World Christian Movement: A Reader*, 3rd ed., edited by Ralph D. Winter and Steven C. Hawthorne. Pasadena, Calif.: William Carey Library.

———. 1999b. “Tribute: Jim Emery (and the Start of TEE).” *Mission Frontiers* (October 1).

———. 2009. “The Kingdom Strikes Back: Ten Epochs of Redemptive History.” In *Perspectives on the World Christian Movement*, 4th ed., edited by Ralph D. Winter and Steven C. Hawthorne, 209–27. Pasedena, Calif.: William Carey Library.

———. and Steven C. Hawthorne, eds. 2009. *Perspectives on the World Christian Movement: A Reader*. 4th ed. Pasadena, Calif.: William Carey Library.

———. and Bruce A. Koch. 2009. “Finishing the Task: The Unreached Peoples Challenge.” In *Perspectives on the World Christian Movement*, 4th ed., edited by Ralph D. Winter and Steven C. Hawthorne, 531–46. Pasadena, Calif.: William Carey Library.

Woodberry, J. Dudley. 2011. “Muslim Missions: Then & Now.” *Christianity Today* 55, no. 9, *http://www.ctlibrary.com/ct/2011/september/muslim-missions.html*. (Accessed September 8, 2011.)

World Council of Churches (WCC). 2009. “History of World Mission and Evangelism.” *www.oikoumene.org/en/who-are-we/organization-structure/consultative-bodies/world-mission-and-evangelism/history.html*. (Accessed December 15, 2011.)

Wright, Christopher. 2006. *The Mission of God: Unlocking the Bible's Grand Narrative*. Grand Rapids, Mich.: IVP Academic.

Wycliffe Bible Translators. 2011. “The Worldwide Status of Bible Translation (2010).” *www.wycliffe.org/About/Statistics.aspx*. (Accessed December 9, 2011.)

Yohannan, K. P. 2009. *Revolution in World Missions*. 35th ed. Carrollton, Tex.: GFA.

Zehner, Edwin. 2006. “Short-Term Missions: Toward a More Field-Oriented Model.” *Missiology: An International Review* 34, no. 4: 509–21.

Scripture Index

Index of Modern Authors and Sources

Subject Index